1993

The recent turn to political and historical readings of Romanticism has given us a more complex picture of the institutional, cultural and sexual politics of the period. There has been a tendency, however, to confine such study to the European scene. In this book, Nigel Leask sets out to study the work of Byron, Shelley and De Quincey (together with a number of other major and minor Romantic writers, including Robert Southey and Tom Moore) in relation to Britain's imperial designs on the 'Orient'. Combining historical and theoretical approaches with detailed analyses of specific works, it examines the anxieties and instabilities of Romantic representations of the Ottoman Empire, India, China and the Far East. It argues that these anxieties were not marginal but central to the major concerns of British Romantic writers. The book is illustrated with a number of engravings from the period, giving a visual dimension to the discussion of Romantic representations of the East.

BRITISH ROMANTIC WRITERS
AND THE EAST

CAMBRIDGE STUDIES IN ROMANTICISM

General Editors:
Professor Marilyn Butler   Professor James Chandler
University of Cambridge   *University of Chicago*

Editorial Board:
John Barrell, *University of Sussex*   Paul Hamilton, *University of Southampton*
Mary Jacobus, *Cornell University*   Kenneth Johnston, *Indiana University*
Alan Liu, *University of California, Santa Barbara*   Jerome McGann,
University of Virginia   David Simpson, *University of Colorado*

This series aims to foster the best new work in one of the most challenging
fields within English literary studies. From the early 1780s to the early 1830s
a formidable array of talented men and women took to literary composition,
not just in poetry, which some of them famously transformed, but in many
modes of writing. The expansion of publishing created new opportunities for
writers, and the political stakes of what they wrote were raised again and
again by what Wordsworth called those 'great national events' that were
'almost daily taking place': the French Revolution, the Napoleonic and
American wars, urbanization, industrialization, religious revival, an ex-
panded empire abroad and the reform movement at home. This was a
literature of enormous ambition, even when it pretended otherwise. The
relations between science, philosophy, religion and literature were reworked
in texts such as *Frankenstein* and *Biographia Literaria*; gender relations in *A
Vindication of the Rights of Woman* and *Don Juan*; journalism by Cobbett and
Hazlitt; poetic form, content and style by the Lake school and the Cockney
School. Outside Shakespeare studies, probably no body of writing has
produced such a wealth of response or done so much to shape the responses
of modern criticism. This indeed is the period that saw the emergence of
those notions of 'literature' and of literary history, especially national
literary history, on which modern scholarship in English has been founded.
    The categories produced by Romanticism have also been challenged by
recent historicist arguments. The task of the series is to engage both with a
challenging corpus of Romantic writings and with the changing field of
criticism they have helped to shape. As with other literary series published
by Cambridge, this one will represent the work of both younger and more
established scholars, on either side of the Atlantic and elsewhere.

TITLES IN PREPARATION

Romantic Correspondence: Women, Politics, and the Fiction of Letters
by Mary A. Favret

*Edmund Burke's Aesthetic Ideology: Language, Gender
and Political Economy in Revolution*
by Tom Furniss

Poetry as an Occupation and an Art in Britain, 1760–1830
by Peter T. Murphy

Allegory in Romantic and Post-Romantic Culture
by Theresa M. Kelley

'Juggernaut', by Thomas Bacon, in *First Impressions and Studies from Nature in Hindostan 1831–36*, 2 vols. (London 1837). Frontispiece, vol. I.

BRITISH ROMANTIC
WRITERS AND THE EAST
Anxieties of Empire

NIGEL LEASK

Queens' College, Cambridge

CAMBRIDGE
UNIVERSITY PRESS

Published by the Press Syndicate of the University of Cambridge
The Pitt Building, Trumpington Street, Cambridge CB2 1RP
40 West 20th Street, New York, NY 10011–4211, USA
10 Stamford Road, Oakleigh, Victoria 3166, Australia

First published 1992

Printed in Great Britain at the University Press, Cambridge

A catalogue record for this book is available from the British Library

Library of Congress cataloguing in publication data
Leask, Nigel, 1958–
British Romantic writers and the East: anxieties of empire/Nigel Leask.
p. cm. – (Cambridge studies in Romanticism)
Includes bibliographical references.
ISBN 0-521-41168-8 (hardback)
1. English literature – Oriental influences. 2. English literature – 19th century – History
and criticism. 3. East and West in literature. 4. Romanticism – Great Britain.
5. Imperialism in literature. 6. Exoticism in literature. 7. Orient in literature. 8. Asia in
literature. I. Title. II. Series.
PR129.A78L4 1993
820.9'325 – dc20   92-11690 CIP

ISBN 0 521 41168 8 hardback

UP

For Evelyn

Contents

List of illustrations		*page* xiii
Acknowledgements		xiv
List of abbreviations		xv
Introduction		1
1 'Byron turns Turk': Orientalism and the 'Eastern Tales'		13
	1 Byron's 'Eastern Tales'	13
	2 The context of the 'Eastern Tales'. 'Samples of the Finest Orientalism'	17
	3 Epics against empire? Samuel Rogers' 'Voyage of Columbus' and Byron's 'The Giaour'	25
	4 Satire against the grain	33
	5 'The Bride of Abydos'	38
	6 'The Corsair'	44
	7 Resolving 'The Corsair': 'Lara' and 'The Island'	54
2 'Sharp Philanthropy': Percy Bysshe Shelley and Romantic India		68
	1 Shelley and India	68
	2 'The Assassins'	76
	3 The word in the wilderness	80
	4 Brahmins, temples and pyres: some Romantic representations of India	91
	5 The European dimensions of orientalism	103
	6 'The Revolt of Islam' and 'Alastor': liberating the Orient?	108
	7 'Revolutions of Empire' or empire as revolution?	118
	8 Engendering India: the poet and the 'Light of Asia'	120
	9 'Alastor: or the Spirit of Solitude'	122
	10 'Can Man be free if Woman be a Slave?': the problem of 'The Revolt's' feminism.	130
	11 The 'Reforming Brahmin' and 'Prometheus Unbound'.	134
	12 'Prometheus Unbound': reorientating Greece	140

13 The role of Asia 146
14 Coda: the Indian writings of Thomas Medwin 154

3   'Murdering one's double': Thomas De Quincey and
S. T. Coleridge. Autobiography, Opium and Empire in
'Confessions of an English Opium Eater' and
'Biographia Literaria' 170
    1 Introduction 170
    2 The 'Confessions': nervous reactions 172
    3 John Brown and the debate about the therapeutic use of
      opium 175
    4 'Two Transcendentalists who are also [opium eaters]' 179
    5 The 'Confessions' and the 'Biographia Literaria' 187
    6 Autobiography as exculpation 190
    7 Stately homes, temples and banks 195
    8 *Merely* a man of letters? 198
    9 Saturday night fever 201
    10 A vision of Liverpool 206
    11 Fear and loathing in Grasmere 209
    12 Opium wars 215
    13 Troubled dreams 220

Notes 229
Index 258

Illustrations

Frontispiece: 'Juggernaut', by Thomas Bacon, in *First Impressions and Studies from Nature in Hindostan 1831–36*, 2 vols. (London 1837). Frontispiece, vol. 1.

1 'The Corsair', *Illustrations to the Works of Lord Byron* (London 1840) unpaginated. *page* 48

2 'Neuha', *Illustrations to the Works of Lord Byron* (London 1840) unpaginated. 65

3 'Tom Raw at a Hindoo Entertainment', in *Tom Raw the Griffin*, by Charles D'Oyly (London 1828), facing p. 182. 81

4 'Tom Raw rejects the Embraces of the Nabob of Bengal', *Tom Raw the Griffin*, facing p. 205. 83

5 'A Mahratta Surdar entertaining Brahmins', in T. D. Broughton, *Letters Written in a Mahratta Camp* (London 1813), facing p. 48. 99

6 'Procession of Hindoo Woman to the Funeral Pyre of her Husband', in William Hodges, *Travels in India* (London 1793), facing p. 84. 117

7 'Raja Ram Mohan Roy', unknown artist, India Office Library and Records. WD 1288. 135

8 'Interior View...of the Temple of Elephanta', in J. Forbes, *Oriental Memoirs*, 4 vols. (London 1813), 1 facing p. 454. 157

9 'Bhadra', an 1830 lithograph by R. M. Grindley of a carving in Ellora caves, *Transactions of the Royal Asiatic Society*, vol. 11 (London 1830), facing p. 327. 159

Acknowledgements

Many people have contributed directly and indirectly to the making of this book. My greatest debt is to John Barrell, who has once again been so generous in sharing ideas and offering inspiration. Thanks are due to him, to Javed Majeed and to Marilyn Butler for their many invaluable comments on the manuscript, and also to Simon Schaffer for his unflagging encouragement and conviviality over the years. Without the benefit of their critical remarks and extensive knowledge this book would be very much the poorer. I also wish to thank Evelyn Arizpe, Bridget Orr, Eivind Kahrs, Sudeshna Guha, Michael Bravo, Pete de Bolla, John Mullan, Anita Herle, Barry Symonds, Ramana Ramaswamy, Namrata Narain, Alfonso Martin del Campo, Marc Silver, Patrick Leech, Daniel Roberts and the undergraduates who attended my Cambridge classes on Romantic Orientalism in Lent Term 1991, all of whom have contributed in various ways. Thanks to Tony Tanner for making me think more carefully about anxiety. My father Reay Mackay Leask, the source of my interest in India, didn't live to see the book completed, but nevertheless is an informing presence throughout in more ways than I can tell. My mother and Alison Dryden helped procure me a word-processor in Scotland at a crucial stage of editing, without which the final draft would have been badly delayed. Josie Dixon at Cambridge University Press has been of indispensable assistance in seeing it through the press. The illustrations are reproduced by permission of the Syndics of the Cambridge University Library and the India Office Library, London. Finally I wish to thank the President and Fellows of Queens' College Cambridge (particularly Iain Wright) for electing me to a Research Fellowship in 1986–9, years in which the bulk of the research for this book was done untrammelled by excessive teaching and lecturing commitments. A version of the first part of my essay on De Quincey has appeared in a special issue of *Prose Studies*, 13, 3 (1991), 'Coleridge and the Armoury of the Human Mind: Essays on his Prose Writings'.

Abbreviations

Chapter 1

BPW   *Byron: Poetical Works*, ed. Frederick Page, corrected by John Jump (Oxford University Press 1970)

CPW   *The Complete Poetical Works of Lord Byron*, ed. Jerome McGann (Oxford: Clarendon Press 1980–)

LJ   *Byron's Letters and Journals*, ed. Leslie Marchand, 12 vols. (London: John Murray 1973–82)

Chapter 2

CL   *Collected Letters of S. T. Coleridge*, ed. E. L. Griggs, 6 vols. (Oxford and New York: Oxford University Press, 1956–71)

CN   *The Notebooks of S. T. Coleridge*, ed. K. Coburn, 5 vols. (New York, Princeton and London: Routledge & Kegan Paul and Princeton University Press, 1976)

MPW   *Poetical Works of Thomas Moore* (London and Edinburgh: William Nimmo 1875)

SL   *Collected Letters of P. B. Shelley*, ed. Frederick L. Jones, 2 vols. (Oxford 1964)

SPW   *Shelley's Poetical Works*, ed. Thomas Hutchinson (London: Oxford University Press 1934)

S Prose   *Shelley's Prose* or *The Trumpet of a Prophecy*, ed. David Lee Clark, new preface by Harold Bloom (1954, reprinted London: Fourth Estate 1988)

WJW   *The Works of Sir William Jones*, ed. Lady Jones, 6 vols. (London 1799)

Chapter 3

BL   S. T. Coleridge, *Biographia Literaria*, ed. James Engell and W. Jackson Bate (Bollingen Series LXXV, Princeton University Press 1983)

C   *Confessions of an English Opium Eater*, ed. Alethea Hayter,

(Harmondsworth 1971). Based on the text as it first appeared anonymously and in two parts, in the Sept. and Oct. 1821 issues of *The London Magazine*, (vol. IV, nos. xxi, 293–312, and xxii, 35–79)

C 1856   *Confessions of an English Opium Eater*, revised 1856 (London and New York: Routledge and Dutton ND)

Mass   *The Collected Writings of Thomas De Quincey*, ed. David Masson, 14 vols. (Edinburgh 1890)

Recoll.   *Recollections of the Lakes and the Lake Poets*, ed. David Wright (Harmondsworth 1970). Text based on the original articles in *Tait's Edinburgh Magazine* between 1834 and 1840

Introduction

During one period of the French Revolution the Brutus head-dress was the mode [amongst the 'fashionables' of England], though Brutus was at the same time considered as the Judas Iscariot of political religion, being indeed at this day to an orthodox Anti-Jacobine what Omar is to the Persians; that is, something a great deal worse than the Devil. 'I suppose, sir,' said a London hair-dresser to a gentleman from the country, – 'I suppose, sir, you would like to be dressed in the Brutus style,' 'What style is that?' was the question in reply. 'All over frizzley, sir, like the Negers, – they be Brutes you know,'... At present, as the soldiers from Egypt have brought home with them broken limbs and opthalmia, they carry an arm in a sling, or walk the streets with a green shade over the eyes. Everything now must be Egyptian: the ladies wear crocodile ornaments, and you sit upon a sphinx in a room hung round with mummies, and with the long black lean-armed long-nosed hieroglyphical men, who are enough to make the children afraid to go to bed. The very shopboards must be metamorphosed into the mode, and painted in Egyptian letters, which, as the Egyptians had no letters, you will doubtless conceive must be curious. They are simply the common characters, deprived of all beauty and all proportion by having all the strokes of equal thickness, so that those which should be thin look as if they had the elephantiasis.[1]

So Robert Southey on contemporary English fashions in his 1807 'translation' of *Letters from England: by Don Manuel Espriella*, in a passage encapsulating many of the concerns of this book. Although it deals with fashion, with hairdressing, interior decoration and shop-sign calligraphy, rather than with those literary texts which we canonize as Romantic, it may serve to draw attention to some of the representational problems, and the proffered solutions to those problems, which characterize British Romantic writing about the East. For the signs of fashion upon which Southey's Spanish 'spy'

I

Don Manuel dwells here are signs of the Other, and moreover of an Other identifiable with the expansion – particularly, although not exclusively, eastwards – of British imperial power. The discovery of these signs embedded in the heart of English culture is subject in Southey's passage to two diverse interpretations, one of them supportive of his culture's claims to superiority, the other troubling to these claims and to the values embodied by its civilization at large.

Because of the influence of Edward Said's seminal study *Orientalism* (published in 1978), there has been a common tendency to view orientalism as being essentially 'a Western style for dominating, restructuring, and having authority over the Orient'.[2] Despite my admiration for Said's project, however, I have chosen in this book to focus upon anxieties and instabilities rather than positivities and totalities in the Romantic discourse of the Orient. It seems to me that whilst Said is right in asserting the links between knowledge of the East (I use both this word, and its synonym, the 'Orient', throughout this book in the full awareness that, as Sir William Jones put it, it is 'a word merely relative'[3]) and the history of colonial power, he is wrong in denominating it 'a closed system'.[4] The (plural) anxieties of empire which I will be examining in the work of Byron, Shelley and De Quincey and numerous other British Romantic writers cannot be laid on any such procrustean bed. Neither can the cultural imaginary of British Romanticism be hermetically sealed from the practical effects, the resistances and accommodations of the colonial encounter so simply as Said would have it in *Orientalism*. While it is true that the oriental Other represented in British Romantic literature is usually a monological construct (the present study discovers only one as it were utopian moment in Shelley's *Prometheus Unbound*, in which a Romantic text can really be said to open itself dialogically to the Other), it is my aim to show that the internal and external pressures determining and undermining such representations are more various than Said's thesis will allow.

To study the manner in which British Romantic writers consciously or unconsciously articulated their anxieties about the Other is neither to claim that they *sought* to subvert the imperialist project (this was largely the work of the colonized peoples who, with the exception of the remarkable Rammohun Roy, are a *silent* but informing presence throughout my book), nor that they sought simply to endorse it. The anxiety which registered a sense of the internal dislocation of metropolitan culture (a dislocation which, as Homi Bhabha has argued,[5] offered itself as a site of resistance for the subjugated), could also lend support to its hegemonic programme. Although to be 'anxious' is a state which normally defines itself in our culture with reference to Kierkegaard or Freud, a glance at the standard dictionary definition (*OED*) may be sufficient to show why it is germane to my thesis in this book: '(1) Troubled or uneasy in mind about some uncertain event; being in painful or disturbing suspense; concerned, solicitous. (2) Fraught with trouble or solicitude, distressing, worrying. (3) Full of desire and endeavour; solicitous; earnestly desirous (to *effect* some purpose).' The anxieties discussed in this book partake of the full semantic range of these definitions; the third in particular shows that if the anxieties which I am addressing sometimes block or disable the positivities of power, they are just as often *productive* in furthering the imperial will.

To render this ambivalence more palpable, let us look more closely at the passage from Southey's *Letters from England* quoted above. The contemporary styles and motifs described by Don Manuel carry the threat that the Same is being *taken over* by the Other, articulating a series of anxieties common in the literature addressed by this book. Here is a list of what seem to be the principal ones occurring in Southey's text, in order of appearance: (1) French Jacobinism, closely connected in counter-revolutionary England with fears of working-class insurgency, is also conflated with the Napoleonic ideology of England's major competitor in the imperial stakes. The suppression of native resistance to British imperial power (such as the defeat of Tipu Sahib in 1799) is also considered to be the defeat of 'Jacobinism' at home and abroad. (2) An as yet unsophisticated discourse of racial difference is here applied to the degenerative principles of the French revolutionaries, implicitly linking French tyrannicides (Brutuses) with negro slaves (brutes). Britain's role as the major slaving nation implicitly troubles this 'reduction'. (3) Wounds inflicted in colonial wars. (4) The outlandish emblems of Egyptian antiquity, undermining the cultural exclusivity of Judaeo-Christian and classical cultural origins. These emblems and antiquities have been wrested (as it were) from French competitors, synecdoches for an 'Orient' rapidly falling under the flag of British imperial power, but their desirability is questionable, as the following make clear. (5) Nightmarish fears of 'long black lean-armed long-nosed hieroglyphical men' haunting English women and children, carrying an innuendo of sexual violation and miscegenation.

(6) Gross inflation of the graphic signifiers of the culture, which, in a troubling metaphor, mimics the effects of glut in swelling the classical line of beauty out of all proportion, the symptom of a tropical disease associated by contemporary orientalists like Sir William Jones with leprosy and syphilis. The fear of Luxury in both its economic and moral sense.[6]

The grotesque colouring of Southey's account recurs frequently in Romantic writing about the oriental Other, although the image-repertoire drawn upon here derives from sources at least as old as Shakespeare's *Antony and Cleopatra*. The passage quoted is itself a source for one of the most celebrated 'set pieces' of Romantic orientalism, the 'Malay dream' near the end of De Quincey's *Confessions of an English Opium Eater*. The dream, which will be discussed in the last chapter, is a wonderful example of the exotic, composite Orient of the Romantic imagination, an Orient invested with an uncanny power to disturb. Although initially prompted by a threatening Malay, De Quincey's dream also registers disquietude at the fashionable Egyptians evoked by Southey in the 1807 passage: 'All the feet of the tables, sophas &c. soon became instinct with life: the abominable head of the crocodile, and his leering eyes, looked out at me, multiplied into a thousand repetitions: and I stood loathing and fascinated.'[7]

Southey's fear of the swamping of English propriety by grotesque oriental forms was shared by his poetic arch-enemy Byron, a poet who (at least nominally) was as opposed to imperialism as Southey was in favour of it. In my first chapter I discuss Byron's *Eastern Tales* in the light of his anxiety that 'they [the purveyors of "romantic" poetry, Byron included] have raised a mosque by the side of a Grecian temple of the purest architecture'.[8] The presiding anxiety as well as the 'frisson' of the *Tales* is of the European subject 'turning Turk'. Byron reduces the imperialist Self to a level with its oriental Other; but in so doing he in effect perpetuates the prejudice of the East/West binary opposition whilst attacking the ideology of empire which it empowers. Byron's anxiety can, as a result, be easily misread by subsequent empire-builders like Benjamin Disraeli and Richard Burton as a mere masquerade. Byron's cultural metamorphosis is more disturbingly registered in the writings of De Quincey, the '*English* Opium Eater', whose feverish fluctuations between the poles of Same and Other ('I was the idol; I was the priest; I was worshipped; I was sacrificed') realizes Byron's worst dreams of the squandering of civic and personal identity in the imperialist project.

Take, for example, De Quincey's *Autobiographical Sketch* entitled 'Introduction to the World of Strife', in which he describes a childhood game of international diplomacy played with his aggressive elder brother William. Thomas rules an imaginary kingdom called Gombroon, a small, underdeveloped tropical island inhabited by a simple, aboriginal people; 'There was no Golden Fleece in Gombroon.'[9] William, on the other hand, is king of a powerful northern state called Tigrosylvania, with undisguisedly imperialist ambitions: 'It seemed that vast horns and promontaries ran down from all parts of his dominions towards any country whatsoever, in either hemisphere – empire, or republic; monarchy, polyarchy, or anarchy – that he might have reasons for assaulting.'[10] The feeble Thomas, here ostensibly taking the part of the victim rather than the perpetrator of aggressive imperialism, agonizes (in 'anxiety and distress of mind'[11]) over polemical strategies for the defence of his threatened subjects. He is able to parry William's claim that diamond mines, useless to the primitive inhabitants, are situated in the heart of Gombroon, and even manages to contest his brother's desired annexation of the island for a time (on grounds of the necessity of a 'civilizing mission') by asserting the 'honour and independence of my islanders'.[12]

But De Quincey's strategy here is, despite appearances, very far from being hostile to imperialism. On the contrary, it is rather the product of an extreme anxiety of empire which identifies with the pariah–victim the better to condemn him to subservience. For Thomas' spurious defence is utterly wrecked when his brother 'discovers' (upon reading Lord Monboddo, who had hypothesized the simian origins of the human race) that the 'primitive' Gombroonians had tails and therefore 'had not yet emerged from this early condition of apedom'.[13] As Southey's barber puts it, 'they be brutes you know'. The anxious solicitous Thomas is forced to bow to objective necessity, to scientific proof; the introduction of a discourse on race provides incontestable evidence that they must submit to the imperial yoke, overriding all other arguments. I will have more to say about some of the ways in which De Quincey deployed the theme of racial development, an argument which he here attributes to his 'tigerish' brother William, to legitimize British imperialism, an argument which would cost its advocates (not to mention the victims of its asseverations) very dear. The arc of racial development very easily becomes the arc of decline, as Daniel Pick has recently shown in his study of European fears of degeneration in the 1848–1918 period; the discourse of racial differences, as yet scientifically unsophisticated in Romantic writing, was haunted by anxieties concerning the blurring of taxonomies as much as it was sustained by the authority of their distinctions.[14]

In fact, fears of miscegenation and cultural degeneration, such as that embodied in Southey's account of swollen, elephantiasic writing, are common in Romantic texts, often (as here) the result of infection by diseases from the East. John Barrell has based his compelling study of *The Infection of Thomas De Quincey* on a typology of such diseases, but De Quincey was by no means unique in his fear of infection.[15] Shelley – whose poetry Christopher Ricks found to suffer from *stylistic elephantiasis* – lived in terror of the disease itself, which was thought to originate in the Middle East.[16] In my chapter on Shelley and India, I argue that Shelley (unlike Byron, Southey or De Quincey) translated British imperialism into a displaced form of revolutionary politics which, in the name of universal enlightenment, alchemized the Other into the Same. What was left out of this convenient (and, for Shelley, potentially salvific) substitution of two political terms was the reality of imperialist violence and appropriation, which returned to undermine the coherence and the totalizing aspirations of his poetry and politics. In Shelley, as in Byron, the Other is often figured as an (often oriental) female who turns out to be an 'epipsychidion' or wishful projection of the ego of the male protagonist. It is therefore perhaps not surprising to discover Shelley's terror of a return of the repressed in the form of a hideous and contagious oriental disease which he feared he would contract from a woman. His biographer T. J. Hogg described his symptomatic behaviour on one occasion: 'One evening, during the access of his fancied disorder, when many young ladies were standing up for a country dance, he caused a wonderful consternation amongst these charming creatures by walking slowly along the rows of girls and curiously surveying them, placing his eyes close to their necks and bosoms, and feeling their breasts and bare arms, in order to ascertain whether any of the fair ones had taken the horrible disease.'[17]

Derek Guiton and Nora Crook, to whose book these comments on Shelley are indebted, have pointed out that the onset of Shelley's panic in 1813 coincided with two cases of elephantiasis, a disease hitherto almost unknown in England, one afflicting an English boy from the Bahamas, the other a 'Miss N', 'daughter of an English officer by a Hindoo woman'. By a curious coincidence, Miss N was treated in the Middlesex Hospital by H. H. Southey, the poet's brother, while the boy was treated by William Lawrence, Shelley's physician.[18] Sir William Jones, who was not alone in linking elephantiasis with syphilis, believed that the disease, which was apparently raging in Calcutta as well as the Middle East and Africa, had been 'imported from *Africa* into the *West India Islands* by the black slaves, who carried with them their resentment and their revenge'.[19] The fear of contagion represented by Southey's infected, Egyptianized letters, as well as Shelley's elephantiasis, can be regarded, along with a mounting fear of cultural and racial degeneration, as one of the paramount anxieties of empire, surely not incomprehensible when we consider the geopolitical ramifications of the great AIDS terror of our own day.

Anxiety as a *suspension* and dislocation of cultural sovereignty does not yet exhaust the affective range of Romantic attitudes to the East, however. As I suggested above, it also solicits resolution, thus empowering as well as simply blocking the furtherance of the imperial will. The signs of the Other presented in Southey's *Letters from England* appear, lest we forget, as *fashion*, functioning here by means of what Stephen Greenblatt terms an assimilative mechanism 'work[ing] like enzymes to change the ideological composition of foreign bodies'.[20] The signs may thus serve as tokens of a 'self-confirming Otherness', rather than of dislocation, in so far as they have power to represent the spoils of empire, exotic exhibits of alien but subjugated peoples. The 'Brutus' hairstyle of the French Jacobin enemy may be grotesquely metamorphosed by the ignorance of a patriotic hairdresser into the hair of negro chattel-slaves and thence into the pelts of animals ('All over frizzley, sir, like the Negers, – they be brutes you know'); the anecdote mobilizes an art of sinking familiar to anti-Jacobin polemic in the period, most famously represented by the simian features of the Frenchman in Gillray's cartoons. But, in working the metamorphic magic of fashion, the loyalist dandy sports the sign of the Other in order to disengage the signifier from any semantic substance, to parody it, and also to *inoculate* himself and his culture from the threat which it poses. To the same ends, the persona of Don Manuel, Southey's Spanish narrator (who, in the tradition of Montesquieu's *Lettres Persanes*, holds a

slightly distorting mirror up to Regency England), serves to disarm
the threat of the Other. Don Manuel, a Catholic 'foreign body' (and
representative of a nation which had long since fallen behind in the
global imperial stakes, soon to be itself incorporated into the
Napoleonic empire), is treated with some indulgence by Southey. No
longer a threat to British power, Spain is replaced by France as the
'enemy'. Accordingly, the anxiety betrayed by Don Manuel in his
account of the orientalism permeating British fashion also serves to
incorporate *him*, to purge him of his foreignness. Differences between
European national cultures (other than the French, which has 'gone
over to the other side') are suspended by consideration of the
difference between Europe and its Others.

Enzymes, antibodies, inoculations; if the diseases of the Other
strike fear into the heart of metropolitan culture, these therapeutical
or assimilative agencies struggle to restore homeostasis, the healthful
ease of the Same. Hence the sheer *demand* for orientalism, the
proliferation of orientalist styles and narratives in the arts of the
Romantic period; the eighteenth-century vogue for Chinoiserie is
diversified into a demand for Egyptian, Ottoman, Mughal and
Hindu motifs, components of what John Barrell calls 'the imagery of
an early but well-established imperialist culture'.[21] Demand and
desire are rationalized in terms of an (always risky) analogy with the
imperial triumphs of the classical world. For the orientalist poet Tom
Medwin, English Romantic literature found a precedent and alibi in
the Athenian practice of incorporating the imagery of its subjugated
enemies into its own culture, Caryatids from the Peloponnese,
flowery eastern capitals from Persia.[22] In line with this precedent,
Medwin's (although, as I will argue, *not* his cousin Shelley's) oriental
poems, just as much as Southey's crocodiles, mummies and 'long-
nosed hieroglyphic men', could be seen as the products of an imperial
heraldry which incorporated the symbols of the conquered into its
own coats of arms.

Even a writer as hostile to (what he considered) the irrationality,
banality and irreligion of oriental imagery as the evangelical John
Foster was not entirely immune to the appeal of imperial heraldry. In
an attempt to mitigate the harshness of his 1811 review of Southey's
epic of Indian mythology, *The Curse of Kehama*, he conceded that 'it
was a thing not to be endured, that, while we are as proud as Kehama
of possessing India, we should not be able to bring to the
augmentation of our national splendour that which India itself deems

its highest glory, its mythology'.[23] In India itself, British 'orientalists' like Sir William Jones (the specialized use of the term in the Indian context will be explained in the second part, and will be signalled throughout this book by inverted commas) sought to interpret – or construct – Indian society according to their ideal of an indigenous classical past. By a process which was in part a 'reverse acculturation' and in part a codification or 'recuperation' of Indian manners and institutions, they sought to refashion the decadent society which they had taken over from the Mughal emperors in what they considered to be *its own terms*. Seen in the light of Foster's 'concession' and my foregoing argument, though, this 'reverse acculturation' reveals itself as, in theory, a hegemonic strategy. To 'go native' might even be a means of reflecting 'our national splendour', at least until that disturbing moment when the heraldry of the Other takes on a life of its own and threatens the familiar with an uncanny absorption and loss of identity.

Foster's concession problematizes his entire argument and is symptomatic of a larger uncertainty in Romantic orientalism. For the ontology of the oriental image is never stable; it is at once *desired* as a heraldic device, but at the same time always tends to shift its meaning from an emblem of symbolic incorporation to one of parasitic tenure. In the same way, if it is rendered necessary as a form of inoculation, it tends suddenly to manifest itself as an infectious rather than a prophylactic agency. For example, in the case of De Quincey, opium (like the term consumption, with its double meaning) becomes a metaphor for imperialism as *both* a cure for national torpor, a stimulant, *and* a compulsive narcotic, a wasting away. Hopes about the invigorating effects of imperial expansion on the metropolitan society turn into a nightmare realization that it has become economically dependent on (or addicted to) its subjugated Other; the relations of power have been grotesquely reversed. Hence the duality of the oriental image, and the attendant anxiety of not knowing any longer where it is exactly that one is standing.

In the three long chapters which follow I explore the mutations of anxiety focussing on the work of three very different writers engaging with three specific areas of Asia; Byron, whose ideology is Whig, and whose 'Orient' is the Ottoman Middle East; Shelley, loosely identifiable with a radical/democratic politics, whose work I interpret in relation to India; and De Quincey, Tory exponent of aggressive free-trade imperialism, whom I discuss principally in

relation to China and the Far East. For Byron, the allure of the East
was in the nature of a fatal attraction, a deadly cure for aristocratic
spleen. For Shelley, it beckoned as an uncluttered site for the fulfilment
of frustrated dreams of liberty, but in practice revealed itself to be
treacherous and obstacle-ridden, the nemesis of revolutionary narcissism. For De Quincey, as I have said, the stimulant turned out to be a
narcotic, although the addicted Self held to the last to a dream of
'untwisting the accursed chain'. The fantasy of detoxification, of
freeing oneself from entanglement with the Other by turning back
the clock of history, is one which still appeals to racists and exponents
of forced repatriation in search of a 'final solution' to cultural
hybridity. Hence the over-arching thesis of this book; for Shelley and
De Quincey, but also to a lesser extent for Byron, the stimulus
afforded by imperialism, the desire for the Other, came to have the
status of what in medical language is called an *iatrogenic* illness, that is
to say, an illness which is caused by that which was intended as a
cure. To alter the metaphor, the compulsive pursuit of an elusive
(and figuratively female) oriental ideal is for the Romantics who are
the subject of this book a form of self-destruction, what Byron
describes in *Childe Harold* as 'the nympholepsy of some fond despair'.
In mitigation of the dark picture which I am painting of the
unbreakable spell of the Other for our (by constitution imperial)
culture and those peoples subjugated in its name, I am aware of
moments – such as in Byron's *The Island* or Shelley's *Prometheus
Unbound* – when the relations of power and desire are actively, and
creatively, rethought against the grain of history.

My introduction would be incomplete without saying a word
about the relationship of this book to Romantic studies in general. As
long ago as 1950, Raymond Schwab suggested that the late
eighteenth-century European 'discovery' of Sanskrit and other
ancient oriental languages stood in the same relationship to European
Romanticism as the 'discovery' of classical humanist texts stood
to the European Renaissance. Schwab's claim has been very
largely overlooked, partly because it was overstated, partly because
of the panglossian tones of the book's vision of 'integral
humanism' in asserting (for example) that since the time of
Montaigne '…it has become a banality to remind Europe that she is
a small promontory of Asia.' After *Orientalism*, Schwab's underestimation of the complicities between enlightenment and empire has
been thrown into sharp relief. Nevertheless, one important claim of

Schwab's book is too important to be neglected by students of Romanticism:

It was logically inevitable that a civilization believing itself unique would find itself drowned in the sum total of civilizations, just as personal boundaries would be swamped by over-flowing mobs and dislocations of the rational. All this together was called Romanticism, and it produced, through its many re-creations of the past, the present that propels us forward.[24]

Schwab's construal of the Romantic Sublime here is immensely suggestive and deserves to be developed in ways beyond the scope of this book; unfortunately, however, at the time it was delivered it fell largely on deaf ears because of its irrelevance to the concerns of contemporary literary studies.

The recent return to political and historical readings of Romanticism has given us a much more complex picture of the institutional, cultural and sexual politics of the period, which the New Criticism had surrendered to (an albeit ironic) aestheticism and structuralist and post-structuralist criticism had incarcerated in the Prison House of Language. History is once again on the agenda, and the political and ideological concerns of poets like Wordsworth, Byron, Shelley and even Keats are now read as being constitutive of their poetry rather than merely 'background' material. On a macro-cultural level, the 're-politicization' of Romanticism has become aware of Romanticism in a national context, at a time when discussion of the history and ideology of nationalism is a very urgent concern.[25] The inauguration of the European Community as an economic, if not yet a civic body (in the words of J. G. A. Pocock 'an association of former imperial states having in common the experience of defeat'[26]) and the inverse movement of the 'nationalities' of Eastern Europe in unsoldering themselves from the post-war Soviet empire have created a new political centre of gravity. The British critical gaze has been accordingly drawn away from a recent history and culture which is, again in the words of Pocock, essentially 'insular, archipelagic, oceanic, and imperial' rather than continental.[27] Despite the controversy aroused by Edward Said in critical circles, Romantic studies (more than Renaissance studies) in Britain have been slow to address the imperial components of the culture, in part due to a culpable blindness on the part of the British Left to the whole issue. The production of Romantic literature may have been predominantly a European phenomenon, even if its consumption was not (as Gauri Viswanathan's recent study *Masks of Conquest* has shown[28]), but the context of that production was strongly marked by a burgeoning global imperialism. The anxieties and transports of Romanticism, I have suggested above, are as much the product of geopolitics as of metaphysics, and an ideological analysis which stops short at metropolitan social relations is only telling half the story. Unfortunately, the 'power-in-spacing' of Romanticism as a Euro-centric phenomenon continues to hold sway, reinforced by the dramatic transformations being wrought in contemporary Europe; it is the mercator projection of the cultural globe, the non-European portions of which are so many side-shows constellated around the Big Top. The internal decolonization of our culture, ethnically hetero-genous and multiracial, *as well as* European, must proceed by brushing our imperial history against the grain, to adapt Benjamin's aphorism. The following offers itself in furtherance of that goal.

CHAPTER I

'Byron turns Turk': Orientalism and the 'Eastern Tales'

BYRON'S 'EASTERN TALES'

Writing to Tom Moore in May 1813, Byron urged the Irish poet to join him on the bandwagon of 'oriental' poetry:

Stick to the East; – the oracle, Staël [Madame De Staël] told me it was the only poetical policy. The North, South, and West, have all been exhausted; but from the East, we have nothing but [Southey's] unsaleables – and these he has contrived to spoil, by adopting only their more outrageous fictions... The little I have done in that way is merely a 'voice in the wilderness' for you; and, if it has had any success, that also will prove that the public are orientalizing, and pave the path for you. (*LJ* III 101)

The present chapter is concerned with Byron's own 'poetical policy' of orientalism, which formed part of a broader cultural engagement with the question of imperialism, productive of so much stimulation and anxiety in Regency Britain. The very tone of Byron's advice to Moore typifies the flippant combination of elation and cynicism which are frequent companions in his own poetical essays in the new style and subject-matter. Byron speaks like a Levantine or East India merchant who has tapped a lucrative source of raw materials in a newly opened up Orient, which he feels will make a splash on the home market. He offers Moore partnership in his business venture which, he has been assured by Europe's leading consultant in cultural capital, cannot fail, as long as the exotic imported commodities are somewhat tailored to domestic tastes. Byron, who was instrumental in the publication of another famous Romantic poem of the Orient in 1816, Coleridge's *Kubla Khan*, obviously had a flair for predicting the market. Moore's *Lalla Rookh*, commissioned by Longman for the gargantuan sum of three thousand guineas, made its author a rich man. Byron's advice, that the two entrepreneurs

13

could only benefit from the negative example of Robert Southey, would continue to pay off. *Kubla Khan* and *Lalla Rookh* enjoyed great popularity in the nineteenth century, whilst the Poet Laureate was left with a warehouse full of unsaleable fictions (the oriental epics *Thalaba the Destroyer* and *The Curse of Kehama*), at once too spicy and indigestible for fastidious British appetites.

In contrast to Southey, Byron had good cause to feel confidence in his business acumen. In mid-March of the previous year he had awoken to find himself famous on the strength of 'the little I have done', namely the first two cantos of *Childe Harold's Pilgrimage: A Romaunt*. In this narrative poem, in the eighteenth-century topo-graphical tradition, Byron took his misanthropic hero on a tour through Iberia to the Levant, based on his own 'grand tour' of 1809–11. Byron was encouraged by his publisher John Murray to make the most of the saleability of poetry with an 'oriental' flavour, and the series of *Eastern Tales* produced between 1813 and 1816 made him the most popular poet in Britain and established the 'Byron Myth' as a European phenomenon. Byron was more than just 'paving the way' for Moore, whose 1817 *Lalla Rookh* was indebted, like most of the oriental poetry which proliferated in this decade, to Byron's *Tales*. If the *Tales* did not fare well with later critics, however, it is partly the fault of their author, who in an 1820 letter to Murray regretted their 'false stilted trashy style, which is a mixture of all the styles of the day, which are *all bombastic*', and two years later considered his early productions 'exaggerated nonsense which [have] corrupted the public Taste' (*LJ* VII 182; IX 161). Later critical depreciation has obscured their immense contemporary popularity and importance, and Byron's subsequent success with the burlesque Italian style of *Beppo* and *Don Juan* has made the early work seem mannered and ridden with Gothic, primitivist and orientalist stereotypes.

Jerome McGann has emphasized how much of Byron's work after 1816 was a critical reflection upon his earlier success in the light of his public disgrace and flight into exile in that year. The second to ninth cantos of *Don Juan*, for example, traverse many of the topoi of *The Giaour*, *The Bride of Abydos*, *The Corsair* and *The Siege of Corinth*. The Isles of Greece, the Seraglio of Istanbul with all its rich oriental paraphernalia, and the Siege of Ismael are reflections, in the later poem, of the topoi which had made Byron famous, subject now, as McGann has shown, to a new inflection which ironizes earlier themes. The figure of the 'sad trimmer' poet of the third canto satirizes more than Southey's political apostasy; he also represents Byron's *own* youthful opportunism, as the poet who had done *better* in the market-place than the Laureate with his oriental 'unsaleables'. As McGann puts it, 'Byron had fun at Southey's Laureate expense, and while he sometimes protested that he never counted his immense popularity or flattered his adulators, he knew that he had in fact "filed [his] mind" (*Childe Harold* iii, st. 113) during his Years of Fame.' For Byron himself, those years were far from innocent of the 'adulations' for which he denounced Southey.[1]

There is a danger of making too much of Byron's later regrets regarding the 'exaggerated nonsense' of his *Eastern Tales*, of having them signal his arrival at a stage of retrospection, at an ironic self-consciousness, which qualifies the earlier writing as sensational or sentimental. Both McGann and Daniel Watkins have recently argued that the *Tales* warrant serious consideration as 'surprisingly comprehensive symbolic formulations of the world as Byron saw it',[2] although Watkins over-seriously reads them as didactic fables of an alternative system of social relations, and more problematically, underplays their sexual politics and orientalism. My argument here is that the *Tales* are indeed worthy of serious critical scrutiny, for the very reason that the later qualifications with which Byron hedged them were *already* implicit in their conception, as well as in their narrative and thematic ambivalence.

Indeed the *Tales* are far more self-conscious than has hitherto been recognized, and enact a conflict between classical and oriental representational norms expanding outwards from questions of style to broader political and social issues. It is easy to overstate Byron's *control* over his material. In his study of *Byron: a Poet before his Public*, Philip Martin criticizes Byron's flippant style and his consciousness of the 'fatal facility of the octo-syllabic verse' in the *Eastern Tales*. 'It is... with considerable self-amusement that he serves up exoticism as a commodity for his reader, an amusement that can be detected in his deliberate indulgence in the art of sinking after the Popean manner... By building a dimension in the verse of which he can be fairly sure his audience will remain ignorant, he is able to dissociate himself from a productive process wherein the poet has become subsumed into the trade of orientalism.'[3] Whilst this may be true of the *Eastern Tales* at a manifest level, it underestimates the depth of Byron's irony and fails to discern the anxiety which accompanies his pragmatic determination to master the popular oriental genre, the jingling *ottava rima* and the adventure ballad, a grave departure from the Horatian and Popean satire more proper to his class and writerly interests. The appeal of Byron's early poetry, as well as the later *Don Juan* style, lies not so much in its 'virtue' as in its 'mobility', as McGann has pointed out.[4] 'Mobility', the very opposite of aristocratic *reserve*, is defined by Byron, in a note to *Don Juan* Canto XVI, as 'an excessive susceptibility of immediate impressions – at the same time without *losing* the past; and is, though sometimes apparently useful to the possessor, a most painful and unhappy attribute' (*BPW*, p. 920). Or, as he memorably put it in the third canto, speaking again of the 'sad trimmer' who represents poetic mobility to a culpable degree:

> His strain display'd some feeling – right or wrong;
> And feeling, in a poet, is the source
> Of others' feeling; but they are such liars,
> And take all colours – like the hands of dyers
>   (*BPW*, p. 696, III, st. lxxxvii)

In the *Tales*, the aristocratic hauteur of Byron's heroes is shown to be itself complicit with the banausic values of the imperialist market which they disdain. Aware of its status as commodity, of the *impossibility* of 'virtue' in the world of the cash nexus, Byron's unhappy poetry of mobility is forced, in contemplating its dyer's hands, to choose between flippancy, pathos or comic evasion. For all the 'official' heroism of the *Tales* (of a kind which, after all, sealed Byron's fame as well as his eventual fate), they finally chose a transgressive path which represented a peculiarly contorted escape from their ideological impasse. As we shall see, Byron was not so sure that he *could* disassociate himself from the lucrative trade in orientalism, any more than he believed that he could stand in Spartan opposition to the corruption of his age and country. Indeed, a point which Philip Martin overlooks in discussing the *Eastern Tales*, the poetic orientalism which Byron was touting in his 1813 letter to Moore itself participates in the discourse of imperialism which to many of his Whig, as well as Tory contemporaries appeared to be the 'manifest destiny' of the nation, the extension of the classical values of 'Pax Britannica' over the world. Despite this participation, Byron (unlike Shelley and De Quincey, the other main protagonists of this book) regretted imperialism as the harbinger of social and cultural corruption, the nemesis of civic order. It was Byron's will to resolve the discursive contradiction in which he found himself implicated that generated the *Eastern Tales*.

THE CONTEXT OF THE 'EASTERN TALES': 'SAMPLES OF THE
FINEST ORIENTALISM'

Although, as I argued in my introduction, orientalism has been recognized, at least since Raymond Schwab's seminal study *The Oriental Renaissance* as a major component of European Romanticism,[5] a criticism limited by the norms of 'internal' textual exegesis has tended to view its powerful mythographic impetus as merely a kind of 'imaginary geography'. Whilst it is certainly true that European knowledge of 'the East' (the geopolitical vagueness of this concept itself characterizes the discursive strategy of orientalism) was opened up by the mythographers, philologists and 'Higher Critics' described by Schwab, Frank Manuel and Elinor Shaffer, exclusive concentration on the scholarly, humanistic origins of orientalism obfuscated its ruling imperative of colonial power.[6] Edward Said's *Orientalism* criticized this tendency by exposing the links between knowledge and power; using Foucault's concept of discourse, Said argued that European knowledge of the 'East' was a distribution and elaboration of beliefs and information which itself constituted, rather than being constituted *by*, its object.[7]

Although I will develop a somewhat different view from Said's in this book, there is no doubt that the body of knowledge known as 'orientalism' – the *relational* meaning of the word is already an index of its subordination to an occidental 'centre' – played a crucial role in the transformation of Asiatic cultures into European colonies and empires. As mercantilist trade relations were replaced by a more programmatic intervention in the affairs of African or Asian nations (a result of the need to stake out securer markets against European competitors manifest in the 'recurrent large-scale [colonial] wars of the period 1741–1815'[8]) the discourse of imperialism grew in strength and resourcefulness, although also, as this book seeks to show, in anxiety. The interaction between imperialism as an administrative/political praxis and literary orientalism in the Romantic period is exemplified by the concurrence of greater British involvement in Indian administration (signalled by Pitt's India Act of 1784, and the 'worthy' resolutions which followed the impeachment of Warren Hastings) with the literary phenomenon described by J. D. Yohannan as the 'fad for Persian poetry' in England between 1770 and 1825. Largely stimulated by the pioneering work of Sir William Jones (to be discussed in the next chapter), heavily doctored translations of Persian poets like Firdausi, Hafiz and Sadi enjoyed a tremendous vogue in England, exercising a strong influence on poets like W. S. Landor, Southey, Coleridge, Byron and Moore. The literary vogue for Persian is clearly linked to the fact that, as the official language of the Mughal Empire, Persian was the medium of official correspondence in British India until 1834, and therefore a language in which British soldiers and bureaucrats had to be schooled.[9]

This is not to say that there had been no interest in oriental topics before the consolidation of Britain's eastern empire. In her 1908 study of *The Oriental Tale in England*, Martha Conant charted four principal varieties of oriental narrative which enjoyed great popularity in the period before 1790, drawing attention to the plethora of oriental tales which were in currency throughout the century. She categorized them into the *imaginative* (tales such as *The Arabian Nights* and Beckford's *Vathek*), the *moralistic* (periodical essays from Addison and Steele to Dr Johnson), the *philosophic* (*Voltaire's Candide* and Johnson's *Rasselas*) and the *satiric* (the tradition of the disguised oriental traveller commenting on European manners and politics in a series of letters home, from Marana's *Turkish Spy* (1684)) through Montesquieu's *Lettres Persanes* (1721) to Goldsmith's *Citizen of the World* (1762).[10] Martha Conant argued that increased first-hand knowledge of the East as well as the plethora of translations of Arabic, Persian and Sanskrit literature initiated by Sir William Jones 'at once and radically differentiat[ed]' orientalist literature of the seventeenth and eighteenth from that of the nineteenth and twentieth centuries.[11] But what she fails to mention is the factor of imperialism, which with the Napoleonic Wars (as much concerned with the 'external question' of the future of European colonialism as with determining the fate of the French Revolution) had become of pressing importance in political and economic terms. The writers of the Romantic age had interests in the 'Orient' to a degree which went far beyond their Augustan and mid-eighteenth-century forebears. As well as Byron and Shelley, both of whom at some point in their lives considered political or diplomatic careers in the East (Byron in 1808 'planned to study Indian and Asiatick policy and manners' (*LJ* 1 199); Shelley's case is discussed in the second chapter), Coleridge, Southey, Lamb, Peacock, Moore, De Quincey and Scott all had personal and/or professional stakes in Britain's oriental empire. De Quincey wrote in 1839, 'everybody has an Indian uncle'; as John Barrell comments, 'for the British middle class that might not have been far from the truth'.[12]

The status of the oriental topos in the pre-Romantic period seems to have been the literary equivalent of an imported luxury commodity, product of the mercantilist economics of the eighteenth-century European involvement with the East Indies. Although this trade had made a significant contribution to Britain's economy since the mid-seventeenth century, by 1713 London was the trading centre of the world and Britain's paramount mercantile expansion was well established. Laura Brown, in her discussion of Pope's *Rape of the Lock* (1712–17), describes how the poem's heroine Belinda 'is adorned with the spoils of mercantile expansion; the gems of India, the perfumes of Arabia, tortoiseshell and ivory from Africa – these are the means by which her natural beauty is 'awakened'…In this dressing scene, the poem identifies her in terms of the products of mercantilist expansion, and it begins to develop a rhetoric of the commodity through which she and her culture can be described, a language of commodity fetishism where objects become the only reality.'[13] Pope's ambivalence regarding Belinda, and the moral anarchy and cultural reification produced by commodity fetishism, is held in loose solution with a contradictory panegyric on Britain's new importance as an imperial power of Roman stature. Byron's abiding fascination with Pope can therefore be seen as more than an aristocratic nostalgia for the values of an inert, Augustan classicism. Rather it partakes in what John Barrell and Harriet Guest have dubbed Pope's 'uses of contradiction' in accommodating the values of the new capitalist order to the quite antagonistic moral paradigms of classical civic humanism.[14] Although the present chapter will argue that Byron rejected the possibility of an accommodation of the Popean kind, the fact that he might have discerned the (self-conscious) tints of 'the dyer's hand' in his poetic master Pope suggests a further dimension to Byron's disaffection with literary modernity.

The great stimulus for the new taste in oriental literary commodities was undoubtedly the *Arabian Nights Entertainment*, translated into English from Galland's 'translation' in the period 1704–12. Rana Kabbani comments 'although Islam continued to be regarded with suspicion and distaste [in the eighteenth century], its sublunary aspects as reflected in *Les Milles et une nuits* produced a passionate desire for additional narrative of this kind ... the fascination with a make-believe location was contiguous to the penetration of real Eastern markets'.[15] Influenced by the *Arabian Nights*, the topography of Voltaire or Johnson's oriental tales, the exoticism and novelty of William Collins' *Oriental Eclogues*, or the encyclopaedic erudition of Henley's notes to William Beckford's 1786 novel *Vathek*, all functioned to displace the Arcadian *locus amoenus* of neo-classicism from a Mediterranean 'Golden-Age' to a 'contemporary' eastern site.

The 'consumer-consciousness' of Byron's letter to Moore cited above was anticipated by Mrs Barbauld's remarks on Collins' *Eclogues*, which she commended for 'open[ing] sources of new and striking imagery which succeeding poets have often availed themselves of', a common apologue for oriental topics in the period.[16] Collins' 'orientalized' pastoralism permitted the representation of (at least nominally) 'transgressive' moral values in a genre which, as Barrell argued in *The Dark Side of the Landscape*, was becoming increasingly committed to depicting only the normative bourgeois values of industry, sobriety and chastity.[17] Beckford's extravagant fable *Vathek* was also praised by contemporary reviewers for the *novelty* of its machinery[18] and its detailed knowledge of eastern manners. Accuracy of what Byron called 'costume' (topographical and cultural description) became an important feature of orientalist literature; Byron himself attacked the poet Campbell's sanctioning of inaccuracy in costume and description in the latter's account of Collins' *Eclogues* (*LJ* VIII 21–2). In a letter of August 1821 he boasted that the description of eastern furniture in Canto III of *Don Juan* was meticulously copied from a contemporary traveller's account of Tripoli and from his own personal experience (*LJ* VIII, 186).

Oriental 'costume' was often, of course, as morally questionable, even transgressive, of western norms, as was the status of 'luxury' in eighteenth-century political and economic discourse. The homo-eroticism of *Vathek* or the 'odalesque' episode in the seraglio in *Don Juan* V and VI attracted a good deal of adverse criticism for being too 'literally' oriental in their portraiture, anticipating the furore over Richard Burton's (un)Victorian notes to his translation of the *Arabian Nights*. Burton took the tradition of oriental 'realism' to an extreme which his hero Byron would not have dreamed of expressing in public; to quote Rana Kabbani again, 'Burton ... [broke] the

Victorian taboo of masking sexuality. Yet he managed to do so only by speaking of sexuality in a removed setting – the East. His was a language of enumeration of perversions, deviations, excesses. He took the traditional seraglio of the Western imagination and shaded in details that would give it the appearance of *vraisemblance*.'[19] Desire and moral scruple merge in this fascination with oriental luxury and its commodification in trade and literature; the absorption of the East in an unworldly dream of licentiousness makes it ripe for moral and economic appropriation by European colonial power.

Increasing concern about the moral probity of orientalist literature by the turn of the eighteenth century seemed to have had its economic corollary in the transformation of India and parts of the Middle East from sources of tribute and producers of luxury goods to real or potential subject states, sources of raw material and consumer markets for home manufactures upon whom Britain was becoming increasingly economically dependent. Critics began to demand that 'oriental' licentiousness such as that represented by the bawdy *Arabian Nights* (widely regarded through the period, with no good warrant, as a specimen of 'genuine' Arabic literature)[20] be subordinated to a moral content defined in European terms. For instance, a 1786 review of *Vathek* excused the work of immorality because it promoted (according to a selective reading!) 'a moral of the greatest importance' in the fate it reserved for those who pursue unlawful pleasures.[21]

Even Robert Southey, whose oriental epics *Thalaba* and *The Curse of Kehama* we saw Byron censuring for the inadequacy of their adaptation to occidental tastes, believed that 'the little of [Persian] literature that has reached us is...worthless', conceding that the *Arabian Nights* alone 'abound with genius', but only because 'they have lost their metaphorical rubbish in passing through the filter of a French translation'.[22] Apologizing later, in 1810, for his 'flattering misrepresentation' of Islamic religion and culture in *Thalaba*, Southey sought to make amends in his treatment of Hinduism in *Kehama*: 'all the skill I might possess in the art of poetry was required to counterbalance the disadvantage of a mythology... which would appear monstrous if its deformities were not kept out of sight... The spirit of the poem was Indian, but there was nothing Oriental in the style. I had learnt the language of poetry from our own great masters and the great poets of antiquity.'[23] His friend Walter Savage Landor, whose oriental poem *Gebir* had been Southey's inspiration for

Thalaba[24] shared his view; in the preface to his translation of Arabic and Persian poetry, he described much of the latter as 'that high-seasoned garbage of barbarians'.[25]

The popularity of orientalist literature in the Romantic period depended very much on this moral 'filtering', as Byron himself sardonically remarked in *Beppo*, indicating once again the consumer appeal of his own orientalism 'mix'd with western sentimentalism':

> How quickly would I print (the world delighting)
> A Grecian, Syrian, or Assyrian tale;
> And sell you, mix'd with western sentimentalism,
> Some samples of the finest Orientalism!
>
> (*BPW*, p. 629)

Byron's account of orientalist literature as a commercial bauble here echoes his admired Pope's gibe at a hack who could 'turn a Persian tale for half-a-crown' or Goldsmith's disdainful remark that 'Mr Tibs [is] a very *useful hand*; he writes receipts for the bite of a mad dog and throws off an eastern tale to perfection.'[26] Orientalist literature could, by the Romantic period, just about pass muster (that is to say, justify its self-evident *brokerage* as a form of 'imperial heraldry') if it had passed through the hands of the moral censors. European orientalism, like European colonialism, had moved from being a commercial venture controlled by literature and financial freebooters or monopolizing joint-stock companies to participation in the civilizing mission of nineteenth-century European culture, or the expansionist dependence on colonial markets. The transformation is finely brought out in Francis Jeffrey's 1817 review of Tom Moore's *Lalla Rookh*. The review combined praise for the luxury commodity of orientalism with a moral indictment of eastern poetry and mythology and a culturist legitimation of imperial policy. Jeffrey commended Moore's judicious blending of eastern 'materiale' with poetic passions proper to the West, echoing the balance sought by Southey in *Kehama*. *Lalla Rookh* is 'the poetry of rational, honourable, considerate, and humane Europe' filtered off from 'the childishness, cruelty, and profligacy of Asia. So far as we have yet seen, there is no sound sense, firmness of purpose or principled goodness, except among the natives of Europe, and their genuine descendants.'[27] The standards being erected for oriental poetry in the Romantic period (like the blend of 'naive' and 'sentimental' which Schiller saw as the goal of modern poetry in general) depended upon the colonization of diverse or 'primitive' cultural forms by a universalized (i.e. European) moral imperative, the literary analogue of the developing style of colonial and capitalist domination of non-European markets. In the second chapter of this book I will examine the cultural analogue of this process in relation to Shelley's negotiations with 'proto-Anglicist' and 'orientalist' styles of colonial hegemony in India. Byron's *Eastern Tales*, however, despite his later cavils, represent a rather different attitude to imperialism in their rebellious and self-conscious flaunting of oriental style as a form of corruption, both in literary and cultural/political terms.

The Orient which Byron described in 1816 as being, before even Venice, 'the greenest island of my imagination' (*LJ* v 129) was composed of what are today Albania, Greece and Turkey, territories of the collapsing Ottoman Empire which he had himself visited, and upon which the eyes of the colonial rivals Britain and France were jealously fixed. Patrick Brantlinger comments that, throughout the nineteenth century, 'the lands between Russia and India...became pawns of the Great Game in Europe'.[28] Although the British government in the early part of the century was concerned to prop up rather than to dismember the tottering Ottoman Empire in order to prevent the creation of a power vacuum which would draw in Russian influence, the possibility of territorial acquisitions was never far removed from its strategic considerations, as Britain's foreign policy in Egypt later in the century would show. Byron's focus on the Levant in his *Eastern Tales*, and particularly on the predicament of Greece, the 'lost source' of European civilization smothered beneath the blanket of the Ottoman Empire, is to some extent complicit in the jealous gaze of British policy. In the notes to *Childe Harold*, the poet who would be hailed as a liberator of Greece even hinted ambiguously (and pessimistically) that Greece might be better off as a British, rather than a Russian colony: 'The Greeks will never be independent: they will never be sovereigns as heretofore, and God forbid they ever should! but they may be subjects without being slaves. Our colonies are not independent, but they are free and industrious, and such may Greece be hereafter' (*BPW*, p. 882).

In the following pages I want to argue that Byron's gaze, fixed like many of his fellow-countrymen on the collapsing fabric of the Ottoman Empire, also turned back reflectively upon his own culture as the world's dominant colonial power, and upon the significance of his own complicity in that power as a poet of orientalism. The pathos of the *Tales* lies in Byron's discovery of the extent to which English (and European) culture had become permeated and corroded by what he regarded as the pernicious influence of imperialism, consistently figured as the abandonment of an aristocratic, re-publican, civic, humanist heritage. On a wider scale, Byron sought to elegize the loss of contact of modern European civilization with its classical, Hellenistic source.

McGann has remarked how *Childe Harold* is 'obsessed with the idea of the renewal of human culture in the west at a moment of its deepest darkness. This means that for Byron... the renewal of Greece as an independent political entity becomes [his] "objective correlative" for this idea.'[29] As the previous quotation makes clear, however, Byron needed to qualify his hopes for the renewal of Greece, a point which McGann perhaps does not sufficiently emphasize. The glimpse of utopia which he permits himself in *The Island*, a final attempt at a resolution and displacement of the dilemma of the *Eastern Tales*, never emerges in relation to the geopolitics of the break-up of the Ottoman Empire. To be sure, Byron's friendship with Ali Pasha and his travels in the Levant had complicated the possibility of his acceptance of a Manichean model of East–West relations, although I will argue at the end of this first chapter that he failed to break free of the sort of binary opposition constitutive of orientalism. It is possible, however, that Byron sensed, as Martin Bernal has argued in *Black Athena*, that European philhellenism, an unambiguously 'liberal' cause in its contemporary context, indirectly sustained a Eurocentrism which lent force to subsequent imperialist apologetics, 'a struggle between European youthful vigour and Asiatic and African decadence, corruption and cruelty'.[30] Philhellenism has in this respect some analogies with Zionism in our own era, at least in the latter's relations to American post-war foreign policy; the 'relocated' Jew takes the place of the Greek as binary opposite of the 'dislocated' Asiatic Other, a taxonomic rearrangement made poss-ible, in Edward Said's words, by 'a transference of popular anti-Semitic animus from a Jewish to an Arab target', facilitated by the fact that 'the figure was essentially the same'.[31]

One of the great ironies of early nineteenth-century liberal imperialism was the manner in which it employed enlightenment attacks on the tyranny and priestcraft of the *ancien régime* to justify the conquest of non-European societies and culture. As I will argue in discussing Shelley's attitude to India in the next chapter, the revolutionary radicalism of 1789 often dovetailed into the imperialism of the 1820s and 30s. Byron's entrapment within an ideological cul-de-sac (to be treated at greater length in my discussion of *The Bride of Abydos*) resistant to the allure both of revolutionary idealism *and* the patriotic nationalism of the era of Waterloo paradoxically protected him from sharing in the enthusiasm for empire. But I will argue that his isolated appeal to the classical ideal as a foundation for both political and poetical practice was nevertheless quixotic at a time when social and cultural forms were beginning to be perceived as ruled by determinants transcending the scope of any single moral vision or agency.

EPICS AGAINST EMPIRE? SAMUEL ROGERS' 'VOYAGE OF COLUMBUS' AND BYRON'S 'THE GIAOUR'

In this section I want to consider a group of narrative poems concerned with colonialism written in the years between 1790 and 1812, particularly Samuel Rogers' *Voyage of Columbus* (1809–12), which provided the immediate context for Byron's *Eastern Tales*. These were produced by a group of liberal poets ranging from Jacobins and Unitarians like Thomas Beddoes and Walter Savage Landor to Whigs of the stamp of Thomas Campbell, Samuel Rogers and Tom Moore, who set up an ideal of rational colonialization and free trade against the belligerent opportunism and monopolist commercial policy of late eighteenth-century British imperialism. Their polemic was centred on a demand for the reform of the East India Company, after the impeachment of Warren Hastings got under way in 1788, and the campaign for the abolition of the slave trade. The issue of the slave trade, as well as American independence, which English radicals and dissenters saw as a blow struck against the spirit of monopoly and a corrupt colonial administration, determined that many of these poems were concerned with America and the West, rather than the East Indies or the Orient, although the political message was the same in both cases. I have written elsewhere about Coleridge and Southey's projected Pantisocracy in the republican Quaker state of Pennsylvania, a scheme in part influenced by anti-mercantilist and anti-slavery arguments of works like Carl Wadstrom's *Essay on Colonization* (1794).[32]

Southey poeticized the pantisocracy scheme in his epic *Madoc*,

148,885

published after an extensive reworking of its original text in 1805. In the original version, the poem's Welsh émigrés formed an egalitarian republic amongst the noble savages of Peru, but in the later, published version the scene was shifted to tyrannical and priest-ridden Aztlan in North America. Madoc's Welsh 'unitarians' deliver the Hoamen, an Indian tribe in vassalage to the Aztecs, converting them to their own brand of 'primitive christianity', defeating and driving out the cruel and idolatrous men of Aztlan to Mexico. Marilyn Butler has written of the 'revised' text of the poem that it stands as 'a frank, very urgent justification of colonialism as a move entirely for the native's own good. Its spirited adventures anticipate what became standard motifs in colonial fiction written for nine-teenth- and twentieth-century British boys, and the implications of such tales, in Southey as in later writers, are 'aggressive and expansionist'.[33] The transformation of *Madoc* also reveals how easily a poem initially conceived as a critique of 'old' imperialism could become an apologue for the new liberal imperialism, a point which will be discussed at more length below in my discussion of India. Southey's next middle-eastern epic *Thalaba the Destroyer* (1800) presented Islam as a rational Unitarian religion, but *The Curse of Kehama* (1810) painted a negative picture of Hinduism as idolatrous superstition, indirectly justifying Christian missionary activity in Britain's new imperial dominion.

Walter Savage Landor also distinguished between benevolent and oppressive colonialism in his 1798 poem *Gebir*, the story of an ill-fated colonial expedition to ancient Egypt by the Iberian prince Gebir. Landor's powerful although elliptical poem is replete with con-temporary political allusions, notably in its praise for Napoleon, 'a mortal man above all mortal praise', and its condemnation of George III, depicted as a damned soul in the underworld. The poem indicted British imperialism whilst obliquely praising the American colonists and the Napoleonic intervention in Egypt. Whilst the younger Southey acknowledged the influence of *Gebir* on *Thalaba* and dedicated *Kehama* to its author, Thomas De Quincey (who declared that Southey and himself were the densely written poem's only readers!) had no doubts as to its political message; he identified Landor's Iberia as 'spiritual England' and described him as having been 'a poet with whom the Attorney-General might have occasion to speak'.[34]

Gebir also had an important influence on the form and theme of *The*

Voyage of Columbus by Byron's friend Samuel Rogers. Rogers' *Columbus* was written, like *Gebir*, in the genre which Marjory Levinson has defined as 'the Romantic fragment poem', although its subject-matter seems also to have been influenced by the American poet Joel Barlow's flatulent 1787 epic of the same name.[35] Byron dedicated the first of his *Eastern Tales*, *The Giaour*, to Rogers, acknowledging *Columbus* as the stylistic model for his own fragment poem of 1813.[36] Although most of Byron's commentators have discussed the stylistic links between the two poems, few have considered the thematic connections, probably because of the occidental and Atlantic, rather than oriental setting of Rogers' poem.[37] Columbus had, after all, inaugurated the age of European imperialism by discovering America (which he considered to be the Far East) in 1492. As Stephen Greenblatt has indicated in *Marvellous Possessions*, 1492 was also the year in which Jews and Moors were expelled from the Iberian peninsula; Columbus hoped that the wealth from the new possessions in the Indies might enable the Spanish king to wrest Jerusalem from Islam and return it to Christendom. The westwards and eastwards expansion of European power was thus linked from the start, a fact which surely would not have been lost on Byron.[38]

To interpret these two poems in the context of a contemporary debate about empire and the colonization of non-European lands is to show how close Byron was to Rogers in *The Giaour*, and also, through Rogers, to the arguments of Southey and Landor. The significant difference in Byron's case is the absence of any form of benign or 'normative' ideal of colonialism or imperialism, which is rather criticized *tout court* from the moral standpoint of aristocratic classical republicanism. To appreciate the ideological differences between Byron and the bourgeois poets of 'rational colonialism', we must look more closely at the stylistic and thematic interrelationship of *Columbus* and *The Giaour*.

In *The Island* Byron wrote that 'one long-cherished ballad's simple stave… Hath greater power o'er each true heart and ear,/ Than all the columns Conquest's minions rear'; (*BPW*, p. 353, lines 87–92). *The Giaour*, like its model *Columbus*, purported to be a 'traditional' ballad, a form which scholars like Thomas Percy and Hugh Blair, leading lights in the primitivist 'ballad revival' (inaugurated in the 1760s), had regarded as the generating medium for epical, visionary and inspired poetry. Rogers' poem purported to redact the frag-mentary manuscript of one of 'the old Spanish Chroniclers of the

16th century' whose rich and superstitious imagination had all 'the freshness of water at the fountain head'.[39] In a similar vein, Byron's *Tale* presents itself as being composed of fragments of 'a Romaic [or] Arnaut ditty' concerning 'a young Venetian many years ago, and now nearly forgotten, – I heard it by accident recited by one of the coffee-house story-tellers who abound in the Levant, and sing or recite their narratives' (*CPW* III, p. 423). Like most Romantic texts of purportedly primitive or oriental provenance, 'traditional' narrative material is presented by a self-conscious redactor from a cultural context 'closer' to the reader (the 'gloss' to Coleridge's *Rime of the Ancient Mariner* is perhaps the most celebrated example). Arguably, the self-conscious antiquarianism of this technique is – paradoxically – the hallmark of Romanticism's sense of its own problematic *modernity*, placing the 'original' ballad within a discontinuous historical or geopolitical field and posing questions about the moral and cultural significance of heroic and epical values in the context of a 'progressive' present.

Like Coleridge's ballad, both Rogers' and Byron's poems developed out of simpler narrative structures which were content to be 'facsimiles' of authentic ballad material.[40] But in the 1812 revision of his 1809 poem, Rogers 'introduced' a narrator, analogous to the Turkish boatman of Byron's *Giaour*. He is represented as one of Columbus' seamen, now turned monk, who had marvelled in a superstitious way at the explorer–hero:

> Oh I was there, one of that gallant crew,
> And saw – and wondered whence his Power He drew,
> Yet little thought, tho' by his side I stood,
> Of his great Foes in earth and air and flood.[41]

The redactor comments upon the fragmentary nature of the monk's 'literary remains', thus placing the reader at a historical third remove from Columbus' heroic voyage: 'these scattered fragments may be compared to shreds of an old arras, or reflections from a river broken and confused by the oar; and now and then perhaps the imagination of the reader may supply more than is lost'.[42] Byron's *Giaour* grew more prodigiously in length and complexity; his 'snake of a poem…length[ened] its rattles every month' (*LJ* III 100) from 344 lines in the first version to 1334 lines in the seventh edition of December 1813.[43] Byron developed Rogers' monk into *two* principal narrators, the Turkish fisherman and a Christian friar who listens to the Giaour's confession from line 787 until the end. Both these characters embody the superstitions of their respective cultures in such a way as to engender a parallelism in their 'naive' representation of events. The Turk's language is rich in the oriental 'materiale' discussed above, and his account of the ruination of Hassan's hall is his own culture's equivalent of the 'European' version of the ruination of Greece by its Turkish overlords (lines 288–315). The friar's language is correspondingly laden with the superstitious machinery of *his* religion, and his demonization of the Giaour is not essentially different from the Turk's:

> Saint Francis! keep him from the shrine!
> Else may we dread the wrath divine
> Made manifest by awful sign. –
> If ever evil angel bore
> The form of mortal, such he wore –
> By all my hope of sins forgiven
> Such looks are not of earth nor heaven!
>
> (lines 909–15)

Two further voices are introduced by Byron into the most structurally complex of all the *Eastern Tales*; that of the Giaour himself and that of the 'redactor', who introduces the *Tale* with an apostrophe to 'the glory that was Greece' and tacitly invites the reader to draw parallels between the corpse of Greece and the poem's dead heroine Leila, slain in the conflict between the Giaour and Hassan.[44] The Giaour's disdainful epitaph to his slaughtered enemy Hassan in lines 675–88, and his confession six years later to the monk (lines 971–1334) establish a symmetry between the two men, one western, one eastern, complimentary to that constructed between the Turkish and Christian narrators. He admits that he too would have destroyed Leila for her infidelity had he been Hassan, thus destroying any possible claims for the moral superiority of Europeans. The power relations of gender transcend cultural difference.

> Yet did he but what I had done
> Had she been false to more than one;
> Faithless to him – he gave the blow,
> But true to me I laid him low;
> Howe'er deserv'd her doom might be,
> Her treachery was truth to me.
>
> (lines 1062–7)

As McGann writes in *Fiery Dust*, 'Hassan can pass his curse to the Giaour because he and his enemy are alike. Traitors both to what Leila represents, both become traitors to themselves.'[45] Byron's reduction of epic (or its vernacular form, ballad) to the fragmentary text of the Giaour's 'broken tale' is the formal equivalent of cultural degradation which is the poem's theme. Islamic and Christian religion are debased to superstition and the violence of the 'curse' levelled by both the fisherman and the monk usurps the place of a moral agency proper to religion. Heroic action, distinguished by love and martial glory in the epic tradition, becomes in the modern world a bloody and vengeful pattern of action and reaction which confounds hero and villain and results in the destruction of the two men's mutual love-object, Leila the Circassian slave. The world of *The Giaour* is a world suppressed under the (modern) sign of imperialism.[46]

How does Byron's treatment of heroism differ from that of Rogers? The character of Columbus emerges from the fragmentary narrative of the superstitious monk as a Dantesque hero whose discovery of America has inaugurated a new era of human history. Like the Pantisocratic heroes of Coleridge's *Religious Musing* (1796) or the 'unitarian' law-giver Madoc of the earlier version of Southey's eponymous epic, Columbus' Christian virtues distinguish him from the dark heroes of Byron's *Tales*, the Giaour, Selim, Conrad, Lara of Alp. Columbus is a bourgeois hero, neither an aristocratic renegade like Conrad nor a kingly voluptuary like Sardanapalus. In the fourth canto Rogers, the 'friend of peace', describes him in the following terms:

> War and the Great in War let others sing,
> Havoc and spoil, and tears and triumphing;
> The morning-march that flashes to the sun,
> The feat of vultures when the day is done;
> And the strange tale of many slain for one!
> I sing a Man, amid his sufferings here,
> Who watched and served in humbleness and fear;
> Gentle to others, to himself severe.[47]

When Columbus' ship arrives in America, his men are struck by the resemblance of the native Indians to Greek 'nymphs of romance'; in a footnote Rogers mentions the American history-painter Benjamin West's comparison of the Apollo of Belvedere to an Indian warrior.[48]

Columbus imagines that he has discovered a terrestrial paradise 'Another Nature, and a New Mankind'; his reaction invites us to compare the rhetoric of his discovery of America with that of the French Revolution. The symbolic links between classical, particularly republican Greece, the new republic of America and the early 'blissful' phase of the Revolution underpin the intensity of the emotion which Rogers evokes in the tenth canto of his poem; subsequent events, which he calls 'the deep tragedy of America' evoke the collapse of the Revolution into tyranny and imperialist war. His introduction of Cora the Indian maid in Canto x looks back to Tamar's nymph in *Gebir* and forward to the Byronic heroine, particularly to Haidee in *Don Juan* or Neuha in *The Island*. Cora, like Marianne (symbol of the Girondin republic) or Leila in *The Giaour*, is a passive embodiment of innocence soon to be ravished by lust, jealousy and imperialist violence; as such she stands for the Arcadian America discovered by the gentle Columbus. The narrator remembers Cora in the eleventh canto in elegaic terms anticipating the Giaour's remorseful confession – could Rogers also be symbolically remembering his blissful visit to revolutionary Paris in 1792?

> That night, transported, with a sigh I said
> 'Tis all a dream' – Now, like a dream, 'tis fled;
> And many and many a year has passed away
> And I alone remain to watch and pray!
> Yet oft in darkness, on my bed of straw,
> Oft I awake and think on what I saw!
> The groves, the birds, the youths, the nymphs recall,
> And CORA, loveliest, sweetest of them all![49]

Between the act and the object of remembrance lies the tragic rape of the New World by the *conquistadores* Cortes and Pizarro, as foreseen by the Indian sage Cazzira who disrupts the idyllic banquet of Canto xi with his tragic vision of the future. The effect is to transform Columbus from a Christian republican hero to a guilt-ridden figure like the Ancient Mariner or one of Byron's heroes, 'Thy reverend form to time and grief a prey,/ a spectre wandering in the light of day!'[50] Rogers is only saved from a 'Byronic' conclusion by a typological identification of Columbus with Washington; the Angel of Canto xii promises that the dove-like spirit of Columbus will be vindicated in the future history of republican America. Providential optimism is balanced, however, by the narrative resolution in which

Cortes and Pizarro themselves visit the monastery of Rabáda, in whose library the manuscript of the poem is kept, and also the site of Columbus' first meeting with his patron Perez. Rogers has it that the poem's coda is written in a different hand from the rest, and at a later date. This is a necessary qualification given the coda's description of the two (disguised) *conquistadores*' confessions to a friar;

> ...deeds of death by tongue untold,
> Deeds such as breathed in secret there
> Had shaken the Confession-chair![51]

The young Franciscan 'turned away and crossed himself again and again' before giving them a copy of the seaman/monk's manuscript, which is of course *The Voyage of Columbus* itself. By this device Rogers puts the (British) reader in the place of the *conquistadore*, conflating the rapine of Spanish colonialism in the New World and contemporary British imperialism in the East, a version of the 'hypocrite lecteur' strategy. The younger man (Pizarro) is silenced, the elder (Cortes) is not 'seen to smile again that night'. 'The curse is heavy', said he at parting, 'but Cortes might live to disappoint it.' – 'Ay, and Pizarro too!'[52]

Rogers' coda clearly inspired the final 657 lines of *The Giaour*, although in Byron's version there is no space for a benign explorer/colonist like Columbus. The Giaour takes on the role of Cortes and Pizarro but it is now the only role; Columbus' visionary discovery of America/Cora becomes the destruction of Leila by the Giaour and Hassan, devoid of the providential optimism which still clings to Rogers' resolution. The Giaour is a Venetian rather than a Spanish freebooter, representative of a 'serenissima republica' turned empire-builder (Venice was a standard 'role-model' for Britain in the seventeenth and eighteenth centuries, as in Thomas Otway's play *Venice Preserved*), and he preys on the Levant rather than Rogers' America. He lives at 'the time [just after 1779] when the Seven Isles were possessed by the Republic of Venice, and soon after the Arnauts were beaten back from the Morea, which they had ravaged for some time subsequent to the Russian invasion' (*CPW* III, pp. 39–40). Byron's historical specification here challenges Marjorie Levinson's argument that 'Although he seems to want history to explain psyche and thus vouchsafe him his heroes, Byron's notion of history – that of great men making great events – psychologizes history, rendering it useless as an explanatory system or even as an abstract logical development.'[53] On the contrary, Byron dramatizes the *failure* of the heroic psyche caught up in the exigencies of contemporary history.

If Rogers could transcend the political deadlock of contemporary Europe by looking to the New World as a source of hope, Byron's vision is here fixed in the moral hopelessness of the war-torn Levant, and by extension, war-torn Europe.[54] Leila, as symbolic embodiment of the Hellenic values underlying European civilization, can find representational space only as a beautiful corpse or as the phantom which returns near the end of the poem to exacerbate the Giaour's remorse. For this reason the poem's opening vision of Themistocles' grave and its rhetorical demand, 'When shall such hero live again?', ironically questions the Giaour's 'heroism': the question will remain unanswered both in terms of a narrative which refuses heroic status, and in a political situation devoid of steadfast principle.[55] Byron's 'disjointed fragments' are the formal correlative of modern history: in looking at his subsequent *Tales*, I will be considering the ideology of the often noted 'psychological parallels' between the poet and his 'heroes'. The ambivalence of the Giaour's heroism (qualified by the modern context of imperialism as nonsensical violence) reflects Byron's ambivalence with regard to the moral value of his own poetry, fitted to appeal to a public corrupted by commodity-fetishism and imperialist war. We know that Byron later came to regret the 'exaggerated & false taste' of his own and his contemporaries' 'romantic' style, which had obscured the classical and Augustan literary norms of a more fortunate age (*LJ* IX 161). If we project this nostalgia back to our reading of the *Tales*, we will be in a position to elaborate the cultural allegory of Byron's mute, heavily gendered heroine, represented by the language of elegy and the imagery of the sepulchre. In Byron's *Tales* the poetic impulse always engenders pathos, just as the heroic impulse on a manifest narrative level always results in *remorse*, the only authentic moral response to a context which seems to prohibit meaningful action.

SATIRE AGAINST THE GRAIN

At this point I wish to pause before continuing with my discussion of the *Tales* to consider the place of satire, the paradigmatic Augustan genre, in Byron's early work. To consider the Gothic, Romantic element of Byron's writing to the exclusion of his satire would be to paint a very partial picture. Although it has been commonplace to separate Byron the satirist from Byron the purveyor of Romantic *weltschmerz*, it is in fact a constitutive tension between the two modes which is most characteristic of his poetry. As McGann writes, 'satire…remained crucial to all Byron's works, even the tales and plays'.[56] When Byron repudiated his early style in 1817–20, his attempt to undo the language corruption which he felt he had helped to foster was manifest in a renewed desire to publish the early *Hints from Horace*.[57] His first satire, *English Bards and Scottish Reviews* (1809), had excoriated the contemporary literary scene in the name of an Augustan propriety which the poem feared had departed from corrupt commercial belligerent Britain. Its critical authority is vouchsafed by the Juvenalian model which exonerates it from the literary barbarism it condemns; but its enabling moral tone lends it at best derivative force.

Childe Harold, particularly in its first, unpublished form of 1812,[58] contains a strong element of satire, although the style of eighteenth-century Spenserianism, with its rich potential for burlesque, has replaced the Popean couplet. Byron debunked the Gothic heroism of Burke's *Reflections* and the fashion for patriotic mediaevalism typified by Scott's *Marmion* (1806) in 'that most unamiable personage Childe Harold' (*BPW*, p. 179). Harold's licence and misanthropy permit a retrospective reinterpretation of Burke's beloved 'age of chivalry'. 'Sir Tristram and Sir Lancelot were no better than they should be, although very poetical personages, and true knights "sans peur", though not "sans reproche"' (*BPW*, p. 179). To send such a character on a tour of the war theatre of the Iberian peninsula and the Levant was Byron's antidote to the 'heroic' deeds of Sidney Smith, Nelson or Napoleon in the Near East, as well as satisfying the tremendous public demand for information about the area. In the notes to *Childe Harold*, packed with just such information, he warned his readers of the imminent publication of 'no less than five tours of the first magnitude and of the most threatening aspect' (*BPW*, p. 882). Byron's protests against the commodification of the Levant are obviously vulnerable to charges of hypocrisy, but the satirical function of the Childe himself is clearly intended to distinguish the poem from conventional travelogues.

This defence is more convincing if we compare Byron's poem with its closest European analogue, Chateaubriand's *Travels in Greece, Palestine, Egypt and Barbary during the Years 1806–7*, which Byron seems to have read shortly after composing the first two cantos of *Childe*

Harold.[59] Chateaubriand, like Byron, invested his autobiographical
protagonist with the mediaeval paraphernalia of a pilgrim/crusader,
in his case on a spiritual quest to the Holy Land. He emphatically
denied any 'worldly' motivation – 'I went in search of images, and
nothing more' – although there is no doubt that Chateaubriand
knew, like Byron, that oriental images made good copy in Napoleonic
France just as they did in Regency England. The French traveller
was (conventionally) disappointed by the Greeks, disgusted by the
Turks, and felt an imperialist pride in Egypt as he beheld the legacy
of the Napoleonic expedition of 1798, 'the remains of the monument
of a new civilization, brought by the genius of France to the banks of
the Nile'. Like Scott in the opening section of *Marmion*, Chateaubriand appealed to the mediaeval past of the crusades to kindle
national spirit, feeling that 'the manes of our chevaliers who fell on
the unfortunate day of Massoura were avenged by our soldiers at the
battle of the Pyramids'.[60]

    In contrast to Chateaubriand's sentimental nationalism, Byron's
Childe 'loathed the bravo's trade, and laughed at martial wight',
remaining unmoved by his country's victories at Talavera or
Trafalgar (*BPW*, p. 200, xl). Byron, child of enlightenment, is
unconvinced by Christianity's claims to moral superiority over
Islam, which is such an important component in Chateaubriand's
'crusading' orientalism, dismissing 'Foul Superstition! howso'er
disguised,/ Idol, Saint, virgin, prophet, crescent, cross' (*BPW*,
p. 201, xliv). Byron's pilgrim searches for the Hellenistic, rather than
the Judaeo-Christian *Ursprung*, so that the tragedy of the modern
Greeks is that they are dominated by Turks, 'men who never felt the
sacred glow / That thoughts of thee and thine on polish'd breasts
bestow' (*BPW*, p. 195, 1). The satirical beginning of Byron's poem is
soon lost in the mood of cultural pathos reworked in *The Giaour*:
ruined Greece becomes the correlative of Harold's own melancholy
state as the exiled conscience of a corrupt Britain. Harold's attitude
is presented as the only morally responsive interpretation of Greece:

> He that is lonely, hither let him roam,
> And gaze complacent on congenial earth.
> Greece is no lightsome land of social mirth:
> But he whom Sadness sootheth may abide.
>
> (*BPW*, p. 208, xcii)

Byron was as yet not ready to translate what he called the 'triteness' of the feelings 'with which the ruins of cities, once the capitals of empires, are beheld' (*BPW*, p. 877) into the metaphysics of sublimation which mark *Childe Harold's* fourth canto, written in 1817. In the early cantos pathos still has a political/satirical function, particularly in Byron's attack on Lord Elgin's removal of the Parthenon marbles, an example of the *wrong* kind of Hellenism and symptomatic of the rapacity of British imperialism from Ireland to India. Byron's attack on Elgin both here and in his unpublished satire *The Curse of Minerva* is an important background to his treatment of the symbolic dismemberment of Greece in the *Tales*. Byron's interiorization of the ruined classical landscape in the self-absorbed melancholy of Harold contrasts with the commodification and expropriation of Greek monuments by the antiquarian Elgin. Byron, unlike his companion Hobhouse, remained a strong anti-antiquarian, preferring, as Carolyn Springer has shown in *The Marble Wilderness*, an image of ruin as effacement to the archaeological endeavour of recovery and attribution.[61]

The scramble by European antiquarians for possession of the ruins of Greece exemplified the war of imperial rivals which Byron explored in *The Giaour*; the very fact of being a foreign resident in Athens implied having a stake in the competition. Byron had to disavow such an interest in his note to Canto II, grounding his critical authority on an 'early prepossession in favour of Greece...[I] do not think the honour of England advanced by plunder, whether of India or Attica' (*BPW*, p. 878). Elgin's 'Hellenism' exemplified the cant of British scholars and patrons who promoted Greek culture as the source of British liberty, studying 'the language and...the harangues of the Athenian demagogues in favour of freedom' while 'the real or supposed descendants of these sturdy republicans are left to the actual tyranny of their masters, although a very slight effort is required to strike off their chains' (*BPW*, p. 882–3).

Byron's philhellenism here sounds more optimistic than is usual in his writings. The 'slight effort' would have involved a major change in British foreign policy which in 1812, as in 1821 when the Greek rebellion actually broke out, was dedicated to propping up the crumbling Ottoman Empire against the claims of Russian and French rivals, and was therefore unsympathetic to the cause of Greek independence. Byron's appeal is rhetorical, a Whig indictment of Tory support for oppression in the Levant and elsewhere. To this more local political end the Greek cause was highly serviceable, even more so than those of 'other cudgelled and heterodox people' like the Irish Catholics or the Jews (*BPW*, p. 882). Greek (meaning in fact *Athenian*) liberty could be equated with Whig liberty, which, as Malcolm Kelsall and Abraham Kriegel have shown[62] was based on an aristocratic classical republicanism quite distinct from the democratic ideology of contemporary 'rights of man' radicalism. Elgin's robbery of the marbles, like Tory foreign policy in general, is construed by Byron as the modern equivalent of the sack of classical civilization by the Goths and Huns.

The Curse of Minerva accordingly connected Elgin with all of Britain's political wrongs; the betrayal of the Danes at Copenhagen, the imposition of 'tyrant empire' on 'Ganges' swarthy race', the currency of paper credit which 'clogs like lead Corruption's weary way', the insurrection of 'starved mechanics' (the Luddites) breaking their 'rusty looms'; all add up to the Tory government's betrayal of 'Pallas' free-born rights' (*BPW* 144–5, lines 213–19; 221; 246; 271). And yet there is a sense in which Byron's representation of the political wrongs of imperialism was hampered by the strict formal imperatives of satire. *Childe Harold* and the *Eastern Tales* provided more adequate vehicles for Byron's particular poetic gifts, the pathos attendant upon what Malcolm Kelsall calls 'an overall historical philosophy of recent events in which frustrations of Whig idealism are placed as part of a larger pattern'.[63] These poems are, I think, of more importance than the satires because they have no easy formal means, no Horatian or Juvenalian paradigm, of resolving (or even, as with Pope, of *utilizing*) their ruling contradictions.

Returning to England from Piraeus on the transport ship Hydra in 1811, Byron, with the manuscript of the *Curse of Minerva* in his writing case, shared ship with 'the last large shipment of Lord Elgin's marbles... accompanied by Lusieri, Elgin's agent and Byron's friend'.[64] Childe Harold became the unlikely hero of a jingoistic British public demanding fresh shares and markets new, just as the marbles would usher in a new era for the British arts, in which modernity fashionably despaired before the lapidary fragmentation which Keats described as 'the shadow of a magnitude'.[65] The tormented exiled conscience of Byron's hero gave a sentimental interest to oriental 'materiale' and the unfamiliar manners of the exotic East, beyond the now unfashionable detachment of satire. The poet's doomed struggle for integrity and authority in the face of cultural forces beyond his control, itself a form of existential fragmentation, had become a spectacular part of the meaning of the 'exotic' places which he described, a point which the *Edinburgh Review* made in connection with *Childe Harold*:

The whole substance...of his poem is, therefore, popular. All the scenes through which he has travelled, were, at the very moment, of strong interest to the public mind, and that interest still hangs over them. His travels were not, at first, the self-impelled act of a mind severing itself in lonely roaming from all participation with the society to which it belonged, but rather obeying the general motion of the mind of that society.[66]

'THE BRIDE OF ABYDOS'

Byron soon capitalized on the success of *The Giaour* with the publication of *The Bride of Abydos*, the second of his *Eastern Tales*, in December 1813. The new poem was superficially different from its predecessor; the complexity of the multi-narrator fragment form was abandoned for a more straightforward ballad narrative ('for the sake of intelligibility [it] is *not* a fragment') (*LJ* III 160) and the setting was now entirely oriental, without the Christian elements of *The Giaour*. The politics of the poem are significantly different also; if the earlier poem deconstructed the 'heroic' claims of imperialism (which we might identify with Tory foreign policy), the new one addressed the dilemma of the Whig opposition and was dedicated to the Whig leader, Lord Holland.[67] *The Bride*'s hero Selim's 'revolt of Islam' fails because he cannot reconcile his notion of heroism with *realpolitik* and the revolutionary values of his pirate band, the only practical means by which he could have overthrown Giaffir's tyranny. Malcolm Kelsall has indicated (in the context of Byron's Venetian plays) that an understanding of Whig 'liberty' in the Regency context must 'turn to Plutarch and Polybius' as much as 'to Paine'.[68] The aristocratic Whig defence of liberty against tyranny turned on a classical republican notion of honour no more happy than Edmund Burke with the ideology of the 'rights of man' or the *petit bourgeois* 'sophists, oeconomists, calculators' responsible for the French Revolution. This aristocratic attitude, later explored in depth by Byron in *Marino Faliero* and *The Two Foscari*, is evident in Selim's description of the politics of his pirate band, 'the last of Lambro's patriots', whose historical counterparts had in 1789–90 inaugurated the struggle for Greek independence. These

oft around the cavern fire
On visionary schemes debate,
To snatch the Rayahs* from their fate
So let them ease their hearts with prate
Of equal rights, which man ne'er knew,
I have a love for freedom too.

(*CPW*, p. 135, I, lines 382–7)

* payees of the Turkish capitation tax

Selim's own political credo typifies the abstraction of Whig 'rational liberty' in a world which tended fatally towards corruption and the destruction of patrician 'independence' by banausic self-interest. Selim sees his pirates as social outcasts rather than as the social vanguard of the Age of Reason, as they see themselves; his view of war as man's natural state is in accord with Byron's sceptical conclusion to *The Giaour*. The pirates are

Friends to each other, foes to aught beside: –
Yet there we follow but the bent assign'd
By fatal Nature to man's warring kind,
Mark! where his carnage and his conquests cease –
He makes a solitude – and calls it – peace!

(I, lines 427–31)

What really seems to threaten Selim, however, is not so much political tyranny, a perennial evil, as modernity itself, an increasingly complex world determined by social and economic structures which exclude 'heroic' action and enforce a bourgeois/Hobbesian state of the war of each against all. Selim's dilemma mirrors that of the Whigs in the years after 1812, caught between the devil and the deep blue sea of Tory triumphalism and the growing tide of unacceptable plebeian radicalism, and with the defection of their most influential supporter, the Prince of Wales himself. Although Selim, like all Byron's heroes, contains elements of the personality of his creator, he is deficient in the one quality which lifts Byron beyond the reach of Kelsall's strictures. Selim cannot see beyond the horizon of his own class ideology, to grasp the socio-economic realities which mould his existence; he is innocent of a knowledge of the cash nexus which Byron scrutinizes in the twelfth canto of *Don Juan* or the Juvenalian satire of 1823 entitled *The Age of Bronze*. Although Byron was by birth and education identified with this aristocratic Whig ideology, which informed his three speeches in the House of Lords (on the Luddites, Catholic emancipation and parliamentary reform respectively), we should not underestimate the extent to which he beat the bounds of Whig libertarianism and assessed the compromises it must make in order to translate into effective political action. The complex narrative form of the *Tales* permitted Byron a freedom to contemplate ideological limits which he could not face in more directly transitive rhetorical contexts (such as the Lords speeches), a fact which Kelsall overlooks in his critique of the impasse of Byron's politics.

Byron's critical stance in relation to his aristocratic hero is evident in Selim's relationship to Zuleika, which, like that of the Giaour to Leila, emblematizes the honour ideal. Selim is doomed, like Orpheus, by his need to keep turning to regard his lover rather than confronting the immediate dangers of his situation:

> Ah! wherefore did he turn to look
> For her his eye but sought in vain?
> That pause – that fatal gaze he took –
> Hath doomed his death – or fixed his chain.
>
> (I, lines 563–6)

Giaffir's men arrive whilst he is explaining the complexities of his genealogy and declaring his love for Zuleika; he is killed in battle on account of his chivalrous regard for her. To read *The Bride* in the context created by the other tales (as I believe one should) suggests, however, that even if Selim *had* got away, he would have become either a predatory freebooter, like the Giaour, or in the end been compromised, like Conrad the Corsair, by a value system inadequate to the exigencies of the modern world. The heroes of the *Tales* live in an existential and moral cul-de-sac.

But *The Bride of Abydos* is more than just an exploration of the limits of Whig ideology. On a formal level, it embodies a struggle to reinterpret its oriental style and 'materiale' (the index of its popularity) by the light of its underlying, and suppressed, classical themes. At the beginning of Canto II, the reader realizes with surprise that the poem's exotic oriental setting is superimposed upon the seascape of the Hellespont made famous by Ovid in the tale of Hero and Leander, and, going further back, upon the mythic landscape of Troy immortalized by Homer.

> Night's descending shadows hide
> That field with blood bedew'd in vain;
> The desart of old Priam's pride –
> The tombs – sole relics of his reign –

All, save immortal dreams that could beguile
The blind old man of Scio's rocky isle!
(CPW, pp. 123–4, ii, lines 22–7)

Byron evokes the Homeric source of Greek civilization only to reveal its weakness and senility, 'old Priam's pride', Homer as 'blind old man'; in lines full of the anxiety of poetic belatedness, Homeric epic is described as 'beguiling', an 'immortal dream'. From the perspective of modernity, which foregrounds the mythic world of all the *Tales*, heroism is devalued, disabled as a programme for action. Anticipating his apostrophe to Rome, the 'Niobe of Nations' in *Childe Harold* iv lxxix, lines 3–4 ('an empty urn within her wither'd hands,/ Whose holy dust was scatter'd long ago'), Byron describes the tomb of Achilles at the opening of Canto ii as 'a lone and nameless barrow':

> Dust long outlasts the storied stone –
> But Thou – thy very dust is gone!
(CPW, p. 125, ii, lines 53–4)

This tomb of Greek heroism is transformed in the narrative present into the grotto 'hewn by nature, but enlarged by art' in which Selim and Zuleika hold their trysts (*CPW*, p. 126, ii, lines 100–1). This is the site of Selim's metamorphosis from effeminate Turkish prince to heroic Greek Galiongee or pirate, so that in the symbolic economy of the tale the hero is figured as an Achilles redivivus. It is also The Bride's highest moment of political optimism, evoking the philhellenism which Byron had heralded, albeit in a qualified fashion, in the notes to *Childe Harold* referred to above. The heroic mood is soon checked, however, by a reflux in the poem's struggle between oriental and Hellenic norms. The political inefficacy of Selim's heroism, which gives victory on a plate to Giaffir's Turks, is echoed on the poem's formal level; the poem itself 'turns Turk'. As Robert Ogle has pointed out, the interweaving of Ovidian motifs in *The Bride* culminates in the metamorphosis of the dead lovers, like Hero and Leander; the poem communicates, therefore, not the tragedy of Zuleika and Selim but the permanence of their memorial in myth'.[69] Yet Ovid's metamorphosis is *itself* metamorphosed into the *oriental* image of the 'rose and the nightingale'. Zuleika's flower blooms in its familiar sepulchral setting;

> A single rose is shedding there
> Its lonely lustre, meek and pale.
(p. 146, ii, lines 672–3)

Meanwhile Selim haunts the cypress grove as a bird singing to the rose

> A bird unseen – but not remote –
> Invisible his airy wings,
> But soft as harp that Houri strings
> His long entrancing note.

(p. 146, II, lines 690–3)

The conclusion has the effect of further submerging and 'oriental-izing' the Homeric and Ovidian sub-text of the poem; the lovers are remembered in the poetic discourse of the Other, the orientalism which Byron equated with the imperialist market-place. First brought into currency by Lady Mary Wortley Montagu's adaptation of a Turkish love-poem by Ibrahim Pasha included in a 1717 letter to Pope from Adrianople, the 'gul u bulbul' or rose and nightingale legend became 'more than sufficiently exploited in the minor [orientalist] poetry of the period [1770–1825]'.[70] Byron paid a fulsome tribute to Lady Mary Wortley Montagu in the fifth canto of *Don Juan*; his first sight of Istanbul had been enriched by his sense that it had once 'charm'd the charming Mary Montagu' (*BPW*, p. 712, iii). Byron's cultural 'translation' of Ovid in *The Bride* also follows in the steps of Lady Mary's account of the genesis of the oriental metaphor: 'The verse is a description of the seasons of the year, all the country being now full of nightingales, whose *amours* with roses is an Arabian fable as well known here as any part of Ovid amongst us, and is much the same thing as if an English poem should begin by saying: Now Philomela sings –.'[71] Byron's Ovidian source has been submerged into the commonplace terms of oriental cliché. Not even the dust remained in Achilles' tomb.

The Bride posits, only to reject a more optimistic political ideology on the narrative as well as symbolic level. The grotto where Selim is transformed from prince to patriot is also the site of the hero's revelation to his 'half-sister' Zuleika that he is not her immediate blood-kin, and that his love for her is therefore (legitimately) more than fraternal. Rather than being the son of her father Giaffir, his real father was Giaffir's brother Abdallah, slain by the former in a political power struggle which Byron describes with great attention to dates and historical detail (pp. 128–32, II, st. 10–15). Selim's revolt is thus doubly legitimized (in the terms of patrician 'honour' culture): first, by his filial duty of revenge, which Gleckner has described as the poem's 'Hamlet' theme; secondly by what is now revealed as his exogamous love for Zuleika, betrothed by her cruel father to an elderly Pasha for political reasons. But Byron originally intended to make Zuleika Selim's sister, and thus also, presumably, half-Greek. The suppressed Greek elements symbolized in the love of the hero and heroine could burst out of the constraining shell of Turkish patriarchal and imperial domination. Such a combination of incestuous love, suppressed Hellenism and revolutionary plotting would have anticipated many of the themes of Shelley's *Laon and Cythna*, published with the incestuous and more radical passages expurgated in 1817 as *The Revolt of Islam*.[72]

By bowing to convention (possibly through fear of drawing attention to his own incestuous affair with his half-sister Augusta Leigh), just as Shelley bowed to pressure from his publisher, and by making Selim and Zuleika cousins, as well as by introducing a revenge-motive for his hero, Byron considerably dampened the poem's political, philhellenic message. Like the revenge motivation of Doge Marino Faliero in the 1817 play of the same name, Selim's motives for joining the plebeian patriots are based on honour (the revenge imperative and chivalrous love) rather than 'principled' political or nationalistic commitment. Byron downgraded the poem's potential radicalism only to deconstruct the 'heroic' alternative in representing the failure of this modern Achilles. As I mentioned above, Selim's sense of honour (like Faliero's) brings about not only his own downfall, but also that of the political cause with which he has aligned himself. In the *Tale*'s background lurks the suggestion that even Troy was taken by guile, not honour, and that Byron was playing Cassandra to his own social peer group in articulating the limits of Whig ideology.

Selim's failure dramatizes the crisis of Byron's own political credo. In *Childe Harold* Byron had resolved the problem of heroism by means of a negative, satirical treatment of the subject; the poem debunked heroism through its hero. *Don Juan* began with the declaration 'I want a hero', and, as Kelsall has written, 'the present age gave him as his *alter ego* Don Juan, en route to hell, in a pantomime'.[73] The formal requirements of the *Tales* and the Venetian plays obviously prohibited either a satirical or burlesque resolution and accordingly reveal more about Byron's dilemma. Underlying these is the suppressed knowledge that effective resistance to tyranny is the prerogative of a more radical political ideology, like that of Lambro's patriot band. And yet Byron is unable to create a narrative link between his hero and such an ideology; he can only contemplate the limits of aristocratic heroism, whilst nurturing a compensatory scepticism about the effects of revolutionary democracy. The course of the French Revolution, man's 'Second Fall', led him to ask in *Childe Harold* IV, 'Can tyrants but by tyrants conquered be?' (BPW, p. 240, st. XCVI), and in an 1820 letter to Murray he wrote concerning the contemporary radicals, 'If we must have a tyrant – let him at least be a gentleman who has been bred to the business, and let us fall by the axe and not by the butcher's cleaver' (*LJ* VII, 44). In *The Bride* Byron recognized the 'visionary schemes' of 'equal rights' but turned the poem's 'fatal gaze' back in the direction of a form of classical republicanism which can now only be represented in elegaic terms.

Peter Burke has shown, in his discussion of the historiography of the Neapolitan Revolt of Masaniello, that plebeian rebellion lay outside the limits of representation available to the classical humanist tradition; 'low' people could not be represented outside the genres of pastoral or comedy, least of all as protagonists of political action. 'This applied particularly to revolution; in Roman history, the patrician conspiracy of Cataline found a historian, the slave revolt of Spartacus did not.'[74] Generic norms of this kind are still very much evident in Romantic writing and criticism, as in Coleridge's 1817 objection to Wordsworth's *Lyrical Ballads* and to the German Gothic drama on the grounds that they treated low subjects in a high style, a practice he termed 'moral and intellectual Jacobinism'.[75] Francis Jeffrey's review of Byron's *Tales* in April 1814 opined that even Byron was sailing too close to the wind in his poetic combination of 'the desperate and reckless valour of a Buccaneer or Corsair of any age, with the refined gallantry and sentimental generosity of an English gentleman of the present day. The combination we believe to be radically incongruous ... [they] never did exist together in any period of society', although significantly this did not mean that such a combination did not fall 'within the legitimate prerogatives of poetry'. Despite his reservations, Jeffrey could accordingly praise the *Tales* in glowing terms.[76] The combinatory power of poetry might (or rather according to Jeffrey *should*) successfully sublimate real contradictions. The pathos of the Byronic hero served to divert the reader's attention from the political possibilities which lie 'beyond heroism'. But, taking a new tack, I wish to argue in discussing *The Corsair* that Byron displaced the political dimensions of a 'radicalised hero' into the terms of gender, thereby finding a way of surreptitiously overcoming the limits imposed upon him by the norms of representation and his own political ideology.

In *The Corsair* Byron managed (momentarily) to get beyond the sort of representational cul-de-sac which marks the earlier *Tales*. I propose to take up Byron's hint to the reader that *The Corsair* be treated together with *Lara*, and that the two *Tales* provide a context for mutual commentary: 'whether the cast of the hero's [Lara's] character, the turn of his adventures, and the general outline and colouring of the story, may not encourage such a supposition [that *Lara* is a sequel to *The Corsair*], shall be left to his determination' (*CPW*, p. 453). As we shall see, Byron's vagueness about the links between the two *Tales* is as important as the fact that they *are* clearly thematically related.

I will concentrate on the heroines of the two later *Tales* rather than the heroes, for it is the women who suddenly spring to life. The representation of Medora, Conrad's wife, picks up much of the symbolism of Leila in *The Giaour* (Zuleika remains comparatively undeveloped in *The Bride*). The Corsair's love for Medora is like that of Numa's love for Egeria in Canto IV of *Childe Harold*, 'the nympholepsy of some fond despair', which McGann interprets as 'the lost dream of a perfect political order'.[77] Such a lament for lost love (a prominent theme in Byron's poetry from *Hours of Idleness* right up to the agony of the last poems at Missolonghi addressed to Loukas Chalandritsanos) occupies a central place in *The Corsair*. The neurotic, passive quality of Medora, which Marina Vitale has described (in a fine reading of the poem's sexual politics) as her 'housewife complex', is due to the fact that she can never satisfy Conrad.[78] She really exists only as a construct of his imagination according to which she is *already* lost and dead, and can therefore never be present to him. Medora's is an extreme version of the female predicament described in Dona Julia's letter in the first canto of *Don Juan* (*BPW*, p. 658, st. CXCIV); her position is summarized by her song in Canto I, stanza 14:

> Remember me – Oh! pass not thou my grave
> Without one thought whose relics there recline:

> The only pang my bosom dare not brave,
> Must be to find forgetfulness in thine.
>
> (*CPW*, p. 162, I, lines 355–8)

Like Leila in *The Giaour*, she really belongs to the narrative past perfect; her appearance in the poem is almost as spectral as that of Leila in lines 1271–80 of that poem, or Francesca's ghost appearing to Alp in a ruined Greek temple in *The Siege of Corinth*. Medora lives a spectral, literary existence: on the rare occasions when she has the wandering Conrad to herself, she likes to 'turn the tale, by Aristo told,/Of fair Olympia loved and left of old' (*CPW*, p. 165, I, lines 439–40), thereby predicting her own fate. Medora is linked with Hellenic republican liberty in the lines which Byron extrapolated from *The Curse of Minerva* at the beginning of *The Corsair*'s third canto. Her symbolic political significance is thus close to that of Cora in Rogers' *Voyage of Columbus* or the figure of Marianne (symbol of the 'aristocratic' early phase of the French Revolution) which Hobhouse spotted on a French consular house, conspicuous amongst the more antique ruins of Athens:

a bas-relief, representing Liberty with her spear and cap encircled with a laurel wreath, and the inscription, *La Republique Française*. Amongst so many memorials of the ages ... I was not a little struck with being thus reminded of the former freedom of another republic, also overthrown and no less to be numbered with the things that have passed away, than the long-lost liberties of the Athenians.[79]

But Conrad's love for Medora, most powerfully evoked in the captivity scene of Canto III (anticipating the pathos of *The Prisoner of Chillon*), seems more pathological than affectionate. His love, more than simply the Corsair's 'sole virtue', is also inextricably involved in his 'thousand crimes', as he explains to Medora when she begs him not to go out on the fatal raid:

> My very love to thee is hate to them [i.e. mankind]
> So closely mingling here, that disentwined,
> I cease to love thee when I love mankind.
>
> (*CPW*, p. 164, I, lines 403–5)

To love the ideal which Medora represents is to hate modernity in all its forms. Like Selim's, Conrad's 'courtly' love belongs to the code of chivalry and is linked to a correspondingly hierarchical political ideology which, like Selim's, is again justified as a natural force:

> 'Tis nature's doom – but let the wretch who toils
> The many still must labour for the one!
> 'Tis Nature's doom – but let the wretch who toils
> Accuse not, hate not *him* who wears the spoils.
> Oh! If he knew the weight of splendid chains,
> How light the balance of his humbler pains!
>
> (*CPW*, pp. 156–7, II, lines 187–92)

The context of these lines makes this statement of Conrad's political beliefs seem to appear in a critical light, like Godwin's portrayal of the aristocratic hero-villain Falkland in *Caleb Williams*; but that final couplet, in style and sentiment worthy of Byron's admired Crabbe, leaves the reader in some doubt. Conrad's treatment of his men is as disdainful as his practical dealings with the woman he idealizes; he appears as little more than a sexual and political tyrant. Transformed into his *alter ego* Lara in the *Tale*'s sequel, he appears to support popular radicalism by freeing his serfs and leading a revolution against the oppressive Barons of Spain; but we learn that his populism is supported by neither a Rousseauesque impulse of pity nor a Godwinian benevolence. Conrad/Lara is an honour-bound aristocrat to the last (a value system which, tellingly, Byron here denominates a form of 'perversity'), at least in his dealings with a democratically defined politics:

> he could
> At times resign his own for other's good,
> But not in pity, not because he ought,
> But in some strange perversity of thought,
> That swayed him onward with a secret pride
> To do what few or none would do beside.
>
> (*CPW*, p. 225, I, lines 337–42)

Conrad is motivated by pride rather than principle; he belongs in the world of Byron's Napoleon or Manfred or Cain, rather than to one ruled by the epicurean generosity of a Sardanapalus or of Torquil in *The Island*.

Conrad's pre-emptive raid on Seyd's stronghold characteristically involves a deed of reckless bravery: the Corsair's penetration of the Pasha's court disguised as a dervish. Like the crucial engagements in *The Bride*, *Marino Faliero* and *Sardanapalus*, the plan is strategically

Plate 1. 'The Corsair', *Illustrations to the Works of Lord Byron*
(London 1840) unpaginated.

botched, the signal to attack being given prematurely, but Conrad's personal valour saves the situation so that he co-ordinates with his pirates and is on the point of defeating Seyd. But victory is thwarted by his chivalrous insistence – in the name of his allegiance to Medora – that the women of the harem be saved.

> Oh! burst the Haram – wrong not on your lives
> One female form – remember – we have wives.
>
> (*CPW*, p. 177, II, lines 202–3)

As improbable as such uxorious behaviour might seem in the context (Byron would give a more 'realistic' impression of the rapine which follows conquest in his description of the fall of Ismail in *Don Juan* Canto VIII), it works out the theme of chivalrous or 'heroic' behaviour jeopardizing effective action. The siege of Ismail is won by the coarse and brutal Russian marshal Suvarov, an effective professional soldier whose job is to win battles and not nurse chivalric scruples. Conrad's courtly hesitation evokes the 'Orphic' quality of Selim's 'fatal gaze' in *The Bride*, anticipating Lara's 'fatal gesture' in Canto II, stanza 15 of that poem (*CWP*, p. 248, II, 1.382), or Alp's fatal hesitation upon hearing of Francesca's death in *The Siege of Corinth* (*CPW*, p. 349, lines 821–30). Ironically, it causes not only his military defeat and captivity, but also his moral defeat at the hands of Gulnare, the Pasha's favourite concubine whom he has rescued from the blazing harem.

The figure of Gulnare is the first woman in Byron's poetry (with the exception of the Maid of Saragossa in *Childe Harold* I) to trespass on the male terrain of action; significantly (unlike the Maid) she is a slave, a harlot and a Turk. Gulnare's irruption into the narrative reveals *The Corsair* to be a 'limit-text'; she breaks the circuit of signification whereby male honour endlessly reproduces itself as revenge and remorse, the circuit we saw exemplified in the narrative parallels of *The Giaour*. According to the logic of this circuit, Conrad accepts his captivity and the fact of his impending execution: although he has been defeated, he has preserved his honour (indeed he has been defeated *because* of his honour), 'Not much could Conrad his sentence blame, His foe, if vanquished, had but shared the same' (*CPW*, p. 183, II, lines 370–1). As Norman Bryson has indicated in his fine reading of David's painting *The Oath of the Horatii*, David's women (whom Bryson sees as representatives, like Leila and Medora, of the painter's desired object, an *original* vision or vision of the origin) do not participate, under the patriarchal mandate, in the system of male metonymies, 'they themselves [become] signs, units to be exchanged between the men in their inter-male alliances'.[80]

The male desire for what Bryson calls 'vision' (in less painterly terms this is equivalent to Byron's myth of the Hellenistic source of European civilization) paradoxically results in the *destruction* of 'vision' by the inexorable logic of signification. The patriarchal order is possessed of an uncontrollable momentum of displacement which can never reconcile desire with its object 'For the men, signs have eaten vision away: they have blinded sight.'[81] Thus Medora, a woman constituted solely by male desire, represents herself in terms of the split temporal logic of her 'sepulchral song' in stanza 14, or, as Ariosto's Olympia, Conrad's wife is only ever present as an absence; at the *Tale*'s beginning she already foretells its tragic conclusion. Nothing changes for Medora: she is always in the same position in relation to the signifying chain of male desire. The position of women under the sign of chivalry resembles that of Byron's modern Greeks, suppressed by the dual burdens of Turkish domination and the 'Hellenism' of Tory imperialists like Lord Elgin.

But things are otherwise for Gulnare, who takes Medora's place – as well as 'mastering' Conrad – in order to defeat tyranny, albeit at the cost of destroying the heroic values for which Conrad had lived. Gulnare, as befits a slave and a prostitute (and therefore a form of female sexuality emancipated from any 'reproductive' wifely role), breaks the symbolic code of the *Tales*, particularly the chain of substitutions represented by Conrad's chivalry, which treats all women with the honour due to other men's wives. She puts herself in Medora's place (as the 'original') whilst refusing to be the object of the metonymic logic of male signification by *accepting* her status as a simulacrum. She doubles as man and woman, Self and Other. Gulnare rejects Conrad's repetitive story:

> Reply not, tell not now thy tale again,
> Thou lovst another – and I love in vain;
> Though fond as mine her bosom, form more fair,
> I rush through peril which she would not dare,
> If that my heart to hers were truly dear,
> Were I thine own – though wert not lonely here.
>
> (*CPW*, p. 200, II, lines 296–301)

Whilst challenging Medora's role as the object of Conrad's desire, Gulnare also reveals that her love for him is intimately linked to her hatred of her master Seyd, and that she is willing to die in the cause of liberty. As a female version of Conrad himself, she disrupts the *Tale*'s sexual economy. But she also reveals herself as *more* than Conrad in her willingness to stab Seyd in his sleep and make good their escape; unhampered by an aristocratic code of honour, she provides the missing link between the Byronic hero (the Giaour/Selim/Conrad) and the revolutionary politics of the pirate band. Gulnare is Byron's solution of discontinuity in rendering the libertarian rhetoric of all the *Tales* a practical possibility – although at a high price for all his ideological and representational norms. In the figure of Gulnare, the European Self is mimicked and ultimately absorbed by its oriental Other. Conrad is reluctant to accept Gulnare's proposal

> To smite the smiter with the scimitar;
> Such is my weapon – not the secret knife –
> Who spares a woman's seeks not slumber's life.
>
> (*CPW*, p. 202, III, lines 363–5)

Conrad's objection that Gulnare owes her life to the same code of honour which would spare Seyd is overruled by her insistence that she will now save *his* by taking Seyd's. Gulnare has mastered the exchange value of the male signifier, although her motivation is the immediate necessity of escape rather than the obduracy of honour. Gulnare emasculates Conrad by taking the helm and usurping his symbolic lordship. In place of the orientalist stereotype of 'white men saving brown women from brown men' – a stereotype utterly deconstructed in the uncanny narrative turn of *The Corsair* and, as we will see, even more drastically exploded in *The Island* – we have a brown woman saving a white man from a brown man. Gulnare reveals, by her very presence and actions, that honour is an exploded system in a world where women and slaves take arms against masters and men. In a complimentary way, Gulnare is unsexed (in Conrad's eyes) the moment he realizes, from a spot of blood on her brown, that she has murdered Seyd. Byron's representation of this crisis of gender is curiously overdetermined:

> ne'er from strife – captivity – remorse –
> From all his feelings in their inmost force –
> So thrilled – so shuddered every creeping vein,
> As now they froze before that purple stain.
> That spot of blood, that light but guilty streak,
> Had banished all the beauty from her cheek!
>
> (*CPW*, p. 204, III, lines 422–7)

Conrad follows Gulnare like a silent zombie from Seyd's palace to the
sea: their boat encounters his followers, bent on vengeance. The
identification between the corsairs (doubtless, like Selim's band,
given to prate about 'equal rights') and Gulnare links her murder of
Seyd to the potential deeds of 'masterless men' in a revolutionary
context. Byron makes it clear that only Conrad's 'mastery' keeps
them within the bounds of honourable practice:

> had they known
> A woman's hand secured that deed her own,
> She were their queen less scrupulous are they
> Than haughty Conrad how they win their way.
>
> (*CPW*, p. 207, III, lines 508–11)

Conrad rather sheepishly permits Gulnare to kiss him, although it
is a symbolic token whose context removes it utterly from any sexual
situation recognizable to the hero; as the narrator apologetically
comments, it is a kiss which 'even Medora might forgive' (*CPW*,
p. 208, III, line 549). The speculation is supererogatory, however,
because the 'abandoned' Medora has (predictably) ceased to exist.
Her acquiescence in and understanding of her husband's code of
honour has caused her to die of grief upon hearing the news of his
captivity. Her reaction would of course have been justified if Gulnare
had not subverted Conrad's value-system, thereby saving his life.
Thus Gulnare's transgression, in the name of liberty and life, has
cancelled out the sepulchral sign of femininity, destroying both
Medora and the one virtue in her husband which is balanced against
'a thousand crimes'. As a result, she defines the representational
system of Byron's *Tale*, being 'at once above – and beneath – her
sex'.

In the poem's sequel *Lara* Gulnare is metamorphosed into the
figure of the hermaphrodite Kaled and Conrad into the brooding
Lara, who has taken on some of the moral ambivalency of the
threatening oriental female; he 'soared beyond, or sunk beneath /
The men with whom he felt condemned to breathe' (*Lara, CPW*, I,
p. 226, lines 345–6). Gulnare and Conrad, cemented together in a
symbolic complicity subversive of all the norms of the *Tales*, can only
now be represented in a sequel, a resolution which is at once a
continuation of *The Corsair* and a different narrative. In the *Tale*'s
confusion of sexual and political order, Byron has crossed the limit of
representational – and, specifically, orientalist – propriety. His sym-

bolic bonding of the active heroine and democratic politics open his discourse up to a revolutionary potential. And yet it is a direction which Byron shuns and suppresses in the conclusion of *The Corsair*.

We have seen how Byron's contemplation of the limits of aristocratic 'honour-politics' nurtured a compensatory scepticism about the effects of democratic radicalism. Byron, who wished to 'restore' rather than 'destroy' the British constitution, disapproved of the political company kept by his friend John Cam Hobhouse which he snobbishly dismissed as 'a pack of blackguards' (*LJ* vii 44). The revolutionary connotations of the Turk Gulnare, who has assumed the symbolic position of the Greek Medora, represent the triumph of 'Asiatic' over 'Hellenistic'/aristocratic values. The cost of *effective* resistance to tyranny is the sacrifice of 'gentlemanly' principles. As Byron wrote in a letter of November 1813, 'The Asiatics are not qualified to be republicans, but they have the liberty of demolishing despots, which is the next thing to it' (*LJ* iii 218). The only revolution which Byron actually came near to witnessing with his own eyes was the Turkish one of 1807, when the Janizaries revolted against the Sultan Selim.[82]

Byron's dedication of *The Corsair* to Tom Moore contains an explicit comparison of Turkish domination of the Levant with British 'imperialism' in Ireland, a situation which, as Abraham Kriegal points out, is 'particularly instructive in demonstrating... the parameters of the Whig conception of liberty'.[83] Whig advocacy of Catholic emancipation in Ireland was associated with repressive policies relating to land and property, typical of an aristocratic double standard in defining the concept of 'liberty', and of course precisely the problematic of the heroes of Byron's *Tales*. But in *The Corsair* Byron had gone beyond the limits of Whig propriety. When Caroline Lamb sought to revenge herself upon her erstwhile lover by showing him off in his 'true light' to Whig society in her 1816 Irish novel *Glenarvon*, she could do no worse than to identify her hero with revolutionary class politics in a domestic situation. Her Irish revolutionaries demand 'an equalization of property, and the destruction of rank and title... since the appearance of Glenarvon [Byron] at Belfort, the whole of the country was in a state of actual rebellion'.[84] Caroline's interpretation of Byron's politics was certainly warranted by a reading between the lines of *The Corsair*, although manifestly to accuse him of 'turning Turk' and betraying his own class values in the advocacy of 'asiatic' revolution was intended as a libel in the contemporary context.

Accordingly Byron struggled to repress the possibilities of his 'limit-text' by bringing *The Corsair* to an unwieldy conclusion, anticipating the sublimatory conclusion of *Childe Harold* Canto IV. The poem's last seven stanzas return to the sepulchral figure of Medora, stretched out in death like *The Giaour*'s opening invocation to the corpse of Greece.

> In life itself she was so still and fair,
> That death with gentler aspects withered there.
>
> (*CPW*, p. 210, III, lines 603–4)

Meanwhile the problem posed by Gulnare is solved by her sudden and unexplained disappearance from the *Tale*; Byron's *dissimulated* version of Conrad's fate is to have him die with his ideal – Medora. As Marina Vitale writes, 'Conrad ceases to exist as a character as soon as Medora dies; he disappears, as if reabsorbed into the landscape and sought by his loyal pirates to no avail.'[85] Or rather, into the *seascape* ('they find on shore a sea-boat's broken chain', l. 685). It is also to the ocean which Byron turns at the climax of his pilgrimage through the ruins of the ancient and modern world, the ocean as the trackless, timeless resolution of all the contradictions of history and ideology. *The Corsair*, like *Childe Harold*, eschews an unthinkable political conclusion for a consolatory aesthetic one. As Francis Jeffrey pointed out in the review quoted above, the proper preserve of poetry is to combine things 'radically incongruous' in real history, to declaim a 'curse of forgiveness' which evokes disorder and pushes contradiction to its limits, only to end by reassuring and forgiving.

RESOLVING 'THE CORSAIR': 'LARA' AND 'THE ISLAND'

Although it is not uncommon for critics to read *Lara* as merely a residue of themes worked – and exhausted – in the earlier *Tales* (Gleckner describes it as 'merely a pot-boiler'),[86] Byron himself, if we believe his wife's testimony, regarded *Lara* in rather a special light. 'There's more in *that* than any of them, [said Byron] shuddering and avoiding my eye. I said it had a stronger mysterious effect than any, and was "like the darkness in which one fears to behold spectres"...He often said the *Lara* was the most metaphysical of his works.'[87]

Even allowing for Annabella's tendency to demonize her estranged husband, there is undeniable truth in her point about *Lara*'s 'mysterious effect'. *Lara* shows Byron as a master of suspense, and there is considerable power in his handling of narrative deferral and chilling denouement. The stripping away of the oriental 'materiale' here does reveal the debt of all Byron's *Tales* to the Gothic milieu of Mrs Radcliffe and Matthew Lewis; the mystery of *Lara* is as good as that of the more ambitious *Manfred* and superior to Byron's other essay in the Gothic, the *Schicksaltragödie Werner*. More accurately speaking, the orientalism of the other *Tales* is here condensed or displaced, rather than stripped away; like *Beppo* (*Lara*'s comic equivalent) it inverts the theme of the *Eastern Tales*, substituting for a 'Gothic' Giaour in an oriental setting an 'orientalized' hero in a Gothic/European setting. Lara himself has the familiar genealogy of the Byronic hero, and yet there is something new and unfamiliar, even *Unheimlich*, about his homecoming, accompanied by the sallow effeminate 'Turkish' page Kaled. An air of macabre mystery hangs over the orphaned Lara's activities 'out east', 'with none to check, and few to point in time / The thousand paths that slope the way to crime' (*CPW*, p. 215, 117–18). Like Childe Harold or the wandering protagonist of Shelley's *Alastor*, the young Lara had left his homeland in search of adventure in 'wondrous wilds, and desarts vast' (*CPW* I 86), abandoning his 'destined bride' to another man and presumably becoming a 'Giaour' figure. Unlike Harold or Shelley's wanderer, however, he *returns* to Europe, a scarred misanthrope, an empty shell, devoid of 'Ambition, glory, love' (*CPW* I 79).

Whatever has happened in 'those far lands where he had wandered lone', it remains utterly repressed in Lara's fatherland; 'it' is manifest only in the hero's symptomatic behaviour, particularly the midnight scream which shatters the silence of the Gothic hall in stanza twelve. Upon awakening from his swoon (the scream is evidently *metaphysical*, in Byron's sense, because of its imaginary, neurotic provenance), Lara recovers his power of speech, but significantly it is the speech of another (oriental) culture:

> his words are strung
> In terms that seem not of his native tongue;
> Distinct but strange, enough they understand
> To deem them accents of another land,

> And such they were, and meant to meet an ear
> That hears him not – alas! that cannot hear!
>
> (*CPW*, p. 222, I 229–34)

Only the arrival of Kaled 'soothes away the horror of his dream' because only Kaled (who is clearly not the cause of Lara's hysterical, remorseful vision) understands the language he speaks. The episode reveals the essence of the *Tale*'s power; its representation of pathological, but apparently unmotivated, behaviour. If it is easy to slip into the critical vocabulary of psychoanalysis in describing *Lara*, it is because the poem's subject is *repression*:

> Or did that silence prove his memory fix'd
> Too deep for words, indelible, unmix'd
> In that corroding secrecy which gnaws
> The heart to show the effect, but not the cause?
>
> (*CPW*, pp. 223–4, I, lines 281–4)

All the *Tales* save *Lara*, as well as many of Byron's other poems, provide a cause or object for their heroes' remorse or corroding guilt (Leila and Medora typify this function), and in many a normative perspective is suggested by a rebuke either from the narrator or another character. Manfred has his illicit, incestuous lover Astarte, and even Alp in *The Siege of Corinth* (a Venetian whose very *name* has been orientalized) is motivated, in the furious Turkish assault he leads on the city, by his love for the Venetian Francesca whose ghost appears to rebuke him for his treachery. The Doge Marino Faliero, whose treason involves betraying his own patrician class by joining the plebeian conspiracy to revenge an insult to his honour, is also rebuked, not by a symbolic woman/lover, but rather by the 'tall warrior's statue' of his noble ancestor (*BPW*, p. 427, l. 87). It forms part of Faliero's political education to learn, albeit tragically, the rules of social justice which must eclipse patrician honour, an index of the play's – and Byron's – growing political insight.

But *Lara* is still suspended between elegaic regret for an evanescent honour ethic and an impulse to accept the 'filthy modern tide' with all its ramifications, ramifications which, as we will see, are represented in the poem as 'barbaric' and 'asiatic'. The conventional female figure is absent in *Lara*, as if, after the usurpation of Medora by Gulnare, no symbolic space could remain for the ideal. Although the narrative's climax will reveal the identity of the woman who truly loves Lara, the real substitute for such a 'normative' figure in the

Tale's symbolic unfolding is Ezzelin, a Spanish knight who 'calls Lara out' at Baron Otho's festival. Ezzelin demands revenge – or at least an explanation – for the hero's imputedly dishonourable behaviour in the 'other lands' from which Ezzelin too has 'now return'd alone... almost a stranger grown' (*CPW*, p. 230, I 471–3). The claims which we saw Medora making on Conrad's conduct in *The Corsair*, 'one virtue' amongst 'a thousand crimes', and which the latter had rejected in complying with Gulnare are here upheld by Ezzelin. Ezzelin's denunciation, like Lara's scream in stanza twelve, evokes a 'return of the repressed'; Lara's reaction now (as in the former instance of the scream) is to reach for his sword. The narrative realization of Lara's gesture is the brutal and clandestine assassination of Ezzelin, uncovered at the *Tale*'s conclusion.

It is significant that Ezzelin's challenge – and Lara's deferral of the satisfaction it demands – 'Tomorrow! ay, tomorrow' (*CPW*, p. 230, I 490) – should be the context for Byron's detailed description of Kaled, the displaced figure of Gulnare, in stanzas 25–8. The crisis of gender which we saw marking the climax of *The Corsair* is crystallized in the exotic, hermaphrodite figure of the page, who 'For hours on Lara he would fix his glance,/ As all forgotten in that watchful trance' (*CPW*, p. 232, I 544–5). Kaled is at once (like Gulnare) the haughty, sneering mirror-image of his master, *and* the object of illicit, and what seems to be specifically homoerotic, description:

> Of higher birth he seemed, and better days,
> Nor mark of vulgar toil that hand betrays,
> So femininely white it might bespeak
> Another sex, when matched with that smooth cheek,
> But for his garb, and something in his gaze,
> More wild and high than woman's eye betrays;
> A latent fierceness that far more became
> His fiery climate than his tender frame.
>
> (*CPW*, p. 233, I 574–81)

Although the baring of the unconscious Kaled's breasts on the battlefield at the end of the *Tale* show 'him' to be a transvestite woman (*CPW*, p. 253, II 516–17), Louis Crompton's (cautious) statement of Lara's homosexuality is a plausible suggestion in the context of the poem's complicated gender exchanges. Quite apart from the suggestive biographical parallels between Kaled and Byron's boy lover Niccolo Giraud,[88] his handling of homoeroticism here is within the conventions established by other contemporary

writers like Matthew Lewis and William Beckford. In *The Monk*
Lewis has Ambrosio pursued by the transvestite Rosario/Mathilda,
thereby exploiting the homoerotic possibilities of the situation before
Mathilda's self-revelation in chapter two.[89] In one of the *Tales*
appended to *Vathek* the 'unashamedly pederastic' love of Prince Alasi
for the boy Firouz is similarly 'legitimized' by what turns out to be
the latter's transvestism.[90]

The hint of an illicit, homosexual relationship between Lara and
his page adds to his image as 'an erring spirit from another [world]'
(*CPW*, p. 255, I line 316). The mystery is added to by the 'latent
fierceness' attendant upon Kaled's oriental origin, and his ambiguous
social position, apparently at once master and slave. Crompton has
argued that the bisexual Byron's periods of homosexual activity
coincided with the failure of his heterosexual love-affairs, and that
there is in Byron a clear association between his homosexuality and
the (less homophobic) Orient, anticipating the homosexual or
bisexual orientalism of writers like Flaubert, T. E. Lawrence and
André Gide. At any rate the focus on Kaled's ambivalent identity at
the critical moment of Ezzelin's denunciation of Lara has the effect of
foregrounding its importance, creating a climax of mystery and
suspense in the replacement of the customary female figure by an
object of homosexual desire.

The non-appearance of Ezzelin at the dual triggers off a dialectic
of retribution familiar from the other *Tales*, with the difference that
Lara is concerned with civil war rather than imperialist freebooting.
Otho takes Ezzelin's absence as tacit proof of Lara's guilt; substituting for him in combat, he is nearly killed by the latter's savage
and unchivalric fighting methods. When his wounds have healed, he
awaits an opportunity to revenge himself, an opportunity afforded
him when Lara betrays his own patrician class by emancipating his
serfs. Otho declares war on the revolutionary (although as we have
seen *undemocratic*) class-traitor, and after a bitter war the rebels are
defeated and Lara slain. Lara's is yet another of the failed revolutions
depicted so often in the poetry of the period, the main focus of the
next chapter of this book: other examples are Wordsworth's *The
White Doe of Rylstone*, Moore's *The Veiled Prophet of Khorassan* and *The
Fire-Worshippers* (in *Lalla Rookh*) and Shelley's *The Revolt of Islam*.[91]
But Lara's relationship to his emancipated serfs is no different from
that of Conrad or Selim to their pirates; as I indicated in the context
of *The Corsair*, the radical transformation which the *Tales* struggle to

portray is played out in terms of a revolution of gender rather than of political principle. The overdetermination of Lara's relationship with Kaled/Gulnare carries considerably more ideological weight than the poem's conventional politics of revolution. Lara's revolution against feudal tyranny really amounts to nothing more than an aristocratic populist invoking the venerable Whig doctrine of the people's 'right of resistance' against corrupt and unrepresentative power.

The smothering, repressed atmosphere of *Lara* is produced by its precipitation (and I think repression) of the representational crisis which Byron had engendered in *The Corsair*. The disturbance of conventions of gender, race and class in that poem is symptomatic of Byron's 'anxiety of empire'; the 'orientalizing' of the classical norms of European civilization which, for Byron, is closely linked to the eclipse of the ideology of aristocratic Whig libertarianism and the simultaneous rise of capitalist economic relations and democratic revolutionary politics. Although it sets out to 'resolve' the oriental *Corsair*, *Lara* is a poem smothered in anxiety, precisely because, more markedly than is the case in the other poems of displaced revolution addressed here, it brings it all back home. Byron struggles to accommodate the consequences of Gulnare's intervention and of Conrad's 'turning Turk', consequences which he had simply 'written out' of the earlier poem by substituting the sublimatory 'tragic' resolution on Medora's death and the hero's disappearance. Byron now represents Lara as 'mastered' by Gulnare, a hybridized, 'orientalized' figure returned to a European context. It is as if Joseph Conrad had reclaimed Kurtz from 'the Heart of Darkness' to wreak an African revenge on the metropolis, a conclusion which is, arguably, the whole point of his novella. As Brantlinger comments, 'Conrad portrays the moral bankruptcy of imperialism by showing European motives and actions as no better than African fetishism and savagery. He paints Kurtz and Africa with the same tar-brush.'[92]

The problem which Brantlinger discerns as qualifying and limiting the scope of Joseph Conrad's critique of imperialism is curiously anticipated in *Lara*. On one level, the figure of Lara represents Byron's fears of the consequences of imperialist intervention in *other* cultures; Lara is in this respect very similar to the Giaour or Conrad the Corsair. Unlike the other figures, though, Lara represents a return to the home base of all the dark forces repressed in the European domination and commodification of the East. The

European who beats the Turk at his own game can only do so by internalizing his enemy's unscrupulous techniques, by sacrificing the 'Hellenistic' values of European civility and becoming 'Asiatic'.

The presiding fear, as well as the 'frisson', of Byron's *Tales* is of 'turning Turk'. In so far as this hinges on anxieties about (as well, as we have seen, of self-conscious participation in) the commodification of society and the overwhelming of aristocratic authority by banausic values, Byron's critique of empire broadens out into a critique of modernity itself, motivated by his fear of infection by forces which negate and subvert Whig liberty and rationalism. If I may be permitted a rather large chronological and contextual leap here, the narrative anxiety of *Lara* has its analogy in the process described by Adorno and Horkheimer, modernist prophets of negativity, as 'the dialectic of Enlightenment'; 'the permanent sign of Enlightenment is domination over an objectified external nature and a repressed internal nature'.[93] *Lara*, like *The Heart of Darkness* and other later works of imperial gloom, anticipates the dark mythic forces of Fascism and totalitarianism which the Frankfurt critics saw as returning to poison the heart of European Enlightenment: 'The modern, fully rationalized world is only seemingly disenchanted; there rests upon it the curse of demonic reification and deadly isolation.'[94] But the Frankfurt critics, no less than Byron, build their cultural pessimism on a culturally exclusive idealization of Enlightenment and European civility; the complicity between Enlightenment and its historical bedfellow, European imperialism, remains unquestioned. In *The Wretched of the Earth*, Frantz Fanon offered another explanation of the 'dialectic of Enlightenment', discerning in the 'curse' of Fascism the return of that estranged next-of-kin. Nazism represented the imperialist subjugation of Europe itself, complete with racist psychosis, a subjugation mirroring the more extreme forms of domination meted out by European liberal democracies to their refractory colonial subjects.[95] The process is uncannily anticipated in Byron's *Tale*; Lara, like European modernity, is cut loose from tradition and custom; morally unrestrained and sceptical of the notion of freedom, in adopting Gulnare's 'Asiatic' values he has accepted a fatalism which Byron would have us believe is foreign to the European/Hellenistic ethical tradition:

> he at last confounded good and ill,
> And half mistook for fate the acts of will.

> (*CPW*, p. 225, I, lines 335–6)

Lara's fatalism threatens to infect Europe with the spiritual anomie identified by western orientalists as the Arabic 'Kayf'. Richard Burton, another rebellious, empire-building misfit whose penchant for oriental disguises and erotica make him a real-life avatar of the brooding heroes of Byron's *Tales*, described 'Kayf' in the following terms in his 1855 *Pilgrimage to Meccah and Medinah :* 'The savoring of animal existence; the passive enjoyment of mere sense; the pleasant languor, the dreamy tranquillity, the airy castle-building, which in Asia stand in lieu of the vigorous, intensive, passionate life of Europe...In a coarser sense "kayf" is applied to all manner of intoxication.'[96] If Burton thrills in disguising himself as an oriental, secure in the knowledge that the world is safely divided into an 'active' enlightened Europe (to which he can return at the drop of his mask) and a 'passive' benighted Orient, Byron is less sure; the 'orientalization' of Lara is no disguise, but rather a permanent stupefaction, a psychosis. In the final chapter of this book I will examine how Byron's anxiety was handled by another writer who registered imperialism as a form of intoxication, and yet suffered all the attendant pathologies of the *addict* – Thomas De Quincey, the 'English Opium Eater'.

Although Byron, unlike Burton, had no confidence in a 'cordon sanitaire' dividing East and West, and, unlike Burton or De Quincey, little sympathy for the project of imperialism, his fears in *Lara* of Asiatic values swamping the West still depend on an orientalist dichotomy between a (fading) European illuminism and Asiatic darkness. Byron's *Tales* are subversive of orientalist discourse only in so far as the qualities attached by the West to the oriental (fatalism, violence, eroticism, intoxication) are now shown also to be charac- teristics of the European imperialist; the Giaour and Hassan are both cast in the same mould. The organizing framework, the deployment of moral values by means of which the dichotomy functions, remains, however, untouched. The scandal of *Lara* reaches out beyond the dying hero's gesture towards the East *(CPW,* p. 251, II 467), his refusal of Christian last unction *(CPW,* p. 251, II 480–1) or even the revelation of Kaled's 'true' sexuality and love for his master *(CPW,* pp. 252–3, II, lines 512–19), in relative terms a weak resolution in comparison with the homosexual tension which it replaces in the narrative's catastrophe. It is not the 'oriental' manner in which the protagonists die which highlights the poem's conclusion so much as the revelation of the 'oriental' manner in which they *lived*, or *acted*, in the description of Ezzelin's assassination.

The poem's penultimate strophe tells the story of a peasant who has purportedly seen a masked horseman dumping the body of Ezzelin in the river on the morning arranged for the duel. There is a clear allusion here to the Turkish fisherman's tale of Hassan's drowning of Leila in *The Giaour*. The crime, an unambiguous evil disguised as 'destiny', is 'oriental' both in its scope and execution. Ezzelin's murder compulsively repeats, in the heart of Europe, Hassan's retribution and the Giaour's revenge or Gulnare's butchery of Seyd. The unspeakable, at least in any intelligible language, manifests itself in the savage destruction of whoever strives to name it or expose it to the light of moral judgement. Accordingly, *Lara* ends not with the beautiful corpse of the classical, 'feminine' signifier, inspiring in its marmoreal repose, but rather, like the 1816 *Parisina*, with female madness expressed as language disorder. Kaled/Gulnare obsessively traces 'strange characters along the sand' before she dies (*CPW*, p. 256, II line 625). Like Byron, forced to work through the repressed themes of *The Corsair* in this its sequel, Gulnare/Kaled's madness is a compulsion to reveal how much she is concealing. With this gesture, *Lara* nearly exhausts the tremendous charge of the *Eastern Tales*; for although both *The Siege of Corinth* and *Parisina* were published in 1816, McGann has provided good evidence to show that their conception, and possibly execution, belongs to the earlier period (*CPW* III, pp. 479–81). At any rate, it is hard to imagine what more Byron could have said about the collapsing, infected world depicted in the *Tales* after the dark 'metaphysics' of *Lara*. Only Byron's strange late poem *The Island* (1823), in some respects a return to the genre of the *Eastern Tales*, remains as a partial mitigation of the negativity of the earlier narrative series.

In 1821 in his *Letter to John Murray on William Bowles' Strictures on the Life and Writings of Pope*, Byron measured the extent of the 'decline' of English poetry in the present age in terms of the degree of its depreciation of Pope, 'The moral poet of all civilization'.

They have raised a mosque by the side of a Grecian temple of the purest architecture; and, more barbarous than the barbarians from whose practice I have borrowed the figure, they are not contented with their own grotesque edifice, unless they destroy the prior and purely beautiful fabric which preceded, and which shames them and theirs for ever and ever. I shall be told that amongst those I *have* been (or, it may be, still *am*) conspicuous

– true, and I am ashamed of it. I *have* been amongst the builders of this Babel, attended by a confusion of tongues but *never* amongst the envious destroyers of the classic temple of our predecessor [i.e. Pope].[97]

A clearer statement of literary orientalism in the period would be hard to find, doubly significant in its deployment of the Hellenistic/ oriental dichotomy to disparage 'the Babel' of British Romantic poetry in general, and more specifically – with the qualification – Byron's own earlier poetry. Byron's sense of artistic *shame* resulted after 1816 in his effort, as McGann puts it in *Don Juan in Context*, 'to return critically upon his own quest (the Pilgrim of Eternity)' and to turn 'what was once romantic to burlesque' (*BPW*, p. 699, IV, st. 3).[98] The pathos which is the dominant strain of the earlier poetry is replaced in *Don Juan* by an urbane irony retraversing (in the first nine cantos) the narrative landscape of the *Eastern Tales*. The characters, some of the episodes, the oriental 'materiale', all are there: and yet the familiar pathos is inflected by the conversational facility (*BPW*, p. 834, XV, st. XIX) of the narrator into a restless critical reflection on the modern world. We saw at the beginning how Byron regarded 'mobility' as 'a most painful and unhappy attitude': the most that Byron can hope to do in *Don Juan* is to transmute his spleen into laughter and ceaselessly unravel the illusions of his age by acknowledging 'the constellation of his own social determinants', to become 'the man who discovers his voice in a conscious and dialectical act of poetic ventriloquism'.[99] In *Don Juan*, Byron disengaged himself from the varieties of modern cant by holding out the dyer's hands for all to see. *Don Juan's* libertine laughter is thus a more effective sublimation of a powerful but exhausted political ideology than the portentous 'curse of forgiveness' amongst the ruins of Rome which concludes Canto IV of *Childe Harold*. As Jean Starobinski notes of Mozart's aristocratic libertine *Don Giovanni* (like the Byronic hero equally at odds with the hypocracy of the *ancien régime* and the 'new men' of 1789), 'le mesure n'est jamais comble, les limites n'existent que pour être transgressés: sa seule religion, c'est la liberté'.[100]

In *The Island*, amongst the last poems which Byron wrote before his death, the impulse which in corrupt Europe emerges as libertinage or, its literary expression, burlesque, develops as a simple, primitive, utopian idyll. Like Shelley's *Revolt of Islam*, Byron's poem tells of another failed revolution (based on the Mutiny on the Bounty) from which is salvaged the happiness of its hero Torquil and his native wife

Neuha. *The Island* reworks many of the themes and narrative techniques of the *Eastern Tales*, focussing upon an amorous, co-operative encounter between European and non-European peoples which is (briefly) free of the imperialist power-relations analysed in the other *Tales*. *The Island* differs significantly from the others not only in its optimistic account of the possibility of miscegenation, its Pacific setting ('further east' than the Orient), but also in the nature of its hero or rather heroes. The stereotypical 'Byronic hero' is still present in the figure of Fletcher Christian, the 'ruddy, reckless, dauntless' leader of the mutineers, but his influence in the *Tale* is eclipsed by Torquil, the 'blue-eyed northern child', who has been 'civilized' by the voluptuous Neuha, and the paradisical delights of the Pacific island upon which the mutineers have settled. The mutineers have rejected the manners of a Europe now revealed as irremediably corrupt, and their decision to 'go native' in the Pacific is the occasion for one of Byron's deepest indictments of European colonialism. The rebellious sailors steer the hijacked ship back to Tahiti to pick up their native wives, an arcadian destination which is significantly described as a journey back in time to

> The goldless age, where gold disturbs no dreams,
> Inhabits or inhabited the shore,
> Till Europe taught them better than before:
> Bestow'd her customs, and amended theirs,
> But left her vices also to their heirs,
> Away with this! behold them as they were,
> Do good with Nature, or with Nature err,
> 'Huzza! for Otaheite!' was the cry,
> As stately swept the gallant vessel by.
>
> (*BPW*, p. 352, I 216–24)

Byron's *Island* is an anticolonial reworking of the theme of *Robinson Crusoe*, in which the condition of castaway is chosen rather than providentially inflicted and in which humanity is seen to depend on the abandonment, rather than the education, of the values of *homo economicus*. The brittle paradise of the mutineers is short-lived, shattered by a punitive expedition of marines against whom Fletcher and the others mount a heroic, last-ditch resistance. Fletcher's last stand represents the Cain-like instinct of heroic rebellion which Byron (in *Cain* and elsewhere) describes as the motor of the ceaseless, palingenetic cycle of human history.

Torquil, however, weaned away from the relentless flux and reflux

Plate 2. 'Neuha', *Illustrations to the Works of Lord Byron* (London 1840) unpaginated.

of rebellion and reaction by his sojourn on Toobanai, is spirited away by Neuha from the slaughter of his fellows.[101] In a sense he disappears from the political world, purged of the mark of Cain which distinguishes all of Byron's other heroes, when he dives into the submarine cavern where Neuha shelters him from retribution. The literal 'disappearance' of Torquil and Neuha represents Byron's second attempt to write a sequel to *The Corsair*. His resolution of the earlier poem is altogether more optimistic than *Lara*: Conrad is metamorphosed into Torquil, and Medora and Gulnare merge together to become Neuha. This time a brown woman saves a white man from other white men. If Conrad, Medora and Gulnare all disappear into a sublimatory seascape to re-emerge (minus the cancelled Medora) as Lara and Kaled, Torquil and Neuha now reappear in the cavern like Shelley's liberated Prometheus reunited with Asia after the dethronement of the vengeful imperial deity Jupiter. Fletcher's last stand is compared to the Hellenistic glory of Thermopylae (*BPW*, p. 364, IV 259) which would have made it the pride and centre-piece of any of the earlier *Tales*, but in *The Island* its significance is dwarfed by Torquil and Neuha's idyllic escape and return to a 'state of nature'; 'A night succeeded by such happy days / As only the yet infant world displays' (*BPW*, p. 366, IV, lines 419–20).

In relation to the earlier *Tales*, *The Island*'s utopianism does represent a limiting simplification, the necessary condition for resolving the aporia of *The Corsair*: the 'liberated' Conrad and his transgressive companion Gulnare can only now survive for Byron in a 'pre-social' state of nature. But perhaps to focus exclusively on the poem's fragile utopianism is not to do it justice; in assessing the manner in which *The Island* stands in relation to the earlier *Tales*, we should rather look to the *quality* of Byron's belated sublimation. Unlike the aristocratic heroes of all the other tales which we have been considering, Torquil is a low-born Hebridean – Byron makes an elaborate and rhetorical excuse for the fact in strophes eight and nine of the second canto – who nevertheless has all the *potential* to fill a conventional heroic role. The point of the poem, however, is that he doesn't. In a reversal of the normal discourse of colonialism, Torquil is educated out of all such heroic aspirations by the simple values of the South Sea Islanders, who 'did more than Europe's discipline had done, / And civilized Civilization's son!' (*BPW*, p. 355, II, lines 270–1). If Neuha is, like Shelley's Asia, a sensual, non-Christian,

non-European woman without the Lady Macbeth-like qualities of
Gulnare, Torquil is a sort of plebeian Sardanapalus exempt from the
responsibilities of monarchy and the tragic destiny which Byron sees
as attendant upon political power:

> His heart was tamed to that voluptuous state,
> At once Elysian and effeminate,
> Which leaves no laurels o'er the hero's urn; –
> These wither when for aught save blood they burn;
> Yet when their ashes in their nook are laid,
> Doth not the myrtle leave as sweet a shade?
> Had Caesar known but Cleopatra's kiss,
> Rome had been free, the world had not been his.
> And what have Caesar's deeds and Caesar's fame
> Done for the earth? We feel them in our shame:
> The gory sanction of his glory stains
> The rust which tyrants cherish on our chains.
>
> (*BPW*, p. 356 II, lines 312–23)

The year after writing *The Island*, Byron died ingloriously (leeched
to death whilst suffering from marsh-fever) at Missolonghi engaged
in what seemed to many at the time a quixotic, although glorious
attempt to free Greece from Ottoman rule. Byron may have thought
that in the philhellenic cause he had found a vehicle upon which to
focus his attenuated libertarianism in the revival of the Hellenistic
source of European civility. The deep cynicism of his late letters and
lyrics does not really encourage such an interpretation, however,
despite the wishes of his philhellenic disciples and nationalist
emulators in the nineteenth century. It is a relief, in reading of the
pessimism of the late Byron, to consider his need, answered by *The
Island*, to finally resolve the dilemma of *The Corsair*. If *Lara* sadly
represents things as they *are* (and have been), *The Island*, its pastoral
qualities aside, offers a fragile vision of hope in terms of the relations
between a predatory Europe and its colonial Others. Along with the
brilliant final cantos of *Don Juan*, the greatest achievement of the late
Byron is his poetic vision of the love of Torquil, voluptuary and
plebeian hero, and Neuha, liberated from the riven condition of the
heroes and heroines of the *Tales* into a utopian space where the
violent dichotomies of culture, class and gender are briefly suspended.

CHAPTER 2

'Sharp Philanthropy': Percy Bysshe Shelley and Romantic India

SHELLEY AND INDIA

Browsing in a Parsi bookstall in Bombay in October 1818 whilst waiting to embark on the long voyage back to England, Lieutenant Thomas Medwin of the 24th Light Dragoons was surprised to come across a copy of his cousin Shelley's recently published *Revolt of Islam* amongst a pile of literary cast-offs from England. Remembering the incident in his 1834 book of fishing tips and memoirs entitled *The Angler in Wales*, Medwin shifted the scene of discovery; his persona Julian picks up Shelley's poem from the counter of a 'Surdaugher's' shop at Kanpur: 'it had been sent out among literary lumber to the markets of India, – a common practice with books that are waste paper at home'.[1] The poem made a greater impact on Medwin – or rather Julian – than it had done on readers in England, where the sales had been bad and the reviews worse. He was 'astonished at the greatness of [Shelley's] genius' and declared that 'the amiable philosophy and self-sacrifice inculcated by that divine poem, worked a strange reformation in my mind'.[2]

Medwin, like Julian, 'with the brevet rank of Captain and half a liver'[3] had been gravely in need of the sort of enlightenment offered by the *Revolt of Islam*. After a love affair with a Hindu woman which had ended badly but which nevertheless had the effect of converting Medwin to the doctrines of the Hindu reformer Rammohun Roy – a figure who will have a prominent role in the story that I am telling – the stability of his cultural identity was shaken no less than his health (according to his biographer Ernest Lovell, he was suffering from amoebic dysentery).[4] The only action which Medwin had seen in five years service with the Company's Indian Army had been in 1818 during the siege and desolation of the Pindari fort of Hathras near Aligarh, part of a punitive campaign to crush the last major

68

resistance to British power by the Maratha chieftains and their freebooting Pindari allies. Medwin had had a rich experience of India to compensate for the lack of military action, however; he had survived the cholera epidemic which ravaged the grand army of Lord Hastings in November 1818, had witnessed at least one incident of *sati* or widow-burning at Mandla on the Narmuda river in 1818, and had toured, with the informed eye of a connoisseur, the classical Hindu temple sites of Gaur, Palibothra (Pataliputra), Jagannath, Karle, and the richly carved and painted caves of Ellora and Elephanta near Bombay.

Medwin's adventures prompted a flood of writing upon his return to Europe; he read his Indian journal to Shelley at Pisa in October 1820, entrancing the poet with his 'relat[ion of] wonderful and interesting things of the interior of India';[5] he contributed a long and scholarly account in French on the temple carvings of Ellora (based on excerpts from the same journal) to the April and September 1821 issues of a Genevan magazine entitled the *Bibliothèque Universelle*. He also published a series of narrative poems with Indian settings heavily influenced by the work of Byron and Shelley, namely *Oswald and Edwin: An Oriental Sketch* and *Sketches in Hindostan* in 1820 and 1821 respectively. Both were edited and corrected by Shelley, and the latter published by Shelley's publisher Charles Ollier at the poet's behest. Sections of the Indian journal and a revised version of the 1821 poem *The Pindarees* also appeared in *The Angler in Wales* in 1834, the poem renamed 'Julian and Gazele'. Medwin's representation of his Indian self in the character of Julian also borrowed much from the character of his cousin Shelley – the choice of name alludes to Shelley's *Julian and Maddalo*, in which the poet had dramatized certain traits of his own character in the persona of another 'Julian'. Finally, Medwin returned to his obsessive theme of a love match between a teenage Hindu widow and an English officer, a convert to the doctrines of the Brahmins, in his short story 'A Bengal Yarn' published in *Ainsworth's Magazine* in 1842, a story which gives the earlier narrative a very significant twist in the light of changing Victorian attitudes to India.

I will return to Medwin's forgotten Indian *oeuvre* as a coda to the present chapter, for it is an *oeuvre* which in poetic terms represents a minor but none the less significant contribution to English Romanticism, and an unacknowledged influence on the Victorian literature of empire studied by Martin Green and Patrick Brant-

linger.[6] I have started my chapter on Shelley and India with
Medwin's discovery of *The Revolt of Islam* in Bombay (or Kanpur) for
two different reasons, however, the first relating to the discoverer, the
second to the place of discovery. Medwin provides an important and
hitherto neglected link between Shelley and India. Shelley was
greatly impressed by Medwin's account of India, although this dose
of first-hand orientalism came too late in the poet's career to leave a
mark on his major poetry, which had depended on more conventional
literary sources for its imagined Orient. But my thesis in the following
pages is that Shelley was *already* a confirmed orientalist and liberal
imperialist, so that Medwin's arrival at Pisa simply confirmed, rather
than initiated, Shelley's interest in India. Indeed, as a coda to the
present chapter, I will argue that the poetry of Shelley and Byron had
a significant influence on Medwin's own poetic representation of
India. For this reason he was an important catalyst in transforming
the poetry of so-called 'High Romanticism' into the idiom of colonial
literature, an often forgotten progeny of Romantic ideology, to
borrow McGann's term.[7]

'Relocating' *The Revolt* in the East highlights the presence of
Romanticism within the actual theatre of imperial power, but also
suggests something more problematic for standard accounts of the
role of European culture in the colonial (in the case of India, more
properly, imperial) encounter. Medwin was not 'overreading' the
poetry of Byron and Shelley in adapting it to his poetic account of life
in early nineteenth-century British India, although he was certainly
reading it against the grain in ways which I hope will emerge in the
course of this chapter. As I have shown in the case of Byron's *Eastern
Tales* and will demonstrate in relation to Shelley's major opus, poetry
was already negotiating the whole question of imperialism, revealing
the extent to which British metropolitan culture was permeated by
this particular discourse of the Other and the attendant anxieties of
empire. As I demonstrated in the introduction, the signs of the
oriental Other were sported as imperial heraldry (or diagnosed as
oriental infections) in the 'heart' of England, revealing the difficulty
of distinguishing between centre and periphery, inside and outside, in
the geopolitics of empire.

This consideration connects my first reason for taking Medwin's
'discovery' as my starting point with my second one, relating not so
much to the person of the discoverer as the *place* of discovery. The
restoration of a (forgotten) imperial history to our contextual

understanding of the work of Shelley and other (for my purposes, Romantic) writers is long overdue. I have been making the case that the production and consumption of Romantic poetry was not limited to the culture of the European metropolis, although nearly all accounts of Romanticism continue to read it as a quintessentially European phenomenon. Medwin's discovery of *The Revolt of Islam* in early nineteenth-century British India draws our attention to the need to reassess the universalizing imperatives of so much Romantic writing – and the *Revolt* in particular, given its title and subject-matter – in terms of historical and political geography. Despite the universalism and abstraction which are, at least in relation to the norms of British Romantic orientalism, its characteristic features, the question of India and of the formation of Britain's second empire was far from being tangential to Shelley's writing. It is well known that in a flush of enthusiasm for India engendered by his cousin's arrival at Pisa, Shelley had written in 1821 to his friend Thomas Love Peacock, poet, novelist, and senior bureaucrat in the East Indian Company, enquiring about his chances of securing a job with the Company in India.[8]

Shelley's interest in India transcends the level of biographical anecdote, however; the oriental *tone* of much of his poetry led the nineteenth-century French orientalist Edgar Quinet to write, in his lecture notes on *Génie des religions*, 'Shelley completely Indian', as well as prompting a recent Shelley specialist to assert that 'Shelley's preoccupation with [India] manifests itself throughout his productive life.'[9] And yet there is a problem; Shelley was no Southey nor Moore, let alone Kipling or Forster, for he wrote only three minor poems explicitly and entirely Indian in character and setting, which hardly constitute a major exploration of the Indian topos; they are the unremarkable *Zeinab and Kathema* (1811), *The Indian Serenade* (1819) and *Fragments of an Unfinished Drama* (1822).

In the light of this discouraging acknowledgement, it might seem that the place of India in Shelley's writing, like the place of the Christian God, is at once everywhere and nowhere. But it *is* possible to be more specific, and it is the aim of the present chapter to be so. The first lead is the fact of the well-established influence of Sir William Jones, pioneering English orientalist, poet and mythographer, on Shelley's poetic style, imagery and subject-matter, whatever the ideological differences between the two writers.[10] Taking a cue from the synthetizing eclecticism of Jones' orientalist project, we should be alert to the fact, as Edward Said has stressed, that for western cultures the 'Orient' is often envisaged as a composite whole, an 'imaginary geography', a 'stage upon which the whole East is confined'.[11] If Said is right here, we should be prepared to find a certain interchangeability in Romantic representations of various Asian cultures. This is certainly the case with regard to Shelley, although I will argue below that he makes a deliberate virtue of eliding cultural distinctions and specificities in a manner which distinguishes his poetry from that of 'orientalists' like Byron, Southey or Moore. The Lebanon of *The Assassins*, the Istanbul of *The Revolt of Islam* or the Kashmir of *Alastor* are easily identifiable one with another, as indeed are the terms in which Shelley castigates Islamic, Brahminical (or for that matter Christian) despotism, superstition and sensuality. Shelley's use of the word 'Islam' in *The Revolt of Islam*, a poem which makes a point of eschewing the cultural and topographical detail of much contemporary orientalism in order to free the narrative for a more universalist reading, might as well refer to *any* people east of the Mediterranean. But my concern here is with showing how these dislocated poems are specifically interested in the question of British India, and why they need at the same time to disavow such an interest.

The Revolt of Islam is as misleading a title for the nineteen-nineties reader as it may have been for Shelley's contemporaries, redolent as it is for us with the jihada rhetoric of the Ayatollah Khomenei or, more recently, Saddam Hussein. The meaning which now informs the poem's title in an age of Islamic fundamentalism is ironic in the light of the secular and 'cosmopolitan' revolution which Shelley had in mind, a humanist rhetoric of 'liberty' since appropriated by western multinational capitalism (witness the 'liberty-rich' speeches of George Bush regarding the Iraqi invasion of oil-rich Kuwait). A more specific interpretation of the title – which actually means 'revolt *against* Islam' (as well as all other 'despotic' religions) – is possible in the light of an argument fairly common in early British India, which I will discuss below in connection with Eliza Hamilton's *Letters of a Hindoo Rajah*. This argument maintained that British power sought to liberate Hindus from the Islamic yoke of the Mughal empire, and restore to them their 'ancient constitution and re-ligion'.[12] I have not taken this interpretation very far, however, because as I will show in further detail, the representation of Brahminism in Shelley's earlier writings is uniformly negative, just as negative as his representation of Islam. Over against the 'Asiatic despotism' of Islam, Shelley's *Revolt* sets up an idealized *hellenism*, not a rejuvenated Hinduism. In the Preface to *Hellas* the poet proclaimed, 'We are all Greeks. Our laws, our literature, our religion, our arts have their root in Greece',[13] and it is evident here and elsewhere that the Hellenistic ideal (standing in Shelley's, as in Byron's thought for civility, progress and European enlightenment) represents the other half of the binary opposition upon which Romantic orientalism is premised, that coercive 'we' speaking in the liberal-democratic interests of an Ideal (European) Reader. Or, more specifically in the present context, the English imperial reader engaged, like Alexander the Great, in the project of carrying Hellenistic values eastwards to the Land of the Five Rivers.

In his critique of the essentialism of the dichotomy between European practical reason and Indian 'dreamy imagination', a dichotomy which he argues has governed western Indology, Ronald Inden writes (cognizant of the metaphor of gender about which I will have a lot more to say):

India...had to succumb to and rely upon the importation of a masculine European hero in order to create order out of her mutually repellent molecules of conflicting castes and races. Just as the man of practical reason was the rational master and maker of the machine and just as God was the one cause of the universe, so the British would become the bearers of rationality in relation to an India that they would make over into a machine of a body politic.[14]

Although Shelley, increasingly uncomfortable with the cut-and-dried terms of such a dichotomy, would distance himself from its assertive rationalism in his later work, it does sustain the metaphoric and narrative energy of poems like *Queen Mab*, *Alastor*, *The Revolt of Islam* and (in a qualified form) the verse drama *Hellas*. Indeed Shelley tells us that *Hellas* is modelled upon Aeschylus' play *The Persians*, identified by Edward Said as the inaugural text of orientalism in western culture, in terms of a Hellenic power of representation defining itself over against an 'Asiatic Other'.[15] In Shelley's earlier poems, 'Greek' values struggle against 'Asiatic' despotism and priestcraft in a universal metaphysical framework, like the elemental battle between the eagle and the serpent in the first canto of *The Revolt of Islam*.

In discussing *The Revolt of Islam*, I will have occasion to compare it with other contemporary narrative poems of (failed) oriental revolution, such as Southey's *Curse of Kehama*, Moore's *Lalla Rookh* and Byron's *Eastern Tales*. The vogue for these poems in the second decade of the century is a cultural phenomenon which as yet awaits its historian, although Marilyn Butler has pointed out these poets' need to 'displace and generalize the revolutions they recreate... whether they envisage the monstrous fall of the state, or the fall of the monstrous state'. She reads displacement more in terms of a revolutionary than an imperialist politics; 'the topic is most dreadful because it implies the rejection and the guilty imagined dismemberment of their own communities'.[16] Although Marilyn Butler subsequently develops the links between the poetic revolutions of the 1810s and Britain's imperial stakes, she is one of the few scholars of Romanticism who does. Most, despite the enormous influence of Said's *Orientalism*, have persisted in reading Shelley's oriental revolt as political allegory, a judgement which is in part warranted by Shelley's *disavowal* of the significance of the oriental setting of his poem (not forgetting that Greece and the Levant were considered to be 'oriental', as we saw in relation to Byron). Take Shelley's remarks in a letter of October 1817:

The scene is supposed to be laid in Constantinople & modern Greece, but without much attempt at minute delineation of Mahometan manners. It is in fact a tale illustrative of such a Revolution as might be supposed to take place in an European nation, acted upon by the opinions of what has been called (erroneously as I think) the modern philosophy, & contending with antient notions & the supposed advantage derived from them to those who support them. It is a Revolution of this kind, that is the *beau ideal* as it were of the French Revolution, but produced by the influence of individual genius, out of general knowledge.[17]

It is important that Shelley needs to disavow the poem's oriental setting in this way, stressing the extent to which he had downplayed the 'minute delineation of Mahometan manners' upon which Southey, Byron and Moore prided themselves. *The Revolt of Islam* is entirely free of the copious footnotes detailing orientalist manners and sources which had become a standard feature of writing about the East at least since Beckford's *Vathek*. In my previous chapter on Byron, I read the currency of 'oriental materiale' in terms of a *literary* commodification analogous to the massive eastwards extension of European commerce from the late eighteenth century on. Lest the reader should mistake his intention, Shelley (in contrast to Byron) needed to reaffirm his poem's genealogy in the tradition of the eighteenth-century oriental tale, a tradition in which the eastern setting served to establish 'a geographical and cultural distance or perspective from which satire and criticism could then be directed at Europe'.[18] Shelley is not of course a lone voice in his disavowal of 'orientalist' machinery, as will I hope become clearer in the next section. James Mill (and to a lesser extent Jeremy Bentham) were engaged in a similar contestation of the 'orientalist' position at about the same time as Shelley, the former working through the massive archive of information which had been amassed on India in order to demolish the 'orientalist' argument in his (ironically titled) *History of British India*. But the general drift of the present book has been to deny the sort of interpretation of oriental literature represented by Shelley's disavowal, by arguing that form is not detachable from content in quite the way that his argument would have it. This is of course not to deny that arguments about the Orient are *also* signs of ideological confrontation in the metropolitan culture, particularly in the case of radical/democratic writers. As Javed Majeed has stressed, 'It is very difficult to make a distinction between colonial and domestic when considering questions of ideology in this period. Indeed, it was crucial to the emergence of Utilitarianism as a rhetoric of reform to ignore any such distinctions.'[19]

The Revolt of Islam hovers in an underspecified space between what for Shelley were the two principal revolutionary sites of the year 1817, neither of which, for different reasons, could conveniently supply him with a literary setting for his political and poetical idealism. The first site was that overshadowed by the spectre of the radical/democratic revolution which, from 1816, he feared was brewing in England, and for which (despite his splendid performance in *The Mask of Anarchy*, stung by the news of Peterloo) Shelley believed the English people were unprepared because too easily swayed by 'the violence of demagogues'.[20] The second, I want to argue, was a revolution in which Shelley placed greater hopes, but which he could not easily *call* a revolution without raising problems for his libertarian polemic: namely the transformation of traditional Indian culture by a British civilizing mission. By taking the colonial Tom Medwin as 'ideal reader' of *The Revolt of Islam* the implications of the poem with regard to this second revolution are foregrounded, a revolution which would tie Shelley in knots when he came to discuss it openly in a passage of the *Philosophical View of Reform* to be examined in some detail below. For Shelley as for many other English liberals, the construction of imperial (and, wishfully for some, *colonial*) power in India was itself part of the '*beau ideal*' of the French Revolution, no less than the project of domestic reform. Nevertheless, Shelley, like other liberal imperialists, could not set his 'beau ideal of the French Revolution' in India without risking a disabling ambiguity. It is not that British India had not known nor *would* not know any social conflicts qualifying to be described as 'revolts' or 'revolutions', as Tom Medwin would well have known. Disputing a wishful reconstruction of 'Pax Britannica' in the official historiography of nineteenth-century India, disturbed only once by a rather troublesome army mutiny in 1857, C. A. Bayly writes that 'in fact armed revolt was endemic in all parts of early colonial India'.[21]

'THE ASSASSINS'

The complex displacements involved in Shelley's attitude to a 'revolution' in British India are brought into sharper relief when we look at his unfinished oriental tale of 1814, *The Assassins*. *The Assassins* represents what is for Shelley an ideal colonial scenario, and as such one which, it should be pointed out, differs from British India as it was in the 1810s, an arrangement whereby Company employees were soldiers and administrators, not colonial settlers. Although the rootless, exiled Shelley nowhere expresses his opinions concerning the settling or colonizing of India, it seems likely that, like many other liberal 'pantisocratizers', he would have been in favour of it. It is certainly possible to read *The Assassins* as an endorsement of colonialism. Shelley's anachronistically named band of Assassins are primitive, gnostic Christians (although their principles are essentially 'Greek') who abandon Jerusalem just as it is about to be besieged and subjected to the imperial yoke of Rome, here representative of the *ancien régime* or 'Islam' of the 1818 poem. The Assassins form an ideal society in the mountainous valley of Bethzatanai in Lebanon.

Like Coleridge and Southey's pantisocracy, the 'Happy Valley' of the Assassins is conveniently devoid of human habitation, so an egalitarian society can be established without the perennial problem of *real* colonialism, namely what to do with the natives. 'It well accorded with the justice of their conceptions on the relative duties of man towards his fellows in society that they should labour in unconstrained equality to dispossess the wolf and the tiger of their empire and establish on its ruins the dominion of intelligence and virtue.'[22] Although Bethzatanai is 'concealed from the adventurous search of man among mountains of everlasting snow', and thus, unlike British Hindustan, hidden and *empty*, it shares with it a splendid antiquity nobler than the remains of 'Caliphs and... Caesars'; 'the men of elder days had inhabited this spot. Piles of monumental marble and fragments of columns that in their integrity almost seemed the work of some intelligence more sportive and fantastic than the gross conceptions of mortality, lay in heaps beside the lake and were visible beneath its transparent waves.'[23] The colony of the Assassins is exempted from the corruptions of a history from which they have fled; its only past is an idealized antiquity. As Bernard Blackstone writes, comparing Bethzatanai with the oriental paradises of Samuel Johnson and Beckford, '[here] the new Golden Age is to be built upon the ruins of and with hints from the old Golden Age; traditional wisdom joins hand with simple piety'.[24]

If the *Revolt of Islam* represents the '*beau ideal*' of the French Revolution, then the valley of the Assassins adumbrates Shelley's '*beau ideal*' of British India, in which European enlightenment joins hands with an idealized Upanishadic age to realize a new utopia. In Shelley's 'utopian' model, the modern natives are left out of the formula, whereas their necessary inclusion in the real plan is contingent upon either a policy of 'reformation' to the antique manners from which they are seen to have degenerated, or 'assimilation' to the modern values of their new masters. These two options, described in relation to British India, are usually designated the 'orientalist' and the 'Anglicist' respectively. The dichotomous use of the two terms, which form the main axes of my argument, and which will be considered in more detail below, developed in the context of a debate about whether Indian education should be conducted in native languages or in English, but broadened into a more general account of different styles of hegemony. Because the Anglicist position with which I will associate Shelley's earlier thinking about India became fully emergent only in the 1830s (the 'orientalist' one had until then been hegemonic), I will use the somewhat awkward term 'proto-Anglicist' to describe it in relation to Shelley and his contemporaries in the eighteen-tens and twenties.

Shelley's 'Assassins', the colonizers of an *empty* Asian valley, are, unlike the cadres of the 'Hon'ble Company', *also orientals* (like the Company's new Indian *subjects*), although orientals fortunate in the possession of all the attributes of Shelley's Hellenes. They can thus be seen to figure the liberal fantasy of oriental peoples *colonizing themselves* in the name of western values – and doubtless to the advantage of the European economies – without the necessity of being subjugated to the imperialist yoke by foreign invaders. In its 'Anglicist' guise, this liberal fantasy represents a wish fulfilment of rational universalism exempted from the violence which marks the real *ambivalence* of colonial discourse. In Shelley's 1814 fragment violence has not disappeared, however; on the contrary, it is manifest even in the title. The Assassins who colonize Bethzatanai are also outcasts from society, engaged (like the Indian 'Thugs' with whom they were often compared) in a *revolution* against the decadent world beyond their sheltering mountains. Indeed, from the purview of the 'outside world', the Assassins are vicious murderers and their gentleness would turn to uncompromising violence if they should leave the Happy Valley to mingle in the corrupt world at large:

No Assassin would submissively temporize with vice, and in cold charity become a pander to falsehood and desolation. His path through the wilderness of civilized society would be marked with the blood of the oppressor and the ruiner. The wretch whom nations tremblingly adore would expiate in his throttling grasp a thousand licenced and venerable crimes.[25]

The violence of the Assassins is at once 'oriental' in its brutality *and* legitimate in terms of Shelleyan political virtue. A rare feature in his later writings (Laon and Cythna *spare* the tyrant Othman in the *Revolt of Islam* and violence is always defensive), Shelley's 'assassination' has more in common with the dark deeds of Byron's *Lara*, Madoc's violent destruction of native Indians in Southey's eponymous epic, or De Quincey's stories *The Peasant of Portugal, The Caçadore* or *The Avenger*.[26] But read as a fable of revolution, *The Assassins* makes more sense in Shelley's generally non-violent opus, as a justification of revolutionary terror, and a vindication of 'the habit of picturing possible forms of society where...crimes would be no longer crimes', like the character of Rivers in Wordsworth's play *The Borderers*.[27] To read *The Assassins* as a fable of empire, however, is more problematic for the libertarian charge of Shelley's writing, particularly in so far as its seeks to *displace* the real violence underpinning the project of imperialism. From the libertarian viewpoint, the Assassins are outcast heroic rebels, colonizers *and* orientals; their violence, far from being inflicted upon a subject

people, is hypothetically aimed at the 'ancien régime' in the world
which they have left. The disturbing fact which is emerging here is
that the rhetorics of liberation and domination, apparently distinct in
the metropolitan context, dovetail one into the other when translated
into the idiom of liberal imperialism. In consequence, when the
European civilizing mission is regarded as *revolutionary*, then violent
resistance to (in real terms, violent *subjugation* of), counter-
revolutionary or indigenous elements becomes a necessary evil. We
will see in the course of the following pages how imperialist radicals
(Shelley not excepted) came to construct cultural 'otherness',
whether of religion, political organization or custom, as counter-
revolutionary. I mentioned that the violence which is represented as
displaced in *The Assassins* vanishes from *sight* in *The Revolt of Islam*. It
is very far from vanishing from the text altogether, however, and I
will argue that its repressed spectre returns to haunt the poetic ideal
of a universal civilizing mission.

In the light of these considerations we can say, then, that Shelley's
radical idealism discovered in the Orient (as the hyperbolic image of
Britain's newly acquired empire in India) both an expansive field –
a fascination or 'interest' – and an aporia, a 'being at a loss' or
blockage. For this reason India is an oxymoronic figure in his poetry,
the site of a revolution which is also a form of imperial domination,
a contradiction which enforces a particularly tortuous deployment of
the metaphors and narrative turns (as well as suppressions) of the
orientalist archive. Critics and admirers alike have tended to overlook
the accommodation which Shelley's radicalism makes with the
question of imperialism; in particular his admirers, in conformity
with a general blindness on the part of the British left towards the
Empire (at least until Raymond Williams' seminal remarks in *The
Country and the City*), have uncritically assumed that Shelley, like
David Erdman's Blake, is a 'Prophet against Empire'.[28] This may to
some extent be based on a failure to understand the nature of early
nineteenth-century imperialist ideology, more commonly based on
liberal notions of a civilizing mission than on belligerent jingoism.
Imperialist writers of the period more often appeal to the diffusion of
civility than to the emergent discourse of racial superiority or the
strategy (common later in the nineteenth century) of justifying
illiberal colonial policies by 'blaming the victims'. Indeed, as Patrick
Brantlinger points out, 'the connections between reform at home and
empire abroad proliferate ... it was largely out of the liberal, reform-

minded optimism of the early Victorians that the apparently more conservative social Darwinian, jingoist imperialism of the late Victorians evolved'.[29] It is in this light that I wish to elaborate the significance of Medwin's discovery of Shelley's *Revolt of Islam* on the Bombay bookstall in 1818.

THE WORD IN THE WILDERNESS

On one level, Medwin's chance find of *The Revolt of Islam* on the Bombay book-barrow partakes of that moment which Homi Bhabha evokes as 'triumphantly *inaugurat*[*ing*] a Literature of Empire...the scenario of the sudden, fortuitous discovery of the English Book played out in the wild and wordless wastes of colonial India, Africa, the Caribbean...at once a moment of originality and authority as well as a process of displacement that, paradoxically, makes the presence of the Book wondrous to the extent to which it is repeated, translated mis-read, displaced'.[30] The English books of Bhabha's 'Signs Taken for Wonders' – whether they be the Gospels translated into Hindustani or Towson's *Inquiry into Some Points of Seamanship* discovered by Marlow in Conrad's *Heart of Darkness* – constitute a discourse of English civility embarked upon a *civil*izing mission.

To be more precise, the discovery of the English book in British India fulfils a *Shelleyan* fantasy of discovery (which, as I will argue, is the message of *The Revolt of Islam* itself), a discovery which has little to do with the historical reality of British empire-building in India in this period. In the following section I will consider Shelley's anxiety of empire in the light of Bhabha's suggestive theory, fully aware of the limitations of that theory in relation to the history of many of the hegemonic strategies with which I will be dealing. For British India was very far from being considered as a 'wild and wordless waste' by the majority of Europeans involved in the process of constructing the edifice of East India Company power in the subcontinent. Most were fully aware that its languages were legion, and soldiers, administrators and missionaries, far from disregarding the indigenous culture and forcing the English book on their native subjects, struggled to make some headway in mastering tongues and manners which might guarantee the success of 'rule by opinion' or Christian conversion. Whatever the historical weaknesses of Bhabha's account (and I will suggest that there are also problems with its notion of the homogeneity of metropolitan 'civility'), it does offer a suggestive model of

Plate 3. 'Tom Raw at a Hindoo Entertainment', in *Tom Raw the Griffin*, by Charles D'Oyly (London 1828), facing p. 182.

the dynamics of Shelley's 'proto-Anglicist' fantasy of revolutionary enlightenment. Whether set amongst the deserted ruins of Bethza-tanai or the cultural wastes of Othman's kingdom in the *Revolt of Islam*, this fantasy carried an implicit ideal of British imperial power as the liberation of its subjects from Asiatic darkness.

One of the advantages of Bhabha's theory of colonial discourse lies in his use of psychoanalysis to problematize the subject–object relationships upon which any such theory must revolve (it is also, arguably, a problem, given the epistemologically privileged, tran-scendental status of psychoanalysis in a theory concerned to deconstruct essentialist and universalizing models of thought).[31] Bhabha argues that 'the institution of the World in the wilds is also an *Entstellung*, a process of displacement, distortion, dislocation, repetition – the dazzling light of Literature sheds only areas of darkness'.[32] Bhabha thereby criticizes Edward Said's notion of a totalizing, monolithic western orientalism, a self-defining structure of intentionality which 'enables Europe to advance securely and *unmetaphorically* upon the Orient'.[33] In deconstructing this notion of the 'one-way march' of imperial power and suggesting that the imperial *subject* was also able to perform an analogous deconstruction 'in the field', his theory is distinct from Gayatri Spivak's insistence on the 'absence of a text that can "answer one back" after the planned epistemic violence of the imperialist project'.[34] In her careful exposition and critique of Bhabha's theory, Benita Parry writes that for Bhabha the displacement of the English book in colonial space results in the mutation of 'the civil discourse of a culturally cohesive community...into the text of a civilizing mission, [whereby] its enunciatory assumptions are revealed to be in conflict with its means of social control, so that the incompatibility of the ideas of English liberty and the idea of British imperialism is exposed'.[35] In his later work (from the essay 'Signs taken for Wonders' onwards) Bhabha's native subject exploits the fault lines of the displaced originary discourse in terms of an indigenous system of cultural meanings as a form of 'defensive warfare' encompassing the categories of 'hybridi-zation' (a category derived from Bakhtin) and 'mimicry' (from Lacan).

How does Medwin's 'discovery' of Shelley's epic of revolution in British India look in the light of Bhabha's theory? I choose the jaded and hybridized Medwin as exemplary reader of *The Revolt of Islam*, rather than a possible Indian client of the Parsi bookstall, in part

Plate 4. 'Tom Raw rejects the Embraces of the Nabob of Bengal', *Tom Raw the Griffin*, facing p. 205.

because I lack the resources to understand what the nature of such a reading might have been, but also because I am concerned – in the present section of my argument at least – to address the anxieties in the British discourse of India rather than the resistances on the part of the Indian subjects of British power. Although a later section of this chapter will consider Shelley's *Prometheus Unbound* as a *dialogue* between 'Hellenistic' rationality and the 'hybridized' Hindu theology of Rammohun Roy, my concern at this point is mainly with the manner in which the imperial context brings out inherent instabilities within the Romantic imagination, the main scope of my study of the 'anxieties of empire'.

This is not simply to differentiate the subject positions of a European writer/reader and an Indian reader/writer, or to suggest that the former acted unproblematically upon the latter. I have already addressed the hybridity of Byron's *Eastern Tales* and, having examined Shelley's tortuous rationalizations, will look in the next chapter at the radical instability of De Quincey's cultural identity. There is space here for hybridized Englishmen as well as hybridized Indians. The anxieties embodied in British Romantic writing about the East – both the assertion of superiority and the fear of instability and absorption – reflect the tenuous nature of East India Company rule in the late eighteenth and early nineteenth centuries, its necessary investment in the Mughal terms of power and its complicated attitude to indigenous idioms. For this reason, an account of colonial discourse as a 'one way' agency would simply – and unhistorically – repeat the binary opposition upon which the whole orientalist project is premised in the first place.[36]

I choose rather to follow Bhabha's radical suggestion that East/West positions are very far from being discrete or even dialectical in the Hegelian sense. The Indian as 'self-consolidating Other' of European subject-hood occupies a place analogous to Freud's fetish-object in psychoanalytic theory, object of an identification which fluctuates wildly between narcissism and paranoia. As such the Indian is always represented *both* as metaphor, a substitution masking absence and difference ('a discoloured European'), *and* as metonymy, which 'contiguously registers the perceived lack',[37] resulting in contradictory impulses of universalist identification and violent aggression. For Bhabha, the other side of the coin ('defensive warfare') is exemplified by 'sly civility', an English missionary's description in 1818 of the evasive acquiescence of Indian subjects resisting conversion. As such it represents the hybridized native's response to the aggression and cajolement – as well as the narcissistic identification – of the British 'civilizing mission'.[38] It is a response which neither refuses nor accepts, but instead offers to mimic its hortatory imperatives, presenting a hybrid version of the European representation in which its anxieties are exposed. Hybridity or mimicry thus play on the ambivalence of the fetishistic will-to-power underpinning the imperialist project, aware of the instabilities which deconstruct its unitary myth.

The story of one of the ways in which the 'fetishized' Indian subject negotiated British hegemony, which had simultaneously encouraged the modernization and enlightenment of native elites whilst denying them the self-determination which is the goal of enlightenment, is told by David Kopf in his books on British orientalism, *The Brahmo Samaj* and *The Bengal Renaissance*.[39] I will be considering an analogous problem in Shelley's attempt to delineate Brahminical enlightenment, particularly in terms of an apparent shift in his thinking about India between *The Revolt of Islam* and *Prometheus Unbound*. A more troubling account of colonial 'enlightenment' is that of Gauri Viswanathan, who, less comfortable than Kopf with an uncritical notion of a 'civilizing mission', whether of an 'orientalist' or 'Anglicist' stamp, exposes the 'discipline of English' in the Indian colonial context as the 'creation of a blueprint for social control in the guise of a humanistic programme of education'.[40] Radically deconstructing the priority of metropolitan centre to colonial periphery, Viswanathan suggests that 'the subsequent institutionalization of the discipline of English itself' in nineteenth-century Britain 'took on a shape and an ideological content developed in the colonial context'. The 'discipline of English' might even be described – by a stretch of imagination – as the descendant of a colonial hybrid.[41]

Taken in tandem with Eric Stokes' arguments in his classic study *The English Utilitarians and India*, Viswanathan's argument provides an important context for 'radical' Shelley's interest in India.[42] Far from being simply perceived as a source of tribute and 'loot' (a Hindi word assimilated unproblematically into English) as in the days of Warren Hastings and the Company's commercial monopoly, India could by 1818 be seen as 'a laboratory of modernity', like twentieth-century French Morocco studied by Paul Rabinow.[43] But if secularist education and the codification of professional and legis-

lative norms were soon to be pioneered in the context of the East
India Company's 'Guardian State', it must not be forgotten that
from the beginning these norms – which in England were associated
with Utilitarianism and radical reform – were developed in the
context of imperialist social engineering and economic expropriation.
Accordingly my discussion of Shelley's interest in India will develop
the notion that for him at least the Orient 'articulated an internal
dislocation within Western culture, a culture which consistently
fantasizes itself as constituting some kind of integral totality, at the
same time as endlessly deploring its own impending dissolution'.[44]

By the same token (a point I touched upon in discussing Byron's
authenticating allusions to Augustan civilization and the poetry of
Alexander Pope), one cannot simply speak of imperialism in this
period as a moment of historical crisis for the civic ideology of a pre-
constituted nation state. It is not as if an 'originary' civil discourse,
developed within a cohesive metropolitan community, was *subsequently* brought into crisis by its misprision within a colonial or
imperial context. The argument of this book is rather that the
national culture was as much a product of imperial expansion, as
imperialism was the 'expression' or exportation of that culture.
Civility by definition excludes in order to include, its identity a
function of difference as much as of an idealized homogeneity. In
their excellent book *The Politics and Poetics of Transgression*, Peter
Stallybrass and Allon White have studied the role of the grotesque
and the carnivalesque in the construction of the seamless, classical
identity of bourgeois civility: 'The very drive to achieve a singularity
of collective identity is simultaneously productive of unconscious
heterogeneity, with its variety of hybrid figures, competing sovereign-
ties and exorbitant demands'.[45] The Same cannot emerge except in
relation to the Other; in a diachronic scale, the varieties of Otherness
are successively incorporated into the Same by the ongoing displacement of the site of the Other.

Despite the fact that they are concerned primarily with a vertical
and 'internal' mechanism of social 'introjection and negation'
Stallybrass and White's Bakhtinian model can be extended to a
horizontal, geographical plane in order to encompass the gradual
extension of the sphere of influence of the metropolitan centre in the
early modern and modern periods.[46] Although it lies well beyond the
scope of the present work, the formation of the modern British state
might be seen in spatial terms as a series of micro-colonizations; from

such a perspective, Wales, Ireland and Scotland represent a British identity-in-difference in relation to American, African and Asian colonies.[47] The political and cultural assimilation of lowland Scotland and the 'Celtic fringe' by the centre historically preceded that of more far-flung territories like the East or West Indies, the acquisition of which was contingent upon more advanced technological and administrative resources, as well as more urgent economic needs.[48] The deployment of subordinate peoples in the construction of empire (Scots and Irish, the metropolitan working class, Bengali sepoys) participated in that triadic power strategy described by John Barrell as a structure of 'this, that and the other', a structure which we will see exemplified in relation to De Quincey and the London working class in the next chapter.[49] To elaborate the 'Same/Other' model in terms of John Barrell's triadic structure, we can say that the excluded 'that' is co-opted by the 'this' in order to reinforce its threatened identity in relation to 'the other'.

A brief example may serve to clarify my argument here. James Macpherson, bardic voice of the highland culture suppressed by the might of the British army after the Forty-five rebellion, becomes in the late seventeen seventies (on the strength of the fame and fortune deriving from his 'translation' of *Ossian*), 'closely involved with the East India Company and...acquired a lucrative position as the London agent for the Nabob of Arcot'.[50] Another Scot of humble birth, James Mill, unlike Macpherson a lowlander and a progressive radical/democrat, bitterly attacks the vested interest and unprofessional practices of the East India Company; under the cloak of a Romantic 'orientalism' associated with Sir William Jones and others, Mill discerns the despotic features of the '*ancien régime*'. In the *History of British India*, Mill quotes from Dr Johnson's strictures on the fecklessness and superstition of the highland character in the *Journey to the Western Isles*, in order to give his British readers a keener sense of the Hindu character.[51] To a radical lowland Scot like Mill, there is little difference between highlanders and Hindus. Both Mill and Macpherson, representatives of a divided Scottish culture with its own anxieties of subordination in relation to its more powerful neighbour, displace their sense of marginality and inferiority onto the Indian Other, a displacement which in both their cases becomes a career. Pursuing the interests of Britain's oriental empire becomes the means of restoring prestige and wealth for these two Scotsmen. Displacing the cultural frontline eastwards in this way functions in a manner analogous to the antiquarianism which is another salient feature of contemporary Scottish culture. Sir Walter Scott in his historical novel *Waverley* – significantly subtitled *Sixty Years Since* – evacuated and resolved the ideological divisions of early nineteenth-century Scotland into a romantic past, thereby constructing an image of the present as serene and untroubled.

The complexity of this structure of displacement is exemplified by Javed Majeed in his reading of Mill's *History* as divided between a negative and a positive view of empire. Mill takes his liberal-democratic critique of the '*ancien régime*' at home to the site of displacement in India, in a movement which is at once the analogue, but also the reverse, of Shelley's displacement in *The Revolt of Islam*. Arguing that the East India Company's possessions in India 'buttress[ed] powerful groups at home', his *History* criticized 'legal, political, and religious institutions in Britain, and... their influence on British rule in India'. Nevertheless, this critique is balanced by a positive account of empire much closer to Shelley's position, viewing the empire as fertile soil for 'a grand Utilitarian experiment'.[52] Mill, whose Scottish origin linked him with many other employees of the East India Company which he execrated (at the same time as he served it), brought his understanding of the eighteenth-century 'modernization' of Celtic society to bear on the civilizing mission in India in linking highlanders – in whose number he would doubtless have included the corrupt 'nabob' Macpherson – with Hindus. And yet he was himself, as a plebeian Scot, an outsider in relation to the centre of metropolitan power, a 'that' seeking to become 'this' in relation to 'the other'. Forced by necessity as well as inclination, like many of his countrymen, to make his way in what he regarded as the fossil institution of the East India Company, Mill was himself the victim of a cramping and custom-ridden oligarchy which he must have regarded as a microcosm of the unreformed British constitution. Moreover, as Stokes points out, Mill's Utilitarianism was not yet acceptable as a hegemonic strategy of empire, and served to place him even further beyond the pale of intellectual and cultural propriety.[53] Mill's situation reveals at once the *heterogeneity* constitutive of what Bhabha describes (oversimplistically) as 'British civility', as well as the anxieties and contradictions which deconstruct the unitary imperative of Britain's 'civilizing mission'. Here we see also how the interest of empire is very far from being supplementary to, or consequent upon, the formation of the British nation state, but rather the manner in which the two are complementary, in a veritable case of 'dog eats dog'.

In contrast to the Scottish Utilitarian James Mill, or the 'Tory Parish' De Quincey, both themselves dangerously identified with an Otherness which they sought to legislate, radical aristocratic Shelley had little use for the triadic structure of 'this, that and the other'. On the contrary, Shelley seems to have preferred a *binary* model whereby the Other is progressively reclaimed (or 'revolutionized') by the Same. As he envisaged his utopian society in *Prometheus Unbound*, 'the loathsome mask has fallen, the man remains / Sceptreless, free, uncircumscribed, but man / Equal, unclassed, tribeless, and nation-less... the king / Over himself' (*SPW*, p. 253, III. iv. 193–7). Like Jean Starobinski's Rousseau in *Transparency and Obstruction*, 'what... he is looking for, and what he will never find, is a state of universal Sameness – whence his desire for transparency, unity, freedom, and a moral and ontological absolute'.[54] Writing in pre-revolutionary France, Rousseau is forced into solitude, the only situation in which he can enjoy an at least partial transparency. Shelley, writing *after* the revolution in a counter-revolutionary, imperialist culture, also makes much of solitude, particularly in his most Rousseauesque poem *Alastor: or the Spirit of Solitude*. In this poem, his protagonist, travelling to India from an 'obstacle-ridden' Europe, is granted a vision of transparency which the poet represents as possessing a dangerous, even fatal, ambivalence. I will argue below that *Alastor* is more cautiously ironic about transparency than many of Shelley's other early poems; but my main point is that, according to Shelley's general binary scheme, it makes little difference whether the Other is Irish or Italian or Bengali (not to mention female) so long as it can be alchemized into the Same, rendered transparent. This quest is central to poems like *Queen Mab*, *Alastor* and *The Revolt of Islam*, poems in which difference is displaced – not unproblem-atically – in the name of universal norms. I will suggest that the Other returns, like the spectre of violence in relation to the civilizing mission, to disrupt the central vision of his poetry, until it is renegotiated in *Prometheus Unbound*.

To turn once again to the terms of Bhabha's theory in order to 'decode' Shelley's binary opposition, the 'revolutionary', homo-genizing prerogatives of his poetry can be seen to correspond with the narcissistic, metaphoric relation to the fetish-object, whilst the (repressed) knowledge that revolution is *also* in this context a form of imperial domination leads to the paranoiac, metonymic relation, registering the absence and difference of the Other. The sensed violence of imperialism which contradicts Shelley's metaphorical relationship (poets mark 'the before unapprehended relations of things and perpetuate their apprehension')[55] requires to be displaced at the level of narrative – as, for example, I have shown in *The Assassins* – and engaged in the transactions of intertextuality. To this latter end, I will show in my reading of *The Revolt of Islam* how Shelley struggled to evade or suppress the unacceptable implications of many of his literary sources. The comforts of narrative (or the dissimulations of literariness) notwithstanding, Shelley's poetry is dogged by anxieties which constantly slip out of the control of its author.

We might say a word here towards a comparison of Shelley's work with Mill's. Published in the same year as *The Revolt of Islam* and ordered by Shelley in late 1821, Mill's *History* would, by the 1830s, become required reading for cadets at Haileybury, the Company's training college, and 'held sway within Indology...until 1904'.[56] And yet the confident and informed judgements of what Inden calls this 'model explanatory text of Utilitarian reductionism and pre-Darwinian evolutionism' are frequently subverted by lapses into a paranoiac prose and exaggerated denunciation of the 'primitive' culture of India which, I have suggested, mark the cultural anxieties of its author.[57] Shelley's secure (although maverick) position within the English ruling class afforded him an authorial credit which exempted his writings from outbursts of the kind which dog James Mill's book, although Shelley's text is very far from being untroubled by the anxieties of empire. Nevertheless, to read Mill's *History* alongside Shelley's *Revolt of Islam* is to restore a lost dimension to the poem, its exact contemporary.

I began this essay by evoking the 'strange reformation of mind' effected by *The Revolt of Islam* on one depressed English reader in Bombay (or Kanpur) in 1818, a relief which, contrary to expectation, would play a part in Medwin's 'final cure and conversion' to the doctrines of Brahminism.[58] It would be strange to think of a reading of Mill's *History* as having any similar effect in the light of its scathing account of Hinduism, although I will suggest that it might in fact have had such an effect on Shelley himself when he came to read it in 1821. Medwin does not make it clear whether his reformation refers to a consolidation of his sense of British purpose in India, or to the opposite position, an ambiguity which suggests that in ideological terms *The Revolt* might have been even for sympathetic contemporary readers far from straight sailing. Medwin's talk of 'cure and conversion' to Brahminism favours the latter option, although the poetry which he wrote upon returning to Europe does not show much departure from a conventionally 'orientalist' attitude to India.

I am now going to leave Shelley for the time being in order to look at the broader panorama of British – and European – attitudes to and representations of India in the late eighteenth and early nineteenth century. I want to establish as wide a context as possible for my discussion of Shelley's oriental poetry – *Alastor, The Revolt of Islam, Prometheus Unbound* – in order to show the various representational pressures and possibilities which that body of poetry negotiates. As my negotiation with Bhabha's theory has I hope shown, variety and heterogeneity must not be sacrificed to theoretical plausibility, although no account of literary orientalism can afford to do without the sort of theoretical groundwork which Bhabha's work offers. As Gayatri Spivak reminds us, the 'class-composition and social positionality' of the British in India 'are necessarily heterogeneous' – and the same may be said for those who wrote about India at home.[59] Also (and here Bhabha proves very useful) in criticizing the essentialism of orientalist representations of the East, it is important not to end up by establishing an essentialism in reverse, a charge which is often levelled at Edward Said's *Orientalism*. Imperialism is a composite of mutable phases and ideologies which transcend the boundaries of specific nation states. In relation to the British experience in India, 'orientalism', Anglicism, Utilitarianism and evangelism all offered different solutions to a plethora of historically localized social conflicts and administrative exigencies. These *local* ideologies were also intersected by conflicting macro-ideologies emanating from a European theatre of revolution and counter-revolution, a factor which must complicate any account of the development of imperial power in this period.

BRAHMINS, TEMPLES AND PYRES: SOME ROMANTIC
REPRESENTATIONS OF INDIA

The present brief survey of the work of contemporary poets, legislators and mythographers, seeks to sketch a 'lexicon of Romantic India' to supply a dimension of intertextuality to my readings of Shelley's poems in the next section. I will consider the links between

literature and politics in the context of British India, before going on
to discuss the European dimension of Indology. In attempting to
delineate a canon of orientalist poetry to which the *Revolt of Islam*
relates, the post-colonial critic is perplexed by an apparent ambivalence regarding the ethics of colonialism in eighteenth- and early
nineteenth-century poetry. There appears a common condemnation
of what we might term 'manifest colonialism', which generally
signifies mercantilist monopoly, the military subjugation of non-
European peoples and the slave trade. At the same time, none of these
accounts (with the possible exception, as I have argued, of the
sceptical Byron, at war with modernity in all its forms) question the
legitimacy of imperialism in its broader, historical guise, the
expansion of the norms of European civilization over the whole
globe.

Take for instance Thomas Beddoes' neglected poem of 1793,
Alexander's Expedition. Here we find the lineaments of the subsequent
ideology of radical imperialism already in place, particularly the
binary opposition of Hellenism and Asiatic despotism. Beddoes,
Jacobin chemist and Bristol friend of Coleridge and Southey, laments
the failure of the genial Alexander to conquer India, wishfully
comparing the imagined cosmopolitanism of an early fusion of Greek
and Hindu culture with the facts of history, namely Mughal savagery
and British Company monopoly;

> And oh! had years matured the fair design,
> Of which thy Genius traced the wondrous line;
> Had GENERAL CONCORD, from her finished fane,
> Shed her pure light, and breathed her strains humane,
> Man's varied race, from far-dissevered lands,
> Her courts had thronged, and pledged discoloured hands...
>
> Mourn, India, mourn – the womb of future Time
> Teems with the fruit of each portentious crime.
> The Crescent onward leads consuming hosts,
> And Carnage dogs the Cross along thy coasts;
> From Christian strands, the Rage accursed of gain
> Wafts all the furies in her baleful train.[60]

In his notes to the poem, Beddoes castigates the familiar villains of
Romantic Indology, the caste system and Brahminism, arguing that
the evils supported by British conquest and monopoly (which in turn
are seen to threaten the metropolis with 'Asiatic' Luxury and

corruption and draining of the national resources) would be dispelled by free trade and its inevitable concomitant social modernization. The East India Company's dominion is like an estate which 'yields no rent, but of which [the nominal proprietor] is obliged to keep the buildings and fences in repair'.[61]

Political idealism characteristically vies with economic pragmatism in diagnosing the malaise of late eighteenth-century British India. Beddoes' paradigm of a Hellenic 'civilizing mission' (in the form of Alexander the Great's expedition) set against 'Asiatic despotism' and the analogous barbarism of European mercantilism is reiterated in Thomas Campbell's 1799 poem *The Pleasures of Hope*. Campbell castigates 'the barbarous policy of Europeans in India' and the first part of his poem concludes with an invocation to 'Seriswattee', 'tenth avatar of Brahma', to 'pour redress on India's injured realm, / The oppressor to dethrone, the proud to whelm'.[62] Such apparent 'anti-imperialism' is a well-worn theme in eighteenth-century poetry, reiterating the sentiments of James Thomson's *The Seasons* ('Summer', lines 747–1051) (1727) and less famously, Richard Savage's poem *On Public Spirit, with regard to Public Works*, a poem whose strictures on colonialism and mercantilism were endorsed and publicized by Samuel Johnson in his *Life of Savage* (1744). Yet Campbell's manifest anti-imperialism is qualified by his approval of another mode of global expansion, this time relating to a quality of civilization rather than simply to the narrow principle of commerce – and one wonders precisely on whose terms 'Improvement' will coexist with 'Seriswattee' on the throne of an India purged of mercantilists;

> Come, bright Improvement! on the car of Time,
> And rule the spacious world from clime to clime,
> Thy handmaid arts shall every wild explore,
> Trace every wave, and culture every shore.[63]

Walter Savage Landor's bizarre poem of 1798 *Gebir*, mentioned above in relation to Byron, takes a more specifically partisan line, attacking in the course of a complex and elliptical narrative Britain's 'colonization in peopled countries' whilst lauding Napoleon's inauguration of 'liberty and equality' in his Egyptian expedition of the same year. In his study of liberal imperialism in nineteenth-century Britain, Bernard Semmel writes that 'the period of the fall of the old colonial system may be viewed as one of the rise of a free-trade imperialism'.[64] To speak of manifestly anti-imperialist discourse in the Romantic period is thus a misnomer, for criticism of the old mercantilist system is normally accompanied by support for the new economic world system which Semmel calls liberal or free-trade imperialism.

The body of poetry being considered here did in fact sound the 'trumpet of a prophecy' in relation to the administration of India. After the impeachment of Hastings,[65] British rule began slowly to shift in favour of the ideology expressed in the poems of Beddoes, Campbell and Landor. With Cornwallis' 'Permanent Settlement' it ceased to be concerned solely with ensuring a steady flow of tribute back to the metropolis and sought rather to construct a controlling 'Guardian State' enabling the conquest of the huge Indian market for British manufactures, which would bring an end to the monopoly of the Company by 1813. The mounting pressure for the creation of a market in India challenged the 'orientalist' ideology of the earlier phase of Company rule, replacing it with a demand for greater westernization of Indian society, obviously a prerequisite in the creation of a consumer demand for British commodities. Despite their opposition to the establishment of missions for converting Indians to Christianity in 1813, on the grounds that aggressive cultural intervention might jeopardize political stability, 'orientalists' (just as much as their Anglicist successors) projected European norms onto their Indian subjects, although disguised in native garb.

Eric Stokes has argued that in their approach to imperial government, Romantic 'orientalists' like Thomas Munro, John Malcolm, Charles Metcalfe and Mountstuart Elphinstone reacted against the 'cold, lifeless, mechanical principles informing the Cornwallis system...impos[ing] English ideas and institutions on Indian society'.[66] But like Burke and Coleridge, these aristocratic civic humanists, prime targets of James Mill's invective in *The History of British India*, were really objecting to the ascendancy of the commercial over the landed principle of society whether at home or in the colonies. Munro and Elphinstone's *ryotwar* land settlement system in Bengal and Western India, securing the peasant in possession of his own land, or Metcalfe's 'village republics' around Delhi and in the Northwest Provinces were in reality 'orientalist' adaptions of physiocratic ideas about the economic primacy of agriculture and neo-Harringtonian principles of 'a prosperous society of yeoman farmers enjoying a freehold property right'.[67] Idealizing the Indian peasant was really the same as refurbishing a cherished principle of Whig political thought, one which was becoming increasingly attentuated at home.

In his thoughtful essay on 'Landholding and the Concept of Private Property' in early colonial India, Ainslie Embree describes the effect of what might be dubbed the 'Wordsworthianization' of India (Munro for one was an ardent admirer of Wordsworth's poetry) in relation to indigenous Hindu and Mughal ideas of property in the Indian subcontinent as 'the distortion of the old system into a form that bore little resemblance to what had actually existed before'.[68] It should be added that whatever the 'hybrid' nature of the colonial land-settlement (which was initially not without some benefits for the Indian peasant), it guaranteed the fixed land-revenues which were still the foundation of the Company's economic power base in the East, amounting to £22 million in 1818.[69]

A further illustration of an homology between varieties of imperial government and styles of orientalist literature is the relationship between the political ideology of the Munro/Elphinstone school and Southey's Indian epic of 1810 *The Curse of Kehama*. In a poem which became the target for much critical censure, Southey followed Sir William Jones' *Hindu Hymns* in combining Indian subject-matter with an innovative western poetic manner. In a bid to neutralize the pernicious effects of Hindu mythology 'which would appear monstrous if its deformities were not kept out of sight'[70] by the 'moral sublimity' of his hero and heroine, Southey told the story of Ladurlad, an Indian peasant yeoman, and his faithful daughter, Kailyal, struggling against the evil Rajah Kehama and the ghost of his murdered son, Arvalan. Drawing on the copious annals of the Asiatic Society of Bengal (founded by Jones in 1784) and other orientalist texts, Southey represented the triumph of the solid Indian peasant – Ladurlad is cast exactly in the mould of Munro's *ryot* – against wicked Brahmins and 'asiatic despotism'. Only a 'peasant's arm' has had the power to slay the evil prince Arvalan, who is otherwise indestructible.[71] In his stagey imagining of Indian mythology – *Kehama* is to the *Ramayana* what the Brighton Pavilion is to the Taj Mahal – Southey exposed the cruelty of *sati* (widow-burning), temple prostitution, child exposure and the Brahmin-instigated sacrifices at Jagannath. In this respect the poem anticipated the popular Victorian and Edwardian genre of 'Imperial Gothic' discussed in Brantlinger's *Rule of Darkness*. Ladurlad's stoic forebearance and Kailyal's constancy finally win out over a grotesque plethora of supernatural terrors as father and daughter are wafted to immortality in a heaven now purged of its grislier mythic monsters.

In the introduction I mentioned the evangelical essayist John Foster's strictures on the poem's pagan imagery and machinery, and suggested that Southey sought to create a form of 'imperial heraldry' which always risked inflecting or subverting its context, in the manner feared by Foster. Southey's poem is characteristically ambivalent in its ideological bearings: although steeped in the work of William Jones and other 'orientalists' to a degree which made it repellent to the likes of Foster, *Kehama* did ultimately lend support to the assimilationist vision of the pro-missionary lobby of Charles Grant and William Wilberforce by exposing the 'fraudulence' of the Hindu religion.[72] The ambivalence of *Kehama* shows that 'orientalist' and assimilationist positions ('proto-Anglicism' and Anglicism proper being the fully-fledged articulations of the latter) are at moments mutually supportive rather than antagonistic.

When Shelley visited Southey in the Lake District in late 1811, brimming with enthusiasm for the recently published *Kehama* (which remained one of his favourite poems and an important influence on his later work, as we shall see), he was baffled by an incongruity between what he took to be the radicalism of Southey's poem and the newly avowed conservatism of the older poet. The two writers discussed the significance of the episode of the three statues in the twenty-third and twenty-fourth cantos of *Kehama*, allegorical figures of accumulated wealth, monarchy and priestcraft. At the end of the twenty-fourth canto, Kehama is himself monumentalized, petrified for eternity, after drinking the ambiguous 'Amreeta cup', thereby adding the fourth evil of the tyrannical 'mighty man' who sets himself up against heaven to the allegorical pantheon of human evils. Shelley reported with some bemusement that Southey was 'an advocate of liberty and equality', although 'he says he designs his three statues in *Kehama* to be contemplated with republican feelings – but not in this age'.[73] He might have added 'and not in *this* country – but in the visionary India of *Kehama*', given the manner in which the poem legitimizes its populist and revolutionary rhetoric by situating it in an imagined Orient. John Foster, in his very suggestive misreading of *Kehama*, argued that the action of the poem could not have taken place in recent history because the despotic actions of Kehama would have been obviated by British intervention; 'it is

impossible that such a person as Kehama should have been in India
at that time, without coming into collision with General Clive, who
would have saved Seeva the trouble of interfering to put him
down'.[74]

The absence of any manifest exponent of British colonial power in
Southey's narrative anticipates Philip Meadows Taylor's popular
novel of 1839 *Confessions of a Thug*, although of course the
mythological setting of *Kehama* is quite distinct from Taylor's
meticulous realism Taylor's native narrator, convicted of thuggery
(a criminal confraternity devoted to the Hindu goddess Kali)
confesses his bloody crimes to a silent British police officer. As
Brantlinger has observed of this De Quinceyan novel (which owes
more to the author of *Confessions of an English Opium-Eater* and *On
Murder Considered as a Fine Art* than merely its title), 'the patiently
listening and recording Sahib is the perfect Benthamite policeman,
an ideal figure of imperial discipline and surveillance, or "panopti-
cism" to use Foucault's term'.[75] As in Southey's epic, the order of
representation is itself the talisman of authority in *Confessions of a
Thug*, relating it to the immense nineteenth-century project of
taxonomizing the subject peoples and cultural practices of British
India, a project which contributed to the birth of the modern
discipline of a social anthropology.[76]

Yet there is still an element of the eighteenth-century oriental tale
in the allegorical elements interfused with *Kehama*'s archival scrupu-
losity, an element which places it in the world of *Vathek* and *Lalla
Rookh* rather than that of the Victorian realist novel. For example, the
character of the corrupt and power-thirsty Kehama contains echoes
of *both* the 'Nabob' Warren Hastings and Napoleon in his role as
orientalist adventurer and challenger of the gods. Kailyal's revolt
against priests and despots thus yokes Britain's construction of a
'traditional' Indian peasant society onto the bandwaggon of loyalist,
Francophobic populism, as well as the displaced republicanism of
Southey himself. Imperialism and radicalism merge into one in the
poem, and a revolution impossible in reactionary Britain is lauded in
a colonial situation in the name of British dominion. The 1810
Kehama is in a sense Southey's version of Wordsworth's championing
of the loyalist and nationalist Spanish guerillas in their struggle
against the Napoleonic invaders in his 1809 pamphlet *The Convention
of Cintra*. Coleridge later described how erstwhile radicals like himself,
Wordsworth and Southey were brought in from the cold in 1809, as

a 'common focus in the cause of Spain...made us all once more Englishmen by at once gratifying and correcting the predelictions of both parties' which had been deeply divided over the cause of the French Revolution and revolutionary war.[77] Southey clearly hoped that the cause of India could produce an analogous consensus, and that an imperial civilizing mission might heal the ideological wounds of a divided England. Although the political agenda of Shelley's *Revolt of Islam* is substantially different from that of *Kehama* (projecting a Jacobinical and Volneyan rather than an 'orientalist' programme), its displaced revolutionary vision owes a great deal to Southey's poem.

The East India Company's construction of a 'traditional' Indian property-owning peasantry in the various different ways mentioned above went hand in hand with attempts to reshape and codify the power of the Brahmins. It is in the context of this programme, and as a preamble to Shelley's opinion of Brahminism, that I want to say a word about the Asiatic Society of Bengal, most notably the work of orientalists of the calibre of Sir William Jones, Henry Colebrooke and H. H. Wilson.[78] The gargantuan labors of these men in inaugurating Sanskrit studies is impressive even by the standards of an age which produced the *Encyclopaedia* in France, the *Decline and Fall of the Roman Empire* in England and the Critical Philosophy in Germany. Nevertheless it is important not to forfeit a critical attitude regarding the ends of the Asiatic Society for an admiration of the scale of its achievements. A recent commentator has written of Jones' 'almost mystical respect for Indian culture as it was embodied in the traditional institutions of the country'.[79] The fact that Jones – a political liberal in England – undoubtedly 'respected' the Sanskrit language and literature, particularly in comparison with the philistinism of Utilitarians like James Mill and 'Anglicists' like Thomas Babington Macaulay, should not blind us to the ultimate rationale of his labours. Jones shows his hand in judgements like the following from the preface to the *Hymn to Na'ra'yena*:

We may be inclined perhaps to think, that the wild fables of idolators are not worth knowing...but we must consider that the allegories contained in the Hymn to LACSHMI constitute at this moment the prevailing religion of a most extensive and celebrated Empire, and are devoutly believed by many millions, whose industry adds to the revenue of *Britain*, and whose manners, which are interwoven with their religious opinions, nearly affect all *Europeans*, who reside amongst them.[80]

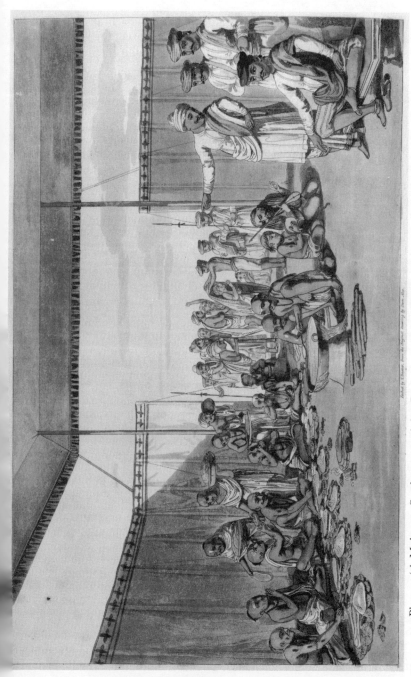

Plate 5. 'A Mahratta Surdar entertaining Brahmins', in T. D. Broughton, *Letters Written in a Mahratta Camp* (London 1813), facing p. 48.

Jones' identification of the common 'Aryan' roots of Sanskrit and
Latin, Greek and the Teutonic languages, his suggestive (and
typically eighteenth-century) comparison of the gods of ancient Italy
and Greece with the Hindu pantheon, his 'discovery' of the pure
deism lying at the Vedic source of Hindu polytheism as well as in the
'revealed' laws of Manu, all these imbued fellow-Europeans with a
respect for Hindu antiquity almost equivalent to that which they felt
for the cultural legacy of Greece and Rome.

Just as Munro and Metcalfe had set about codifying Indian land-
settlements on physiocratic and 'Neo-Harringtonian' principles, the
'orientalists' of the Asiatic Society, in dialogue with Brahmin pandits,
set about codifying the immense corpus of Hindu literature in terms
of the interpretative skills in which they were learned, namely the
exegesis of Graeco-Roman literature, the Bible and English common
law. Although Jones was always concerned to give priority in terms
of antiquity, rationality and moral clarity to the Judaeo-Christian
tradition, his own liberal deism entailed his acceptance of 'classical'
Hinduism as a legitimate, although flawed, form of natural religion.
The ideological bent of his work – subsequently doctored by the
evangelical John Shore in his biography of Jones – set the tone for the
(predominantly) Whig opposition to the evangelization of India after
his death in 1794. This is exemplified in the Revd Sydney Smith's
1808 article in the *Edinburgh Review*, in which Smith feared that the
loss of caste undergone by Indian converts to Christianity would
seriously threaten both the cohesion of Hindu society and the
exchequer of the British 'Guardian State'; converts would naturally
be the wards of their Christian proselytizers. Conversion (which
many argued was impossible in the case of Hindus) would antagonize
native elites and threaten the political as well as the economic hold of
the Company on India. A missionary might write home that 'he
makes a Christian,' wrote Smith, 'when in reality, he ought only to
state that he has destroyed a Hindoo. Foolish and imperfect as the
religion of a Hindoo is, it is at least some restraint upon the
intemperance of human passions.'[81]

Whig opposition to the evangelizing of India was bulwarked by a
distrust of interference in cultures ruled by their own 'customary
laws' – a lesson learned from the Irish Edmund Burke and applied
everywhere but Ireland – which rationalized British intervention in
India as a project aimed at restoring Hindu culture to its 'original'
purity. In her *Letters of a Hindoo Rajah* of 1796, the Scottish/Irish

writer Eliza Hamilton built her argument on an analogy between the
Islamic conquest of large parts of Hindu India and the impact of the
French Revolution on Europe. In both cases it was the role of Britain,
as the leading counter-revolutionary power, to redress the wrongs
done to a traditional culture by newfangled ideas, whether based
upon the Koran or the Rights of Man. 'In those provinces
which ... have fallen under the dominion of Great Britain, it is to be
hoped the long-suffering Hindus have experienced a happy change ...
Their ancient laws have been restored to them; a translation of them
into the Persian and English languages has been made, and is now the
Guide of the Courts of Justice, which have been established amongst
them.'[82]

Hamilton's Islam takes on an ideological meaning exactly the
reverse of Shelley's, without pre-empting the standard libertarian
rhetoric of imperialist discourse. Hamilton's idealized Hindus are
then used to satirize the corrupt manners of Britain, as her virtuous
Rajah tours the loose-living country houses of the metropolitan
homeland, and reports home in the familiar eighteenth-century
manner of Montesquieu's *Persian Letters*.[83] The inference is that
Britain had better learn from the good works being performed
abroad and from the pure manners of her new subjects to set her own
house in order. Hamilton is here blind to the threatening, infectious
aspects of the Orient which we observed in Southey's *Letters from
England* but one can see why. Her appeal is to the sense of moral
responsibility attendant upon the imperial civilizing mission in order
to urge the moral reformation of the British ruling class. This is really
an orientalist version of a common idealization of the thrift and piety
of the 'deserving poor' by middle-class evangelicals in their bid to
reform the manners of the opulent and powerful. Hamilton's
patrician evangelism is more concerned, in the troubled ideological
climate of 1796, to 'christianize' Britain than India. Thus evangelicals of a socially conservative temper like Eliza Hamilton (not just
disaffected radicals) found an ideological use for imperialism beyond
the rich economic rewards to be reaped. By 1813 they were on the
offensive, so that with the influence of the Clapham Sect in Parliament,
the establishment of an evangelical mission in India was assured.

A position relative to India which is closer to the Whig Sydney
Smith than to the evangelically minded Eliza Hamilton is taken by
the Irish novelist Sydney Owenson (Lady Morgan) in her 'oriental
Gothic' novel *The Missionary*, published in 1811. It is a work which

will feature prominently in the pages to come, so I will discuss it only briefly here. Lady Morgan's novel draws heavily on William Jones in idealizing the monotheism and deism of its heroine, the Vedanta priestess Luxima, based on the figure of Shakuntala, in Kalidasa's drama of the same name, which Jones had 'translated' in 1789.[84] *The Missionary* follows Jones in reading Hinduism as a form of European deism, just as it names its heroine Luxima after the Hindu deity Lakshmi whilst managing to Latinize her into meaning something approaching 'the light of Asia'. In Morgan's novel, Hinduism as embodied in the doctrine and example of Luxima is preferred to the intolerant asceticism of the Catholic missionary Hilarion who falls in love with and in the end destroys her. But Hinduism as represented by the 'orthodox' Brahmins who excommunicate the heroine because of her entanglement with Hilarion is shown, on the other hand, to be just as pernicious as the doctrines of the sinister Jesuit villains who link the novel to the Gothic tradition of Radcliffe and Lewis.[85] Luxima's nature-worship and exquisite sensibility had a great impact on Shelley, who, in 1881, thought *The Missionary* to be 'a divine thing... Since I have read this book I have read no other – but I have thought strangely.'[86] I will be making the case that Shelley's radical scepticism regarding Hindu culture was offset by his admiration for Luxima, a character-type to which he returned obsessively in his oriental poems.

As I indicated above in relation to Sir William Jones, it is not difficult for modern critics to idealize British 'orientalist' discourse of the Romantic period; its fascination with Indian culture and apparent resistance to the more aggressive forms of cultural imperialism make it considerably more attractive than the ideologies which succeeded it. 'Orientalists' may have negotiated with indigenous culture in a manner quite distinct from their 'Anglicist' successors, and their own position within India was riddled with instabilities quite different in character from the aggressive imperialism of later nineteenth-century British India. Nevertheless, it should not be forgotten that the 'positive' knowledge of Hindu culture, emblematized in the figure of Morgan's Luxima, was the product of an instrumental construction of the Indian Other, just as Shelley's more negative version sought (also for instrumental ends) to homogenize the Other as the Same.

A practical example of 'orientalist' negotiation (or misprision) is offered by Lata Mani in her essay on 'The Production of an Official

Discourse on *Sati* in early 19th Century Bengal'. Anxious not to interfere legally with a religious practice obnoxious to the British (and to many Indians) on humanitarian grounds, Company officials sought, in collaboration with their Pandits, to find a 'scriptural' ground for prohibition. Because *sati* was a localized, customary practice without codification, this was impossible, the very quest depending upon a mistaken analogy between the nature of Christian and Sanskrit 'scriptures'. Mani describes the effects:

The colonial rewriting/reinterpretation of the pandits' *vyaswathas* (edicts) as invariable scriptural truths and their enforcement as law is analogous to [Paul Ricouer's] textualization of discourse. Opinions pronounced on particular cases became rules applicable to all cases. Thus the meaning of *sati* became 'fixed'; in other words, a *sati* that met certain criteria could be identified as authentic – The textualization of the pundit's discourse on *sati* also had as a consequence the elimination of human agency... [which] effectively put the operation of Hindu culture into a timeless present in which passive natives remained eternally yoked to religion.[87]

This sort of procedure was of course castigated by Utilitarians and progressives like James Mill, who wrote (with considerable plausibility) attacking the 'orientalist' legal apparatus, 'the Shasters and the Khoran were just about as well calculated for defining the rights of the people of India, as the Bible would be for defining those of the people of England'.[88] The result of this 'orientalist' mummification of Hindu culture, despite the elephantine rationalizations of the 'Anglicist' camp which would swing to the opposite extreme in its assimilationist programme, was that, in C. A. Bayly's words, 'hierarchy and the Brahmin interpretation of Hindu society which was theoretical rather than actual over much of India as late as 1750 was firmly ensconced a century later'.[89]

THE EUROPEAN DIMENSIONS OF ORIENTALISM

To understand the complexity of the orientalist discourse in which Shelley's major poetry takes its place, it is necessary not only to see it, in the terms of Edward Said, as a corollary of empire, of power over the East, but also as a conflict of ideas in a European context. I have referred above to the importance of India in the process of British nation formation in terms of the triadic model 'this, that and the other'.[90] Orientalism – a point perhaps inadequately stressed by Said – was saturated from the beginning by the nationalist or proto-nationalist claims of rival European states, each of which developed competing accounts of the East, albeit based on a limited, shared body of information. Said reproaches himself in *Orientalism* for ignoring the enormous contribution of German scholarship to the field, but justifies his exclusion on the grounds that 'there was nothing in Germany to correspond to the Anglo-French presence in India, the Levant, North Africa'.[91] Said's omission does create a serious problem for his argument, however, narrowing the scope of his critique and removing orientalism from the mutations of its historical and polemical sites of production.

Let us pause for a moment to consider the case of Germany. Britain had nothing to fear from Prussian competition in the stakes of empire in the late eighteenth century in the way it had from France, but none the less the orientalism of Prussian and other German scholars was contested by hegemonic British intellectuals just as energetically as was that of the French. Clearly there are links between the empiricist idiom of British orientalism and the administrative demands of colonial rule, just as there are links between the transcendentalist idiom of German scholarship and the incongruous relationship between a sophisticated, but, in practical terms, frustrated in-telligentsia within the backward, pre-nationalist German princi-palities. The 'Odyssey of Spirit' articulated in the huge philosophical systems of post-Kantian philosophers like Hegel and Schelling represent at one level the sublimation of a more literal 'odyssey' to southern hemispheres made in the same period by British and French intellectuals and administrators. Yet this is not all; as Gayatri Spivak has tirelessly reiterated, the 'Orient' (and particularly India which assumed the role of a European *Ursprung* for the Romantic movement) was Europe's self-consolidating Other[92] at a time when questions of origin were of paramount importance *both* at an epistemological level and in terms of the formation of canons of national identity.

European mythographers thus tended to interpret Brahminism according to their own most advanced ideologies and it was reviled or exalted according to these internal ideological pressures. The French scholars Volney and Dupuis castigated Brahminism just as they castigated any form of priestcraft, claiming it shared with Judaism a common Egyptian origin; this was an argument which, although quite familiar to the Enlightenment, took new force from post-revolutionary France's imperial designs on Egypt.[93] Nevertheless, the inheritors of the French Enlightenment were prepared to make compromises in the interests of securing colonies. Edward Said has described how Napoleon profited from Volney's oriental expertise in dealing with Islam during his unsuccessful Egyptian expedition of 1798; his instructions to his deputy Kléber upon leaving him in charge of the new acquisition, 'to administer Egypt through the orientalists and the religious Islamic leaders whom they could win over... [because] any other politics was too expensive and foolish' are not very different from the policy of British 'orientalists' in India surveyed above.[94] And if Volney and Dupuis regarded Hinduism as bigoted and obscene, they could nevertheless use it to expose the Christianity championed by the counter-revolutionary powers Britain, Austria and Russia as a sham, derived at third hand from Egyptian mythology. Volney infuriated Christian apologists in Britain by arguing that 'Christ' was etymologically connected to 'Christna', and that 'Abraham' and his wife 'Sarah' were derived from 'Brahma' and his wife 'Saraswadi'.[95] Notwithstanding the expediency which Volney had urged on Napoleon in governing Egypt 'orientally', on the home front the French ideologues Volney and Dupuis could be more scientific in breaking down the complex elaborations of religious myths into their basic elements, showing them to originate in a zodiacal system derived from astronomical observations. 'These various theological opinions are mere chimeras', wrote Volney, '...allegories and mysterious symbols, under which moral ideas, and the knowledge of the operations of nature in the actions of the elements and the revolutions of the planets, are ingeniously depicted.'[96] The whole world was exposed in its transparency to the penetrating gaze of reason and natural law, the official, cosmopolitan ideology of the new French regime and its sympathizers (like the young Shelley) abroad.

In hostile England, the East India Company's 'official' mythographers, after the early death of William Jones in 1794, were Thomas Maurice and George Stanley Faber, both of whom fought a rear-guard action against French principles, later to be represented at home by radicals of the stamp of Shelley and James Mill. In arguments which matched in bulk and paradox those of the querulous Whig bishop William Warburton, Maurice attacked Volney on his own terrain, supporting Mosaic revelation against the challenge posed by the Hindu zodiac and mythology. Denying the superior antiquity of the Sanskrit texts, he developed Jones' account of Indian religion by regarding Hinduism as 'the shattered remains of one grand primaeval system' which had revealed a primordial trinitarianism to the ancient world, and of which Anglicanism was (of course) the most pristine modern survival.[97]

But G. S. Faber's *The Origin of Pagan Idolatry* (1816) outdoes even Maurice in polemical complexity, denying the connections between the triads of Hinduism and other oriental religions and the Christian Trinity. In particular Faber attacked the Hindu doctrine of metempsychosis and of the avatars (or successive manifestation of Brahma in the shape of diverse deities) as a form of serial repetition quite inferior to the sequential eschatological narrative of Trinitarian Christianity. In an argument which exposes the polemical pre-occupation of his book, Faber connected the Hindu scheme of the avatars with palingenesis, the materialistic doctrine of cyclical resurrection elaborated by Cuvier and the Swiss/French scientist Charles Bonnet, and subsequently developed by Lamarck in his doctrine of transformism.[98] It must be stressed that Faber's brand of mythography, which seems such an intellectual byway to the modern reader (particularly in the light of George Eliot's portrait of the mythographer Casaubon in *Middlemarch*), had an ideological urgency in its own time and culture, however crude its method in relation to that of the German 'Higher Criticism' or seen from the perspective of modern Sanskrit studies. His book carries the stamp of the evangelism which had triumphed with the insertion of a 'pious clause' inaugurating Indian missions in the 1813 Charter Act. Faber denied that Hinduism contained even a distorted ray of revelation, arguing instead that it is based on a confused historical memory of the triadic genealogies of Adam and Noah. As such it cannot challenge scripture in the way that Volney or Dupuis had sought to do, but neither can it be privileged as an acceptable substitute for Christianity on Jones' and Maurice's grounds that it was 'the shattered remains of one great primaeval system'. Christianity 'solely rests on the declarations of the inspired volume; nor does it either admit or require any extraneous assistance from the demon-theology of paganism'.[99] Although *Pagan Idolatry* was read with curiosity by Shelley, possibly providing him later in his career with the source for 'hermaphroditus' in *The Witch of Atlas*,[100] its author, along with Rowland Hill and other prominent divines of an evangelizing tendency, was singled out by the author of *The Necessity of Atheism* and his undergraduate friend T. J. Hogg as a target for atheistical squibs. In a letter of 1811 Shelley described Faber (not without a note of grudging respect) as one of a band of 'Armageddon-Heroes [who] maintain their posts with all the obstinacy of cabalistical dogmatism'.[101]

Last but not least, the Germans, 'Everything, absolutely everything, is of Indian origin,' wrote Friedrich Schlegel in 1803.[102] Schlegel was voicing the extreme views of Englishmen like Francis Wilford and Reuben Burrow, the latter of whom had written, with a confidence certainly not shared by other Fellows of the Asiatic Society, 'that the Druids of Britain were Brahmins is beyond the least shadow of doubt'.[103] Despite Hegel's relegation of India to an early stage in the self-development of *Geist*, before it had come to terms with matter, thus representing Indian art and culture as 'always outside history, static, immobile, and fixed for all eternity',[104] the Germans were soon to become the masters of Indology. The immense prestige enjoyed by Sanskrit in German Romanticism (and indeed right through the nineteenth century) is unmatched either in England – where it was killed off after 1830 by 'Macaulayism'[105] – or in France, more concerned for practical purposes with elaborating an Arabic-based orientalism after the collapse of its power base in India.

Two related ideas are tentatively proposed here to explain a phenomenon to which Said's *Orientalism* fails, by its own admission, to do justice. The first is connected with a sociological difference between the French and German Enlightenments which influenced the manner in which they interpreted Brahminism and caste society. In the words of Raymond Schwab, while in France everything was ascribed to the sacerdotal domains in order to reproach them for their exploitation of credulity, in Germany this was done in order to venerate them as the preservers of the great secret of the universe'.[106] The Freemasonry of German philosophers like the young Schelling, the Schlegels and Creuzer followed, in relation to India, the suggestion of Starck's *Hephestion* (1775) in identifying the new German philosophy with 'the esoteric religion of the mysteries'. Starck located the origin of this hermetic, perennial philosophy in 'Egypt, in Tibet, in India, everywhere there was a strongly organized priestly caste'.[107]

The second idea involves the quest for origins mentioned above, involving the German belief in the common Aryanism of the Teutonic and Sanskrit languages and races, both of which were thought to have originated in the mountains of the Caucasus. Postulating (against biblical orthodoxy) a theory of linguistic and racial

polygenesis which distinguished the roots of the Aryan and the
Semitic languages, German scholars led by Friedrich Schlegel
argued, in the words of Martin Bernal, that 'just as the Germans were
supposed to be purer Caucasians because they were the last to leave
the *Urheimat* or original homeland, German was thought to be purer
and more ancient than other languages in the family'.[108] In England
Coleridge, who had sympathetically traced the emergence of the
German argument, followed his Teutonic mentors by associating
Hinduism with the pantheism of Spinoza. By the second decade of
the nineteenth century, however, he was supporting the missionary
cause (in his 1818 *rifacciamento* of *The Friend*) and censuring Indian
religion for its failure to distinguish between the Creator and his
Creation.[109] As Elinor Shaffer has pointed out, 'of all the forms of
Oriental thought, Coleridge had least sympathy with Hinduism, at
least in his later years'.[110] Coleridge's change of heart about Indian
religion, related to his advocacy of missionary activity, is also a
change of heart about Germany and the threat of transcendental
idealism and the pantheism of the *Naturphilosophie* to orthodox
Christianity of a conservative, Anglican caste.[111] He was glad to
observe a similar change of heart in the later work of his old mentor
Schelling, whom he quoted in the *Friend* expressing regret for a
current turning away from 'Hebrew Sources...now we hear of
nothing but the language and wisdom of India'.[112]

'THE REVOLT OF ISLAM' AND 'ALASTOR': LIBERATING THE
ORIENT?

In the ninth canto of *The Revolt of Islam*, Shelley's feminist heroine
Cythna invokes the contemporary post-revolutionary mood, 'This is
the winter of the world; – and here / We die, even as the winds of
Autumn fade':[113] but they are verses which achieve their *relève* in the
1819 *Ode to the West Wind*, 'If Winter comes, can Spring be far
behind?' The Stendhalian ennui and disenchantment of post-
Napoleonic Europe is relieved for Shelley by a glimpse of dawn in the
East; *lux ex oriente*. The faith of *The Revolt of Islam*, *Prometheus Unbound*
and *Hellas* lies in a *ricorso* of liberty spreading over the world from the
revolutionary liberation of the long oppressed East.

    The displacement and apotheosis of revolution from epic narrative
into elegy, of unprocessed European history into the 'timeless
present' of orientalism which I take, using Stephen Greenblatt's

phrase,[114] to be hallmarks of the 'social energy' of *The Revolt of Islam* are the literary analogues of the legal/administrative imagining of India which saw the construction of Britain's imperial apparatus. I will return in more detail below to the resemblances between Shelley's and Karl Marx's visions of 'revolution in the East', although the former's faith in the European 'civilizing mission' in India partook (unlike the latter's) of the liberal imperialism which dominated nineteenth-century British policy towards India and other colonies, a faith we have discerned in the poems of Beddoes, Campbell and Southey, as well as in the work of a selection of mythographers, novelists and administrators. These writers all sought to distinguish British 'rule by opinion' from 'Roman' conquest of the kind which liberals had struggled to exorcize during the impeachment of the freebooting Warren Hastings. As an Edinburgh Reviewer wrote in an 1805 article on the best means of civilizing India, 'we trust that those of our countrymen who may have been seduced into Roman schemes of conquest abroad, will never be *honoured with a triumph at home*'.[115]

Revolution in the East was more than a dislocation of frustrated political idealism, however; it was also a *cure* for vitiated European nerves, a point which I will elaborate in my discussion of De Quincey in the final chapter of this book. Writing to Hogg in October 1821 and referring to his project of enlisting in the East India Company, Shelley complained of 'nervous irritability' and 'la noia e l'affanno della passata vita. – I have some thoughts, if I could get a respectable appointment, of going to India, or any where where I might be compelled to active exertion'.[116] After Peacock had vetoed Shelley's idea, he complained to his friend: 'I wish I had something better to do than furnish this jingling food for the hunger of oblivion, called *verse*: but I have not, & since you give me no encouragement about India I cannot hope to have.'[117] I am not simply suggesting here that Shelley's poetry was a sublimation of his desire to be an administrator in the service of the East India Company, but rather that both his poetic achievement and his nervous 'itch' to go to India are the common fruits of a displaced revolutionary desire looking beyond the current condition of Europe for its fulfilment. It is a structure of feeling to which I will return in discussing the 1815 poem *Alastor*.

'*The Revolt of Islam*' and Tom Moore's '*Lalla Rookh*'

I want now to look at some of the ways in which the dislocation and disavowal which I discussed above in relation to Shelley's attitude to India is worked out at the narrative level and in terms of the intertextuality of his oriental poems. Although I will discuss *Queen Mab*, *Alastor* and *Prometheus Unbound* in some detail, this section will flout chronology by taking *The Revolt of Islam*, the most problematic of Shelley's oriental poems, as its starting point. I will consider the relationship of the *Revolt of Islam* to three of the sources I mentioned above, Tom Moore's *Lalla Rookh*, Volney's *The Ruins* and Lady Morgan's *The Missionary*.

On one level, Laon and Cythna's revolt against the Sultan Othman figures Shelley's reaction against the negativity of Tom Moore's 1817 account of oriental revolution, 'The Veiled Prophet of Khorassan' in *Lalla Rookh*. Azim, the hero of the 'Veiled Prophet' is inspired by the noble ideals of ancient Greek liberty to join a revolution against Islam by the perfidious Mokanna, the 'Veiled Prophet'. He is horrified to discover the sexual tyranny and luxury of the prophet's harem, particularly when he meets his beloved Zelica reduced to the status of a concubine, having been raped (officially 'married') by Mokanna in a charnel-house with 'blueish death-light round them cast'.[118]

Shelley's Greek hero Laon is brought up 'In Argolis, beside the echoing sea' (line 676) and like Azim is inspired by the libertarian principles of Greek antiquity. There is no hint that Laon is a noble peasant like Southey's Ladurlad; as Richard Holmes points out, 'Laon and Cythna are heroic leaders out of an ancient, aristocratic mould that owes more to Spenser's mythical knights than to [the world of the contemporary English radical movement].'[119] Shelley's radicalism, true to its Godwinian roots, is premised upon rational benevolence and nobility of spirit rather than the idealization of a propertied freehold peasantry. Brought up in the colonized Peloponnese ('Tyrants dwelt side by side / And stabled in our homes') (lines 695–6) Laon shares his home, like Southey's Thalaba, with an orphan girl who subsequently becomes his lover. In the poem's first version of 1817 published as *Laon and Cythna* the lovers are brother and sister, but Shelley excised the incest theme along with some of the more extreme radicalism and atheism for the 1818 republication entitled *The Revolt of Islam*. Laon, a poet, converts Cythna, his 'second self' (line 875), to the 'Hellenistic' principles of republicanism, feminism and free-thought and teaches her to sing his poems and hymns to liberty.

Unfortunately Cythna is kidnapped by a marauding band of the Sultan Othman's men and, as we learn from her retrospective narrative in Canto VII, she is, like Moore's Zelica, thrown into the harem and raped by the tyrant, to whom she later bears a son. The kidnapping scene is a reworking of an earlier oriental poem by Shelley entitled *Zeinab and Kathema* set in an idyllic Kashmir; the poem's theme, borrowed from an idea suggested by William Jones in his *Essay on the Poetry of the Eastern Nations*[120] (although Lawrence's *Empire of the Nairs* is also an influence) is based on the lament of the Indian Kathema for his lover Zeinab kidnapped by British marauders and carried to a life of prostitution in England. Laon's dream of Cythna's putrefying body in Canto III (stanza xxvi) is based on Kathema's discovery of Zeinab's corpse swinging on an English gibbet, complete with worms and blue unnatural light.[121] This modification of the 1811 poem is the first of a number of passages in which Shelley reworked his sources in order to *avoid* casting his victims as Indians and his tyrants as British, important in assessing the manner in which the poem *disavows* an Indian colonial setting which nevertheless, I have suggested, represented the 'social energy' of the poem itself.

Whereas Moore's idealistic Azim is duped into joining forces with the evil Mokanna, Shelley's Laon, severely wounded and bound by Othman's henchman, is succoured by an old hermit who is a composite figure of Shelley's mentors Dr Lind and William Godwin. After seven years of illness, Laon recovers and is told by the old philosopher – whose benevolence and philanthropy are a marked contrast to Moore's Veiled Prophet – that his poems have spread enlightenment in the 'Golden City' (Othman's capital Constantinople); 'the pure law / Of mild equality and peace, succeeds / To faiths which long have held the world in awe, / Bloody and false' (lines 1541–4). He also informs Laon that a 'maiden fair' has led a feminist uprising against the sexual and political tyranny of Islam, motivated by his (Laon's) own principles. Laon, not suspecting that she is his Cythna (whom he believes to be dead) promptly sets off over the 'Asian mountains' to join the camp of the 'friends of liberty', assembled on a plain outside the Golden City. The tyrant strikes the first blow against the assembled patriots, but they are rallied by Laon and overwhelm Othman's forces and capture the Golden City, where Othman is deposed and, accompanied by his child (it later transpires that the child's mother is Cythna), is set free, rather than executed, by the rebels. To this point the poem clearly represents a '*beau ideal*' of the French Revolution in which the king is pardoned rather than guillotined, and also a departure from the violent vengefulness of *The Assassins* mentioned above.

Shelley's poem plays off the sexual tyranny of Moore's revolutionary Mokanna over Zelica by having Cythna overcome Othman. I will address the problem of the poem's feminism below, but note here that none the less the active role of Cythna sets *The Revolt* ideologically apart from Southey, Byron and Moore's poems of eastern revolution. When Cythna appears at the revolutionary 'Festival of Federation', having taken the name of her lost mentor 'Laone', 'a veil shrouded her countenance bright' (line 2115), placing her in the numerous company of 'veiled maids' haunting Shelley's poems. The culmination of the diabolical career of Moore's Veiled Prophet is to poison all his followers at a banquet after they have been defeated by the loyalist Caliph of Abbas; as they die, he lifts his silver veil in Moore's Allegorical exposé of the 'true face' of Jacobinism:

> Not the long-promised light, the brow whose beaming
> Was to come forth, all-conquering, all-redeeming,
> But features horribler than hell e'er traced
> On its own brood; – no Demon of the Waste,
> No churchyard ghole, caught lingering in the light
> Of the blest sun, e'er blasted human sight
> With lineaments so foul, so fierce as those
> Th'Impostor now, in grinning mockery, shows.[122]

Zelica, whose only remaining virtue is fidelity to her oath to Mokanna, is spared, but assuming the self-immolated prophet's veil, she is unwittingly murdered by her lover Azim who has in the meantime conveniently switched his loyalties to the counter-revolutionary Caliph. Shelley points the contrast between his revolt and Moore's by having Laon and the now unveiled Cythna escaping from the ruins of their revolution after Othman's forces have struck back; making their way to a ruined Greek temple they consummate their love before offering themselves as heroic martyrs on the tyrant's *auto-da-fé*. Both revolutions are failures, but whereas Shelley's inspires future hope for radical change in the growth of love between committed individuals, Moore's stands as a warning to his fellow Irishmen against the 'French' principles which had led to such disastrous consequences in Ireland in 1798. Nevertheless Moore's poem provides the bridge between Byron's oriental revolutions, led by unprincipled but noble heroes like Conrad and Lara, and Shelley's 'reorientation' of radical politics in *The Revolt of Islam*.

The political message of Moore's oriental revolution seems to be most fully intelligible in his native Irish context. The patriot Azim backs an imposter but realizing his error returns to the legitimist forces of the Caliph. The second unsuccessful revolt of *Lalla Rookh* (set against the more light-hearted tone of 'Paradise and the Peri' and 'The Light of the Haram')- is that of the Persian 'Fire-worshippers' against their Islamic conquerors, the setting for the tragic love-affair of Hinda and Hafed. The poem reworks the love story of Selim and Zuleika in Byron's *Bride of Abydos* in a context allegorical of the predicament of Irish nationalists under the yoke of British domination. As Moore writes of the Fire-worshippers (followers of a more ancient religion – Zoroastrianism/Catholicism – than that of their conquerors – Protestantism/Islam), 'I should not be surprised if this story of the Fire-worshippers were found capable of a...doubleness of application.'[123] Moore – a Whig 'orientalist' of the school of Jones rather than a reformer of the school of Mill or Shelley – is sympathetic to the claims of a romantic, organic nationalism which, he implies, must free itself from the imposture of Jacobin cosmopolitanism and French atheism.

A comparison of this with Shelley's famous intervention in Irish politics is instructive, particularly as his approach to the colonial situation in Ireland touches on his perception of the situation in India.[124] Shelley's negotiation of both situations is indebted to Volney's exposure of the equivalence of all religious system in *The Ruins*, as we will see shortly; more pragmatically, his 1812 *Address to the Irish People*, in its accommodation of the rationalist reduction to Catholicism, is very similar to Volney's advice to Napoleon on ruling the Egyptians through a 'reconstructed' Islam. Shelley's *Address* ostensibly supports the sort of nationalism idealized by Moore in *The Fire-worshipper*, a national independence founded on Catholic emancipation and the repeal of the Act of Union. At the same time he seeks to 'enlighten' his address by recommending 'Liberty, benevolence, peace and toleration' to the superstitious but oppressed Irish. As he wrote to Elizabeth Hitchener in January 1812 of the *Address*, 'It is *secretly* intended also as a preliminary to other pamphlets to shake Catholicism at its basis, and to induce Quakerish and Socinian principle[s] of politics without objecting to the Christian religion, which would do no good to the vulger just now.'[125] For Shelley the 'superstitions' of colonized peoples are a useful curb on their passions, means of social control (a fact which the British had grasped in India but not in Ireland, for rather different historical reasons) and even, as here, incitements to revolution against social injustice; they must, however ultimately give way to the rational transparency of the modern state. Hence Shelley writes, remarkably, in the *Address*, 'Were Ireland at this moment peopled with Brahmins, this very same Address would have been suggested by the same state of mind. You have suffered not merely for your religion, but some other causes which I am equally desirous of remedying.'[126] Judging from what Shelley has to say elsewhere about Brahmins, his sympathy for the religious persecution of Irish Catholics might be construed as a rather superficial affair.

' The Revolt of Islam' and Volney's 'Ruins'

In *Queen Mab*, printed in the summer of 1813, a year after the Irish adventure, Shelley casts the Brahmins in a very different light. In this most Volneyan of his poems, they epitomize the universal conspiracy of priesthood and credulity against liberty of thought and action:

> The name of God
> Has fenced about all crime with holiness,
> Himself the creature of His worshippers,
> Whose names and attributes and passions change,
> Seeva, Buddh, Foh, Jehovah, God, or Lord,
> Even with the human dupes who build His shrines,
> Still serving o'er the war-polluted world
> For desolation's watchword; whether hosts
> Stain His death-blushing chariot-wheels, as on
> Triumphantly they roll, whilst Brahmins raise
> A sacred hymn to mingle with the groans.[127]

Shelley's distillation of chapters 19–24 of Volney's *Ruins* (in a poem whose narrative framework – the dialogue between Mab and Ianthe – is based on the dialogue between Volney's protagonist and the 'Genius of tombs and ruins')[128] is reworked in the tenth canto of *The Revolt of Islam*. Shelley's counter-revolution rewrites Volney's chapter XVIII, entitled 'The consternation and conspiracy of Tyrants'.

Whereas Volney's liberated nation stands fast against the counter-revolution (Volney was writing in 1790 full of revolutionary optimism), Shelley, writing in 1817 with historical hindsight, has his pike-wielding citizen army defeated by superior force. Othman's counter-revolutionary armies are gathered from far and wide – 'Tartar and Frank, and millions whom the wings / Of Indian breezes lull' (lines 3835–6) – a mercenary eclecticism which Moore had stressed as a characteristic of the Veiled Prophet's *revolutionary* army, and which we will see informing Tom Medwin's description of the insurgent Pindari army in his poem of 1820 discussed in the coda to this chapter. The ferocious *anarchy* of tyranny (as in the title *The Mask of Anarchy*) is evident in the plethora of superstitious creeds which threaten the unity of the counter-revolutionaries; in his freak-show of 'Otherness' Shelley returns to the Volneyan 'panopticon' of religions presented in *Queen Mab*:

> And Oromaze, Joshua, and Mahomet,
> Moses and Buddh, Zerdusht, and Brahm, and Foh,
> A tumult of strange names, which never met
> Before, as watchwords of a single woe,
> Arose; each raging votary 'gan to throw
> Aloft his armèd hands, and each did howl
> 'Our God alone is God!'

> (lines 4063–9)

The warring factions are prevented from tearing each other apart by the intercession of an 'Iberian priest' who plays an important part in the sanguinary conclusion, but who seems peculiarly out of place in a poem about the Orient; even Leigh Hunt, in the *Revolt*'s most generous review, censured Shelley's 'violation of costume' as contributing to its uncommonness and obscurity.[129] Although Shelley explains that the priest has joined forces with Islam because he hates atheists and radicals even more than Muslims, and the 'cruel' Orient gives him licence to practise tortures banned in Europe, his manifest role of demonstrating the equivalence of all religions is achieved somewhat at the cost of narrative plausibility.

' The Revolt of Islam' and ' The Missionary'

A glance at Shelley's main source for the final cantos, Lady Morgan's novel *The Missionary*, reveals that the inclusion of the Iberian priest is pure pastiche, although what is *excluded* in the pastiche work is perhaps of more interest than what is included. Near the end of *The Missionary*, Hilarion returns to Spanish-controlled Goa (the novel is set in early seventeenth-century India) with the beautiful Brahmin priestess Luxima, who has been excommunicated and deprived of caste on account of her love for the Missionary, an unclean foreigner. The Dominican Hilarion is charged with having sexually corrupted his Indian neophyte (who has not in fact converted to Christianity) by a Spanish Jesuit and is tried by the Inquisition who sentence him to burn. Lady Morgan's *auto-da-fé* is quite clearly the model for Shelley's in *The Revolt*, just as her conniving Jesuit, a Gothic stereotype in the tradition of Matthew Lewis' *Monk*, is the model for Shelley's 'Iberian priest'.

As the pyre is about to be lit, Luxima, who with Hilarion's help has given her captors the slip, appears in front of the assembled Goans. 'A form scarcely human, darting with the velocity of lightning through the multitude, reached the foot of the pile, and stood before it, in a grand and aspiring attitude.'[130] Shouting 'Brahma receive and eternally unite our spirits!' she leaps onto the pyre; Hilarion embraces her, puts out the flames and fights off the Jesuits, who fatally wound Luxima. In Shelley's version, the defiant Laon's pyre is about to be lit when Cythna arrives on horseback, 'a steed / Dark and gigantic, with the tempest's speed, / Bursts through their ranks' (lines 4516–18). She springs from her horse and takes her place beside Laon; the couple exchange 'Looks of insatiate love' (4581) as the flames rise. That Luxima's attempted self-immolation is a form of *sati* (particularly as she dedicates her sacrifice to Brahma) is an embarrassment for Shelley's text; *his* heroine dies unflinchingly as an atheist in order to strike a blow at priestcraft, of which *sati*, as constructed by British colonial discourse, is a most salient example.[131]

In Morgan's novel, Luxima's action is the signal for an armed rebellion of the Indians against Spanish colonial authority; 'the Spaniards fought as mercenaries, with skill and coolness; the Indians as enthusiasts, for their religion and their liberty, with an uncurbed impetuosity; the conflict was long and unequal'.[132] Shelley, having kept Morgan's 'Iberian priest' in the most unassimilated form for the affective purposes of his poem, dispenses entirely with the insurrection; Laon and Cythna die in order to be *re*surrected and elegized in the Temple of the Spirit of the framing cantos. Anti-colonial revolt in Lady Morgan is replaced by the republican suicide of the nameless character (in the poem's early version, an 'Atheist and Republican',

Plate 6. 'Procession of Hindoo Woman to the Funeral Pyre of her Husband', in William Hodges, *Travels in India* (London 1793), facing p. 84.

terms elided from the 1818 version) who 'sheathed a dagger in his heart' (line 4716) after delivering a stirring epitaph to Laon and Cythna. As in his 1817 incorporation of *Zeinab and Kathema*, the revolt of Indians against colonial tyranny – the gist of both these sources – is suppressed in *The Revolt of Islam* and translated into a 'Jacobinical' and Hellenistic revolt against Asiatic tyranny in which Brahminism takes its place along with Catholicism as the religion of the oppressors. Shelley's poem of displaced revolution is also a poem of inverted imperialism in which, in a remarkable anticipation of Kipling's 'White Man's Burden', the colonial subject is represented as a tyrant and the colonizing power as a heroic martyr to its own idealism in struggling to enlighten the dark places of the earth.

'REVOLUTIONS OF EMPIRE' OR EMPIRE AS REVOLUTION?

In June 1853 Karl Marx, writing in the *New York Daily Tribune*, described how British power was breaking up the village communities of traditional agrarian India. (The part played by British 'orientalists' in propping up the village system before the triumph of Anglicist policies is here ignored by Marx.) He regarded this as no bad thing, as village life had always been 'the solid foundation of Oriental despotism...restrain[ing] the human mind within the smallest possible compass, making it the unresisting tool of superstition, enslaving it beneath traditional rules, depriving it of all grandeur and historical energy'. Although no admirer of the blend of greed and 'sharp philanthropy' which characterized British imperialism, he felt that the British had 'produced the greatest, and to speak the truth, the only *social* revolution ever heard of in Asia'.[133]

Thirty-four years earlier Shelley had used the same word to describe the impact of British colonialism on Indian culture in a long passage in his *Philosophical View of Reform*, written (but not published) in late 1819. As it is Shelley's longest comment on India, I want to quote the passage in full and remark briefly upon its rhetorical complexity, its entanglement in a discursive structure of 'contradictory doubling'.

Revolutions in the political and religious state of the Indian peninsula seem to be accomplishing, and it cannot be doubted but that the zeal of the missionaries of what is called the Christian faith will produce beneficial innovation there, even by the application of dogmas and forms of what is here an outworn encumbrance. The Indians have been enslaved and cramped in the most severe and paralyzing forms which were ever devised by man; some of this new enthusiasm ought to be kindled among them to consume it and leave them free, and even if the doctrines of Jesus do not penetrate through the darkness of that which those who profess to be his followers call Christianity, there will yet be a number of social forms modelled upon those European feelings from which it has taken its colour substituted to those according to which they are at present cramped, and from which, when the time for complete emancipation shall arrive, their disengagement may be less difficult, and under which their progress to it may be the less imperceptibly slow. Many native Indians have acquired, it is said, a competent knowledge in the arts and philosophy of Europe, and Locke and Hume and Rousseau are familiarly talked of in Brahminical society. But the thing to be sought is that they should as they would if they were free attain to a system of arts and literature of their own.[134]

Although the qualified sympathy for the missionaries is unexpected coming from Shelley, 'atheist' and admirer of Lady Morgan and Volney, his account of the 'modernization' of Indian elites is without doubt both perceptive and prescient in terms of the story told by David Kopf, namely the galvanizing effect of evangelism in establishing Hindu reform movements such as the Brahmo Samaj and the Dharma Sabha. As well as the changes being wrought by Rammohun Roy, to which I will return in detail below, the Eurasian Jacobin Henry Derozio was teaching Locke, Hume, Rousseau and Paine to the Bengali elite in the Hindu College at Calcutta in the late 1820s, a rationalist, progressivist philosophy which would have a profound influence on the Bengali Renaissance of the mid-century.[135]

But perhaps the most remarkable thing about Shelley's passage is the awkwardness of its last sentence, and in particular the faltering, unpunctuated conditional 'as they would if they were free'. The main body of the text has described a 'revolutionary' liberation from the straight-jacket of Brahminism, albeit a gradual one; the last sentence is forced, surreptitiously, to admit that the European values which are to free them are also those which enslave them. Phrases like 'complete emancipation' become by this token problematic; emancipation from Brahmins or from the British? What are we to think of a revolution which enslaves rather than liberates, or a discourse of revolution which admits that it is also a discourse of domination? The 'contradictory doubling' of the whole passage exemplifies Bhabha's account of the construction of the colonial subject as fetish canvassed in a previous section of this chapter, in which competing Anglicist and 'orientalist' policies of hegemony are shown to be complicit in a vacillating structure of metaphor and metonymy, narcissism and aggression, liberation and domination.

I have argued above that a *manifest* discourse of India based on universalizing Volneyan norms of the reduction and equivalence of cultural systems is forced into a strategy of substitution and displacement by its suppressed knowledge of the violence of imperialism. But Shelley would also negotiate the question on another level, in which metaphors of gender and the narratives of desire complicate his account of the rationalization of the oriental Other. As Rana Kabbani points out, 'The European was led to the East by sexuality, by the embodiment of it in a woman or a young boy'.[136] The question of cultural difference becomes entangled with that of sexual difference, and a binary opposition which is almost a cliché in orientalist discourse (that which sets the figure of the male/European against the female/Asian)[137] is problematized by Shelley's manifest feminism in *Alastor*, *The Revolt of Islam* and *Prometheus Unbound*. In order to trace this theme, I am going to go back to Shelley's 1815 poem *Alastor*, a poem in which the ambivalence of an erotic 'encounter' (again modelled on *The Missionary*) is mapped onto an explicitly Indian landscape.

ENGENDERING INDIA: THE POET AND THE 'LIGHT OF ASIA'

A story familiar to readers of Shelley criticism tells how the poet is weaned off the radical atheism and French materialism of his youth by a Platonic idealism hospitable to the apotheosis of imagination evident in later works like *Prometheus Unbound, Adonais* and *The Defence of Poetry*.[138] If one is studying the influence of Platonism on the poet, then it is the Platonizing summer of 1818 at Bagni di Lucca which effects Shelley's sea-change; if on the other hand one is more concerned with the influence of Sir William Jones and Sanskrit studies, then 'his transition from the rational materialism of the early writings to the mystical pantheism of his mature works was largely due to his study of Jones'.[139] John Drew, in his recent book *India and the Romantic Imagination*, rather fancifully conflates the two in an elaborate account of ancient hermetic links between Sanskrit theology and the western Neoplatonist tradition which he sees as central to the thought of Sir William Jones, Coleridge and Shelley alike.[140]

There is no doubt but that the strong influence of Volney which I have been tracing through the poem up to 1817 is linked to a materialism whereby 'spirit' can be explained in terms of matter and motion. Shelley's caution in the 1821 *Defence* against taking materialism and scepticism to an extreme position 'as some of the French writers have', of 'defac(ing)...the eternal truths charactered upon the imaginations of men', undoubtedly represents a qualification of his earlier position. I do not propose to add to the scholarly debate partly because it seems to me far from evident that there was any hard-and-fast distinction in the English radical tradition of Priestley, Godwin, Erasmus Darwin and the young Coleridge between 'materialist empiricism' and 'Neoplatonism',[142] and secondly because the sceptical basis of Shelley's 'Intellectual Philosophy', of which C. E. Pulos' *The Deep Truth* is still the best study, has both a 'positive' and a 'negative' side which cannot be easily written into a genetic account of Shelley's thought. The most important of Shelley's philosophical mentors after 1814 were David Hume and Sir William Drummond; if Hume's scepticism limited rational enquiry to the task of discerning the 'constant conjunction of objects' through observation and experiment, thereby demolishing metaphysical dogmatism, he also 'sometimes exhibits a willingness to give qualified assent...to conclusions regarding the unknowable, basing his right to do so on the imagination and feeling'.[143]

Returning to the question of gender, Shelley apparently conceived : relationship between the negative and the positive side of his scepticism in terms of two (stereotypical) metaphors. One is based on the conventional gender opposition of 'masculine' rationality and 'female' imagination. The second is a geopolitical metaphor of Europe and Asia; in the words of Sir William Jones' *Second Discourse* of 1785, 'reason and taste are the grand prerogatives of *European* minds, while the *Asiaticks* have soared to loftier heights in the sphere of imagination.'[144] Because I want to maintain that Shelley's metaphors for the dichotomy reason/imagination were loaded with the weight of material history (imperialism and patriarchy), rather than generated by some disinterested epistemological decision, the relationship between the two terms will be viewed in the present discussion as troubled and unstable rather than as a balancing act in the constitution of a symmetrical, integrated humanism. If, as we have seen above, much of Shelley's writing is carried by the force of the stereotypical binary oppositions West/East, male/female, reason/imagination, it is apparent that to reverse the power current in any one pair upsets the general economy of equivalences. Shelley's feminism seems to have had this effect in relation to the binary opposition East/West: granted Cythna's rhetorical question in *The Revolt of Islam*, 'Can man be free if woman be a slave?', a critique of the *partiality* of what for Rousseau or Paine is universal reason, what are we to make of a poem in which the liberation of men *and* women is premised, albeit at a subliminal level, upon imperial domination? We will see how this problem emerges with *Prometheus Unbound*, in an attempt to circumscribe the very project of universal reason, as the role of the subordinate terms Asia/female/imagination is redefined in a poem which seeks through a radical exercise of imagination to rethink the binary stereotypes.

'ALASTOR: OR THE SPIRIT OF SOLITUDE'

The exhilaration (and exhaustion) or sexual desire, most famously treated in *Epipsychidion*, is also an informing theme of *Alastor: or the Spirit of Solitude* (1815). Although it seems to me that the protagonist's dream of the 'veiled maid' is the most interesting and problematic aspect of the poem, I want to say a preliminary word about *Alastor* as an orientalist poem and therefore a poem concerned with empire, a theme which has been consistently overlooked by its critics. The 'poet' protagonist of *Alastor* on one level typifies the career of the Volneyan orientalist visiting the ruins of past civilizations, Athens, Tyre, Baalbek, Jerusalem, Babylon, Memphis, Thebes and 'Dark Aethiopia' (*SPW*, p. 17, lines 107–15), seeking the equivalence of all mythologies in the motions of the heavenly bodies, the immutable laws of nature. Like Volney and Dupius, he discovers amongst the ruins 'the Zodiac's brazen mystery' and by 'poring on memorials / Of the world's youth' he seeks to establish 'the thrilling secrets of the birth of time' (*SPW*, p. 18, lines 119–28). But the 'poet' (nameless, this his only designation) is driven further East beyond the Egyptian/Ethiopian *Ürsprung* of the French mythographers, to the Kashmir which Bernier, Maurice, Wilford and Germans like Schlegel and Johann Müller regarded as the 'terrestrial paradise of the Indies', birthplace of Hinduism, Zoroastrianism and religious mysticism.[145]

The poem's impulse to move 'further East' reiterates a contemporary fantasy of European power, like Napoleon carrying a translation of the *Rig-Veda* with him on his expedition to Egypt, the gateway to the East, in 1798.[146] The *Alastor* 'poet' figures the expansive, imperial mission of European reason to secure its destiny in the discovery of its genesis (or genetrix). It prefigures Max Müller's remark to an Indian Civil Service candidate in 1882 that his heart should not sink when approaching the shores of India, for he was 'going to his "old home", full of memoirs, if only he can read them'.[147] The 'poet' is a figure of the same stamp as Captain Walton or Victor Frankenstein in Mary Shelley's novel begun in 1816, the year after the publication of *Alastor*. Walton is an explorer seeking the North Pole, which he believes to be, like the 'poet's' Kashmir, 'a land surpassing in wonders and beauty every region hitherto discovered on the habitable globe',[148] and Victor seeks to conquer for science the secret of life itself. The lesson of both Shelley's poem and Mary's novel is that 'The Poet's self-centred seclusion was avenged by the furies of an irresistible passion pursuing him to speedy ruin.'[149] Walton and Victor discover in the high latitudes of the globe the kingdom of abstract reason, a physical and moral wilderness of ice and death, void of humanity. In the same way *Alastor*'s 'poet', pursuing his visionary 'prototype' out of Kashmir, ends up (ironically) in a premature grave in the Caucasus, the barren mountain range where J. F. Blumenbach had located the birthplace of the human race.

Unlike the Arctic explorer Walton or the mad scientist Victor Frankenstein, however, the *Alastor* 'poet's' Orient is figured as an idealized woman, his quest motivated by sexual desire rather than scientific hubris. We will see when we come to look at Medwin's Indian poems how the *Alastor* 'poet's' quest for his female 'prototype' could be read as an unmasking of Britain's desire for its Indian Other. The 'poet' is a composite figure who contains elements of Wordsworth's 'Solitary' in the *Excursion* as well as the figure of Rousseau whom Mary Wollstonecraft attacks in the *Vindication of the Rights of Woman*. Wollstonecraft's Rousseau is the solitary, misanthropic architect of the revolutionary 'Virtue' of 1793, whose sexist idealization of women and refusal of domesticity damns him into a feverish and masturbatory dissatisfaction with 'things as they are'. The analogy is evident in the *Alastor* 'poet's' negligence of the timid 'Arab maiden', who falls in love with him in lines 129–39 of the poem, and his vain pursuit of a dream-maiden projected by his frustrated need to embody his ideal.

I will discuss this aspect in more detail below; for the moment I wish to draw attention to *Alastor* as a poem about the 'psycho-pathology of empire'. The *Alastor* 'poet' prefigures the Victorian empire-builder, moving ever further and outwards, employing ever more powerful resources in his search for an intellectual beauty which always seems to give him the slip. Shelley's *Alastor* just as much as the popular adventure stories which are the subject of Martin Green's *Tales of Adventure, Deeds of Empire*, inaugurates a nineteenth-century myth which became history in the lives of men like Richard Burton and William Gifford Palgrave, Edward Stanley or T. E. Lawrence. Shorn of its heroics, the poem desublimates into the image of the young Collector upholding the Empire in some dusty corner of British India with a Sanskrit grammar and a copy of either Plato's *Republic* or the Bible (depending upon his ideological proclivities), dedicated to upholding 'Pax Britannica' before falling victim to loneliness, madness, dysentery or drink.

Joseph Raban has reiterated, in one of the rare readings of the poem sensitive to its geography, that the journey of Shelley's 'poet' from the Middle East to Ethiopia, Arabia, Persia and Kerman Shah (Iran), over the Hindu Kush to the aphelion, Kashmir, then north-west via Aornos and Petra, Balk and Parthia to Chorasmia (Uzbekistan) and the Caspian Sea to the Caucasus, 'closely approximates that of Alexander the Great during the triumphant years between his initial conquests in the Near East and his glorious extension of his empire beyond the borders of the Persian domains'.[150] I have mentioned the importance of Alexander as a positive paradigm for European expansionism in India in the context of Thomas Beddoes' poem of the same name, in which the activities of the Company are weighed and found wanting. One can speculate that Beddoes' poems might have stimulated Shelley's interest in Alex-ander's Indian expedition, an interest evident from his avid reading of its classical historians Arrian and Quintus Curtius, the merits and demerits of whom he discussed with Hogg in a letter of July 1817.[151]

Considering Shelley's distaste for Alexander as desecrator of the Greek republics, Raban argues that the other classical source for *Alastor*'s journey, also entailing an invasion of India – a mythological rather than historical source – was that of the god Dionysus, as narrated in Nonnus' poem *Dionysiaca*. Shelley ordered the poem in 1817, although he may of course have read it earlier. Although the case Raban makes for the *Alastor* 'poet' as a Dionysian figure is, I think, unconvincing, Dionysus' conquest of India could have

represented for Shelley, as Alexander's expedition represented for
Thomas Beddoes, a 'civilizing mission' (or synonymously, a 'Hellen-
izing' mission) against which to set, for either positive or negative
comparison, Britain's 'revolutionary' impact on India. The fact that
Dionysus, god of both civilization and revolutionary energy, had
been brought up on Mount Nyasa, identified by William Jones with
Mount Meru in the Indian Caucasus or Hindu Kush[152] before
moving west to Egypt, and *later* returning to conquer India, would
allow Shelley to construct the Indian empire, much as Schlegel
would construct German culture, as England/Europe returning to
an Indian point of origin. England's Indian empire might thus be
construed, with the help of a little mythology, as a *ricorso* of liberty.

Shelley was not the only major Romantic poet interested in the
Dionysiac invasion of India. In the 'Song of the Indian Maid' in
book iv of *Endymion*, John Keats, like Shelley, combined the 'imperial'
story of Dionysus/Bacchus with the erotic interest of the Maid in a
poem which at one level constitutes a 'response' to *Alastor*. Keats
mobilizes the full panoply of Indian imagery behind the Miltonic
fascade of this passage, the Maid's account of Bacchus' 'disen-
chanting' of India; 'Great Brahma from his mystic heaven groans,
/ And all his priesthood moans; / Before young Bacchus' eye-wink
turning pale.'[153] The Maid has followed Bacchus back from India,
but has left him, satiated with sensual pleasures; she appeals to the
Greek Endymion, whose heart is dedicated to the divine Cynthia, for
love and protection. Keats' 1818 poem offers both a revision and a
critique of Shelley's *Alastor*; the Indian Maid who apparently offers
a 'practical' alternative to the shepherd/prince's visionary love for
Cynthia (like the 'Arab maid' and 'veiled maid' respectively in
Alastor) turns out to be another manifestation of the goddess, a means
of testing the hero's dedication to the ideal. In the poem's final lines,
the dark Indian maiden undergoes a racial transformation into a
blonde Greek goddess, revealing her oriental incarnation as a lure.[154]
For Keats' poem, unlike Shelley's, orientalism is primarily a question
of style, an imperial heraldry uncomplicated by the anxiety of
empire; India is merely an appendage to classical Greece, the exotic
imagery on the capital of a Corinthian column. Keats' poem is
another protest against Shelley's sacrifice of poetic manner and
imaginative experience to political 'magnanimity', and as such he
clearly read *Alastor* as a *critique* of its dreamy protagonist, a critique
with which he disagreed as a disciple of the 'truth of imagination'.

The nympholepsy of *Endymion* brings us back to the central event of *Alastor*, the poet's dream of the 'veiled maid', as he lies asleep 'beneath the hollow rocks (of) a natural bower' in 'the vale of Cashmire' (line 147; 145). John Drew notes the derivation of the poem's 'veiled maid' from the character of the Kashmiri 'Vedanta' priestess Luxima in *The Missionary*, although he misses the crucial transformation that Shelley's has wrought upon her.[155] Morgan's novel, which as I have argued drew heavily and sometimes verbatim on Jones' essays (notable *On the Philosophy of the Asiatics* and *On the Mystical Poetry of the Persians and Hindoos*) in describing the theology of its 'Brahmachira' heroine, is a source-book of orientalist stereotypes articulated as metaphors of gender. For example, look at the contrast between the 'towering', 'energetic' and 'vigourous' missionary Hilarion, 'a being created to resist and command', and the soft lustre of Luxima, 'a being created to feel and to submit', 'enthusiastic in her brilliant errors'. Morgan exploits the related metaphors of gender and geography in her account of the dawning love between Christian and Hindu: 'Silently gazing, in wonder, upon each other, they stood finely opposed, the noblest specimens of the human species, as it appears in the most opposite regions of the earth; she, like the East, lovely and luxuriant; he, like the West, lofty and commanding.'[156]

When Hilarion first sees Luxima through her veil in her palanquin, she seems 'like one of these splendid illusions, with which the enthusiasm of religion brightens the holy dream of its votarist, like the spirit which descends amidst the shadows of night upon the slumbers of the blessed'.[157] Hilarion gets closer to Luxima, too close for comfort, as he begins to lose a grip on his personal 'civilizing mission': Luxima's Vedantin 'religion of mystic love' troubles his asceticism and her warm sensibility in the end overcomes his own powerful sense of purpose in preaching 'the doctrine of a self-denying faith, in the land of perpetual enjoyment'.[158] The fact that Hilarion is a seventeenth-century Portuguese Catholic allows Lady Morgan a certain freedom in criticizing the limitations of European rule without ever directly implicating current British policy, still in 1811 based upon the 'orientalist' policy approved of by Morgan, although already being challenged by the increasingly influential arguments of the evangelical party.

We saw above Shelley's comment on Morgan's novel in June 1811: 'Luxima the Indian is an Angel. What pity that we cannot incorporate these creations of Fancy; the very thought of them thrills the soul. Since I have read this book I have read no other – but I have thought strangely.'[159] Shelley's 'reincorporation' of the visionary Luxima in *Alastor* passes an ironic comment on the same poem's protagonist, who fails to realize that his 'veiled maid' is only a dream, and pays for his error with his life. The poet dreams while he sleeps by a 'sparkling rivulet' in the vale of Kashmir, the very setting of Hilarion's dangerous encounter. Luxima's locks 'enwreathed with beams, sparkled with the waters of the holy stream'; she 'stood so bright and so ethereal…that it seemed but a transient incorporation of the brilliant mists of morning'.[160] In his vision, Shelley's protagonist admires, 'by the warm light of their own life / Her glowing limbs beneath the sinuous veil' before 'fold[ing] his frame in her dissolving arms', in what the unromantic reader may unproblematically identify as a 'wet-dream' (*SPW*, p. 19, lines 175–191). Shelley intensifies the erotic value of Morgan's Luxima whilst never letting the reader forget that she is 'a creature of Fancy'; yet once again he alters the ideological content of his source. If Morgan's Vedantin priestess is a word-for-word mouthpiece for Jones' orientalism, then Shelley's 'veiled maid' is spokeswoman for revolutionary enlightenment, but also a figure who is revealed as a self-conscious *projection* of the author of *Address to the Irish People* or the 'poet protagonist' who dreams her into existence:

> Her voice was like the voice of his own soul
> Heard in the calm of thought; its music long,
> Like woven sounds of streams and breezes, held
> His inmost sense suspended in its web
> Of many-coloured woof and shifting hues,
> Knowledge and truth and virtue were her theme,
> And lofty hopes of divine liberty,
> Thoughts the most dear to him, and poesy,
> Herself a poet.
>
> (*SPW*, p. 18, lines 153–61)

Shelley's 'veiled maid' collapses – or refuses – the neat dichotomies around which Lady Morgan had constructed her plot. Far from finding a 'self-consolidating Other' in the Vale of Kashmir (for Luxima figures the similarity-in-difference, the metaphoric link between Vedantin Brahminism as constructed by colonial power and Morgan's enlightened European deism), Shelley's 'veiled maid' represents a narcissistic discovery of the *same*, a secular/revolutionary rather than religious enlightenment of the sort which, after Jones' *On the Philosophy of the Asiatics*, was the more usual object of visionary experience in the Vale of Kashmir.

Shelley elides the Brahminism of his source in the same way as he would suppress the Indian context of *Zeinab and Kathema* in Canto III of *The Revolt of Islam*, or a possible reading of the *auto-da-fé* as a *sati* in Canto XII of the same poem. Her Brahminism gone, Luxima is recast as the 'prototype' (what Shelley would later term the 'Epipsychidion') of the poet-protagonist; for which reason, presumably, we are informed that she is 'herself a poet'. This is Shelley's ideological equivalent of the racial transformation of Keats' Indian maid into the blonde goddess Cynthia: 'Her long black hair swell'd ampler, in display / Full golden; in her eyes a brighter day / Dawn'd blue and full of love.'[161] The polemical thrust of Morgan's novel is to show that evangelical policies of cultural assimilation cannot succeed; rather than 'making a Christian' Hilarion only succeeds in 'destroying a Hindu', and he himself ends up as a hybrid rather in Homi Bhabha's sense.

The novel constructs a definition of Hinduism which is acceptable to the 'orientalist' European mind (that is to say, a definition 'feminized' into the subordinate term of the binary opposition), distinguished from the sinister priestcraft of the Brahmins who excommunicate the heroine. But Shelley's *elision* of the Hindu elements of Luxima in representing his 'veiled maid' is rather different, equivalent to his displaced *Revolt of Islam* – a break with the orientalist discourse of Jones and Lady Morgan, a fantasy of the universalism of revolutionary reason. *His* Luxima disrupts the economy of the orientalist binary opposition; she is at once *more* sensual than her source, but also the spokeswoman of an aggressive libertarian rationalism which belies the image of the soft and luxurious oriental woman 'a being created to feel and submit'. Shelley's 'Light of Asia' (like Marx's) casts the beams of European revolutionary progress, 'knowledge and truth and virtue', onto the darkness of the Asiatic mode of production.

And yet we must not lose sight of the ambivalence of *Alastor*'s visionary maid. Shelley makes it clear that the 'veiled maid' is merely a masturbatory fantasy, a wish-fulfilment, a figure of displaced desire. 'Luxima the Indian Priestess', he had written in 1811, '*were* it possible to embody such a character, is perfect' (my italics).[162] The reason why Shelley's *Alastor* is more sensitive than *The Missionary* to what I have suggested was an as yet barely articulated sense of the *violence* of imperialism is that, despite its most cherished longing to do so, it *fails* to discover in the East *either* a 'self-consolidating Other', as in the orientalist canon, or a spectral reflection of the same, the more usual Shelleyan figure for dealing with the East.

I suggested above that Shelley's feminism disrupted the economy of the orientalist/patriarchy metaphor; if we read *Alastor* as a poem powerfully motivated by Wollstonecraft's critique of Rousseau, then we can see the source of its ambivalence regarding cultural difference emerging from its awareness of sexual difference. Rousseau, according to Wollstonecraft, 'debauched his imagination' by refusing the ties of the domestic affections and dreaming of a perfect but unrealizable woman, like Pygmalion and Galatea. The impact on the poem of Wollstonecraft's analysis here is evident if we remember its full title: *Alastor: or the Spirit of Solitude.* '[Rousseau] then sought for solitude', Wollstonecraft continued, 'not to sleep with the man of nature, or calmly investigate the causes of things under the shade where Sir Isaac Newton indulged contemplation, but merely to indulge his feelings.'[163] The 'self-centred seclusion' of Shelley's protagonist drives him to mistake his own projection for reality, like Wollstonecraft's Rousseau who 'skilfully exhibits the objects of sense most voluptuously shadowed or gracefully veiled; and thus making us feel whilst dreaming that we reason, erroneous conclusions are left in the mind'.[164] The prurient, unsocialized nature of Rousseau's visions of universal reason was commonly perceived as the root cause of the failure of the French Revolution by liberal and conservative critics alike, a fact which was not lost on Shelley in his unfinished poetic meditation on Rousseau *The Triumph of Life.*

The uncharacteristic ambivalence of *Alastor* (at least in relation to *Address to the Irish People* or *Queen Mab*, if not to later poems) regarding Rousseau or the Volneyan doctrine of rational equivalence evinces a cultural self-awareness which rejects *both* 'orientalist' and assimilationist strategies in constructing India. The poem's 'negative' knowledge reveals the expansive purposiveness of European reason as similar in kind to Rousseau's famous paranoia; solitary, unsocialized, narcissistic, driven, it is in the end consumed by its own metaphors of power, like the protagonist 'avenged by the furies of an irresistible passion pursuing him to speedy ruin'. Accordingly the poem's dominant mood is one of detumescence, absence, disenchantment, as the 'poet' wakes from his dream; 'His wan eyes /

Gaze on the empty scene as vacantly / As ocean's moon looks on the moon in heaven' (*SPW*, p. 19, lines 200–2). But his imagination soon fills the void. Leaving Kashmir the poet journeys in search of his 'prototype': if the first stage of his travels figures an eastward path from Europe to the origin of cultures in Kashmir, the second leads north-west to the Georgian Caucasus, where Blumenbach had located the 'autocthones of mankind'.[165]

The 'poet' discovers the landscape through which he passes to be vitally metaphorical, as he follows the philogenetic stream back to its source; 'O stream!' he asks, '/ Whose source is inaccessibly profound, / Whither do thy mysterious waters tend? / Thou imagest my life' (*SPW*, pp. 25–6, lines 502–5). Although sympathetic to what the Preface terms the protagonist's 'generous error', the poem's narrator has a very different perspective on the poet and the landscape through which he travels, maintaining the detumescent mood of lines 200–5. The protagonist's metaphors are recast as metonymies, the Caucasian source is represented as a stony mountain wasteland, a landscape of absence. Like Rousseau in *The Triumph of Life* whom the narrator mistakes for 'an old root which grew / To strange distortion out of the hill side',[166] the *Alastor* 'poet' becomes himself a metonymy of the barren Caucasus in which he seeks the elusive 'prototype';

> A gradual change was here,
> Yet ghastly. For, as fast years flow away,
> The smooth brow gathers, and the hair grows thin
> And white, and where irradiate dewy eyes
> Had shone, gleam Stony orbs.
>
> (*SPW*, p. 26, lines 532–6)

'CAN MAN BE FREE IF WOMAN BE A SLAVE?': THE PROBLEM OF 'THE REVOLT'S' FEMINISM

I have been arguing that the Wollstonecraftian sub-text of *Alastor* opens the poem up to a sense of sexual and cultural difference which problematizes the 'colonial' impulse of Shelleyan reason. The feminism of one of his sources for the poem (Wollstonecraft) effectively neutralizes the 'orientalist' oppositions of another (Morgan's *The Missionary*) as well as the Volneyan equivalences which we have seen motivating Shelley's 'assimilationist' attitude to India. In *The Revolt of Islam* by contrast, a strongly motivating although suppressed ideology of imperialism/revolution negates the poem's feminism; it is as if the contradictions in Shelley's radicalism are constantly displacing the object of his critique. In discussing the clichéd gendering of orientalist discourse above, I suggested a domino effect whereby the undoing of the stability of one metaphorical pair caused all the others to collapse. In *The Revolt of Islam* the same thing happens in reverse: a manifest feminism is undone by the poem's investment in a discourse of latent imperialism. Indeed, in contrast to the critique of a stereotypical sexual difference in *Alastor*, Shelley's feminism becomes itself a form of colonial discourse in *The Revolt*.[167]

In her introduction to *Romanticism and Feminism* Ann Mellor describes Shelley's feminism as categorically narcissistic, involving an assimilation of the Other. 'Shelley carried to an extreme this dual strategy of deifying the male ego even as it cannibalized the attributes of the female. In his *Essay on Love* he defined the beloved female as the antitype of the male, "a miniature as it were of our entire self, yet deprived of all that we condemn or despise, the ideal prototype of everything excellent or lovely that we are capable of conceiving as belonging to the nature of man".'[168] A glance back to the mechanism of displacement in *The Revolt of Islam* endorses Mellor's point, enabling us to see how the 'social energy' motivating Shelley's representation of revolution forced him into the very trap which he had so successfully avoided by *dramatizing* in *Alastor*.

An undeniable problem facing the reader of *The Revolt of Islam* is that of identifying with the self-congratulatory, priggish hero Laon. Laon is the sole source of enlightenment in the poem; the other characters, including Cythna, simply refract or reflect his self-generated radiance. Cythna's feminism is hardly given a chance, considering that Laon takes sole credit for its conception and propagation; she is no more than his mouthpiece. The fact that Shelley wrote the brother–sister relationship of Laon and Cythna out of his 1818 version of the poem is thus really immaterial given that Cythna remains as Laon's 'prototype' or 'Epipsychidion'. 'As mine own shadow was this child to me, / A second self, far dearer and more fair', says Laon in the second canto of Cythna, the 'orphan [who] with my parents lived' (ii, lines 874–5; 847). The question of incest which so fascinated Shelley is really another version of his favourite theme of discovering the Same in the Other, which I have linked on an existential level with Rousseau and on an ideological/philosophical level with Volney.

The 'undissolving radiancy' Cythna sheds on Laon's onerous life identifies her as another version of Luxima or the 'veiled maid' of *Alastor*, except this time she is 'embodied' as a fleshly character, at least in so far as the poem can be said to trade in creatures of flesh and blood at all. Shelley identifies so strongly with Laon that at times he seems to forget that there is *any* distinction between himself and his creation, unmindful of his self-conscious exposure of just such a projection, and its fatal consequences, in *Alastor*. When Cythna sings (like the 'veiled maid' of *Alastor*) Laon describes her 'wild melody' as 'Hymns which *my* soul had woven to Freedom' (II, lines 914–15) (italics mine); when she sits in contemplation she does so 'on the wing / Of visions that were *mine*' (II, lines 926–7). At times it seems as if Shelley must be dealing ironically; note here the qualifying metaphor of bondage informing Laon's boast that 'all things became / Slaves to my holy and heroic verse, / Earth, sea and sky, the planets, life and fame / And fate, or whate'er else binds the world's wondrous frame' (II, lines 933–6). Although Shelley allows Cythna to initiate the revolt of Islam, it is in the name of Laon and *under* his name, for 'Laone was the name her love had chosen, / For she was nameless, and her birth none knew' (V, lines 1882–3) – despite the fact that we already know her as Cythna. Laon's egomania does not stop short at Cythna, for the old hermit who saves him in Canto IV (a composite figure for Lind and Godwin, as I mentioned above) also admits that he is a mere mouthpiece for Laon's 'aspirings bold' (IV, line 1516). He confesses, 'For I have been thy passive instrument... thou hast lent / To me, to all, the power to advance / Towards this unforeseen deliverance From our ancestral chains' (IV, lines 1549–54), a startling piece of impudence on Shelley's part if we take the biographical Godwin/ Lind identification at face value. And such is the talismanic power of Laon's name that its very sound is enough to rout the tyrant's army in 'sudden panic' (V, lines 1779–91).

It would be possible to multiply instances of this sort, but I think that the point is sufficiently established. Laon is a reincarnation of the *Alastor* poet (even to the extent of sharing his physical characteristics, 'my thin hair / Was prematurely grey, my face was lined / With channels' (IV, lines 1668–70) and Cythna, who actually implements the revolution during Laon's seven-year illness in Canto IV, is that poem's 'veiled maid'. If we read *The Revolt* as a palimpsest which 'includes' its precursor poem of 1815, as well as *The Missionary*, the Hellenistic cultural identity of hero and heroine can be seen as a sublimation (incorporating that which it cancels or transcends) of the *Indian* Luxima/'veiled maid' set against the *European* Hilarion/*Alastor* protagonist. The fact that Cythna is a nameless orphan in the 1818 version, leaving the question of her origins unresolved, is I think of less importance than the symbolic links which connect her to Luxima in the poem. Shelley's attempt to elide cultural, racial and kinship differences from the hero and heroine (to make them *both* Greek, and, in the earlier version at least, brother and sister, rebelling against Asiatic despotism, superstition and misogyny) represents the triumph of Volneyan equivalence and universalism; it also distinguishes the *Revolt* from *Prometheus Unbound*, in which the 'lovers' embody cultural difference.

The only difference which remains in *The Revolt* is one of gender, and without that (itself a questionable difference in Shelley's handling here) the 'feminist' revolution would lose half its point. The eventual failure of the revolution seems very secondary, however, in relation to what the poem represents as its principal success, certainly its moment of maximum tension, the love-making of Laon and Cythna in Canto VI, lines 2623–76. If we read this in terms of the precursor poem – linguistically its rhetoric of sexual consummation is very close to that of *Alastor*'s 'wet-dream' in lines 161–91 – we can see it as the death of Shelley's problematization of sexual and cultural assimilation as plotted out in *Alastor*. Shelley has in a manner of speaking had his cake and eaten it: he has maintained an awareness of Cythna's fantastical character, her *impossibility*, but then he has proved her to be flesh and blood and permitted his protagonist to *possess* her in the flesh, in effect to *be* her flesh. It may be that Shelley's narcissism in this poem is no greater than the assimilationist imperial will which, at an identical moment in history (1817–18), was constructing British rule by 'imagining India' as a laboratory of modernity whose natives were *subjects*, brown-skinned Englishmen, and not simply figures of 'self-consolidating Otherness'. Eric Stokes quotes a nineteenth-century spokesman for free-trade and universal values asserting that 'We may be assured that in buying and selling, human nature is the same in Cawnpore as in Cheapside.'[169]

I have presented Shelley's poem as a complex mechanism of displacement, a palimpsest upon which a previous text (*The Missionary*/*Alastor*) is written over but which can be made to reappear by exegetical 'processing'. To recap: Shelley's central female protagonist (Luxima, the 'veiled maid', Cythna/Laone) is revealed

Plate 7. 'Raja Ram Mohan Roy', unknown artist, India Office Library and
Records. WD 1288.

in my reading to be at once a Brahmin priestess, the 'masturbatory'
fantasy of a revolutionary or empire-building poet, and a 'Hel-
lenized' woman who leads a revolt against oriental tyranny, the
'beau ideal' of the French Revolution. If we think back to Shelley's
remarks on India quoted above ('Locke and Hume and Rousseau
are familiarly talked of in Brahminical society'), we can read the
Cythna figure as an embodiment of an ideal of a native elite which
leads a revolution against itself (not its colonial masters) *without being
prompted or coerced*, thereby cancelling the contradiction between
revolution and imperialism. *The Revolt* seeks to perform at a more

complex level (because cognizant of the necessity of hegemonizing a native population) the narrative sublimation which we observed in *The Assassins.* Shelley's awareness of the way in which imperialism violates difference, even (or particularly) in the name of a universal discourse of revolutionary liberation, is evident in both the ambivalence of *Alastor* and the uncertain tone which concluded the passage from *Philosophical View of Reform.* Shelley desires that the Brahmins discussing Locke and Rousseau 'should as they would if they were free attain to a system of arts and literature of their own'.

Although the consummation of Laon and Cythna's love in Canto VI appears on one level to satisfy the frustrated desire of *Alastor* and figure an 'integrated humanism' wedding East and West, I have preferred to argue that it rather heralds the triumph of the Same, the reduction of all differences to an equivalence of reason, the totalizing programme of the West. Despite its rhetoric of political and sexual liberation, it is no more possible to read the poem in the belief that it depicts 'revolution from below' – either Cythna's as a woman or the Asiatics' as victims of social paralysis – than it is to believe that British policy in India simply represented the 'beau ideal' of the French Revolution, the triumph of enlightenment and self-determination over Asiatic darkness. The reason for this impossibility, as I have suggested, is discernable in the nature of Shelley's protagonist Laon, a figure of 'self-centred seclusion' whose priggish voice echoes with the bad faith of self-negating humanism.

THE 'REFORMING BRAHMIN' AND '*PROMETHEUS UNBOUND*'

In June 1817, whilst Shelley was engaged in the composition of *Laon and Cythna* in Buckinghamshire and James Mill was publishing his *History of British India,* the unitarian *Monthly Magazine* published the first in a series of articles on the idolatrous worship of the Hindus. Its author dismissed the arguments of 'orientalists' like Sir William Jones that modern Hinduism was essentially monotheistic and that 'all objects of worship are considered by [modern Brahmins] as emblematical representations of the Supreme Divinity'. Whilst maintaining that Hinduism of the Upanishadic age *had* been monotheistic, he insisted (echoes of Southey, Shelley and Mill) that nineteenth-century Hinduism was polytheistic; 'the Hindoos of the present day have no such views of the subject, but firmly believe in the real existence of innumerable gods and goddesses, who possess, in their own departments, full and independent power'.

Anticipating Shelley's censure of the 'severe and paralyzing forms' of Hinduism in the *Philosophical View*,[170] or Mill's vitriolic judgement that 'the Hindu, like the eunuch, excels in the qualities of a slave',[171] the *Monthly*'s author complained of the 'injurious rites introduced by the peculiar practice of Hindoo idolatry, which, more than any other Pagan worship, destroys the texture of society'.[172] Unlike Southey, Shelley or Mill, however, the author was himself a Brahmin called Rammohun Roy, founder in 1829 of the Hindu reform movement Brahmo Sabha (precursor of the more celebrated Brahmo Samaj) which, according to David Kopf, in its various manifestations 'played a crucial role in the genesis... of every major religious, social and political movement in India from 1820 to 1930... Brahmos were the first social reformers, and the first to extend full equality to women.'[173]

Rammohun Roy's articles in the *Monthly Magazine* (in addition to the June 1817 article two more appeared, in January and March 1818) were excerpted from his book *Translation of an Abridgement of the Vedant*, published in London in 1817 by his friend and former colleague John Digby upon the latter's return from Calcutta. They offered a liberal metropolitan readership excerpts from the author's translations of Vyas' Vedanta, from the Ishopanishad, and the Kena Upanishad. By translating the hieratic literature of the Vedanta into Bengali and English – the work had already come out in Calcutta in 1815–16 – Rammohun had 'profoundly offended the susceptibilities of his fellow Brahmins... infringing, as it were, the copyright which the Brahmins claimed in perpetuity on sacred knowledge'.[174] Although Rammohun had not explicitly attacked the caste system and had left the question of the observance of Hindu ritual and dietary regulations to the discretion of individuals (he was of the opinion that, although not essential to the Hindu religion, they could usefully serve as what Coleridge termed 'Aids to Reflection'), the very publication of the book aimed a blow at Hinduism as a 'religion of distinctions'.

Sure enough, a controversy soon broke out in which two orthodox Brahmins, Sankara Sastri and Mritunjaya Vidyalankar (teachers at the College of Fort St George, Madras, and the College of Fort William, Calcutta, respectively) employed violent invective against Rammohun in defence of 'the worship of the attributes of Deity'. If, as it is often argued, Rammohun Roy's criticism of Hindu traditionalism represented a parroting of western assimilationist policies, it should be noted that the two Brahmins who turned on him were both servants of the same Company which, suspicious of his reformist ideas, had already hijacked his career as a civil servant in the Revenue Department.[175] As Iqbal Singh notes, 'an influential section of the East Indian Company... was willing to give moral support – and often more than moral support – to the Brahminical hierarchy from the touch-lines even if it considered it impolitic openly to enter the arena'.[176] I argued above that the coalition between religious and political conservatism cemented by British 'orientalists' served the purposes of imperialism just as much as the secularizing policies and assimilationism of *The Revolt of Islam* or Mill's *History*. Rammohun Roy's intervention seems to me to be distinct from both; his interpretation of the Vedanta broke from Hindu traditionalism whilst at the same time, according to Kopf, 'updated and revitalized by contemporary progressive values from the West', it 'served as the Bible of the Hindu reformers', goaded into action by the 'heavy-handed hard-sell' of Christian missionaries.[177]

Rammohun attributed the social evils in Hindu culture to the corruptions of the pure monistic doctrines of the Upanishadic era, which proclaimed the unity of the Supreme Being as sole ruler of the universe. But he also equated the 'corruptions' of Hinduism with Trinitarian Christianity, and it is arguable that his 1820 publication entitled *The Precepts of Jesus: The Guide to Peace and Happiness* angered the Anglican establishment in India and the Baptist missionaries even more than his *Translation from the Vedant* had infuriated orthodox Brahmins.[178] The ensuing debate resulted in Rammohun's publication of a magazine entitled *The Brahmunical Magazine, or The Missionary and the Brahmun*, which ran spasmodically from 1821 until 1823 and parried the 'indiscreet assaults made by Christian writers on the Hindoo religion' in the name of 'the mild and liberal spirit of universal toleration, which is well known to be a fundamental principle of Hindooism'.[179] Whilst there is undeniably a correspondence between Rammohun Roy's theology and that of the British and American Unitarians who championed his cause and in whose midst he died during a visit to England in 1833, it was by no means merely an attempt to pass off Unitarian Christianity in Hindu costume; many Unitarians were disappointed, for example, that the Brahmo Samaj assumed primarily a Hindu Indian rather than a 'universalist' form.[180]

David Kopf has argued that Rammohun Roy and other Hindu reformers owed a major debt to British orientalists of the school of Jones, an argument which doubtless exposes them to the charge, in Gayatri Spivak's words, of early participation in a tradition of 'native informants for first-world intellectuals interested in the voice of the Other'.[181] But on the other hand, B. N. Ganguli, in a study of Rammohun's political and economic thought, makes the point that 'the rationalist mould of his social philosophy had been cast before he learned the English language and came into contact with Western thought' through his Arabic and Persian studies, and his engagement with the *Upanishads* and the *Mimamsa* philosophy.[182] Although Rammohun had been elected to the Parisian *Societé Asiatique* as a corresponding member in 1824, he was never deemed fit for membership of the Asiatic Society of Bengal (founded by Sir William Jones), a clear indication that he was considered to be a thorn in the side of the British establishment in Bengal. A truly hybrid theology, Rammohun's interpretation of Hinduism was thus based on the Vedantin tradition of Shankara and Ramanuja, bearing traces of its author's Islamic and Sufi training as well as his later acquaintance with the rational dissenting Christianity of the European Enlightenment. When writing for an English public, Rammohun Roy appropriated the colonial construction of Hinduism and brought out a radical potential in English orientalism, at just the historical moment when British hegemony was beginning to veer towards a strategy of aggressive Anglicism.

However much Rammohun is seen as the exponent of a 'social philosophy of acceptance and accommodation'[183] with regard to the imposition of European institutions in India, the fact remains that as a Brahmin who refused conversion to Christianity and the loss of caste which that would have entailed, he retained in his capacity as member of a native elite strong links with the fabric of Indian culture, and thus avoided the fate of becoming a 'brown Englishman'.[184] This distinguished him from the radical and progressivist secularism of the students of David Hare and Henry Derozio – a colonial reflection of the ideology we have been examining in Shelley's *Revolt of Islam* – who would constitute the core of the 'Macaulayite' Young Bengal movement of the nineteenth century.[185] Any attempt to assess the strengths and weaknesses of Rammohun's manner of negotiating colonial power should consider the fact that, to quote Iqbal Singh again, he was 'writing at a time when British ascendancy was unchallenged and unchallengable; when Indian public opinion could impose no check upon the exercise of absolute and arbitrary power by the British – and for the obvious reason that as yet no organised body of public opinion had crystallised'.[186]

Upon hearing of the defeat of the Neapolitan revolution in 1821, Rammohun was plunged into a gloom no less deep than Shelley's at the same time. His comment in a letter to the radical journalist James Silk Buckingham nevertheless goes beyond the position of the author of the *Revolt of Islam* in its equation of the European *ancien régime* with European (and, reading between the lines here, British) *imperialism*: 'I am obliged to conclude that I shall not live to see liberty universally restored to the nations of Europe, and Asiatic nations, especially those that are European colonies…'[187] In the midst of a plethora of conciliatory remarks regarding British power in India, this is the most we get from Rammohun Roy, at least in *explicit* terms, but it is enough, for in a sense he was performing at an elite level the disturbance of hybridity wrought by Homi Bhabha's plebeian appropriators of the 'English Book' in 'Signs Taken for Wonders'. 'Hybridity is the revaluation of the assumption of colonial identity through the repetition of identity effects. It displays the necessary deformation and displacement of all sites of discrimination and domination. It unsettles the mimetic or narcissistic demands of colonial power, but re-implicates its identifications in strategies of subversion that turn the gaze of the discriminated back upon the eye of power.'[188]

Rammohun Roy clearly made quite a splash in metropolitan intellectual circles at an early stage of his publishing career, as is evident from Coleridge's relation, in a letter to Southey dated 31 January 1819, of 'A Brahmin [who] has, I hear, arisen to attempt what we have both so often wished – viz, to be the Luther of Brahminism – and with all the effect, that could be wished – considering the times'.[189] But how would Rammohun Roy's agenda have touched Shelley, scourge of Brahminism and imperialist radical? Unlike his cousin Medwin, Shelley nowhere mentions Rammohun Roy, for which reason my argument that Rammohun had a significant influence on *Prometheus Unbound* must remain at the level of conjecture. Nevertheless, even if Shelley never saw a copy of Digby's London edition of the *Translations of an Abridgement of the Vedant*, there is a good chance that the poet had read at least the three articles published in the *Monthly Magazine*, and that this reading might have contributed to the substantially revised representation of India in *Prometheus Unbound*. The June 1817 issue of the *Monthly* (referred to above) carried, in addition to Rammohun's translation, reviews of Moore's *Lalla Rookh*, his friend Peacock's *Melincourt* and Bentham on Parliamentary Reform, all of which would have been of interest to Shelley. The January 1818 issue carried a review of Shelley's father-in-law William Godwin's *Mandeville* along with its excerpt from the *Abridgement of the Vedant*. The March 1818 issue, in addition to carrying Rammohun's translation of the Kena Upanishad (which, I will argue, resembles part of *Prometheus Unbound*, begun in the Autumn of the same year), also contained a short and unfavourable review of *The Revolt of Islam*, the first after Leigh Hunt's friendly treatment of the poem in the *Examiner* in February, and one which Shelley may have taken pains to get hold of on the continent.[190]

I am not going to try and argue that reading Rammohun Roy turned Shelley against the implicit (or explicit) imperialism of some of his earlier writings, or wrought upon him 'a final cure and conversion' like that apparently effected by the Hindu reformer upon his cousin Tom Medwin at about the same time.[191] Chronology suggests otherwise; Shelley had barely finished working on *The Revolt* when the articles were published, and he was still to write on the 'revolution' of British India (with its qualified support for mission-aries) in the 1819 *Philosophical View of Reform*.[192] Moreover, in mid to late 1821 he was soliciting Peacock for a job in the Company's administrative machine. But I want to speculate that Rammohun Roy's articles did sow a seed of doubt in Shelley's politics of assimilation, a doubt which is perhaps already evident in that strange qualifying sentence at the end of his account of the Brahmins in the 1819 *Philosophical View*, 'the thing to be sought is that they should as they would if they were free attain to a system of arts and literature of their own'.[193] I will argue that this seed bore fruit in the 'polyphonic' texture of Shelley's major work, *Prometheus Unbound*, unsettling the norms of both 'orientalist' and assimilationist discourse and permitting the emergence of a new account of the relations between East and West.

'PROMETHEUS UNBOUND': REORIENTATING GREECE

The deployment of myth in *Prometheus Unbound* represents a departure from the Volneyan manner of *Queen Mab* and *The Revolt of Islam*. Ostensibly, of course, Shelley's 'Lyrical Drama' is Greek, a reworking of the final play in the Aeschylean trilogy, although it exchanges Aeschylus' setting of the Georgian Caucasus for the *Indian* Caucasus or Hindu Kush and its principal female protagonist, the Greek Io, for a female figure called Asia. And yet, as John Drew comments of Shelley's Prometheus, 'unlike the Prometheus of Alexander's men, he is not simply a defiant Greek figure who has been moved geographically east. His re-orientation, his re-location in the Orient... is indicative of an corresponding (and wholly appropriate) psychological shift in his character.'[194]

Prometheus is not the first Shelleyan protagonist to find himself in the mythological *Ursprung* of the Hindu Kush, the mountains above the terrestrial paradise of Kashmir; this is, after all, the landscape of the *Alastor* 'poet's' vision of the 'veiled maid'. Shelley's odyssey eastwards (like the protagonist of *Alastor*'s) from the classical Mediterranean crescent participates in a widespread Romantic reorientation of the roots of Greek culture, particularly manifest in the widespread contemporary interest in the Indian origins of the Dionysian mysteries.[195] In the Preface to *Prometheus Unbound*, Shelley's account of his emulation of the imagery of the Greek poets 'drawn from the operations of the human mind, or from those external actions by which they are expressed' (*SPW*, p. 205), suggests a linkage in his mind between the Greeks and the oriental poets discussed by Jones in his *On the Poetry of the Eastern Nations* and *Essay on the Arts, called Imitative*.[196] Friedrich Schlegel argued that 'the obscurity of Aeschylus, especially in the choruses, appears highly Oriental, although clothed in an Hellenic form'.[197] We might recall at this point Quinet's statement that 'Shelley is completely Indian' and remember the feelings of bafflement with which contemporary readers responded to Shelley's unsettling metaphors and the restless movement of what John Barrell has described as 'the flight of syntax' in poems like *Epipsychidion*.[198]

If Shelley's linguistic vehicle now breaks the terms of the binary opposition Greek/reason, oriental/imagination by deriving the former genetically from the latter ('Reason is to imagination as the instrument to the agent; as the body to the spirit; as the shadow to the substance'[199]), the political geography of his poem gives a new autonomy and agency to Asia. Writing to Peacock about the completed first act of *Prometheus* in January 1819, Shelley reiterated the rationalist imperative of his earlier writing (he was after all addressing the friend of Mill and Bentham and future author of *The Four Ages of Poetry*): 'I consider Poetry very subordinate to moral & political science, & if I were well, certainly I should aspire to the latter; for I can conceive a great work, embodying the discoveries of all ages, & harmonizing the contending creeds by which mankind have been ruled.'[200] Despite this statement of intent, Shelley was an *invalid* and as such the instigator of a 'valetudinarian poetics' rather than a vigorous expansive rationality. It is no longer the figure of the rationalist Volney which towers over Shelley's writing as 'harmonizer' 'of the contending creeds' of man, but rather the Romantic 'higher critical' approach typified by Friedrich Schlegel who wrote, 'Mythology presents the most complicated structure ever devised by human intellect; inexhaustibly rich, but at the same time most variable in its signification.'[201] Despite Shelley's cautionary remarks, *Prometheus Unbound* displays a new confidence in the possibilities of the poetic imagination, exploring 'the difficulty of definition, the problems of communication, the cramping boundaries of language'.[202]

One of the common Romantic orientalist stereotypes which we have surveyed (exemplified in *The Missionary*) sets up a figure of western male rationality against the 'dreamy imagination' of a feminized Orient, so that, in Inden's words, 'The features that constitute human nature are, for the Romantics, distributive and not, as they are for the empiricist and rationalist, cumulative in Western man. It would seem, therefore, that no society as such could embody the whole of human nature, unless all its members had first become transformed by understanding of the Eastern or Western Other.'[203] Although *Prometheus Unbound* is based on a distributive human nature, its geopolitical terms are dialogic rather than discrete. The poem reworks the cultural and sexual oppositions of Shelley's earlier writings: the inward, valetudinarian nature of Prometheus (his decisive action is sceptical, 'negative', in revoking the Curse) qualifies his conventional role as paragon of western instrumental reason, and the active, educated character of Asia – manifest in her dialogue with Demogorgon and her role in instigating the rebellion against the empire of Jupier – complements her role as embodiment of imagination and love. If, according to my preceding argument, *The Revolt of Islam* pulled its (suppressed) Indian setting westwards into the Hellenistic world, and sought to homogenize the Orient in occidental terms, *Prometheus Unbound* functions by an antithetical movement, namely in the orientalization of Greek myth, a reverse acculturation which frees the Orient from its formerly negative or supplementary connotations.[204]

Prometheus' function as the epitome of Europe is not open to doubt, and his bondage and eventual release from the Caucasus mountains (in the conventional version of the myth) associates him with the 'Caucasian' races, a term coined by Blumenbach in 1775. As Martin Bernal indicates, 'Not only was [Prometheus] the son of Iapetos, plausibly identified as the third son of Noah and the ancestor of the Europeans; but his heroic, beneficial and self-sacrificing action – of stealing fire for mankind – soon came to be seen as typically Aryan. Gobineau saw him as the ancestor of the principal white family.'[205] In Shelley's treatment of the complex mytheme, Prometheus' mountain prison is moved far to the south-east so that, as part of his torture, he can gaze down on the 'lovely vale in the Indian Caucasus, the terrestrial paradise of Kashmir' (*SPW*, p. 227), where he had once wandered with Asia "drinking life from her loved eyes" (*SPW*, p. 210, I, line 123) and where she remains biding her time and awaiting the release of the defiant Titan.

In contrast to the conquering Dionysus or the (historical) empire-building of Alexander of Macedon (figures whom I discerned underpinning the symbolic fabric of *Alastor*), Prometheus' (western) presence in the space of India is figured as a form of captivity, of bondage. The Titan's Curse, which in Shelley's version is fore-grounded as the principal cause of his captivity and torture (rather than the theft of fire of the Greek original), represents the blight of anthropomorphic religion which divides Europe from Asia, Christian from Hindu. By foregrounding the Curse and placing the theft of fire in the background, Shelley is able to condemn religion without casting aspersions on that other Promethean quality, the gift to mankind of technology and 'progressive' civilization. In her speech to Demogorgon in Act II, scene iv, Asia recalls how Prometheus inaugurated the first 'world system' through his institution of the sciences and arts, as well as the commerce between nations (doubtless Shelley had in mind what Bernard Semmel terms 'free-trade imperialism'): 'He taught to rule, as life directs the limbs, / The

tempest—wingèd chariots of the Ocean, / And the Celt knew the
Indian' (SPW, p. 238, II.iv.92–4). The intercourse between the
different hemispheres in the utopian time of Acts III and IV, when
man is 'Sceptreless, free, uncircumscribed...Equal, unclassed, tribeless, and nationless' (SPW, p. 253, III.iv.194–5) remains unspecified;
Shelley is characteristically better at imagining the negativity of
Prometheus and Asia's retreat than the positive lineaments of a
'decolonized' world system.

    Not until Prometheus revokes the Curse can Panthea convey the
god's new vitality to Asia and thereby initiate the overthrowal of
Jupiter and the reunification of the lovers (the fact that Shelley uses
the Roman Jupiter rather than the Greek Zeus, more appropriate in
the Aeschylean context, suggests a connection in his mind between
patriarchal religion and 'Roman' imperialism).[206] By casting the
relationship between Prometheus and Asia in this way, Shelley has
modified the connection between male and female protagonists as
portrayed in Alastor and The Revolt of Islam (a modification which is
all the more evident given the common Kashmiri setting of Asia's
exile, The Missionary and Alastor). Prometheus is now aware of his
own guilt in cursing Jupiter and the part that this has played in
blighting and dividing the work, including his separation from Asia.
Earth's cryptic narrative of Zoroaster's vision of his double in Act I
lines 190–218 brings about Prometheus' recognition that the world of
myths from which religion is generated is no more nor less than a
kind of poetry, 'Dreams and the light imaginings of men, / And all
that faith creates or love desires' (SPW, p. 212, I, lines 200–1).
Zoroaster's encounter with his doppelganger in Earth's speech at line
191, although obscure, appears to symbolize the self-conscious
syncretism which inaugurates the sceptical project of comparative
mythology.

    According to Volney, Zoroastrianism was the transitional moment
between zodiacal mythology and the moral dualism underlying
religion properly so-called:[207] to Friedrich Schlegel it represented the
bridging point between Hinduism and other oriental religions on
the one hand and Christianity on the other.[208] Shelley, writing to
Peacock from Mont Blanc in 1816, had discerned in the Zoroastrian
evil principle Ahrimanes (the title of the Zoroastrian epic upon which
Peacock was working between 1812 and 1815)[209] a primitive, poetic
response to the terror of the natural sublime; his poem Mont Blanc
insisted that the tendency of the imagination to anthropomorphize

the laws of nature, above all the inexorable and impersonal power of necessity, must be resisted.[210] For Romantic mythographers, Zoroastrianism is the portal which leads from the moral dualism and anthropomorphic basis of contemporary Christianity back to an understanding of the beginnings of myth in a poetic response to nature. As the religion of the Persians, it also occupied the geographical as well as world-historical mid-point in the 'passage to India' from the patriarchal monotheism of the Judaeo-Christian tradition to an Indian source in the Vedantic religion of poetry, love and nature.

The phantasm of Jupiter, evoked by Prometheus in his bid to unsay the Curse, represents the sceptical power of imagination to undo the negative work of its myth-making propensities. For Shelley the Curse afflicting western man is idolatry to creatures of his own imagination, 'those foul shapes, abhorred by god and man, – / Which, under many a name and many a form / Strange, savage, ghastly, dark and execrable, / Were Jupiter, the tyrant of the world'. (*SPW*, p. 253, III.iv.180–3) In his *Second Defence of the Monotheistical System of the Veds*, published in Calcutta in 1817, Rammohun Roy had mounted an attack on Hindu idolatry very similar in tone to Shelley's *Prometheus Unbound*, above all censuring the tendency of worshipping the Supreme Being as an earthly king; '[those] who know the feeble and dependent nature of earthly kings, as liable to sudden ruin, as harassed by incessant cares and wants, ought never, I presume, to dissimulate the contemplation of the Almighty power with any corporeal service acceptable to an earthly king'.[211] Although Prometheus defies rather than worships Jupiter as a 'sceptred curse' (*SPW*, p. 262, IV, line 338), he is guilty of precisely the error described by Rammohun, an error remitted in his evocation of the phantasm. In suggesting that Europeans, no less than Asian subjects of the Company, are guilty of idolatry, Shelley is appropriating the language of the 'civilizing mission' and turning it back upon its western source, although as I will suggest below, it is in the second rather than first Act of *Prometheus* that Rammohun's polemical writings are closest to Shelley's poetic purpose.

In a sense the evocation of the phantasm of Jupiter embodies in miniature the purpose of Shelley's sceptical mythographical poem, as a return of political and religious despotism to its mythic source, a 'harmonization of all the contending creeds by which mankind have been *ruled*' (emphasis mine). Prometheus proclaims to the phantasm or *image* of the patriarchal God, 'Tremendous Image, as thou art must be / He whom thou shadowest forth' (*SPW*, p. 213, lines 246–7). The patriarchal, monological Jupiter/Jehovah must be returned to the order of representation, the dialogical intercourse of language, if his absolute power over man's will is to be broken.[212] The first Act of *Prometheus* appeals to the sceptical imagination of those poets described in *The Defence of Poetry*, whose 'vitally metaphorical' expression 'marks the before unapprehended relations of things', but always tends to harden into a dogmatic language in which words 'become, through time, signs for portions or classes of thoughts instead of pictures of integral thoughts; and then, if no new poets should arise to create afresh the associations which have been thus disorganized, language will be dead to all the nobler purposes of human intercourse'.[213] I have argued above that the metaphors through which Shelley controlled the power relations of *The Revolt of Islam*, despite the poem's manifest radicalism and feminism, were 'disorganized' stereotypes motivated by a monological imperialism; *Prometheus Unbound*, on the other hand, reveals Prometheus' Curse as a fading echo which is superseded by a new language constructive of before unapprehended relations between the poem's different symbolic figures.

THE ROLE OF ASIA

In his *Essay on Christianity*, probably written in late 1817, Shelley stated that 'The Universal Being can only be described or defined by negatives which deny his subjection to the laws of all inferior existences. Where indefiniteness ends idolatry and anthropomorphism begin.'[214] Earlier in the same year, in his *Second Defence* from which I quoted above, Rammohun Roy had written:

Language can convey a notion of things only either by the appellations by which they are already known, or by describing their figure, accidents, genus and properties; but God has none of these physical circumstances: the Ved therefore attempted to explain him in negative terms (that is by declaring that whatever thing may be perceived by the mental faculties, or the external senses, is not God).[215]

In his excellent essay on 'Negatives in *Prometheus Unbound*', Timothy Webb points out possible sources for Shelley's language of negatives (like 'unimaginable', 'tongueless', 'inarticulate', 'uncommunicating' and 'wordless') in Plato's *Symposium* and Aquinas' *Summa Theologica*.[216] The close resemblance between Rammohun Roy and Shelley on the use of negatives goes beyond mere verbal similarity, however; when we consider the geopolitical role of Asia in the poem (consistently ignored or underplayed by commentators), it assumes an important thematic relevance as well. The education of Asia by Demogorgon (not, significantly, by the 'western' Prometheus) and the ensuing rebellion against Jupiter suggest that Shelley may have known by 1820 if not before that a Brahmin had appeared on the scene who was instructing 'Brahminical society' not merely in the principles of Locke, Hume and Rousseau, but also in 'a system of arts and literature of their own', 'as they would if they were free'.[217] He may also have known that Rammohun had in 1817 begun campaigning for the abolition of *sati* and was championing the education of Indian women, arguing in 1820 against orthodox Brahmins that 'If, after instruction in knowledge and wisdom, a person cannot comprehend or retain what has been taught him, we may consider him as deficient; but as you keep women generally void of education and acquirements, you cannot...in justice pronounce on their inferiority.'[218]

As I have already said, *Prometheus Unbound* significantly revises the stereotyped hero/heroine roles of the earlier poetry, a revision which represents more than just a move from a Utilitarian 'assimilationist' position to a more conservative 'orientalism' of the Jones/Lady Morgan school. A thematic parallelism runs through the first two Acts; Asia's education by Demogorgon is analogous to Prometheus' accession to self-knowledge through the mediation of Earth (a symmetrical pattern is also evident whereby each is 'instructed' by a mentor of the opposite sex). Prometheus' sceptical revocation of the Curse exemplifies the most enlightened use of rational imagination, but is insufficient in itself to ensure his 'unbinding'. His act of forgiveness makes him feel all the more keenly the physical absence of Asia, his interlocutor and lover, 'Most vain all hope but love; and thou art far, Asia!' (I, lines 808–9).

In Shelley's complex allegory (Mary tells us that he purposed to write notes which would have 'served to explain much of what is obscure in his poetry'[219]) Panthea is the messenger of the new spirit, and as John Drew suggests, 'represents' 'that pantheism which – though *through* it the truth of the soul may be glimpsed – can be fully apprehended only by the still greater power Asia embodies –

the Imagination'.[220] Asia's descent into the cave of Demogorgon represents Shelley's belated attempt to come to terms with the 'Vedantin' doctrines idealized by William Jones and Lady Morgan, which he had rejected in his portrayal of the veiled maid in *Alastor*.[221] If the elusive dream-maid had preferred 'western' 'knowledge and truth and virtue' to Luxima's rather elaborate 'Brahminical' cosmology, the rejected body of 'orientalist' doctrine would assume a radical new meaning for Shelley in 1818–19 in the knowledge that it had been appropriated and redefined as the pretext for Rammohun's hybrid programme of religious and social reform.

Readers have always found Asia's oracular instruction by Demogorgon in Act II scene iv to be one of the most compelling passages of *Prometheus Unbound*. Drew points out the resemblance between Demogorgon, 'a mighty darkness…neither limb, / Nor form, nor outline', 'the snake-like Doom, coiled underneath his throne', and the Hindu Seshanaga, according to Jones 'the sovereign of Patala, or the infernal regions' and 'the king of Serpents'.[222] Shelley's Seshanaga/Demogorgon embodies a Dionysian energy quite distinct from Southey's 'Christianized' Satanic Seshanaga in *Kehama*[223] and symbolizes the divine power as described in the *Essay on Christianity*, 'the interfused and overruling Spirit of all the energy and wisdom included within the circle of existing things'.[224] Enthroned in the nether world (suggesting by a common spatial metaphor the southern hemisphere), Demogorgon is associated with a potential hitherto unrealized by the doyens of the 'upper world'; 'In the world unknown, sleeps a voice unspoken' (III.i.190–1). The education of Asia by Demogorgon realizes this potential and brings both teacher and pupil up from the depths on the chariot of hope and the chariot of revolution (the car of the Hour) respectively.

The idea that Demogorgon seeks to convey, both in the formless embodiment of energy which he represents and the sceptical negative method of his catechistic dialogue, is precisely the message of the *Translation of the Abridgement of the Vedant*, or Shelley's adage that 'where indefiniteness ends, idolatry and anthropomorphism begin'. For Asia is not innocent of error: in the mountains above Demogorgon's 'mighty portal', her admiration of Earth's magnificence drives her to imagine an anthropomorphic creator whom she might worship like a king; 'Like its creation, weak yet beautiful, / I could fall down and worship that and thee' (*SPW*, p. 234, II.iii.15–16). When in scene iv she questions Demogorgon as to the source of evil, she repeats Prometheus' error by demanding that Demogorgon 'Utter his name: a world pining in pain / Asks but his name: curses shall drag him down' (*SPW*, p. 236, II.iv.29–30). Herein lies Asia's fault, for the twin impulses to worship and to curse initiate the moral dualism underlying religious idolatry; a vindictive patriarchal God and a suffering and rebellious subject return us to the dilemma of the poem's opening scene.

The dialogue between Asia and Demogorgon bears a close resemblance to Rammohun's translation of part of the *Kena Upanishad*, the only one of the translations which employs the form of dialogue between a pupil and 'spiritual parent'. The first translation from the Vedanta in the *Monthly's* series, in which is to be found the declaration that 'All descriptions which I have used to describe the Supreme Being are incorrect' and that the act of loving God is in itself a moral act, anticipates the mainspring of Shelleyan ethics, 'the great secret of morals is love, or a going out of our own nature and an identification of ourselves with the beautiful which exists in thought, action, or person, not our own'.[225] But it is in the *Kena Upanishad* that we find an anticipation of the dialogue between Asia and Demogorgon. The pupil asks his 'Spiritual Father',

Who is he... under whose sole will, the intellectual power makes its approach to different objects? Who is he, under whose authority, breath, the primitive power in the body, makes its operation? Who is he, by whose direction, language is regularly pronounced? And who is that immaterial Being, that applies Vision and hearing to their respective objects?

Answering the pupil's enquiry into the nature of God, the 'Spiritual Parent' declares, 'He alone, who has never been described by language, and who directs language to its meaning, is the Supreme Being; and not any specified thing which men worship: know thou this.'[226] Asia asks Demogorgon, 'Who made the living world? (*SPW*, p. 236, II.iv.7), ... Who made all / That it contains? Thought, passion, reason, will, imagination? (II.iv.9–10) ... Who made that sense which, when the winds of Spring / In rarest visitation, or the voice / Of one belovèd heard in youth alone, / Fills the faint eyes with falling tears... And leaves this peopled earth a solitude / When it returns no more?' (II.iv.13–18). When Asia asks Demogorgon, 'Whom calledst thou God?', he retorts, 'I spoke but as ye speak, / For Jove is the supreme of living things' (*SPW*, p. 238, II.iv.112–13). When Asia, unsatisfied but realizing the inadequacy of her attempt

to grasp linguistic absolutes and anthropomorphic definition, goes on
to demand, 'Who is the master of the slave?', the reply is:

> If the abysm
> Could vomit forth its secrets...But a voice
> Is wanting, the deep truth is imageless:
> For what would it avail to bid thee gaze
> On the revolving world? What to bid speak
> Fate, Time, Occasion, Chance, and Change? To these
> All things are subject but eternal Love.
>
> (*SPW*, p. 238, II.iv.114–20)

The indefiniteness of Demogorgon and his message in Shelley's
celebrated lines referred to above seems to echo the *Kena Upanishad*'s
declaration that 'He alone, whom no one can conceive by vision, and
by whose superintendence every one perceives the objects of vision, is
the supreme Being; and not any specified thing which men worship:
know thou this.'[227] Asia's 'generous errors' are whittled away as part
of her education in scepticism, leaving her, like the recalcitrant
Prometheus, possessed of love, which as the ethical kernel of
imagination represents the 'positive' element of both Shelley's
'intellectual philosophy' and Rammohun Roy's Vedantism.

If my conjecture regarding Shelley's allusion to Rammohun's
articles is correct, then the *Monthly Magazine* could truly be said to
have succeeded (beyond its wildest imaginings) in its vaunted aim of
'encourag[ing the] intercourse, and...render[ing] our miscellany a
medium of communication between the learned of the East and the
West'.[228] The active role assumed by Asia in the poem signals the
entry of Rammohun Roy's hybridized discourse into the heart of the
western literary canon, an interweaving of the Demogorgonic voice
from the depths, from the underworld, into the polyphonic texture of
Shelley's 'Hellenic' lyrical drama. The incorporation should disturb
rather than console the West in its unrelenting quest for a 'self-
consolidating Other', however. The instruction of Asia, which allows
her to transcend her stereotypical role in the combined discourse of
orientalism and patriarchy, questions the self-proclaiming universalism of western truth by bringing down Jupiter and leaving his
throne unfilled.

The proof of Asia's instruction is her moral and physical
transformation in the faith that 'Common as light is love...It makes
the reptile equal to the God' (*SPW*, p. 241, II.v.40–3). The
remainder of the poem is dedicated to implementing the effects of the

positive side of Shelley's 'intellectual philosophy' after the sceptical 'working through' of the first two Acts, particularly the political, moral and cosmological ramifications of love, the precondition for any effective moral change in the cosmic system. As Shelley put it in *Essay on Christianity*, 'In proportion to the love existing among men, so will be the community of property and power. Among true and real friends all is common, and were ignorance and envy and superstition banished from the world, all mankind would be as friends.'[229] Unfortunately, as I remarked above, the economic basis of Shelley's 'decolonized' world system is not specified in any more detail than this; the utopian 'positivity' of Acts III and IV represents, at least for this reader, a falling off in terms of dramatic and psychological intensity. Jupiter's drinking of the 'Daedal cup' (*SPW*, p. 243, III.i.26–32), the ascent of Demogorgon and Asia to Olympus and the dethroning and fall of Jupiter owe much to the rather wooden epic action of the final scene of Southey's *Kehama*, in particular the tyrant's quaffing of the ambiguous 'Amreeta Cup' and subsequent downfall.[230] The disappearance of Prometheus and Asia into their cave, with its allusion to the 'Cave of Congelations' in *The Missionary*,[231] whilst essential at the thematic level, disperses the dialogic energy of the earlier 'negative' scenes and leads to an increasing lyrical abstraction in the remainder of the poem. Nevertheless, in terms of the symbolic weight which Shelley affords to Asia, the narrative represents a major revision of the terms of the earlier poems and the admission of a principle of hybridity and difference into the work of a poet strongly attracted by abstract universals and totalities.

The emergence of hybridity and a new confidence regarding the poetic imagination in *Prometheus Unbound* accompanies Shelley's increasing disengagement from Utilitarianism in the period after finishing the poem and writing his *Philosophical View of Reform* in late 1819. In the latter work Shelley included Bentham with Godwin, Hazlitt and Hunt in the august band of literary men whom he exhorted to petition the House of Commons in favour of Reform, declaring that 'Poets and *philosophers* are the unacknowledged legislators of the world' (emphasis mine).[232] But by the time of writing the *Defence* in early 1821 Shelley's moral and political philosophy (the two are not really distinguishable in Shelley's writings) followed his new-found poetic confidence in affording priority to imagination rather than reason: 'Reason is to imagination as the instrument to the agent; as the body to the spirit; as the shadow to the substance.[233]

As a questioning of the sufficiency of analytic reasoning, the *Defence* attacks the 'social geometry' at the foundations of Utilitarianism and by implication the work of its advocates, Shelley's reformist allies Bentham and James Mill. Only 'Poets' (by which Shelley means the advocates of artistic, political or ethical principles based on imagination rather than analytic reason) and *not* 'philosophers' now qualify for the term 'unacknowledged legislators of mankind'.[234] The whole *Defence* is a rejoinder to Peacock's Utilitarian/progressivist theory of culture entitled *The Four Ages of Poetry*, a work which identified poetry and works of imagination with a primitive level of civilization, moral philosophy and science with progress and modernity. Although Shelley did not order Mill's *History of British India* until October 1821,[235] several months after he had completed the *Defence* (assuming he had not read the 1818 work before ordering his own copy), one can speculate that at the later date it would have confirmed his dissatisfaction with Utilitarianism in general, and in particular the unqualified application of Utilitarian principles to India by James Mill, if not by the more cautious Bentham. In book II chapter 8 of his *History*, Mill, Peacock's friend and colleague in the administrative machinery of the East India Company, had dealt with Hindu culture according to the same principles as Peacock had dealt with poetry and the arts in the *Four Ages*, although with an often savage iconoclasm quite distinct in character from Peacock's polished irony.

If my conjecture that Shelley had encountered the writings of Rammohun Roy sometime between mid-1818 and early 1821 is correct, then he would have been in a position to acknowledge an indigenous current of Brahminical reform dependent neither on English missionaries nor Utilitarians. During his sojourn in Liverpool, London and Paris in 1831–3, Rammohun met many of the leading philosophical and literary lights of the liberal establishment: the historian William Roscoe, the phrenologist Spurzheim, Tom Moore, William Godwin, Jeremy Bentham and Robert Owen.[236] Like Shelley, Rammohun's thought converged in many points with the reformist spirit of these men, but like him also he negotiated it on his own terms, wary of the social effects of (in Shelley's words) 'an unmitigated exercise of the calculating faculty'.[237] One can imagine how Rammohun (as well as Shelley) might have read Mill's *History*, a work which superficially resembled his own in its critique of the institutions of orthodox Hinduism and its concern with establishing a good system of judicial procedure. None the less, the aggressive Utilitarianism of Bentham's pupil must have caused him, like any other Indian reader of the time, great offence. Moreover, as Eric Stokes points out, Mill 'strenuously resisted any suggestion for establishing representative institutions for India... the only control that could properly be exerted over the administration was that of Parliament and the Home Authorities'.[238] The internal contradictions of Mill's 'radicalism' cannot have been lost on the author of *Prometheus Unbound*, particularly after his knowledge of the state of British India had been considerably enhanced by the arrival of his garrulous Anglo-Indian cousin Medwin in Pisa in late 1820.

At any rate, there is little trace of the Volneyan spirit of Shelley's earlier oriental poetry, particularly *The Revolt of Islam*, in either *Prometheus Unbound* or the *Defence*, despite the failure of the latter (unlike the former) to consider the significance of oriental art or literature in its historical canon, (this notwithstanding the much greater knowledge of Asian art and literature which Shelley must have gleaned from reading Medwin's journals). In this respect, the *Defence* is a disappointment after the reorientations of *Prometheus Unbound*, and it is difficult to read in terms of the discourse of imperialism given such slender warrant from the text. To be sure, its attack on Peacock's Utilitarian argument moderates the sceptical rationalism which was so pronounced in Shelley's earlier poems, and censures Volneyan reductionism: 'While the sceptic destroys gross superstitions,' Shelley warns, 'let him spare to deface as some of the French writers have defaced, the eternal truths charactered upon the imaginations of men.'[239] The qualities of dialogue and difference which a post-Rammohunian Shelley had set up against the hegemonic strategies of both 'orientalism' and 'proto-Anglicism' fail, however, to emerge in the *Defence of Poetry*. If anything, the *imagination* which Shelley sets up against rationalist reductionism (and therefore an oriental/female principle in terms of the system of binary equivalences at which we looked above), is privileged in a repetition of the discourse of Jones and Lady Morgan.

Shelley's critique of universal reason thus falls short here of constituting a critique of imperialism itself, in so far as the latter depends on the binary opposition which Shelley had surpassed in *Prometheus*, but which seems to reabsorb his argument in the *Defence*.

The term 'empire' is used as a metaphor for scientific rationalization rather than territorial and cultural appropriation. Only by a rather forced reading of this term and of the slavery metaphor employed alongside it can we coax anything more than a conventional Romantic poetry/reason dichotomy out of the following passage. Having done so, we are left with nothing more nor less than an anxiety of empire which is, as we have seen, no stranger to British orientalism. It is, namely, the fear of an elephantiasic, slave-borne disease returning to infect the masters of space, of the 'external world'. As Shelley writes, 'The cultivation of those sciences which have enlarged the limits of the empire of man over the external world has for want of the poetical faculty proportionally circumscribed those of the internal world, and man, having enslaved the elements, remains himself a slave.'[240]

CODA: THE INDIAN WRITINGS OF THOMAS MEDWIN

In the context of a discussion of the Romantic and Utilitarian attitudes to India in the 1820s, Eric Stokes writes:

At a time when Bentham was feeling 'as if the golden age of British India were lying before me', when Charles Trevelyan thought that it could not but 'be conceded that India is on the eve of a great moral change', Metcalfe was meditating on the mortality of empire, 'Empires grow old, decay, and perish. Ours in India can hardly be called old, but seems destined to be short-lived. We appear to have passed the brilliancy and vigour of our youth, and it may be that we have reached a premature old age.'[241]

The Indian writings of Thomas Medwin, discoverer of Shelley's *Revolt of Islam* in the Bombay bazaar, are steeped in the *Weltschmerz* of Metcalfe's Romanticism. Metcalfe and Medwin's epitaph for British 'orientalism' in India anticipates not the end of British power, but the end of *their* definition of power. For it was shortly to be superseded by the reforms of Lord William Bentinck's administration (1828–35), so strongly influenced by Utilitarianism and the assimilationist policies of evangelicals and Macaulayites. Before we take Medwin's attitude as paradigmatic of the 'literary' discourse of imperialism influencing Shelley after 1820, however, we should balance the account by considering the following entry from the Italian journal of Edward Ellerker Williams.

Williams, like Medwin a former Indian cavalry officer, whose regiment had also participated in the Maratha campaign of 1817–18 before he had retired on half pay to a life of mildly bohemian leisure in Switzerland and Italy, has gone down in literary history as the 'husband' of Jane Williams (subject of Shelley's 1822 love lyrics) and as the other unfortunate drowned with Shelley in the Gulf of Spezia on the evening of 8 July 1822. But Williams, it transpires from his journal, was also an enthusiastic imperialist: 'It is a singular fact that the sun never sets upon the British dominions,' he entered jingoistically in his journal for November 1821. 'The Roman Empire, in all its glory, contained 120,000,000 souls, one half of whom were slaves. The British Empire, in its present state, contains about 95,220,000 souls, all of whom are *freemen*. In the scale of nations she is, then, the greatest in the world.'[242] Williams' triumphalism is premised upon a *liberal* confidence regarding the moral probity of empire, however questionable the truth of his conclusion in overlooking the wage slaves of Birmingham or the plantation slaves of Trinidad. One can only speculate how assertions of this sort were received by the author of *Song to the Men of England* or *The Triumph of Life*, if Williams was in the habit of airing them in company. The ambivalence which we have discerned at the heart of imperialist discourse is highlighted by a comparison of Williams' assertion with the anxiety present in Medwin's Indian writings, and particularly in 'Julian's Journal', published in the *Angler in Wales* in 1834, but based on the journal Medwin had kept whilst his regiment was stationed at Boorwa Sangar in June 1817. Here a self-hating Julian, inflicted by a Byronic sense of remorse, asks himself, 'Why...am I haunted by a demon, who is ever gnawing insatiably at my heart's core...?',[243] while contemplating the fragility of British power in India. As he ruminates upon a well-tended garden of English plants in the dusty cantonment, he writes:

We are exotics in the animal, as many of [the English flowers] are in the vegetable kingdom ... [I] sighed and exulted over the concluding paragraph from Gibbon, whilst speaking of the overthrowal of the Mogul Empire. 'Since the reign of Aurungzebe, their empire has been dissolved – their treasures of Delhi rifled by a Persian robber, and the richest of their kingdom are now possessed by a company of Christian merchants, of a remote isle in the *Northern* ocean.' The train of thought gendered by the recollection of this remarkable sentence, threw a gloom over my mind.[244]

Although there is undoubtedly a fashionable (and Byronic) stageyness to this, Julian's creator Medwin was certainly *entitled* to a genuine sense of remorse. He had recently seen action in the Pindari wars with Lord Hastings' grand army, participating in the siege and bombardment of Hathras by seventy-one mortars and howitzers and thirty-four 18- and 24-pounder battering guns, a military siege technology greater than any yet deployed in the subcontinent.[245] It is not hard to imagine that the exercise of such a formidable apparatus of imperial power may have taken its psychological toll on the assailants (one nevertheless scarcely comparable to the physical toll inflicted upon the Pindari garrison). Julian's self-hatred in this context reveals the other side of the coin from Williams' liberal jingoism, providing the absent imperialist context for the interpretation of Shelley's monitory remarks in the *Defence* that 'man ... having enslaved the elements, remains himself a slave'.[246] For Julian, Medwin continues, 'feared that he had become "a half-mad, desponding hypochondriac"!' and (even more melodramatically) 'At the mess every one said I was a madman. I am – I am.'[247]

In the course of his sojourn in India, however, Julian finds a means of easing his conscience, temporarily relieving himself of his corrosive guilt by falling in love with a young Hindu woman whom he rescues from death by *sati* on the banks of the Sutlej river. As Gayatri Spivak writes of the English fascination with *sati*, it is a case of 'White men ... saving brown women from brown men ... The protection of women ... becomes a signifier for the establishment of a *good* society, which must ... transgress mere legality.'[248] Julian's 'Gizele' – she is called Seta in other versions of Medwin's tale – becomes as devoted to her English rescuer as Shelley's Asia is to Prometheus during his three thousand years of suffering; ('Hast thou forgotten one who watches thee / The cold dark night, and never sleeps but when / The shadow of thy spirit falls on her?').[249] Julian recalls Gizele's devotion in the following terms: 'She tended me during those days and nights of howling, and would allow no doctor to approach me, and with the healing medicine of her spirit charmed away the fiend that preyed on me. But she died ... After her death I became a Manichaean, and supposed the world governed by some malignant genius.'[250]

It is at just this moment that the disconsolate Julian discovers Shelley's *Revolt of Islam* on a 'Surdaugher's' stall at Kanpur, and the poem 'worked a strange reformation in my mind', although the whys and the wherefores are, as we have seen, left unspecified. But, we learn, the dislocated – and, as I have argued, fragile – optimism of Shelley's poem was ultimately insufficient to redeem Julian from the blue devils, and he began to take instruction from a Guru at Benares.

Plate 8. 'Interior View...of the Temple of Elephanta', in J. Forbes, *Oriental Memoirs*, 4 vols. (London 1813), 1 facing p. 454.

'In process of time and instruction, I embraced the doctrines of Bramah, and continued for many years a correspondence with that excellent person Ram Mohun Roy, whose opinions and my own are little different: and I agree with him in thinking that "the worship of Idols (that finds no place in the Vedas or Vedantis) was directed by the Shastras merely as a concession made to the limited faculties of the vulgar".'[251] In Anglo-Indian terminology, Julian has 'gone native'.

In the absence of any detailed contemporary evidence, we will never know the extent to which Julian's experiences in India corresponded with Medwin's. Nor does it matter for my present purposes, concerned with Medwin's use of Shelleyan and Byronic themes in representing India, which I suggested at the start of the present chapter constitute a unique if minor genre of English Romanticism and contributed to the development of a Victorian literature of empire. Medwin was a learned orientalist, as is evident from his articles (in French) on the Ellora temple carvings in the Genevan Journal *Bibliothèque Universelle* in April and September 1821.[252] As well as showing a considerable knowledge of Hindu mythology and literature (including the *Mahabharata* and *Ramayana*), the articles censure Brahminical priestcraft and mount a scholarly attack on the theory that Hinduism was pure deism until it suddenly declined into 'un polythéisme bizarre' in the ninth century; they quote Arrian, Strabo, Plutarch and Clement of Alexandria to support their arguments. Medwin prefers the explanation (which Julian attributes to Rammohun Roy in the above cited passage) that idolatry was an instance of 'double-doctrine' comparable to that of the Pythagoreans or the priests of Egypt.[253]

By the time he came to write *The Angler*, however, Medwin had moved away from Rammohun's reformism to a more conventional orientalist 'acceptance' of orthodox Hinduism. Speaking through the 'hybridized' Julian, he no longer saw cause to censure Brahminical 'double-doctrine'; 'the ignorant and unenlightened, who can form no metaphysical notion of the attributes of a God, must have some type of his goodness or power, by which to be taught to acknowledge him. The true Brahman is like the philosophers of old.'[254] Even in 1821, Medwin's 'reformist' attitude to Hindu polytheism is mediated by his admiration for classical Indian plastic art, which he has no hesitation in comparing with that of ancient Greece. Although Indian antiquities are infinitely superior

Plate 9. 'Bhadra', an 1830 lithograph by R. M. Grindley of a carving in Ellora caves, *Transactions of the Royal Asiatic Society*, vol. II (London 1830), facing p. 327.

to Egyptian (an index of Medwin's Romanticism in Martin Bernal's terms),[255] their relative inferiority to the Greek is explicable by the fact that whereas the Greeks were 'citoyens libres, et soldats', the Hindus, subordinated to the caste system, a hostile climate and mercenary habits, 'étoient étrangers au sentiments de la liberté qui encourage et vivife les arts'. Nevertheless, 'Malgré tout de désavantage, on trouve, dans plusiers de leurs statues, l'expression de la beauté idéale...'[256]

It was not as a learned orientalist but as a poet of contemporary British India, however, that Medwin sought to describe the predicament of an Indian 'ideal beauty' glimmering through the obscurity of 'Asiatic' priestcraft and imperialist war. Medwin's poems are perhaps the earliest to treat colonial life in India in 'serious' Romantic style; in this respect they differed from poems like the anonymous *Rinaldo, or the Incipient Judge. A Tale of the Writer's Building* (1822) or Charles D'Oyly's *Tom Raw, the Griffin: A Burlesque Poem in 12 Cantos* (1828) which sought to satirize the drudgery of life in the Company's employ in the flippant comic style of Byron's *Don Juan*, a poem which had appeared in Calcutta in 1819 to great plaudits. Medwin's 1821 collection *Sketches from Hindostan* reworked the earlier *Oswald and Edwin: An Oriental Sketch* (February 1820) in its opening poem 'The Lion Hunt' and its principal offering 'The Pindarees' germinated from section xxiii of the 1820 poem. Both these earlier works were corrected and edited by Shelley himself, who thought the 1820 poem was 'highly fit for popularity, considered in its subject; there being a strong demand in the imagination of our contemporaries for the scenery & situations which you have studied, I admire equally the richness & variety of the imagery with the ease & profusion of language in which it is expressed'.[257] The 'Pindarees' was in turn extended and elaborated into 'Julian and Gizele' published with copious notes in the *Angler in Wales* in 1834; Julian's tragic love-story was reworked one last time as a magazine piece entitled 'A Bengal Yarn' in 1842. Unlike the brief trajectory of the *Alastor* protagonist's fatal quest, Medwin's obsessive pursuit of his Indian 'ideal beauty' spanned almost a quarter of a century.

Despite their appearance of being mere pastiche versions of Byron's *Eastern Tales*, appropriating Byron's verse couplets as well as elements of character and narrative, Medwin's Indian poems are also indebted to Shelley, especially in the manner in which they adapt the male and female protagonists of *Alastor*, *The Revolt* and *Prometheus Unbound* to their author's own experience of India. The character of Edwin in 'The Lion Hunt' is evidently based on a version of the *Alastor* 'poet', and the poem's epigraph cites lines 429–30 of Shelley's poem. 'He sought in Nature's dearest haunt some banks, / Her cradle and his sepulchre.' The poem's ostensible theme, its exploration of male

friendship between the lion-hunters Edwin and Oswald, collapses
under the strain of its evidently greater fascination with the 'hybrid'
character of Oswald. If Edwin is the *Alastor* 'poet', Oswald is closer
to Byron's Giaour or Conrad the Corsair: 'But on his brow a cloud
of mystery hung, / ...And in his very smile you might detect / A
sneer, for those he knew not to respect.'[258] Like Byron's Alp in *The
Siege of Corinth*, Oswald has 'gone native' in religion and manners:

> Though Christian born, he followed Brahma's laws;
> His faith ascribed to many a various cause.
> And Oswald practised strictest abstinence;
> The Yoga's life – without the priest's pretence.[259]

The narrator tells of speculation amongst the British community as to
the cause of Oswald's 'conversion – he is considered to be either a
dedicated Sanskritist (like Colonel Pollier of the East India Company, the first European to succeed in collecting copies of all four
Vedas) seeking to 'cheat the Brahmins of their Veda lore', or, in
anticipation of Kipling's *Kim*, a political spy involved in the 'great
game of Asia'. But consensus has it that the cause of his 'strange
apostasy' is his love for Seta, a high-caste Hindu girl, an affair which
is however downplayed in a hunting poem concerned with male
friendship.[260] Medwin's poem recalls itself to the matter in hand (the
hunt) and to the fate of Edwin rather than the more compelling
character of Oswald, returning to the task (with great attention to
local detail) of bringing the lion to bay. It ends rather abruptly with
Edwin being himself eaten by his quarry (apparently an essential
element of Anglo-Indian sporting memoirs) and an account of
Oswald's reflections on bereavement.

The central theme of Oswald and Seta is, however, developed in
the second part of 'The Pindarees' which followed it in the 1821
volume. Seta's village is raided by the Pindaris, and Oswald (like
Medwin, a cavalry officer), sets off on a retaliatory raid despite Seta's
exhortations that he should not go. The Pindaris are defeated and
suffer heavy losses, and Seta's brother Singha, one of Oswald's
sepoys, is killed in the fighting. News gets back to Seta that Oswald
has perished as well as Singha, and she dies of a broken heart. When
Oswald returns, 'an empty urn is all that fills his arms',[261] – leaving
him in exactly the same position as Owenson's Hilarion in *The
Missionary* who retires to his Kashmiri cave bearing an urn full of
Luxima's ashes. Oswald gradually pines away: 'The store that fed

the lamp, diminished more and more; / Till in the socket glimmering, it but threw / On the dark future a despairing hue'.[262] The
poem as a whole is indebted to Byron's *Corsair*, its description of
Zalim's Pindari band a pastiche of Conrad's pirate band, exchanging
Levantine for Indian 'costume', and Seta's exhortations and tragic
death being closely based on the story of Conrad and Medora.

But the character of Oswald now owes more to Shelley than to
Byron, in particular to the protagonist of *Alastor*. Medwin's poem
seems to illustrate the dictum of the Preface to *Alastor*, to the effect
that, 'that Power which strikes the luminaries of the world with
sudden darkness and extinction, by awakening them to too exquisite
a perception of its influences, dooms to a slow and poisonous decay
those meaner spirits that dare to abjure its dominion'.[263] Referring to
Oswald's bereavement and alienation, Medwin asks 'Who that has
owned in all their thrilling force / Would seek an unendearing
intercourse / With those, who make of life a cold pursuit; / And
laugh at passions in their bosoms mute?'[264] By concentrating upon
the sympathetic rather than the critical element of Shelley's
treatment of his protagonist, Medwin represents the imperialist
project (symbolized by the uncertain and ephemeral 'possession' of
Seta) as a heroic vocation for which the price to be paid is alienation
from kith and kin, even a form of hybridity or semi-absorption in the
Other. In the 'Lion Hunt, the Briton who has stayed at home, like
Shelley's 'meaner spirit', is possessed of 'A brain of figures and a
heart of ice; / With microscopic eyes to grope his way, / And scales
of gold his every thought to weigh'.[265] We see before our eyes the
transmutation of the Romantic quest poem into the nineteenth-
century epic of empire as revolutionary or Romantic idealism
becomes imperial heroism.

In his reincarnation as Julian in *The Angler in Wales*, the 'Byronic'
Oswald of 'The Lion Hunt' has undergone a further shift in the
direction of Shelley. Although Julian is clearly modelled on Medwin
in his Indian period (whilst the book's other interlocutor Stanley
evokes Medwin in his subsequent European character), the change of
names from Oswald to Julian suggests Shelley's self-dramatization in
Julian and Maddalo. Julian retains Oswald's 'hybrid' character; as
Stanley remarks, 'I found my old friend a person neither English nor
Indian, Christian nor Hindu.'[266] Forced to return to England for his
health's sake, he feels profoundly alienated; he denies that Britain is
his native country and expostulates, 'Call it exile – call it what you

will. India was *my* country. There I had friends, a home, congenial employments – pursuits to rouse the mind to energy: here all is torpor – stagnation – death!'[267] Julian's vision of the tonic effect of the colonies echoes Shelley's 1821 letter to Peacock requesting employment in the Company's service, as well as De Quincey's equation of opium and imperialism as stimulants discussed below. Shelley's poem *Alastor* relates how its protagonist 'left / His cold fireside and alienated home / To seek strange truths in undiscovered lands' (*SPW*, p. 17, lines 75–7).

Julian, speaking as Shelley's character might have done on his stony deathbed in the Caucasus, emphasizes that if colonial service is a stimulant, an addiction, it is also a price to be paid for a fall from innocence. He describes how 'a depraved imagination drove me from [the arms of the blissful protection of those to whom I owe my being] – a cursed destiny urged me to venture on a world of which I was ignorant, and for which I was unfitted – a fiend...dragged me with unmeaning steps over half the globe'.[268] His overland journey to India, 'through the Don country, over the Caucasus into Georgia, thence travers[ing] the Persian empire, and crossing the Desert to Bushire...to headquarters in the Upper Provinces', nearly follows the itinerary of the *Alastor* 'poet', although Julian's destination, a British military cantonment in Kanpur, casts the harsh light of contemporary history on the mysterious, orientalist journey of Shelley's character. And of course Julian's obsessive pursuit of India takes a toll on his health similar to that of his Shelleyan prototype; Julian's '"winter of strange sorrows" had prematurely furrowed his brow and thinned his hair which had become almost grey'.[269]

Medwin's reworking of 'The Pindarees' in *Julian and Gizele* elaborates the earlier poem's division of its Indian subject-matter by means of reduction and idealization, similar to the narcissism and aggression which for Bhabha characterize the construction of the colonial as fetish object.[270] Whilst his account of the Pindaris seeks to evoke in its readers the same frisson as Schiler's Robbers, Byron's Corsairs or Phillip Meadows Taylor's Band of Thugs in the 1839 *Confessions of a Thug*, Medwin contributes to the hegemonic construction of tribal peoples – the poem's Goorkhas, Thugs, Brinjarries and Arab nomads who compose the Pindari band – as criminal elements. This is the *reductive* element in Medwin's representation. C. A. Bayly describes how in these years the development of a cavalry arm (of which Medwin's regiment was part) and improved siege technology, such as that used at the siege of Hathras, allowed the Company to strike at what Wellesley termed the 'freebooting system' threatening the land revenue yield in western and central India, its main source of income.[271] The importance of private property in land to Company rule – discussed above – was threatened by 'nomadic' elements such as the Pindaris, represented by Medwin as colourfully *machista*, although none the less criminal in type and ideology:

> 'Tis nature's ordinance, – man preys on man;
> Our's not the fault, – condemn the general plan!
> Call us Pindarries, Cossacks – to the strong,
> All that the weak protect not, should belong.[272]

In these years, according to Bayly, the British 'were seeking not simply an increase of their revenues but a monopoly of all sources of political authority throughout Indian society... If other chiefs [i.e. outside the arbitrarily designed category of 'native princes'] resisted they were rebels, or plunderers, or bandits, defined out of existence by a power which perceived itself to be unitary and unchallenged as no other had done before it.'[273] I suggested in my discussion of *The Revolt of Islam* that Medwin's strategy of 'defining out of existence' revolt against British power, in representing the Pindaris as nomadic criminal elements, borrowed from Shelley's description of the diverse Asiatic desperadoes composing Othman's counter-revolutionary army in Canto x. Protecting the weak – the *ryots* settled by the British on their private property – against the 'Asiatic despotism' of nomadic freebooters becomes the truly revolutionary task of the East India Company, Medwin's 'Guardian State'.[274] The nature of the Pindaris calls for the suspension of British civility and an equivalence of aggression such as that which we saw Shelley exorcizing in *The Assassins*. When Julian's punitive band discover the carnage wrought by the Pindaris on Gizele's native village, their thirst for revenge is aroused; the British force decimates the rebels and Julian kills Zalim their leader with his own hands, 'No quarter's given; 'twere vainly ask'd of those / Who treat as fiends in human shape their foes.'[275]

The second element of Medwin's representation of India is *idealization*, bearing many of the narcissistic traits I have discussed in Shelley's *Alastor* and *Revolt of Islam*. In the 1820 'Pindarees', Oswald has saved Seta from the depredations of the Pindaris, who in true *machista* fashion know only one way to treat their women. In *Julian and Gizele*, however, Julian has saved his lover from *sati* – 'white men saving brown women from brown men'. The interference of a non-caste Hindu has of course resulted in Seta's loss of caste, and she becomes dependent on the Englishman. By the time of writing the poem, the abuses of Brahminism (and, as we have seen, this is quite consistent with Julian/Medwin's adoption of the reformist Hinduism of Rammohun Roy, a leading Indian campaigner against *sati*), have replaced the banditry of the defeated Pindaris at the top of the agenda of Indian incivilities to be reformed by the Guardian State. Although Medwin's horrific footnote description of the voluntary, unintoxicated adult *sati* he had witnessed at Mandula concluded that 'no instance of heroism could be greater than this',[276] Gizele's account of her *sati* here contains all the stereotypes noted by Lata Mani:

> I did not, could not pine
> For *that*, whose loss has made me thine –
> Link'd as it was – is – must be now,
> With those who urged the barbarous vow;
> For though betroth'd, I was a child,
> And therefore easily beguiled,
> And till I reach'd the fatal pyre,
> I knew not what a Suttee's rite.[277]

If Shelley's 'revolt of Islam' had sought to save a Hellenistic 'ideal beauty' from the ravages of Asiatic despotism – which, I have argued, read in an Indian context involved the imperialist *imposition* of 'universal' rational norms upon Indian society – Medwin's 'orientalist' agenda is premised upon the discovery and salvation of a classical *Indian* 'ideal beauty' from the barbarism of degraded Hindu modernity. A certain similarity is again evident here with Rammohun Roy's idealization of a pure Upanishadic age, although as I have suggested in discussing the possible influence of Rammohun's doctrines on *Prometheus Unbound*, the latter's Brahminical status recontextualizes and radicalizes doctrines which have points in common with both the orientalism of the Jones school *and* utilitarian and evangelical reform. If I am right in suggesting that it was this *recontextualization* which influenced Shelley's change of heart concerning India in his representation of Asia in *Prometheus Unbound*, rather than merely any late conversion to Medwin's style of orientalism, then it becomes possible to exempt Asia from the strategy of sexual/colonial narcissism which determines Shelley's earlier works and all Medwin's poems. *Prometheus Unbound* might then be seen to transcend the discursive protocols determining nearly all other representations of the relations between Europe/England and India, pointing the way forward to a *decolonized* account of cultural difference. Medwin's Indian poems fail to meet the challenge of his cousin's masterpiece in their role as colonial discourse.

Gizele is therefore presented as an embodiment of Indian antiquity, her sensuality distinguishing her at once from Byron's personification of Greek antiquity in *The Corsair*'s Medora. Her love of nature, her 'saumur' (thrush) and 'favourite tree' evoke the nature-loving heroine of *Shakuntala* (in Jones' 'translation') by Kalidasa,[278] her Vedantin religion evokes Owenson's Luxima in the *Missionary*, and her very form is described in terms of the classical Indian (albeit, in this case, Mughal) architecture and sculpture of which, as we have seen, Medwin was a well-informed student:

> a shape of Ind
> In infant slumberings on a couch reclined:
> Pale as the Tajh's marble was her cheek,
> Her features and her form half breathing speak,
> The love that animated them, each line
> Might pass in sculpture's language for divine.[279]

Gizele's long declaration of love to Julian, as she exhorts him not to set off on the punitive raid against the Pindaris, whilst in *narrative* terms deriving from Medora's speech to Conrad, rather takes its idiom and breathless syntax from Shelley's *Alastor*, Canto VI of *The Revolt of Islam* or *Epipsychidion* lines 575–91:

> 'Twas you first taught this heart of mine
> To throb in ecstasy with thine,
> To beat in mystic ebb and flow,
> Self-conscious of thy joy, or woe.
> ...Why said I two? We are but one –
> One heart – one mind – one soul – one breath –
> And shall we not be one in death?[280]

Only in death can the lovers be united, it transpires, for Gizele, like Medora, dies on account of a tragic piece of misinformation. There is a dawning sense in the conclusion of Medwin's poem of the tragic impossibility of the imperialist project, of the manner in which its narcissism is incompatible with its aggression, its idealizations negated by its reductions. The savagery of Julian's reprisal against the Pindaris is intrinsically connected to the death of his Hindu lover, in an allegory of the way in which the violence of one aspect of British imperialism in India – of imperialism per se – always qualifies its desire to 'reconstruct' the purity and integrity of its object. Julian himself is left vacillating between a corrosive nostalgia for his lost love and an inability to return to his own cultural base, 'Estranged from man henceforth he ran his race. / ... Year after year, waned lingering moons away, / And Julian's hair turn'd prematurely grey.'[281] Medwin's poems, no less than Charles Metcalfe's vision of the impossibility of continuing British power in India, elegize the 'orientalist' project as it is eclipsed by the new guardians, their aggression towards Indian culture enhanced by disdain rather than problematized by desire.

The final collapse of Romantic India is signalled by Medwin in 'A Bengal Yarn', published in *Ainsworth's Magazine* in 1842. Its mood is iconoclastic, anti-romantic, counter-sublime, and I believe that it is on just such a note that any study of British Romantic India should end, if only to counteract the 'Jewel in the Crown' type nostalgia which has of late crept into our collective memories of the British Raj. Medwin's 'Yarn' reworks the familiar story of Oswald/Julian in the character of 'Major B—', an exemplary orientalist and Sanskrit scholar, who 'became a Hindu, at least as far as doctrine went, for they admit of no converts'. He 'used to contend that Christianity was borrowed from India; that our Saviour was only the reflex of Chrishna, the Shepherd God, whose concealment by the Gopees, and the mystery that hung over his education, were but types of the flight to Egypt: that the doctrine of the Incarnation, the Trinity, were derived from the Hindus'. 'B—' is a hybrid like his precursors in Medwin's opus – in the mess his brother officers call him 'the Pundit', 'the Hindu', 'the Brahmin'; he is also a disciple and correspondent of Rammohun Roy and therefore 'no believer in mysteries' or the abuses of modern Hinduism.[282] Like Julian, Major B— rescues a beautiful twelve-year-old girl, once again called Seta, from *sati* (despite the outlawing of the practice by Governor-General Bentinck in 1829 Medwin claims that at least 500 *satis* have been recorded in the previous year, 1841). Perhaps it is significant that B—'s child bride – for she becomes his lover and bride – is described now in terms of Hellenistic rather than Hindu classical beauty. Although an 'odalisk', 'her face, a perfect oval, would not have lost in comparison with that of a Greek statue, so finely moulded was it, and set off to advantage by the classical disposition of her hair, fine, black, and luxuriant, whose great charm consisted in its simplicity'.[283]

The days of Major B—'s connubial joy are limited, however, for he has the misfortune to live in the treacherous thirties and forties, an era of increasing disturbance leading up to the violence of 1857.[284] After his regiment is disbanded, he obtains command of an irregular corps: Seta, although an outcast, uses her influence with B— to get places for her relatives. But his native troops mutiny in protest at B—'s rigid disciplinary regime; the mutiny is quelled, but it is evident that his irregular horsemen are really no better than the freebooters and opportunists who composed Zalim's Pindari band in Medwin's 1820 poem. Worse is to come, however, and B— is to learn the hard way that 'native women make bad wives'. No sooner has he made over all his property to Seta than she decamps into the jungle with everything he possesses. 'Why had he not a mirror by which he could read the workings of her soul and detect the falsehood, the inconceivable and almost incredible treachery of that fiend in human shape!'[285] In a finale which parodies the tragic death of Julian's Seta or the love-lorn wanderings of Shelley's *Alastor* 'poet', the stunned and heart-broken Major B— rides into the jungle, only to be promptly eaten by a tiger. Meanwhile Seta 'the faultless and infamous Hindu' emerges and uses the defunct Major's money to buy her way back into Hindu society. Time and changing circumstances had clearly transformed Medwin's 'orientalist' desire for India, and the bathos of 'A Bengal Yarn', despite the lip service it pays to Rammohun Roy and the Indian *Ursprung*, announces that in the end it is all superstition and chicanery:

> By her munificent gifts to the Brahmans, and through the mediation of a Yogi of great sanctity, who had, as an atonement for her sins undertaken to perform the penance of living for five years in a hole in the ground, the ban was removed from her, and she was again restored to her caste.[286]

The perfidious Seta signals the end of a Romantic tradition of idealization: Shakuntala, Luxima, the 'veiled maid', Cythna, Asia, Gizele, all these different inflections of the imperialist desire for India. All end here, a strange anticipation of the terrible anger of 1857 and particularly British reactions to the 'Well at Cawnpore'. In September of that year, we hear De Quincey evoking a very different feminine ideal from Shelley or Medwin, the voices from 'the bloody graves of our dear martyred sisters, scattered over the vast plains of India...':

We from our bloody graves, in which all of us are sleeping to the resurrection, send up united prayers to thee, that upon the everlasting memory of our hell-born wrongs, thou, beloved mother, wouldst engraft a counter-memory of everlasting retribution, inflicted upon the Moloch idolatories of India. Upon the pride of *caste* rests for its ultimate root all this towering tragedy which now hides the very heavens from India.[287]

De Quincey's is an extreme voice, speaking at a moment of national humiliation: Medwin's late fiction perhaps provides a more representative sample of changing British attitudes to India in the first half of the nineteenth century. If at least Medwin spared his Major B— the fate of a cuckold, he did portray him as a foolish figure with his youthful odalisk and his orientalism. Macaulay and his Victorian acolytes would not forget the fact in their campaign to implement an Anglicist cultural homogeneity – which concealed a racial apartheid – in British India. I have suggested that Shelley might have realized too late, upon reading Mill's *History*, how his 'revolt of Islam' could be interpreted by a colonial reader browsing on the book-barrows of Bombay. His unique attempt at a cultural dialogue – inspired by the hybrid intervention of Rammohun Roy – and his depiction of a 'decolonized' relationship between Prometheus and Asia remains in mitigation of his earlier thinking upon the subject. *Prometheus Unbound* however, represents a brief ray of light in the gathering gloom of nineteenth-century English writing about India; as Patrick Brantlinger puts it, 'If a humanist text can be imagined which will break down national, social class, religious, racist, and sexist barriers to understanding, then nearly all nineteenth- and many twentieth-century accounts of the Mutiny are versions of its antithesis.[288]

It is tempting for admirers of the radical energy of Shelley's poetry, and those who are tolerant of the utopian optimism which breaks through the despair of much of his writing, to believe that he was searching for a voice to say, albeit late in his short poetic career, what no other contemporary British writer even dreamed of saying. Namely, that the colonial encounter need not exhaust the possibilities of the meeting of different cultures, and that the option might remain, however apparently counter-factual, of imagining communities premised neither upon paranoiac discriminations nor fetishistic identification, the twin pathologies of imperialism.

CHAPTER 3

'Murdering one's double'; Thomas De Quincey and S. T. Coleridge. Autobiography, Opium and Empire in 'Confessions of an English Opium Eater' and 'Biographia Literaria'

> Any of us would be jealous of his own duplicate; and, if I had a
> *doppel-ganger* who went about personating me, copying me, and
> pirating me, philosopher as I am I might (if the Court of
> Chancery would not grant an injunction against him) be so far
> carried away by jealousy as to attempt the crime of murder upon
> his carcase; and no great matter as regards HIM. But it would be
> a sad thing for *me* to find myself hanged; and for what, I beseech
> you? for murdering a sham, that was either nobody at all, or
> oneself repeated once too often.
>
> (Mass. XI 460–1)

INTRODUCTION

The relative critical neglect of De Quincey's *Confessions of an English Opium Eater* compared with, say, Wordsworth's *Prelude* or Coleridge's *Biographia Literaria*, is perhaps all the more remarkable given the deconstructive mood which dominated Romantic Studies in the nineteen-eighties. For De Quincey's work set out to challenge what its author considered to be the flawed idealism – and voluntarism – of the 'High Romantic Argument.' Perhaps this is partly because *The Confessions* has always stood in a somewhat uneasy relationship to the literary canon in its prostration to the 'dark idol' of opium. Arguably, it took the drug culture of the nineteen-sixties to reawaken interest in the relationship between narcosis and creativity in De Quincey and Coleridge, as well as writers of narcosis like William Burroughs, Aldous Huxley, Henri Michaux, Baudelaire and Edgar Allen Poe implicitly or explicitly influenced by them. The revival of more popular interest is exemplified in Alethea Hayter's 1968 study *Opium and the Romantic Imagination* and a first Penguin edition of the *Confessions* in 1971, although critics were slow to take up the challenge. Hayter was anxious to disassociate her book from the drug culture, despite the fact that it barely disguised its fascination with the phenomenon and its ramifications for artistic creativity.

Treatments of drug experience in the period drew on a consistent range of stereotypes: the hedonistic – or in newspeak 'recreational' – use of drugs revealed a quasi-mystical site of truth in the psyche, in many cases a vessel for spilt religion or repressed sexuality and creativity. This was balanced by an anxiety about the moral consequences of instant pharmaceutical gratification, 'fear and loathing' of the Hunter Thompson stamp induced by gross overconsumption, and paranoiac visions of alien, exotic – usually oriental – cultures from the beginning associated with western narcosis; Francis Ford Coppola's film *Apocalypse Now* – a reflection on the mood of the sixties – is a case in point. Above all (an attitude which more than any other hails De Quincey as progenitor), the compulsion to *confess* one's bondage to, or liberation from, the pleasures and pains of drugs. In an illuminating recent study of the cultural mythology of heroin, Marek Kohn selects the Coleridgean figure of the Ancient Mariner as paradigmatic of much contemporary drug literature: '[The Narcomaniac] is sentenced to confess eternally, like those devotees who believe that their drug dependency is a life sentence, in the manner of original sin...The compulsion to testify to addiction replaces the compulsion to act it out by taking the drug. Addiction is seen as a permanent component of the soul.'[1] In the present chapter I wish to explore some of the cultural and political ramifications of drug confession, or rather of what I take to be its inaugural moment, De Quincey's *Confessions of an English Opium Eater*. I will suggest that De Quincey represented the pleasures and pains of opium upon his sensitive nervous system as a metaphor (or a symbol, in the Coleridgean sense) for the effects of capitalism, in its newly developed imperialist phase, upon the body politic. I will first explore the medical discourse of opium therapy in order to read the *Confessions* as a materialist 'assassination' of Coleridge's *Biographia Literaria*. But De Quincey's apologia for opium is also an apologia for imperialism as the means of stimulating a torpid and internally fissured national culture, and of displacing domestic anxieties onto the oriental Other. In conclusion, I argue that De Quincey (and a by now well-defined imperialist ideology) was plagued by a return of these displaced anxieties magnified fourfold, radically threatening to stable self-identity.

THE 'CONFESSIONS': NERVOUS REACTIONS

Although De Quincey's title evoked the *Confessions* of St Augustine and Rousseau, the declared subject of his book was impersonal, 'preternatural', pharmaceutical, rather than autobiographical, natural or spiritual, not 'the subject of the fascinating spells, but... the fascinating power. Not the opium-eater, but the opium, is the true hero of the tale: and the legitimate centre on which the interest revolves' (*C* 114). De Quincey sought to domesticate this exotic 'hero', just as we have seen writers like Southey, Byron, and Moore domesticating oriental 'materiale' as a species of 'imperial heraldry'; as Virginia Berridge writes, 'The majority of descriptions [of opium-eating] available up to that time had presented the habit, along with opium-smoking, as a peculiarly Eastern custom. De Quincey's eulogy of the drug proved the reality could be different, and that English opium-eating was possible.'[2] When De Quincey republished the *Confessions* in 1856, he had padded out the 1822 text (it had originally appeared in the September and October 1821 numbers of *The London Magazine*) to almost three times its original length with mainly autobiographical material. Perhaps for this reason, the passage just quoted had been cut; the true hero of the tale was now the author rather than the drug, and the *Confessions*, removed from the troubling no man's land of the elegant case-history or pathology, settled comfortably into the genre of literary autobiography. Henry Crabb Robinson's brief comment on the *rifacciamento* conveys this exactly, 'It is delightful, but it is now become more autobiographic.'[3]

Response to the original anonymous *Confessions* had been extremely favourable, making the 'English Opium-Eater' 'famous in his time': between 1821 and 1823 some fifteen reviews appeared, nearly all enthusiastic.[4] Although the *Confessions* had first appeared in a literary journal, and was clearly the work of a man of letters (the sub-title of the first magazine instalment read 'Being an extract from the life of a scholar'[5]), contemporary readers tended to take it at its word by reading it as a medical account of opium addiction and an intervention in a current debate about the therapeutic value of opium, a point to which I will return below. At the same time, the literary merits or demerits of what De Quincey called his 'florid or Corinthian order of rhetoric' (Mass. x 106) were noticed. One Dr Christen in a medical monograph *On the Nature of Opium* thought the work badly written and, as far as its medical credibility was concerned, a mere 'romance'. The latter suspicion was also canvassed by James Montgomery in *The Sheffield Iris*, to which De Quincey himself replied in a letter to the readers of the December 1821 issue of the *London Magazine*. The *Medical Intelligencer* replied to Christen's criticisms by finding De Quincey's language 'a fine specimen of nervous, classical, and grammatical English' and the *Confessions* as a whole 'a valuable addition to our stock of medical information'.[6]

From the beginning, however, there was uncertainty about the work's moral tendencies, perhaps understandable when one looks at the 'reader's response' to the *Confessions*, which make the tears shed over Richardson's *Clarissa* or Rousseau's *Nouvelle Heloise* seem rather tame by comparison. The hyperaesthetic and hypnagogic vistas of the dreams with which De Quincey concluded his book, and which he declared were 'the real object of the whole' (*C* 126), caused many readers to experiment with opium. In 1823, at the inquest into the death of a young man who had overdosed on opium, the reporting doctor 'claimed to have direct knowledge of four cases in which the patients, when questioned, gave [the *Confessions*] as their inspiration for taking a near-fatal dose'.[7] De Quincey's closest friend John Wilson, in his 'Noctes Ambrosianae' series in the October 1823 issue of *Blackwood's Magazine*, had his fictional interlocuter discuss the 'fifty unintentional suicides' caused by the *Confessions*, concluding in the author's favour; only six had actually died, a fact which 'only shows the danger that dunces run into, when they imitate men of genius'.[8]

Wilson's glib humour aside, these complaints echoed the objection of the naval surgeon Thomas Trotter, in his 1807 *View of the Nervous Temperament*, to a literature which candidly advertised the qualities of opium, '...the dose of opium concludes what was begun in the circulating library. A little more secrecy and discretion are certainly wanting in the general use of this dangerous narcotic.'[9] Sensitive to the criticism that his work contained an 'overbalance on the side of the *pleasures* of opium' and not enough on the *pains* to act as a deterrent to would-be opium-eaters, De Quincey promised readers of the *London Magazine* a Third Part to remedy the situation (*C* 119–20). The fact that this was never written and that the 1856 revision was unrepentant in its representations of the pleasures and therapeutic benefits of opium (it even urged insurance companies not to discriminate against opium dependants in transacting Life Insurance policies), reveals De Quincey's dogged advocacy of the drug's positive effects despite his personal failure to free himself from dependence, upon which such an advocacy largely rested.

De Quincey's doggedness notwithstanding, this morbid 'reader's response' to the book reinforced its enemies' arguments, based on a well-established and by now generally accepted opposition to the therapeutic use of opium in medical circles. A sanctimoniously titled medical journal, *The Family Oracle of Health*, opined in January 1824 that 'this wicked book' (the *Confessions*) must be held responsible for the misery caused by 'its lying stories about celestial dreams, and similar nonsense. Drunkenness is not confined to the use of fermented liquors', it continued; 'The tipplers of laudanum are sots, although of another sort.'[10] In taking this line, the *Family Oracle* was alluding to another work by Trotter entitled *An Essay on Drunkenness*, the first medical work to pathologize intoxication by alcohol or drugs. Whilst allowing for the utility of opium as a panacea for terminal illness, Trotter regarded its habitual use as causing 'debility, emaciation, loss of intellect, palsy, dropsy, dyspepsia, hepatic diseases and others which flow from the indulgence of spiritous liquors'.[11] Like all the medical opponents of opium, Trotter argued that dependence on drugs, like alcohol, was unbreakable, a charge which De Quincey denied, despite personal evidence to the contrary.[12]

The *Confessions*, without mentioning Trotter, also denied his thesis that opium caused this impressive list of diseases, or that it was an intoxicant like alcohol. The latter point he argued against the authority of the surgeon John Abernethy, himself a laudanum addict on 450 drops a day (an inconsiderable dose compared to De Quincey's 8–9,000 drops daily at his peak addiction period). Abernethy's mistake in supporting Trotter, he concluded, was semantic, based on the 'logical error of using the word intoxication with too great latitude, and extending it generically to all modes of nervous excitement' (*C* 76). In a recent polemic with the radical surgeon William Lawrence, Abernethy had defended a vitalistic position against what he took to be the atheism and French materialism of the latter's theory. In thus attacking Abernethy's authority, De Quincey was also having a dig at Coleridge, whose *Essay on Scrofula* contained a tribute to Abernethy, and whose *Theory of Life* attacked Lawrence's definition of life as a function of organization, rather than as a superinduced principle. De Quincey might have sought to discredit Trotter's argument about intoxication, but on one count at least (which incidentally proves his knowledge of the uncited *Essay on Drunkenness*) he was willing to concede. Trotter was the source for the contemporary theory that intoxication caused spontaneous combustion, fear of which – the terrible fate overtaking Krook the rag-merchant in Dickens' *Bleak House* – De Quincey tells us in the 1856 *Confessions*, caused him seriously to attempt a reduction of his laudanum consumption. This withdrawal attempt was probably contemporaneous with a bizarre story in the *Westmoreland Gazette* (which De Quincey was editing from July 1818 until November 1819) concerning an 'Incombustible Man', together with a recipe for an ointment of marshmallows, eggs and radishes with which concerned readers could fireproof their own flesh. Whatever Trotter's medical errors, the opium-eater was not taking any chances on this one.[13]

JOHN BROWN AND THE DEBATE ABOUT THE THERAPEUTIC USE OF OPIUM

Trotter's *Essay on Drunkenness* opposed the use of opiates to remedy physiological and psychological complaints, preferring the well-tried 'opiates of the soul', 'religious and moral sentiments'.[14] In emphasizing the narcotic and sedative rather than the stimulating effects of opium, and by presenting disease and dependence as pathological consequences of the drug, Trotter's work challenged a body of medical theory based on the teachings of the Edinburgh doctor John Brown (1735–88), known as the 'Brunonian system'.[15] The title derived from Brown's Latin *Elementa Medicinae* (1780) which ensured the work great popularity on the continent, particularly in Germany and Italy. Reinterpreting the work of his mentor, William Cullen, Professor of Clinical Medicine at Edinburgh, Brown argued that the nervous system was composed of excitable tissue, highly sensitive (or 'sensible') to its environment. As Christopher Lawrence has remarked of the eighteenth-century Scottish theorization of the nervous system, the monistic and essentially materialist psychology which it developed implied that 'all man's higher attributes – taste, imagination, and indeed the capacity to reason – would, in the last analysis, depend on his condition of existence, diet, weather, labour and so forth... Sensibility [was] in the end related to the individual's mode of life and should, in the healthy state, be properly adjusted to it.'[16] Medicine was thus a preternatural means of resolving natural maladjustment.

Brown classified all diseases as 'sthenic' or 'asthenic', according to whether they increased or decreased the state of excitement of the nervous tissue. For asthenic diseases (caused by understimulation), he recommended 'stimulating remedies, in particular brisk exercise or opium'; he believed that most doctors, including Cullen, misunderstood the properties of opium 'instead of allowing it to be the strongest stimulant in nature, they made it a sedative... Another property they ascribed to it was that of bringing on sleep: whereas, it is the most powerful body of all others in producing and keeping up the watchful state.' The debate between the Brunonians and the Cullenites (as well as with the followers of F. J. V. Broussais who advocated bloodletting by leeches, which, as Robert Woof has pointed out, is a submerged concern of Wordsworth's 'Leech Gatherer'[17]) survived into the beginning of the nineteenth century, although medical consensus increasingly lay with the Cullenites who accepted that the primary effect of opium was its narcotic rather than its stimulating influence on the nervous system.[18]

There is no doubt that De Quincey's *Confessions* is permeated with the increasingly unfashionable discourse of Brunonianism, albeit in a somewhat modified form. 'The primary effects of opium are always, in the highest degree, to excite and stimulate the system', he wrote in the section entitled 'The Pleasures of Opium' (*C* 77). By the same token, he denied that the drug led, at least in his own highly refined English nervous system, to 'torpor and stagnation, animal and mental', whatever its effects may be on the 'coarser' sensibilities of Turks or Orientals; 'I honour the Barbarians too much by supposing them capable of any pleasures approaching to the intellectual ones of an Englishman' (*C* 77, 78). Opium 'greatly increase[s] the activity of the mind generally' (*C* 79); whereas wine 'disorders the mental faculties', opium 'introduces amongst them the most exquisite order, legislation and harmony' (*C* 73). The essential effect of opium is to restore the condition of the finely balanced nervous system to a condition of homeostasis: for this reason we need not read De Quincey's account of its 'controlling power' over 'nervous irritation' or its efficacy as an anodyne and 'tranquillizer of nervous and anomalous sensations' as contradicting its primary function as a stimulant (*C* 212).

Stimulus resolves the condition described by Foucault as 'a sensibility which is not sensation', when 'the sensibility of the nervous organ itself overcharged the soul's capacity to feel, and appropriated for its own advantage the multiplicity of sensations aroused by its extreme mobility...Since madness [the extreme form of nervous maladjustment] can be dumb immobility, obstinate fixation as well as disorder and agitation, the cure consists in reviving in the sufferer a movement that will be both regular and real, in the sense that it will obey the rules of the world's movements.'[19] It is important to stress that the reality and regularity of the world's movements to which the sufferer is restored are precisely *not* the flux of incoming impressions (which have stretched and irritated the sensibility), but rather the capacity of the soul to feel and to reflect. Opium thus offered an *induced* artificial recovery of the sort of natural equanimity sought by Rousseau or Wordsworth beyond the forms of modern sociability; as De Quincey put it, 'a healthy restoration to that state which the mind *would* naturally recover upon the removal of any deep-seated irritation of pain that disturbed and quarrelled with the impulses of a heart *originally* just and good' (italics mine) (*C* 74). As a form of *inoculation* (a word which De Quincey uses in the *Confessions* (pp. 92–3) to describe his own drug experiments) he recommends a controlled dose of stimulant to remedy a general overstimulation, which has paradoxically resulted in what Wordsworth described as the almost oxymoronic state of 'savage torpor'; it is a homeopathic pattern which we will see recurring in De Quincey's writings.

Perhaps the clearest summary of De Quincey's representation of the Brunonian system was offered by the *Medical Intelligencer* in the review of the *Confessions* referred to above; it is moreover an account which we know De Quincey to have read as he cited it approvingly in the 1821 letter to the *London Magazine* (*C* 120).

Opium is found, in the first place, to lessen the sensibility of the *nervous system*, and thus check the transmission of sensations or impressions to the sensorium, whether painful or pleasant. The reduction of *sensation* in the brain and nervous system does not appear to reduce the activity of *reflection*; – on the contrary, the intellectual operations are quickened under the influence of opium – a proof that its action is not uniformly sedative or stimulant on all parts of the system.[20]

The enduring importance of the Brunonian system in De Quincey's writing is nowhere more evident than in his numerous sketches of contemporary men of letters, as characteristic in the genre as Hazlitt's sketches in *The Spirit of the Age*. Crabb Robinson's reaction to perhaps the most famous of these sketches, *The Last Days of Immanuel Kant*,

identifies this characteristic: 'He has made much of the bodily
constitution of a great man, with no allusion to his mind or
philosophy.'[21] What is particularly noteworthy about the sketches is
the manner in which De Quincey *medicalizes* his literary subjects,
subordinating their ideas to their bodily pathologies. For example,
writing on Herder, 'the German Coleridge', in the *London Magazine*
for April 1823, De Quincey felt that 'opium would have been of
service to [the German writer]'. He diagnosed his malaise as being
characteristic of the age: 'weariness of daily life, inirritability of the
nerves to the common stimulants which life supplies...he was sick of
the endless revolution upon his eyes of the same dull unimpassioned
spectacles' (Mass. IV 384).

Herder's *Weltschmerz* is in stark contrast to the 'exquisite' health of
Immanuel Kant, as described in *The Last Days of Immanuel Kant* (in
Blackwood's Magazine for February 1827). Until the philosopher's
rapid mental and physical decline (marked by gnawing stomach
pains for which De Quincey hypothetically prescribed 'a quarter
grain of opium, every eight hours' (Mass. IV 359)), Kant's setting
'the highest value upon...the Brunonian theory' (Mass. IV 342) had
ensured his enjoyment of a 'state of positive pleasurable sensation'
and 'the absence of pain, and of irritation, and also of *mal-aise*...'
(Mass. IV 338). Kant's famous solitary post-prandial walk was an
important article of his adherence to a Brunonian regime, an example
of the brisk exercise which De Quincey elsewhere recommended as
'omnipotent against all modes of debility or obscure nervous
irritations' (*C* 208).

Another figure who enjoyed a privileged and, like Kant, somewhat
Oedipal position in the De Quinceyan pantheon was Wordsworth,
who thrived on the natural stimulus of walking rather than the
preternatural one of opium, and was also a byword for sobriety. In
his 1839 article on Wordsworth in *Tait's Magazine*, De Quincey
calculated that Wordsworth had walked a distance of 175–180,000
miles – rivalling even the eccentric Scots Jacobin and Pantheist
'Walking' Stewart (the subject of another pair of articles by De
Quincey), who had walked everywhere, including Tibet and back.
Wordsworth's 'mode of exertion', he wrote, stood (him) 'in the stead
of wine, spirits and all other stimulants whatsoever to the animal
spirits; to which he has been indebted for a life of unclouded
happiness, and we for much of what is most excellent in his writings'
(*Recoll.* 135). In a rather pathetic attempt to emulate Wordsworth

and Stewart's naturalism, a desperate late bid to cut down on his
laudanum dose in 1843, De Quincey walked round and round his
tiny cottage garden in Lasswade, having calculated that 'forty
rounds were exactly required for one mile'. Keeping track of the
number of circuits with marker pebbles, he was able to announce that
he had walked a thousand miles in ninety days.[22] This anecdote
reveals that De Quincey never abandoned the hope of a natural cure,
rather than the preternatural agency of opium with its pathological
duplication and multiplication of symptoms, symbol of the artificial
condition of the modern subject. I will now go on to read the
Confessions as an interpretation of the 'bodily constitution' of
Coleridge, or more exactly, of his *Biographia Literaria*, aware that its
author, like De Quincey himself and unlike the privileged Wordsworth, poet of nature, was dependent upon the preternatural stimulus
of opium.

'TWO TRANSCENDENTALISTS WHO ARE ALSO [OPIUM EATERS]'

Not all of the *Confessions*' first readers were blind to an ulterior motive
which supplemented its role as medical polemic. In one of his
characteristic semi-insights Henry Crabb Robinson found the work
'a melancholy composition, a fragment of autobiography in emulation of Coleridge's diseased egotism'.[23] Robinson refers to the
Biographia Literaria (1817), a work whose author sought, in the words
of the book's epigraph, 'to spare the young those circuitous paths, on
which he himself had lost his way' (*BL* 1 3). The *confessional* aim
announced in this quotation from Goethe had remained unrealized,
however, and Coleridge's book had encountered the world as, in his
own words, an 'exculpation' (*BL* 1 5). On a formal, public level,
Coleridge proclaimed his philosophical and moral system to be based
on the Will, his aesthetics upon the Imagination, which he offered to
theorize in chapter 13's 'transcendental deduction', and his political
system to be anchored on fixed principles, exposing the shallow
pragmatism of Jacobin and utilitarian 'metapolitics'.

The actual effect of the *Biographia* on its readers was quite different,
however, inasmuch as it failed to score a hit as public discourse; its
defensive, querulous tone was the mark of a personal style of the kind
described by Robinson as 'diseased egotism'. Coleridge constantly
undermined his stated aims before the reader's eyes; instead of a Will,

he displayed his 'constitutional indolence', 'procrastination' and 'mental cowardice' (*BL* 1 45); instead of a transcendental deduction of Imagination he inserted a 'letter from a friend' in the middle of chapter 13 which represented his theorization as unintelligible and unpublishable; instead of demonstrating the steadfastness of his political principles and thereby 'exculpating' himself from damaging charges of political apostasy, he indiscreetly falsified his early political and theological ideas in the light of his later position. Coleridge seemed to be laying himself open to charges of inconsistency such as those made against him by Hazlitt in his celebrated 1821 essay *On Consistency of Opinion*.

The worst attack on Coleridge came, ironically, from an erstwhile member of his own camp, the Tory John Wilson. Wilson had, like his close friend De Quincey, been a fringe member of the Lake School until financial misfortune had driven him to embark upon a journalistic career in Edinburgh. In a notorious anonymous review of the *Biographia* in *Blackwood's Magazine* of October 1817, Wilson tore Coleridge to pieces, at the worst employing scandalous charges of a private nature picked up when he had enjoyed the confidence of Coleridge and his friends in the Lakes. The review, which reiterated the charges of 'inveterate and diseased egotism',[24] surprisingly began in an elevated and lyrical vein before stooping to pick up the mud. It complained that the *Biographia* 'does not contain an account of his opinions and literary exploits alone, but lays open, not unfrequently, the character of the Man as well as the Author ... without benefitting the cause either of virtue, knowledge or religion [it] exhibit[s] many mournful sacrifices of personal dignity, after which it seems impossible that Mr Coleridge can be greatly respected either by the Public or himself'.[25] Coleridge would have been better off letting sleeping dogs lie; as an erstwhile member of the poet's (albeit outer) circle, Wilson knew the facts about Coleridge's political past as well as the squalid details of his drug addiction, to which the *Biographia* seemed, at least to the initiate, to make constant veiled references. Wilson placed the *Biographia* in the same class as Rousseau's *Confessions* and Hume's *Autobiography*: it '[tore] away that shroud which oblivion may have kindly flung over his vices and his follies ... instead of composing memoirs of himself, a man of genius and talent would be far better employed in generalizing the observations and experiences of his life, and giving them to the world in the form of philosophical reflections, applicable ... to the universal mind of Man'.[26]

Wilson was here probing a weak point in Coleridge's defences, for the *Biographia* had found itself forced, by its perceived failure to match its declared aspirations, to announce itself as a mere prolegomena to just such a work of public and universal relevance, a projected systematic work on the 'PRODUCTIVE LOGOS' (*BL* I 136). Like the 'chapter on Imagination', the 'critical essay on the uses of the Supernatural in Poetry' (*BL* I 306) and a host of similar schemes, the projected work lay beyond the capabilities of the 'damaged archangel', entangled in the tortuous contingencies and compulsions of a life of addiction, with its grim auxiliaries 'procrastination' and 'mental cowardice'. When De Quincey announced a parallel work in the *Confessions*, the grandiosely titled *De Emendatione Humani Intellectus*, he was quick to confess that it was a mere chimera; there was no attempt to 'exculpate' himself from possible charges of irresolution because he was writing, after all, in the character of an 'opium-eater'. Unlike Coleridge, De Quincey felt that the *magnum opus* was part and parcel of the visionary architecture of his opium dreams, and thus 'it was likely to stand a memorial to my children of hopes defeated ... of foundations laid that were never to support a superstructure – of the grief and ruin of the architect' (*C* 99).

Wilson's criticism of Coleridge is, I believe, an important link between the *Biographia* and the *Confessions*, and the verbal parallels between Wilson's article and De Quincey's address to the reader at the beginning of the early version of the work are so close that it is remarkable that they have escaped notice. Indeed one is led to wonder whether De Quincey himself might not have been the author of at least the rhetorical *bravura* which opens the review. This is not at all unlikely given the pastiche composition methods of contemporary review articles, and Wilson's frequent letters to De Quincey begging him for material either for *Blackwood's* reviews or for lectures, after his rigged election to the Chair of Moral Philosophy at Edinburgh University in 1820.[27] The parallels between review and book endorse Crabb Robinson's interpretation of the *Confessions* mentioned above, enabling an identification of the *Biographia* as the occasion and pretext of De Quincey's work. One example will suffice: when De Quincey writes that 'Guilt and misery shrink, by a natural instinct from public notice: they court privacy and solitude' (*C* 29), he echoes Wilson's point that 'the true confessional is not the bar of the public ... there are feelings ... which, in the silence of solitude and of nature, are known only unto the Eternal'.[28]

De Quincey's strategy was to *materialize* the *Biographia*, in his very title naming the term which Coleridge's need to 'exculpate' himself had caused him to repress, and which his fellow opium addict believed to be the secret of the work's 'diseased egotism'. As Crabb Robinson would realize upon reading the 1856 revision of the *Confessions*, the earlier version was not really egotistical at all, mainly because it was *impersonal*, 'not the opium-eater, but the opium, is the true hero of the tale' (*C* 114).[29] Wilson complained that the *Biographia* 'rambles from one subject to another in the most wayward and capricious manner',[30] a fact which made perfect sense to De Quincey, who read it as the narrative of an opium addict. In a term which De Quincey developed in his later writings, the *Confessions* is the 'Dark Interpreter' of the *Biographia*, a 'dark figure on [its] right hand, keeping pace with [it]self', *stimulating* its abstracted, self-absorbed precursor, wasting itself in interminable reverie, 'revealing the worlds of pain and agony and woe possible to man'.[31]

De Quincey's starting point was to address the issue of hedonism, a consistently negative term in Coleridgean ethics; 'If opium-eating be a sensual pleasure, ... [I] am bound to confess that I have indulged it to an excess', exceeded only, he hinted, by Coleridge himself (*C* 30). De Quincey admits luxury to be the sovereign principle of his work, as it is the *secret* principle of the contemporary narcotic freemasonry, 'the whole class of opium-eaters', including Wilber-force, Dr Milner, Lord Erskine, Henry Addington, Coleridge, Abernethy and Sir James MacKintosh. 'I confess it, as a besetting infirmity of mine, that I am too much of an Eudaemonist: I hanker too much after a state of happiness, both for myself and others' (*C* 87). What distinguishes De Quincey from the others, he claims, is both a willingness to *confess* and furthermore positively to *advocate* both the pleasurable and therapeutic agency of the drug. Whatever the negative status of either eudaemonism or opium (as we shall see, the moral and pharmaceutical terms are closely, and literally, linked) in the ethical or medical views of Wilberforce or Coleridge or Thomas Trotter, De Quincey, playing somewhat the role of the devil's advocate, is unabashed in admitting that 'An inhuman moralist I can no more endure in my nervous state than opium that has not been boiled' (*C* 88). I will return to the social and economic implications of luxury as a Brunonian 'stimulus' later in the chapter.

When Coleridge first revealed the secret of his addiction to the young De Quincey in 1807 (*Recoll.* 43), it is quite likely that he mentioned the name of his Bristol mentor Dr Thomas Beddoes, whom we encountered above as the author of *Alexander's Expedition*. Beddoes was also a partisan of Brunonian medicine and author of a 'Life of John Brown' prefixed to the 1795 second edition of Brown's own translation of his *Elementa Medicinae*. Beddoes, like Erasmus Darwin, whose medical treatise *Zoonomia*, also influenced by Brown's system, exerted a strong influence on the young Wordsworth and Coleridge, recommended opium as both an anodyne and a stimulant. He is usually held responsible for Coleridge's own opium habit, although the latter had almost certainly experimented with the drug whilst a Cambridge undergraduate. The fact that the young Coleridge, like the mature De Quincey, had subscribed to the Brunonian system chapter and verse (cf. *CN* I 388–9) rather qualifies the terms of the acrimonious debate in later years as to whether Coleridge and De Quincey had first taken opium as an anodyne to relieve pain or as a source of pleasurable sensations. That debate, stimulated by De Quincey's accusations in *Tait's Magazine* after Coleridge's death in 1834, was based upon a false premise, although not one that would have been visible to the public in 1834; if both men had subscribed to the Brunonian theory of disease and cure, and shared Brown's underestimation of the addictive powers of opium, then there was no moral reason for either *not* to have taken it.

In Coleridge's case, however, experience of the 'pains of opium' and a rejection of the philosophical materialism which underpinned Brown's system had by 1807 caused him to reject it, although he would suffer in the most palpable terms for the rest of his life the effects of the 'false theory' of his youth. This is clear from a notebook entry dated January 1830, quoted in Gillman's 1838 *Life* of Coleridge, a rejoinder to the *Tait's* article of 1834, which in turn drew from De Quincey the bitter attack in his 1845 article *Coleridge and Opium-Eating*. Coleridge blamed 'the necessity of daily poisoning by narcotics' not on a quest for pleasure, but rather 'pain, delusion, error, of the worst ignorance, medical sciolism'. The latter clearly refers to the Brunonian system closely linked as it was to radical materialism. He went on to imprecate 'mercy on the author of the "Confessions of an Opium Eater"', if...his book has been the occasion of seducing others into this withering vice through wantonness'.[32] De Quincey is thus represented as an advocate of 'medical sciolism' and therefore a voluptuary; by 1830 Coleridge could or would not distinguish between radical materialism and wanton self-indulgence. Addressing the Irish writer Thomas Colley Grattan two years before this, in 1828, Coleridge denied ever having used opium for 'hedonistic' purposes or in excess. His remarks on the *Confessions* in this passage are of particular interest in so far as they repeat the criticisms levelled at his own *Biographia* discussed above:

> He spoke with utter abhorrence of the *Confessions*..., called it 'a wicked book, a monstrous exaggeration', and dwelt with great reprobation on the author for 'laying open his nakedness to the world'. He considered him to have behaved grossly in bringing him [Coleridge] into the book, as an authority for the excesses he avowed; and declared that 'when he suspected Mr De Quincy [*sic*] of taking opium, he had on several occasions spent hours in endeavouring to dissuade him from it, and that gentleman invariably assured him in the most solemn manner that he did not take it at all, while by his after confessions it appeared that he was drinking laudanum as other men drink wine'.[33]

Coleridge's remarks in the later years of his life confirm the anti-Brunonianism of his maturity. Already, in the *Biographia*, he had unambiguously rejected Brunonian medicine, praising the English physician Richard Saumarez' *New System of Physiology* (1798), whose 'detection of the Brunonian system was no light or ordinary service at the time' (*BL* I 162–3). The voluntaristic scheme of the *Biographia*, like the partially completed but unpublished *Theory of Life*, was dissatisfied with a system which 'made life an effect instead of a cause', and equated life, 'the contradictory *inert* force', with the capacity for 'excitability' or irritability, and the 'exciting powers' as stimuli created by external forces'.[34]

Because Coleridge wished to argue that Imagination, far from being merely a reflex of sense data, a product of *sensibility* as the condition of a highly refined nervous system, was 'first put in action by the will and understanding, and retained under their irremissive, though gentle and unnoticed, controul...' (*BL* II 16), he found it necessary to devote the whole of chapter 2 of the *Biographia* to denying 'the supposed irritability of men of Genius'. Coleridge's ideal of the unconditioned Will, his quest for 'exculpation', could never repress the dark truth which haunted it in the shape of the body, of physical dependence: De Quincey, a less convinced transcendentalist but fellow opium-eater could read that diseased, irritable body all too clearly between the lines of Coleridge's text. De Quincey exposes the tone of chapter 2 as redolent of the feigned innocence described by Michel Foucault: 'The innocence of the nervous sufferer, who no longer even feels the irritation of his nerves, is at bottom only the just punishment of a deeper guilt: the guilt which makes him prefer the world to nature.'[35]

Coleridge of course categorically denied the pathological account of genius; true men of genius are characterized by 'sanity of mind' and 'a calm and tranquil temper in all that related to themselves' (*BL* I 33). Whilst these men are clearly not irritable, there exists a class of 'false' geniuses, the simulacra of the first, whose irritability is based upon 'an ill conformation of body, obtuse pain, or constitutional defect of pleasurable sensation' (*BL* I 37). These are the modern hedonists, who seek in luxury a stimulus for torpid sensibility, who seek preternatural and worldly substitutes for their natural deficiencies. These men, of whom the opium-eaters clearly form a class, compose the great party of 'mere men of letters', the 'manufacturers of poems' and the anonymous critics 'fit instruments of literary detraction, and moral slander' (*BL* I 42). Coleridge disassociates himself from this class, although he lacks the confidence to place himself in the category of healthy, unconditioned, genius. He inhabits both worlds and neither, being at once a critic and victim of 'false theory'. As his pseudonymous 'letter from a friend' in chapter 13 asserts, in a strikingly anti-Brunonian metaphor, 'arguments drawn from your own personal interests more often act on you as narcotics than as stimulants' (*BL* I 304).

According to De Quincey's reading, Coleridge first took opium as a *stimulant*, became addicted, suffered the 'pains of opium' and rejected the 'medical sciolism' and materialistic epistemology upon which the demand for stimulation was based. He found himself left with a narcotic, a repressed guilt which constantly threatens the manifest voluntarism of the *Biographia*. This he articulated with sufficient clarity for a fellow addict (like De Quincey) to comprehend; he names his mysterious ailment as 'constitutional indolence, aggravated into languor by ill-health; ... procrastination ... mental cowardice ... which makes us anxious to think and converse on any thing rather than on what concerns ourselves' (*BL* I 45). Of course this passage, with characteristic irony, qualifies the content by the form of its argument; instead of talking about the exquisite health of men of genius, Coleridge talks only about himself and his own pathological compulsions, a clear instance of Robinson's 'diseased egotism'.

This is exactly what the *Confessions* sets out to expose in denying every tenet of chapter 2's argument. As valetudinarian and addict

Coleridge falls beneath every moral and critical standard which his work avows, showing himself the most 'irritable' of authors (in the technical sense of one suffering from a morbid nervous system), but also his prognosis of the cause of his malaise is shown to be at best mistaken, at worst hypocritical. Coleridge follows the medical theory of William Cullen in identifying opium as a narcotic, rather than a stimulant, as the Brunonian and De Quinceyan argument would have it. This means, paradoxically, that, while believing in free will, he accepts the deterministic Cullenite opinion on the unbreakable nature of addiction. Coleridge has no warrant for trying to kick the habit. On the other hand, De Quincey, following the Brunonian line which stressed irritability rather than voluntarism, an essentially materialistic and necessitarian epistemology, insisted with Brown that opium was not necessarily addictive and thus he *did* have a warrant to 'unwind the accursed chain'. Because this paradoxical relationship of the two addicts to their drug structures their relationship to each other, it is worth quoting in full a relevant passage from the 1856 *Confessions*.

I, boasting not at all of my self-conquests, and owning no moral argument against the free use of opium, nevertheless on mere *prudential* motives break through the vassalage more than once, and by efforts which I have recorded as modes of transcendent suffering. Coleridge, professing to believe (without reason assigned) that opium-eating is criminal, and...having, therefore, the strongest *moral* motive for abstaining from it – yet suffers himself to fall into a captivity to this same wicked opium, deadlier than was ever heard of...A slave he was to this potent drug not less abject than Caliban to Prospero – his detested and yet despotic master. Like Caliban, he frets his very heart-strings against the rivets of his chain. (*C* 144)

One of De Quincey's tasks in the *Confessions* is to show that the affliction which produces the guilt and egotism of the Coleridgean text is, if not a positive virtue, at least not a positive vice. De Quincey *rewrites* the *Biographia* in a pathological rather than a normative moral/aesthetic register, showing Genius, Imagination, Will and Principle to be conditioned by the complex nervous organization of civilization and all its discontents, in particular, the conditioning of what I call the 'preternatural stimulants' of opium on the body, or luxury and its systemic concomitant, imperialism, on the body politic, about which I will have more to say later in this chapter.

De Quincey's shift from exculpation to confession implies a transformation of what Foucault calls the 'regime of truth', a metamorphosis such as the latter finds written across the history of sexuality in the modern era, from 'the heroic or marvellous narrative of trials, of bravery or sainthood' to 'a literature ordered according to the infinite task of extracting from the depths of oneself, in between the words, a truth which the very form of confession holds out like a shimmering mirage'.[36] Confession presupposes an abandonment of the particular claim to discursive authority which towers over the ruinous surface of the *Biographia*, the Will or 'Productive Logos', exchanged now for an immanence in which the author addresses his public as 'the authority who requires the confession, prescribes and appreciates it, and intervenes in order to judge, punish, forgive, console and reconcile'.[37] Just as Hume and the Adam Smith of the *Theory of Moral Sentiments* had theorized civil society as a macrocosmic nervous system, a 'structure of interacting sensibilities binding together and controlling the whole' through sympathy,[38] the De Quinceyan politics of authorship were founded upon a legitimacy of *fact* opposed to a Coleridgean legitimacy of *principle*. De Quincey confessed to, and on behalf of, a public which sheltered in its hidden places a 'whole class of opium-eaters', a freemasonry which bound with secret links the addicts of High Society to their numerous fellows amongst the working classes of the great industrial cities like London and Manchester (*C* 31).

THE 'CONFESSIONS' AND THE 'BIOGRAPHIA LITERARIA'

Although the *Confessions* contains no sustained discussion of the *Biographia* (Coleridge's work is not even mentioned in the 1823 text), its structural fabric and thematic development are parasitic upon that book, from the sporadic biographical narrative of its early sections to the fragmented dream visions with which it concludes and which, we are told, are the rationale of the whole (*C* 126). De Quincey's parasitism bears out Crabb Robinson's judgement that 'he is too much a disciple and admirer to have anything of his own' although in the case of Coleridge the admiration is clearly inverted,[39] a fact which has bearing on the charges which he levelled against the *Biographia* for containing 'barefaced plagiarism' of Schelling in the 1834 *Tait's* article (*Recoll.* 40).[40] If De Quincey regarded discretion as the better part of valour in the *Confessions*, he was literally spoiling for a fight in the *Letters to a Young Man whose Education has been Neglected* published in the *London Magazine* two years later. Challenging

Coleridge to 'sally out of his hiding place into a philosophic passion and to attack me with the same freedom', he considered that

> Such an exhibition must be amusing to the public. I conceive that two transcendentalists, who are also two [opium-eaters], can hardly ever before have stripped in any ring... I wish he would leave transcendentalism to me and other young men; for, to say the truth, it does not prosper in his hands, *I* will take charge of the public principles in that point, and he will thus be more at leisure to give us another *Ancient Mariner*. (Mass. x 21–22)

The many parallels between the *Biographia* and the *Confessions* are of course in part attributable to what John Beer has described as De Quincey's 'slow reenactment of Coleridge's career',[41] his paradoxical 'plagiarism of the plagiarist', although at the narrative level these parallels are often deliberately crafted.

For example, De Quincey's account of his schooling at the hands of his 'Archididascalus' Charles Lawson, headmaster of Manchester Grammer School, alludes to Coleridge's description of James Bowyer, headmaster of Christ's Hospital (*C* 36–7; *BL* i 8–11). Both boys were accomplished Greek scholars and received their initiation into the pleasures of poetry at school, Coleridge through the sonnets of William Bowles, De Quincey through Wordsworth and Coleridge's *Lyrical Ballads*. Characteristic of the difference between the two texts, however, is their representation of authority. Coleridge found a liberating commonsense in Bowyer's authority (a kind of 'anti-authoritarian authority'), whereas De Quincey was depressed by the 'meagreness' of Lawson's understanding (*C* 36), and even more so by the master's neglect of his charges' health, an accusation considerably elaborated in the 1856 version. The abuse of De Quincey's delicate nervous system and the neglect of his guardians (his father having died in 1793 when Thomas was eight) caused him to run away from school and wander 'down and out' in Wales and London. This 'fatal error in my life' (*C* 163) which he in later years regarded as a sort of original sin or fall from grace resulted in permanent damage to his stomach from sixteen weeks of gnawing hunger, a complaint for which he later (in 1813) began taking heavy doses of laudanum, thus ending the pleasurable 'honeymoon' stage of experiencing the drug (*C* 35).

Coleridge had also traced the aetiology of his current 'mental disease' ('delving in the unwholesome quicksilver mines of meta-physic depths') to his comparable 'friendless wanderings on our *leave-*

days (for I was an orphan, and had scarcely any connections in London) (*BL* 1 16). If De Quincey mingled with 'peripatetics' of the street-walking variety like Ann of Oxford St during his friendless wanderings in London (*C* 50), Coleridge preferred the company of peripatetics in the Aristotelian sense of the word, so that he could 'direct ... [the conversation] to my favourite subject, Providence, fore-knowledge, will, and fate...' Indeed Coleridge's comment on this 'preposterous pursuit' (in chapter 11, as we shall see, he made it quite clear what he thought about philosophers on the streets) would seem more appropriate to De Quincey's starvation regime – or whatever else he was doing amongst the 'peripatetics' – than Coleridge's philosophical discussions 'injurious both to my natural powers, and to the progress of my education' (*BL* 1 16). Characteristically overdetermined judgements on intellectual affairs are pathologized in De Quincey's account into gastric, nervous and, possibly, venereal complaints. Whilst insisting upon the 'Platonic' nature of his relations with the street-walkers, there is a subliminal suggestion that De Quincey contracted venereal disease either during or shortly after this first sojourn in London (we know from a diary he kept at Everton the following year that he was regularly visiting prostitutes in 1803).[42]

The account of his 'slumming' in the East End of London related in the 'Pleasures of Opium' section of the *Confessions* appeared to be couched in the contemporary sexual slang which Derek Guiton and Norah Crook have discussed in their study of *Shelley's Venomed Melody*.[43] 'I came suddenly upon such knotty problems of alleys, such enigmatical entries, and such sphinx's riddles of streets without thoroughfares...' De Quincey admits that he 'paid a heavy price in distant years' for his midnight cruising (*C* 81) and that his wife Margaret became '*infected* with the spectacle of my dread contest with phantoms and shadowy enemies' (*C* 59). This may of course refer only to the opium addiction which was also an indirect result of his youthful excursions into the East End (a figure from the Far East which would assume a more threatening aspect as a source of addiction and infection in his later writings). None the less, his pun on the 'antimercurial' quality of opium in *Confessions*, p. 72 suggests an allusion to its contemporary indication either as a counter to the iatrogenic illness caused by a regime of mercury pills, the principal contemporary cure for the 'lues venerea', or as a cure for venereal disease itself.[44]

The main point of the autobiographical account of his earlier years, as De Quincey made clear, was to demonstrate how London and Ann of Oxford St provided the 'image repertoire' for his later opium dreams, as well as to demonstrate the grim 'organic' continuity of a life held together by the parasitic narratives of drug addiction and possibly syphilis in its developing stages. De Quincey organicism is far removed from the principle of high Romantic autobiography, the Wordsworth assertion that 'the child is father of the man'. It is appropriate that he described the unifying principle of *his* life in part two of the *Confessions* with the Coleridgean image of the Upas tree, the 'noxious umbrage' 'overshadow[ing] and darken[ing] my latter years, connected organically with the experiences of the young pariah, years that were far asunder were bound together by subtle links of suffering derived from a common root' (*C* 67).

AUTOBIOGRAPHY AS EXCULPATION

A central issue in the literary representation of the self must be the philosophical question of personal identity. The *Biographia Literaria* tells the story of how its author's encounter with Wordsworth, both man and work, has returned him to a sense of spiritual health and organic identity anchored in the transcendental agencies of Imagination and Will. At least, Wordsworth serves, after his critical redefinition in the book's second volume (and like the promised *magnum opus* on the 'Productive Logic'), as a guarantor of a healthy organicism at which the valetudinarian author can only gesture. If Coleridge describes himself as having been 'newly couched' by Wordsworth (*BL* I 40), then De Quincey's first encounter with the poet 'was marked by a change even in the physical condition of my nervous system' (*Recoll.* p. 207). The curious neurotic malaise from which the young De Quincey suffered was for a time attenuated by the natural stimulus of Wordsworth's genius (in part a product, as we saw above, of his exquisite health), although he would later discover the poet's '*einseitigkeit*, or one-sidedness' (*Recoll.* p. 381). Disenchantment with Wordsworth would soon drive him back into the arms of the preternatural stimulus of opium and the darker organic ligatures of addiction.

In a passage of the *Confessions* which indirectly reflects on the autobiographical manner of Coleridge and Wordsworth (whose manuscript draft of *The Prelude* he had been one of the few men of his generation fortunate enough to read), De Quincey described his visit to a Jewish money-lender named Dell in London – during his sixteen weeks of 'gnawing hunger' – in quest of credit to support himself and repay his debt to Ann the prostitute who had sacrificed her last savings to preserve him from starvation. Because of his renegade status, he needed to prove that he was Thomas De Quincey, beneficiary of his deceased father's will; he also needed a possible escape clause, in case Dell attempted to alert his guardians of his whereabouts. He was suspected initially of counterfeiting his own identity in order to gain credit; 'It was strange to me to find my own self, *materialiter* considered ... accused ... of counterfeiting my own self, *formaliter* considered' (*C* 55).

The equivocation was solved, and De Quincey's personal identity guaranteed, by his aristocratic connections, Lord Altamont and his father the Marquis of Sligo. Dell promised him credit if he went to Eton to get a signed testimony from Altamont, whom the Jew hoped might prove a lucrative business connection. Arriving at Eton to find Altamont gone, the starving De Quincey managed to get a letter from his cousin Lord Desart; he returned to London but found that not only did Dell refuse Desart's terms, leaving him penniless, but that he had lost Ann, whose patronymic he had forgotten to note. This episode, replete with anxiety concerning the instability of personal identity linked to a failure to repay a debt which may have caused the death of an innocent young woman, is vintage De Quincey. The loss of Ann in 'the mighty labyrinths of London' is described as the 'heaviest affliction' of his life (*C* 64); mapped onto the death of his sister Elizabeth and of the young Kate Wordsworth, it is fashioned and refashioned into the nightmare visions of his later opium dreams, described in the *Confessions* as well as *The English Mail Coach* and *Suspiria de Profundis*. Ann, whom De Quincey loved 'as affectionately as if she had been my sister', had been 'the saviour of my life' (*C* 57). De Quincey the pariah fails Ann just as he will tell us, in the *Autobiographical Sketches*, that he blamed himself for the death of his real sister Elizabeth, a death which both Hillis Miller in *The Disappearance of God* and John Barrell in *The Infection of Thomas De Quincey* read as being fundamental to his subsequent belief system or psychopathology.

Reminiscent of De Quincey's problem of identity with the money-lender is Coleridge's account in chapter 4 of the *Biographia* of the logical solecism called a 'bull'. Discussing the problem of equivocation concerning the meaning of the personal pronouns 'I' and 'me', Coleridge warns of the danger of confusing the *ego contemplans*, the *act* of self-consciousness constitutive of personal identity (corresponding to De Quincey's 'self, *materialiter* considered') with the *ego contemplatus*, 'the visual image or object by which the mind represents to itself its past condition, or rather, its personal identity under the form in which it imagined itself previously to have existed' (De Quincey's 'self, *formaliter* considered') (*BL* I 72). The importance of autobiography for both Wordsworth and Coleridge – particularly the latter – was largely 'exculpatory' in so far as it sought, by demonstrating a consistency of principle between present and past selves (very far from being a 'given' in the contemporary ideological climate), to gain the *credit* of personal identity.

Ideally considered, as exemplified by Wordsworth at full poetic strength, this entailed the nourishment of a tranquil and composed present self by the 'vivifying virtue' of the past, like *The Prelude*'s 'spots of time' where 'feeling comes in aid / Of feeling...if but once we have been strong'.[45] Coleridge, less happy with objects or histories ('I may not hope from outward forms to win / The passion and the life, whose fountains are within'[46]) based his 'Dynamic Philosophy' on the linchpin of the *ego contemplans* or *act* of self-consciousness. 'The self-conscious spirit...is a will; and freedom must be assumed as a *ground* of philosophy, and can never be deduced from it' (*BL* I 280). In reviewing his past lives in the *Biographia* Coleridge sought to confound the associationist psychology of Hartley and others by theorizing consciousness as an act of *will* rather than the aggregate of sense data and memory. In a related discussion, he subordinated the aesthetics of Fancy ('a mode of Memory emancipated from time and space') to Imagination, a power 'first put in action by the will and understanding, [which]...reveals itself in the balance or reconciliation of opposite or discordant qualities' (*BL* I 305; II 16).

In the midst of his long critique of associationism in chapters 5–8, Coleridge considered an episode which demonstrated the imperishable nature of 'the reliques of sensation...in the very same order in which they were originally impressed' upon the mind. Commenting on his chapter 6 anecdote of the polyglot German maid, he argued that past impressions could only be fully recovered in their original order by madness (the maid was afflicted by 'nervous fever') or divine inspiration; the '*body celestial* instead of the *body terrestrial*' would 'bring before every human soul the collective experience of its whole past existence. And yet this, this, perchance, is the dread book of judgement, in whose mysterious hieroglyphics every idle word is recorded!' (*BL* 1 114). Whilst Coleridge rather forcedly relegated the return of the past to a form of preternatural consciousness, policed, as it were, by the free will and 'absolute self', De Quincey played upon the involuntary memory, an opium-induced 'body celestial' (reminiscent of Baudelaire's 'homme-dieu'), as the paramount law of mind. In the *Confessions* he alluded to Coleridge's passage in discussing 'the dread book of account, which the Scriptures speak of, is, in fact, the mind itself of each individual ... there is no such thing as *forgetting* possible to the mind' (*C* 104).

I will have more to say about the De Quinceyan dreaming faculty in relation to Coleridgean imagination later; it will be sufficient to note here De Quincey's development of the *Confessions'* 'dread book of account' in the 'Palimpsest of the Mind' section of *Suspiria de Profundis*. De Quincey is troubled by the 'grotesque collisions of ... successive themes' threatening 'the grandeur of human unity', as he is disturbed by a 'horrid alien nature' repeating, doubling and multiplying the self in *The English Mail Coach* (Mass. XIII 347; 292). In the *Confessions'* 'dark interpretation' of Coleridge's proclaimed 'absolute self', the autobiographical will, the *ego contemplans* is rewritten as a structure of dependence which interprets the Coleridgean myth of origins as a recurrent narrative of suffering, loss and addiction. De Quincey's past is irredeemable; the scene which returns to haunt him tells of a past in which the self is *already* revealed as a counterfeit, both of itself and of the sense impressions ineradicably inscribed upon it, 'those profound revelations which had been ploughed so deeply into the heart, from those *encaustic* records which in the mighty furnaces of London life had been burnt into the undying memory by the fierce action of misery' (*C* 205). Because the *Confessions* presents itself as a case history rather than an 'exculpation', it is dedicated to represent rather than efface the traces of the past, which in the *Biographia* are subject to the selective 'task of retrospection and revaluation' of the Coleridgean imagination. De Quincey accordingly substitutes irritability for will; 'Not in the energies of the will, but in the qualities of the nervous organization, lies the dread arbitration of – Fall or Stand' (*C* 129).

If opium stands in relation to the De Quinceyan self as a simulacrum, a substitute for personal identity, like the dark projection which hovers on the right of Symons the murderer as he rushes on his hellish career in the 'Dark Interpreter' essay in *Suspiria de Profundis*,[47] the *Confessions* exposes the fraud of the *Biographia*'s ontology by revealing Coleridge as De Quincey's opium-eating double.[48] Like Dell, the money-lender, De Quincey suspects his subject of 'counterfeiting' his former self in order to gain credit; Coleridge has sought to transform the dark penumbra of addition and his shadowy political past into a halo of imagination, representing his life as a consistent and organic unity by an act of interpretative will. De Quincey might have given, as one counterfeit amongst many, the example of the *Biographia*'s chapter 23. Coleridge republished his 1816 criticism of German 'Jacobinical' drama and Maturin's play *Bertram* in that chapter immediately after the very similar polemic in 'Satyrane's letters', purportedly written from Germany in 1798. The juxtaposition is intended to show 'in proof, that I have been ... falsely charged with any fickleness in my principles of taste' (*BL* II 208). His consistency in aesthetic matters is analogous to the political consistency which Coleridge claims to have demonstrated to the public in the 1818 *Friend*, where he had inserted 'extracts from the Conciones ad Populum, printed ... in the year 1795, in the very heat and height of my anti-ministerial enthusiasm: these in proof that my principles of *politics* have sustained no change' (*BL* II 208).

In reality, however, as any one as close to Coleridge and his circle as De Quincey had been might have known, the attack on German drama, with the appended critical dialogue, composing Satyrane's letters (and thus 'officially' dated 1798), were in fact 'written afterwards, possibly for the 1808 lectures or for *The Friend* (1809) no. 16'.[49] Coleridge is disingenuously passing off opinions of 1808 for those of a decade earlier in an attempt to 'exculpate' himself from charges of apostasy. Not only that, he refers in the same passage to his republication of the 'Conciones' in *The Friend* as a further alibi. A closer examination of this republication reveals that he had been forced to omit approximately 250 lines of the original 1795 text on account of their unpalatable radicalism.[50] The philosophical question of personal identity here becomes identified with the ideological issue of apostasy, problematizing Coleridge's claims to organic integrity. From the viewpoint of the 'Dark Interpreter', Coleridge's claims for credit, founded upon the postulate of free will, come to look like a freedom wilfully to falsify the truth of the past self, the ineradicable

('encaustic') traces of which De Quincey reads clearly inscribed
upon the body of his Coleridgean double.

STATELY HOMES, TEMPLES AND BANKS

In De Quincey's exemplary encounter with the Jew Dell, the proof of
personal identity (the patronymic) is only supplementary to the
aristocratic connections which underwrite his claims to credit.
Coleridge's equivalent of De Quincey's surety Lord Altamont was
Lord Liverpool, Tory Prime Minister, to whom in 1817 he sent a
copy of the *Biographia* with a long and metaphysical covering letter.
Although, as I have discussed elsewhere, Coleridge's intervention
coincided with a legitimation crisis for the British establishment, he
nevertheless based his statement of principles upon the authority
symbolized by Liverpool and 'the good sense of the English people,
and of that loyalty which is limited to the very heart of the nation by
the system of credit and the interdependence of property' (*BL* I 213).
Although the system of credit backed by landed property might seem
consistent with the Tory principles which De Quincey had pro-
pounded as editor of the *Westmoreland Gazette* in 1818–19 (and indeed
with many of his subsequent political pronouncements), we should
not be too hasty in taking De Quincey at his word when he described
himself, in 1847, as 'a specimen of the fossil Tory' (Mass. XI 404). The
Confessions first appeared in the radical *London Magazine* in a deliberate
snub to the Tory *Blackwood's* (with whose editor he had had a series
of altercations), at a time when the memory of his dismissal from the
Westmoreland Gazette by the paper's proprietors, acting upon the
wishes of Wordsworth's patron the Tory MP Lord Lowther, was
fresh in his mind.[51]

In the money-lending incident, De Quincey actually *failed* to get
credit on the strength of his aristocratic connections, despite the
generosity of Lord Desart, Altamont's surrogate. The failure is
metonymically linked to the loss of Ann, devoid of a patronymic,
swamped by the myriad of faces composing the London crowd, and
De Quincey's own fears of being submerged in the ocean of
undifferentiated humanity. But De Quincey takes the opportunity of
his failed credit to criticize the elevated station of society; he is proud
to be the 'son of a plain English merchant' and judges 'a station
which raises a man too eminently above the level of his fellow-

creatures [as]...not the most favourable to moral, or to intellectual qualities' (C 61–2). Whilst believing, in conventionally Burkean terms, that the aristocratic 'British constitution may be properly called a work of nature' protecting national institutions, in neo-Harringtonian fashion, from 'the madness of the population', it is clear from De Quincey's article 'On the Approaching Revolution in Great Britain' written on the eve of the Reform Bill that he considered the ancient equilibrium of forces to have been ruined by the spirit of Jacobinism, 'the spirit of plebeian envy'... 'low-minded jealousy against the aristocracy'.[52]

In one of his *Westmoreland Gazette* editorials, De Quincey was critical of conservatism of the Coleridgean type based upon *principle* which subordinated national feeling and opinion to a transcendental authority. 'Principles in themselves are inert,' he wrote 'but national feeling is the power by which only a people can be predisposed to bad principles, or by which good ones can be made operative.'[53] De Quincey viewed the body politic as an organism in the sense of a complex nervous system, governed by mutual sympathies rather than by a sovereign will. Drawing upon the eighteenth-century Scottish account of civil society as a nexus of commercial interests in which according to Smith 'all things find their level', rather than the neo-Harringtonian civic humanist discourse underpinning the political thought of Wordsworth and Coleridge, he regarded national 'feelings and sentiments' as creating an autonomous system of credit (in the etymological sense of mutual confidence) at once 'causative, diffusive, contagious and vital'.[54]

De Quincey's writings are full of panegyrics to the organic power of capitalism, a network of communications across the nation forged by technological advance, first of the mail coach system, then by telegraphs and railways. *Travelling in England in the Old Days* (1834) and 'The Glory of Motion' in *The English Mail Coach* (1849) hymn the pleasures (as well as the pains, developed in the 'anarchies' of his dreams) of the age of capital. The former essay envisaged the expansion of the 'system of intercourse' in early Victorian England in terms of an organicism more often associated by Romantic thinkers with a pre-capitalist age; 'then first will be seen a political system truly *organic* – i.e., in which each acts upon all, and all react upon each' (Mass. 1 271).

One of his most revealing reveries on the birth of capitalism occurred in the unlikely setting of an 1842 *Blackwood's* article on 'The

Pagan Oracles'. De Quincey described how the temples of ancient Greece, built with the strength of fortresses, involuntarily provided the conditions for the birth of a money economy. The temples, built in a subsistance economy in which it was considered 'that if any man drew a profit, a something *extra*, from the employment of his money, that profit must take its rise in some unlawful source' (Mass. VII 90), were gradually transformed into strongboxes for money, although this was a role strictly supplementary to their civic and religious functions (VII 92). Eventually the temples were metamorphosed into banks, supporting the organic links of society mentioned above 'bring[ing] scattered interests into communication, and remote interests into contact' (VII 92). In modern terms the temples clearly have their analogue in the civic role of the landed aristocracy and the Erastian national church, institutions which De Quincey believed had served as seedbeds for the germination of capitalism, but which, he hints, might have served their historical purpose. We can fit this model of supersession into the general terms of De Quincey's discourse of the nervous system and of cultural politics; the 'natural' 'healthful' authority of the constitution and aristocracy is in the course of replacement by the 'preternatural' organism of capital in which an initially parasitic growth becomes independent of its host and reproduces itself in an autonomous way, 'money, to the confusion of the incredulous ... is found to produce money' (I 92).

According to the De Quinceyan prediction, Coleridge would have driven the brokers out of the temple, on the grounds that such economic libertarianism acted upon the nation's well-being more as a narcotic than as a stimulus. It comes as no surprise, then, to discover that the most visible point of difference between De Quincey and the older 'Lake Poets' lies in their treatment of political economy, the radical 'new science' which had emerged from the Scottish Enlightenment in the middle of the previous century. In the *Confessions* De Quincey described the moment in 1818, in the midst of one of his most chronic periods of addiction, when Wilson sent him a copy of Ricardo's *Principles of Political Economy and Taxation* (1817) to review for *Blackwood's* (C 100). The book aroused his admiration by reducing the 'unwieldy chaos' of economic facts and figures 'into a science of regular proportions, now first standing on an eternal basis'.

Coleridge, whom De Quincey considered (along with Wordsworth and Southey) 'ignorant of every principle belonging to every question alike in political economy ... obstinately bent on learning nothing'

(*Recoll.* 242), believed just the reverse. 'Political economy...can never be a pure science', he was recorded as saying; 'an abstract conclusion in a matter of political economy...is not a truth, but a chimera – a practical falsehood'.[55] In a *Tait's* article of 1839, De Quincey demolished Coleridge's theory of taxation and his ethical qualms about the legitimacy of a credit economy; he considered his remarks in *Table Talk* to be at least two hundred years out of date (*Recoll.* 242). The 'dismal science' provided the opium-eater with the perfect intellectual pursuit, incapacitated as he was by the 'pains of opium'; his sustained study of Ricardo was the equivalent of Coleridge's study of Kant when in the grips of chronic addiction, an analogy highlighted by the 'Kantian' title of De Quincey's projected work on the subject *A Prolegomena to all future Systems of Political Economy*. 'Though it is eminently an organic science (no part, that is to say, but what acts in the whole, as the whole again reacts on each part),' he wrote in the *Confessions*, 'yet the several parts may be detached and contemplated singly' (*C* 99–100).

MERELY A MAN OF LETTERS?

De Quincey picked up this same point two years later in the *Letters to a Young Man whose Education has been Neglected* in the context of a sustained criticism of Coleridge, this time particularly his exhortation in chapter 11 of the *Biographia* to 'be not *merely* a man of letters!' (*BL* I 229). Whilst respecting the reasons for Coleridge's advice that literature should be pursued as a supplement to an ecclesiastical, pedagogic, medical or legal profession, he again opposed the 'legitimacy of fact' to Coleridgean idealism; Coleridge, like him, *is* merely a man of letters, just as Coleridge, like him, is an opium-eater. De Quincey argued for literature as a trade: not, like Coleridge, as an aspect of the pastoral work of the Clerisy or National Church, or a fireside leisure activity for professional men.

Characteristically, De Quincey met Coleridge's argument not by direct refutation, but by a *diagnosis* of the pathology which he believed impelled it. Because Coleridge is 'a voluptuary in his studies; sparing himself all toil, and thinking, apparently, to evade the necessity of artificial power by an extraordinary exertion of his own native power' (Mass. X 17), he can only think in generalities, lacking the analytical discipline of considering particularities, such as was provided by the study of political economy. Coleridge's plan of study is 'dependent...on the incidents of individual will, or the caprices of momentary feeling springing out of temper or bodily health' (Mass. x 13–14), a deficiency which has led him to that characteristic misanthropy which De Quincey complacently compared to his own 'great overbalance of happiness' (x 16). Little wonder that Coleridge yearned for a profession, such as the church, in which 'he may cherish a rational hope of being able to unite the widest scheme of literary utility with the strictest performance of professional duties' (*BL* 1 226). Coleridge's plan of study is a product of the particular pathology which De Quincey diagnosed in his essay *Coleridge and Opium-Eating*, '[Opium] defeats the *steady* habit of exertion; but it creates spasms of irregular exertion. It ruins the natural power of life; but it develops preternatural paroxysms of intermitting power' (*C* 128).

The spasmodic effect of opium on the psyche is analogous to the effect of the critical boom-and-recession cycles of capitalism upon the nation, the nature of which Coleridge had himself analysed in the second *Lay Sermon* of April 1817. De Quincey found in the 'organic' discourse of political economy the solution to both the 'preternatural' agencies of opium and the caprices of the market, just as we will discover him, in a chiasmic reversal of this resolution, proposing opium as a solution to Britain's balance of trade with the Far East, itself a problem of political economy. What he praised as the 'detachable' nature of Ricardian economics had supported De Quincey during the terrible lulls in the 'preternatural paroxysms' of opium, 'perpetual influxes of pleasure, from the constant sense of success and difficulty overcome' (Mass. x 17). This was the basis for De Quincey's account of the *complementarity* of the literature of knowledge and the literature of power, first outlined in the same essay, *Letters to a Young Man*, a point which is often missed by commentators on this most famous De Quinceyan critical distinction. Thus Robert Maniquis is correct in describing De Quincey as a 'bourgeois pariah';[56] like the hero/villain of Marx's *Communist Manifesto*, melting all that is solid into air, profaning all that is holy, the opium-eater eschewed the aristocratic or professional norms which underpin the cultural politics of Wordsworth and Coleridge, replacing the 'sovereign principle' of Romantic conservatism with a commercial vision of civil society and free-trade imperialism. This is (disturbingly) inflected in the metaphor of a diseased nervous system in the grip of dependence on the 'preternatural stimulus' of opium.

At the conclusion of chapter 11, Coleridge cited Herder as an exemplar of his doctrine of a 'clerisy', 'combining literary utility with ... professional duties'; the celebrated German writer worked as a schoolmaster and assistant pastor in a church at Riga. Coleridge quoted a passage from Herder's *Letters on Theological Studies* (1790) attacking literary professionalism in which the dissemination of letters is equated with a masturbatory 'spending'; 'certain secretions, as with certain thoughts, ... must be taken up again into the circulation, and be again and again re-secreted in order to ensure a healthful vigour' (*BL* 1 231). This critique of literary 'spending' echoes eighteenth-century attacks on imperialism and luxury as a squandering of national resources, and unsurprisingly the agrarian civic humanist Coleridge showed little enthusiasm for the economic 'solution' represented by imperialism.

As was mentioned above, De Quincey's diagnosis of Herder differs from that of Coleridge's here in its portrayal of the German writer as a victim of nervous torpor resulting from the drudgery of his professional duties, and prescribing a Brunonian opium stimulant to awaken him from his somnambulistic state. Although De Quincey half-heartedly embarked upon a professional career as a lawyer, professional men, particularly those pursuing a 'supplementary' life of letters, do not fare well in his writings. This is evident from the portraits, in the *Confessions*, of the schoolteachers Edward Spencer and Charles Lawson, and the shady attorney Brunell to whom the young De Quincey was referred by Dell the money-lender in his search for credit. Despite Brunell's seedy existence, De Quincey described him, in the 1856 version, as possessing 'the deepest, the most liberal, and unaffected love of knowledge, but, above all, of that specific knowledge which we call literature' (*C* 198). Brunell had been forced to interrupt his studies by his father's death, and the only benefits he had reaped from a profession in 'the lower branches of law' were 'daily temptations ... surrounding him with opportunities for taking advantages not strictly honourable' (*C* 198). Just as the failure of De Quincey's aristocratic surety was metonymically linked to the loss of Ann, so the failure of his professional surety, the cold and hunger of the attorney's house at 38 Greek Street, Soho, is linked to the loss of his young neglected female companion (Brunell's maid or illegitimate daughter) with whom he slept under a bundle of rags. The whole episode can be read as a severe satire on Coleridge's exhortation to men of letters to pursue a professional career, on the grounds that 'the *necessity* of acquiring [money and immediate reputation] will in all works of genius convert the stimulus into a *narcotic*' (*BL* I 224). Whatever hardships it might entail, the opium-eater was vocal in praise of literature as a trade, to him a stimulant rather than just a compulsive narcotic.

SATURDAY NIGHT FEVER

One of the most problematic areas of the opium-eater's social discourse is his adoption of what we might call, adapting Arthur Lovejoy's term, Wordsworth's 'uniformitarianism' in his representation of the London working class. The notion of 'uniformitarianism' is problematized by David Simpson's demonstration of an unresolved tension between Wordsworth's identification with the Spartan values and linguistic economy of the Lakeland farmers and a simultaneous displacement from that community. If *identification* supports the critical rhetoric of a poem like *Gypsies*, then *displacement*, the fear of being 'merely a man of letters', generates the sublimatory figure of the leech-gatherer in *Resolution and Independence*.[57] If Wordsworth resolved his anxieties by an identification at the scene of production, De Quincey as bourgeois pariah and pioneer of 'slumming' (that favourite occupation of Victorian bohemia), identified with the urban working class at the scene of consumption. De Quincey overrode the Wordsworthian fear of the productive insubstantiality of men of letters ('What then was Saturday night to me more than any other night? I had no labours that I rested from; no wages to receive', *C* 80) by sympathizing with the pleasures and the luxuries, rather than the labours and the hardships, of the poor.

De Quincey describes how 'I used often, on Saturday nights, after I had taken opium, to wander forth...to all the markets, and other parts of London to which the poor resort on a Saturday night, for laying out their wages' (*C* 80). Again opium provided him with a solution of social discontinuity; as an opium-eater he is at one with the poor on Saturday night, *no longer* poor and overworked, but 'rich' and at leisure, with 'some luxury of repose' to enjoy. Hence De Quincey's London is a very different place from that of Mayhew or Dickens or Booth, or indeed of Frederick Engels' joyless 'world of atoms' in *The Condition of the Working Class in England*.[58] It is an urban, laudanum-soaked version of the pastoralism of William Paley's *Reasons for Contentment addressed to the Labouring Part of the British Public*

202 'Murdering one's double': De Quincey and Coleridge

(1792), levelling all the grievances and divisions of the scene of production into a uniformitarianism of consumption. In his 1831 article on Samuel Parr, De Quincey objected to Paley and his mother's evangelical friend Hannah More 'sitting in luxurious saloons... lecturing their poor, hard-working fellow countrymen upon the enormity of the blessing which they enjoy' (Mass. v 121). But De Quincey takes the same message into the saloons (or saloon bars) of the poor, where they indulge 'the luxury of repose'; more significantly, he addresses his reasons for contentment not to the poor but to the anxious bourgeoisie, who may be relieved that, echoing Wordsworth's *Preface to Lyrical Ballads*, 'the poor are far more *philosophic* than the rich':

Sometimes there might be heard murmurs of discontent: but far oftener expressions on the countenance, or uttered in words, of patience, hope, and tranquillity. And, taken generally, I must say, that, the poor are far more *philosophic* than the rich – that they show a more ready and cheerful submission to what they consider as irremediable evils, or irreparable loss. (*C* 80–1)

De Quincey's echo of Wordsworth's ('a more permanent, and a far more philosophical language, than that which is frequently sub-stituted for it by Poets'[59]) almost parodically transforms the poet's exemplar of a rustic language and subsistence economy based on habits of independence, industry, sobriety and a Spartan rejection of luxury. Again the difference between 'natural' and 'preternatural' stimuli is evident in the distinction between Wordsworth/Coleridge and De Quincey; the latter's narcosis against what John Beer has described as the Wordsworthian 'element of strenuousness... always deliberately undrugged'.[60] At the same time De Quincey undoubt-edly endorsed the (albeit transformed) uniformitarianism of Words-worth's *Preface* against the objections made by Coleridge in the second volume of the *Biographia*; he regarded the former as 'the most finished and masterly specimen of reasoning which has in any age or nation been called forth by any one of the fine arts', and thought that the *Biographia* had 'fail[ed] altogether of overthrowing Mr Words-worth's theory'.[61]

De Quincey might have thought with Wordsworth (and against Coleridge) that the poor were more philosophic than poets or professional philosophers for some of the reasons we looked at in the last section, but only on terms very different from those of

Wordsworth's and limited to the exceptional (and shared) conditions of 'Saturday night fever'. In order to understand the motives for the *Confessions'* bizarre uniformitarianism, it is necessary to understand what De Quincey thought about the poor at any other time than Saturday night. Writing to William Blackwood in 1842, he described how he 'look[ed] upon the working poor, Scottish or English, as latent Jacobins – *biding their* time'.[62] In 1819 he had no doubts about his opinion of the Peterloo Massacre '[The Magistrates]...have discharged their duty under trying circumstances in a way satisfactory to the country.'[63] By 1831 he was convinced of the 'approaching revolution in Great Britain' because the lower orders were motivated by a fundamental spirit of revenge, 'plebeian envy in every society arms a certain body of low-minded jealousy against the aristocracy'.[64] De Quincey's journalism of the 1830s through to the 50s is replete with scathing attacks on the Radical party and the global conspiracy of 'Communists and Red Republicans'.[65]

And yet De Quincey's manifest class hatred, like the race hatred to be discussed below, is more complicated, and more disturbing than it first seems, on account of his seemingly perverse identification with the victims. De Quincey's liasions with working-class prostitutes and his marriage to Margaret Simpson, with her 'Jacobinical' small-farming family, were the biographical equivalents of his literary obsession with revenge, the paradigmatic structure of feeling amongst the poor. This is particularly manifest in his fiction; from the 1827 and 1828 stories *The Peasant of Portugal* and *The Cacador*, through the Gothic novel *Klosterheim* (1832) to *The Avenger* (1838), revenge is a major, and, I suggest (against Grevel Lindop), far more than 'an essentially private concern' in his narratives.[66] In the *Confessions*, the 'original sin' of running away from school was in part vengeance against Lawson and his indifferent guardians, 'punished' by his sixteen weeks of 'gnawing hunger' and the consequent 'pains of opium'. In 1856 the cause of this *jacquerie* was described as 'lurk[ing] in what Wordsworth, when describing the festal state of France during the happy morning-tide of her First Revolution (1788–1790), calls the senselessness of joy' (*C* 1856 65). Indeed in a passage from the autobiographical *Introduction to the World of Strife*, which balances, without necessarily contradicting, the passage quoted above about the philosophical nature of the poor, De Quincey represented Jacobinism as a natural impulse which, if not repressed, invited its own chastisement. Writing of his first childhood experience of class conflict, he described the factory boys who ambushed his brother William and himself on the Oxford Road bridge. Although ostensibly loyalists and anti-Jacobins (the episode occurs during the first war with revolutionary France), the boys manifested 'a personal Jacobinism of that sort which is native to the heart of man, who is by natural impulse (and not without a root of nobility, though also of base envy) impatient of inequality, and submits to it only through a sense of its necessity, or under a long experience of its benefits' (Mass. 1 70). What is remarkable about the Saturday night passage in the *Confessions* is that this natural Jacobinism is completely put out of sight along with the 'yoke of labour'. Or rather put out of mind, by 'philosophic' habits induced by cheap gin, porter and laudanum, the latter 'cheaper than beer or gin, cheap enough for even the lowest paid worker', and which claimed a massive number of addicts in all the industrial cities of early nineteenth-century England, as well as rural Yorkshire, Cambridgeshire and Lincolnshire.[67] Berridge quotes Samuel Flood, a surgeon in Leeds in the 1840s, describing how Saturday night purchases of laudanum pills and drops were as common as the buying of meat and vegetables; 'in the public market place...are to be seen...one stall for vegetables, another for meats, and a third for pills!'.[68] If De Quincey went slumming in order to promote the philosophical benefits of opium, and to feel himself at one with the humblest fellow addicts, he also performed the role of what Marx called 'a sycophant of capital',[69] a political economist. Indeed the two roles were really complementary:

If wages were a little higher, or expected to be so, or the quartern loaf a little lower, or it was reported that onions and butter were expected to fall, I was glad: yet, if the contrary were true, I drew from opium some means of consoling myself. For opium (like the bee, that extracts its materials indiscriminately from roses and from the soot of chimneys) can overrule all feelings into a compliance with the master key. (*C* 81)

Just as opium offers a preternatural restoration of 'exquisite order, legislation and harmony' to the taut, irritable and self-absorbed nervous system, it expands 'the heart and the benevolent affections' of man as a social being, remedying the deleterious effects of class fragmentation and the division of labour. It should be pointed out, however, that De Quincey's approval of an intoxicated working class was perhaps as uncharacteristic of the 1820s as his subscription to the articles of the unfashionable Brunonian system of medicine. This is

evident if we consider the foundation in 1831 of the British and
Foreign Temperance Society and a plethora of alarmist reports such
as the one cited by Berridge; 'the Westminster Medical Society was
told in 1840 that "the consumption of opium was increasing among
the working-classes to a frightful extent"'. Neither was the action of
opium upon them perceived to be a sedative one, for it 'affected all
that was good and virtuous in women, it acted as an aphrodisiac, and
subverted all morality'. It is interesting that it was *Blackwood's
Magazine*, with its De Quinceyan connections, which took a more
lenient view of the working-class 'stimulant' use of opium. It
enquired, in 1830, whether 'when eighteen hours toil out of the four
and twenty have bowed down body and soul to the dust, a few drops
of laudanum may not be, in the best terms, a blessing?'[70]

Bondage to opium, 'prostration before the dark idol' (Mass. XIII
337) serves as a paradigm of that fetishization of the commodity
which converts alienation and expropriation into the vicarious
happiness of unquenchable desire. At the heart of De Quincey's
'Saturday night fever' is the spectre of a working class undrugged,
obeying the voice of a *natural*, and, he is forced to concede, *noble*
resistance to inequality. He might have imagined what Coleridgean
Will and Principle would have meant to an unintoxicated proletariat; civic virtue to such a class could mean *only* systematic
Jacobinism. Hence his need to reassure the bourgeois reader (who
might have surmised such a possibility) that public men like
Coleridge are in reality closet hedonists and opium-eaters. De
Quincey observed with satisfaction in 1827 that Coleridge was 'too
fat to be a person of active virtue' although he was 'undoubtedly a
worthy Christian' (Mass. XIII 14). Fortunately happiness, like literature, is now a trade, a commodity, rather than a moral programme;
'happiness might now be bought for a penny, and carried in the
waistcoat pocket: portable ecstasies might be had corked up in a pint
bottle; and peace of mind could be sent down in gallons by the mail
coach' (*C* 72). In a pre-emptive inversion of the Coleridgean idea of
a National Church with its East End settlements and its Christian
Socialism, De Quincey urged that opium be the religion of the
people. As the most effective, even Utilitarian, reification of
consciousness, opium was the true hero of De Quincey's social vision,
just as it was the organizing principle of his own life, both as written
and lived. The moral vision of the opium-eater's social eudaemonism
is almost as dismal as that of Malthus' 'principle of population', but

at least its author cannot be accused of double standards like Malthus, Paley or Hannah More. The uniformitarianism of luxury, of addiction, is a great leveller.

A VISION OF LIVERPOOL

It should be by now evident that the agency of opium in the *Confessions* is a material simulacrum of the agency of imagination in Coleridge's *Biographia*, controlled by hedonism rather than Christian asceticism. The narrative effect of opium is rather different from the selecting, unifying and harmonizing agency of imagination, however, in its working upon the 'encaustic' records of the mind. Opium produces an 'elaborate intellectual pleasure' of the signifier; like Marx's commodity, that 'crystal of social substance' whose 'mysterious' quality is a function of the fact that in it 'the social character of men's labour appears to them as an objective character stamped upon the product of that labour', opium has both aesthetic and anaesthetic qualities.[71] The moral anaesthesia of the *Confessions* is what saves it from the 'diseased egotism' of the *Biographia*; its narrative voice is not in pain as it describes the suffering of its subject, and its 'impassioned prose' is more concerned to draw attention to its brilliant linguistic surface, 'the florid or *Corinthian* order of rhetoric' (*Mass.* x 106). The 'elaborate intellectual pleasure' of opium disguises the misery which is all too visible even on Saturday nights in the East End, and the fellowship of consumption with fellow addicts stultifies the claims of a bourgeois social conscience. Because the opium-eater, like the bee, derives aesthetic nourishment from high and low, opera and slop shop alike, all he needs is his five shilling fix and the pain of the world or the self may still be seen, but cannot be *felt*. Experience is aestheticized, becomes an elaborate musical form,

a chorus [at the opera]... of elaborate harmony, displayed before me, as in a piece of arras work, the whole of my past life – not as if recalled by an act of memory, but as if present and incarnated in the music; no longer painful to dwell upon; but the detail of its incidents removed, or blended in some hazy abstraction; and its passions exalted, spiritualized and sublimed. All this was to be had for five shillings. (*C* 79)

De Quincey's raid on the moral 'disinterestedness' of Romantic aestheticism in the final sentence here is further developed in his 1827 satire on Kant's *Critique of Judgement*, the paper entitled *On Murder Considered as a Fine Art*, a work which appears to have grown out of *Confessions of an English Opium Eater* via a projected novel called *Confessions of a Murderer*.[72] Yet there is a profound instability in these modest proposals of De Quincey's, whether based on an anaesthetization of guilt by the intoxication of a whole vengeful class or, in the more extreme version, of a murdering of the murderers, a vengeance wrought upon the avengers. The London section ends with an account of the price paid for these voyages of exploration into the terra incognita of darkest London, the 'anguish and remorse' of a conscience only temporarily besotted and consoled for the loss of innocence, figured by Brunell's female charge or Ann of Oxford St. In the complex finale of 'The Pleasures of Opium', De Quincey described how he subsequently dismissed the dream fugues as 'sensual and gross', the London crowds as 'an oppression'. Unlike Coleridge, his retreat into 'the cave of Trophonius' (*C* 82) (an allusion to chapter 13 of the *Biographia*) to brood in solitude upon the wrongs of the world has been only a temporary recourse. Refusing to succumb to 'hypochondriacal melancholy' he had sought the homeopathic remedy of 'forc[ing] myself into society, and keep[ing] my understanding in continual activity upon matters of science' (*C* 82).

The section ends with a bravura passage about another city which seems to resolve, at least to sublimate, the feverish uncertainty of London. De Luca describes the opium reverie overlooking Liverpool as 'the most eloquent expression in De Quincey's writings of that Wordsworthian faith in a secular and internalized centre of transcendence'.[73] The passage certainly evokes the customary Wordsworthian 'spot of time' in which 'the tumult, the fever, and the strife, were suspended', replaced by a 'tranquility that seemed no product of inertia, but as if resulting from mighty and equal antagonisms; infinite activities, infinite repose' (*C* 82-3). And yet the preternatural calm of the vision has the effect of drawing attention to the unheard bustle of Liverpool, a mile distant from Everton, in an unWordsworthian trope, 'a distinct alternative to the Wordsworthian perceptual mode'.[74] De Quincey does not hide anything (in the way, for example, that Marjorie Levinson has shown Wordsworth to be doing in *Tintern Abbey*)[75] but *reveals* it in an anaesthetized form. Liverpool is represented as off-centre, 'its sorrows and its graves left behind, yet not out of sight, not wholly forgotten' (*C* 82). The off-centre is often the position of that which is to appear as *naturalized* within our field of vision, the position of an incongruous object which solicits our acceptance without having to give an account of itself.

If we should ask for a specification of the sorrows and graves which are unforgotten but unworthy of remark, the answer would have to lie in the material history of Liverpool, for De Quincey had no personal associations with this city as he had with Manchester. Not only was Liverpool the great imperial entrepôt (in an 1856 addition, De Quincey described it as 'the many-languaged town of Liverpool') (C 1856 200), but it had more than any other British city waxed fat on the slave trade, employing 132 ships solely for that purpose in 1792. Liverpool was also one of the main British ports to import Turkish opium in this period, taking in 120 lbs in the year 1792.[76] What I am suggesting is that Liverpool as a synecdoche for Britain's imperial power substitutes for 'darkest' London in De Quincey's narrative, displacing anxiety about wage slavery at home onto darker continents and a more literal bondage. In the words of Marx, 'the veiled slavery of the wage-workers in Europe needed, for its pedestal, slavery pure and simple in the new world'.[77]

The rhetoric of this displacement functions according to the structure described by John Barrell as 'this, that and the other' which I referred to above in the context of the links between nation formation and imperialism in British India.[78] We have seen how De Quincey had placed the East End wage-slaves on a pedestal of Saturday night consumption, expropriators in their turn of the labour of slaves and Far Eastern coolies. To be an *English* opium-eater was to consume (although maybe, as I will go on to suggest, to be consumed by) the East, to enjoy the diversion of luxuries whose grievous scenes of production were over the horizon, but which could be none the less *represented* by a distant view of the imperial entrepôt of Liverpool. De Quincey is thus performing a double displacement of the vengeful 'natural Jacobinism' characteristic of the prime victims of capitalism, the producers. He identifies with the metropolitan proletariat only in their capacity as consumers (they are only visible on Saturday night), and more particularly as opium-eaters; but he also identifies with them as English men and women all alike threatened by the potential violence and incipient vengefulness of those races upon whom their consumption was dependent, and who were subject to British imperial power. The English proletariat is thus no longer a 'that' but rather a 'this' when considered in relation to the oriental 'other'.[79] In the next section I want to look at some of the ways in which De Quincey found in the discourse of imperialism a 'negative' legitimation, a 'preternatural stimulus' to restore order and harmony to a body politic which he believes is unified in pleasure rather than regulated by repressive social discipline. I will also suggest that the creation of the hybrid figure denominated the 'English Opium Eater' generated another set of anxieties in which it was feared that East and West might become interfused, and alien natures blended into one another, creating a swamp of undifferentiated and vindictive humanity.

FEAR AND LOATHING IN GRASMERE

One of the most dramatic episodes of the *Confessions*, introducing the 'Pains of Opium' section, is the account of the visit of a Malay to De Quincey's cottage (Dove cottage) in Grasmere. Although Grevel Lindop surmises that the Malay might have stepped out of the frontispiece of a book like Marsden's *History of Sumatra*, there is no necessary reason to doubt his reality given that English ships had been employing Chinese and Lascar seamen since the beginning of the French revolutionary wars; the Malay might have been one such as these on his way to the port of Whitehaven or Workington, as De Quincey himself suggested.[80] De Quincey's servant, Barbara Lewthwaite, disturbed her master in his study to inform him of the arrival of 'a sort of demon below, whom she clearly imagined that 'my art could exorcise from the house' (*C* 90). Barbara's reaction to the Malay is evidently not merely connotative of her credulity or ignorance, however, for her scholarly master soon afterwards also refers to him as a 'tiger-cat' (*C* 91).

It is not poetic licence which commands De Quincey's account of the dark figure standing too close for comfort to Barbara in the kitchen downstairs ('her narrative spirit of mountain intrepidity [contending] with the feeling of simple awe', *C* 90), but rather a current racial stereotype. Shelley's friend Edward Trelawney reported the Malays (conventionally considered to be devoted opium-eaters) as being 'the most fierce, treacherous, ignorant and inflexible of barbarians' and the Revd Sydney Smith (whose opposition to British missionaries in India was referred to in the previous chapter) described them in 1803 as 'the most vindictive and ferocious of living beings. They set no value on their own existence, in the prosecution of their odious passions; and having thus broken the tie which renders man...capable of being governed, and fit for society, they are a constant source of terror to all those who have any kind of connection...with them...we cannot help thinking, that, one day or another, when they are more full of opium than usual, they will run *amock* from Cape Cormorin to the Caspian.'[81] Homi Bhahba has ascribed the stereotype to the field of fetishism, 'the primary point of signification in colonial discourse'; 'the stereotype impedes the circulation and articulation of the signifier of "race" as anything other than its *fixity* as racism. We always already know that blacks are licentious, Asiatics duplicitious...'[82] In a stark contrast to his *repression* of class hatred in London or the off-centring of the liminal place of Liverpool, De Quincey in this passage mobilizes the full armoury of racial discrimination, 'racial typology, the analytics of blood, ideologies of racial and cultural dominance or degradation';[83] all are implicit or explicit in his overworked 'tableau-vivante' in Dove Cottage kitchen. Skin equals culture in this telling confrontation between an English servant girl and the oriental Other:

the beautiful English face of the girl, and its exquisite fairness [illumination; youth; innocence; justice], together with her erect [morally upright] and independent [political liberty of *even* a subaltern class and sex] attitude, contrasted with the sallow [etymologically 'dirty'] and bilious [querulous, vengeful] skin [not face] of the Malay, enamelled or veneered with mahogany ['sleek enamelled neck' of the Miltonic serpent] by marine air, his small, fierce, restless eyes [reptilian, degenerate], thin lips [cruelty], slavish gestures and adorations [the meaningless rituals of oriental super-stition and social deference]. (*C* 91)

The Malay's presence introduces a racial, sexual and social paranoia into De Quincey's narrative; his skin proclaims his difference, already a threat; he stands too close to Barbara, and is therefore a sexual menace, opening the possibility of unhallowed miscegenation; unable to speak English, he stands outside the system of symbolic exchange which encodes social hierarchy, and therefore threatens the master's authority in the eyes of his female servant. What distinguishes the episode from its subsequent repetition in De Quincey's 'dream fugues' is his success in mastering his own feared impotence. De Quincey does not here 'ratify for himself the original transgression' by 'lying down before the lion' (Mass. XIII 304). Perhaps his resolution of the crisis is already determined by his establishment of the stereotype, but the violence of the stereotype is dissimulated by the feigned civility of the giving of gifts.

The first of these is a 'gift' of language; unable to lay his hands on either a Malay dictionary or Adelung's *Mithridates* (a work which translated the Lord's Prayer into 500 different languages), De Quincey addresses the Malay 'in some lines from the *Iliad*' (*C* 91). The choice of text is felicitous (the defeat and slaying of the Trojan (Asian) Hector by the Greek Achilles) as is the language, which is the nearest approximation to an oriental language which De Quincey can muster. To address the Malay in Greek is already to conquer him, for, as De Quincey wrote elsewhere, the classical languages are 'the sublime masonic tie of brotherhood we ourselves possess, we members of Christendom' (Mass. v 87), and, by extension, 'within the next two centuries all the barbarous languages of the earth (that is, those without a literature) will be one after one *strangled* and *exterminated* by four European languages, – namely the English, the Spanish, the Portuguese, and the Russian' (italics mine) (Mass. x 33).

De Quincey thus unequivocally reveals the civilizing mission (symbolized here, as with Byron and Shelley, by the Hellenistic legacy) as a deadly gift for the Other. The legacy of Greek civilization to the four principal imperialist powers of Europe is that of *literature*, specifically the 'literature of power' theorized in the *Essay on Pope* and the *Letters to a Young Man*. The possession of a literature of power is at once the evidence for a legitimation of one's destiny as an imperial nation, as is shown in De Quincey's 1857 advocacy of war with China, on the grounds that it is devoid of the literature of power which guarantees participation in the league of 'organic' nations fit to colonize the world. De Quincey scorns 'the pretended literature and meagre civilization' of this 'putrescent... tribe of hole-and-corner assassins'.[84] Like the nineteenth-century inaugurators of systematic racism, De Quincey does not lump all subject peoples into the same category, however, but rather deploys a taxonomy of cultural development. If savages possess the *negation* (= 0) of imaginative power, he argued in 1824, then orientals possess the *negative* (= −imagination), an observation by which, if my argument about De Quincey's 'negativing' of Coleridgean imagination is correct, he risks tarring himself with his own brush, an issue to which I will return below (Mass. x 444). But Greek is the perfect language for the Grasmere Malay, given that 'It is not for knowledge that Greek is worth learning, but for power', and, sure enough, 'he worshipped me in a most devout manner, and replied in what I suppose was Malay' (Mass. x 51; *C* 91).

De Quincey tells us that he owed the notion of a literature of power
to Wordsworth, admired surrogate for De Quincey's absent father
(just as Coleridge is the despised older brother/double William). It is
perhaps, then, not surprising to learn that he believed Wordsworth to
be the poet whose work is best adapted to the British colonies, and
which he evidently foresees as participating in the 'strangulation'
and 'extermination' of the language and culture of 'the countless
myriads of future America and future Australia, no less than
Polynesia and Southern Africa' amongst whom it will be dis-
seminated (*Recoll.* 144). While it is hard, as René Wellek has argued,
to get much critical purchase on the 'vagueness and multiplicity of
meaning' of the term 'the literature of power',[85] the context of the
present discussion draws our attention to the fact that the psychology
of creation around which the notion of power is deployed is already
thoroughly infected with the interests of imperialism, *mutatis mutandis*.
Not only is his notion of a literature of power, exemplary site of a
privileged subjecthood, complicit with a Eurocentric cultural hegemony in the sense of Gayatri Spivak's remark that 'there is an
affinity between the imperialist subject and the subject of humanism',[86] but the very description of that mode of production
saturates a discourse of psychology with the geopolitics of the
civilizing mission. For De Quincey, what is *power* if not

to feel vividly, and with a vital consciousness, emotions which ordinary life
rarely or never supplies occasions for exciting, and which had previously lain
unawakened, and hardly within the dawn of consciousness – as myriads of
modes of feeling are at this moment in every human mind for want of a poet
to organize them? I say, when these inert and sleeping forms are organized,
when these possibilities *are* actualised, is this conscious and living possession
of mine *power*, or what is it? (Mass. x 48)

De Quincey's first gift to the Malay, the literature of power, is also a
mode of *possession* proleptic of the self-proclaimedly 'organizing' and
'actualizing' role of official imperialism (although in the passage
quoted above, the equivalent terms were 'strangle' and 'exter-
minate'). In his essay on Ceylon, De Quincey described India as
a 'monument' to British civilization, a word which already opens
up to the ambivalence everywhere present in his writings on
imperialism:

We found many kingdoms established, and to these we have given unity;
and in process of doing so, by the necessities of the general welfare, or the

mere instincts of self-preservation, we have transformed them to an Empire, rising like an exhalation, of our own – a mighty monument to our own superior civilization. (Mass. VII 429)

The hybridization which both celebrates British power and creates a monumental edifice, an epitaph for something which has passed away, is also evident in Thomas Macaulay's 1835 *Minute on Indian Education* in which the absence of 'power' from Indian literature and culture legitimated the project of creating a class of Indian 'mimic men', 'Indian in blood and colour, but English in tastes, in opinions, in morals and in intellect'.[87] Indian and Englishman become, in relation to one another, 'either nobody at all, or oneself repeated once too often' (Mass. XI 461).

If De Quincey's literature of power cast an orphic spell over the oriental 'tiger-cat', it also worked wonders upon the frightened Barbara Lewthwaite and the little child from a neighbouring cottage who clung to her apron and gazed at 'the turban and the fiery eyes beneath it' (C 91). Her master's taming of the Malay doubtless taught Barbara a lesson about the usefulness of inequality, against which as a member of the lower orders her 'naturally Jacobin' heart rebels. The incident gives her a vicarious eminence, from which her intrinsic social and gender qualifications would otherwise have excluded her ('what work of imagination' asked the opium-eater in 1824 'owing its birth to a woman...has exerted any memorable influence, such as History would notice, upon the mind of Man?', x 442). The fact that neither Barbara *nor* the Malay understand a word of Greek, but that their relative positions are resolved around the Homeric text, exemplifies Foucault's account of the 'economy' of discourses, 'the effects of power which underlie them and which they transmit – this, and not a system of representations, is what determines the essential features of what they have to say'.[88] Without collapsing the complexities of De Quincey's text into historical allegory, the episode represents the fetishistic possibilities of imperialism – in 1816, the date of the Malay's visit, Britain had just emerged from the Congress of Vienna laden with the spoils of a second empire – in stimulating a crisis-ridden and enervated national culture into what De Quincey represents as a condition of organic integration.

The fact that the episode in Dove Cottage kitchen so well fits the account of Marx himself and Marxist historians like Victor Kiernan about a hegemonic 'playing off' of subject races against the metropolitan proletariat is only part of the story we are unfolding, however.[89] De Quincey gave the Malay a second gift which was also perhaps a disguised attempt to murder him. Being an 'orientalist' he presumed that the Malay would be an opium-eater; before his departure he accordingly presents him with a lump of opium which the Malay instantly swallows whole. De Quincey is 'concerned' at this prodigious consumption, for the opium was 'enough to kill three dragoons and their horses'; in the 1856 version, by an appropriate irony, after the opium war had forcibly opened up the Chinese markets to the biggest narcotics consumption in history, the quantity had become 'enough to kill some half-dozen dragoons together with their horses' (C 1856 212). Although Malays and Chinese did have a reputation as prodigious opium-eaters by the beginning of the nineteenth century, the 'orientalist' presupposition which legiti-mized De Quincey's potentially fatal 'gift' was built on shaky foundations of fact, like many orientalist presuppositions. 'From a historical point of view, opium was primarily a plant of the occidental cultures. Notwithstanding popular opinion, China was never a classical "opium country" in a medical sense. The association between China and opium and its relevance as an important social factor in the historical development of the late Chinese empire was, in fact, only established with the extension of the British colonial influence in the Far East.'[90]

There is a note of disingenuity in De Quincey's concern, 'I felt some alarm for the poor creature; but what could be done?' (C 91), but there is no call for guilt, as no body is ever found in the vicinity. The supposition that De Quincey intended to poison the Malay in order to protect the English child and maidservant is supported, as John Barrell indicates, in a note to the 1856 text, 'a reparative version of an earlier narrative which had ended unsatisfactorily'. The note evoking the Malay incident tells how De Quincey's young daughter Margaret administered 'yoddunum' to a sick caged finch: next morning, watched by De Quincey, Barbara Lewthwaite and Margaret, the finch falls dead from its perch. The metamorphosis of the Malay from 'tiger-cat' to caged finch might seem implausible, but as Barrell puts it, in the narrative of reparation the animal impersonating the threatening Malay 'had to be one that De Quincey could square up to with a measure of confidence in the likely outcome of the struggle'.[91] According to my reading, however, there might be a rationale for the 'unsatisfactory' resolution of the earlier narrative; from the point of view of De Quincey's *imperialism*, the *survival* of the Malay might be of as much importance as the fact that he is *nearly* poisoned, and the threat he poses dismissed.

De Quincey's declaration of the inappropriateness of guilt here is legitimized by his belief that the cruder nervous systems of inferior races, whilst depriving them of any refined *enjoyment* of opium ('I honour the Barbarians too much by supposing them capable of any pleasures approaching to the intellectual ones of an Englishman', *C* 78), afforded them a far higher tolerance to the drug's deleterious effects. This will be another justification for British drug-trafficking in China, although one that is still not cleared of anxiety. According to Marek Kohn, 'linking the ideas of racial drug immunity and the corruption of vulnerable white females' is still a potent item in the pharmacopoeia of the popular mythology of drug abuse.[92]

OPIUM WARS

If De Quincey's first gift, the classical test upon which the civility of British 'liberty' was founded represented the 'official' discourse of imperialism, the second gift of opium compromises the libertarian rhetoric of the civilizing mission by guilefully resorting to violence and coercion. I have argued that De Quincey mobilized a discursive violence in criticizing the vestigial civic humanism of Coleridge's *Biographia*, that the 'Pleasures of Opium' effectively undermined the Coleridgean 'sovereign principle' which failed to recognize its own investment in a capitalist world order ruled by the sign of luxury. I now wish to read the 'Pains of Opium' as the consequence of that recognition, as the simulacrum of the (cancelled) authority of Will found itself literally petrified, objectified into the image of an Orient which it had claimed the right to expropriate. Or, in Homi Bhabha's account of this crisis, 'What is the image of authority if it is civility's supplement (i.e. both extension *and* replacement) and democracy's despotic double?'[93]

The prescription of opium/imperialism, in best Brunonian fashion, to stimulate the torpid nervous fibres of the body politic invited the real danger that the cure might be worse than the disease, that the regime of luxury might create its own parasitic and iatrogenic pathology. I take it that the function of the dreams which conclude the 'Pains of Opium' section of the *Confessions*, 'the real object of the whole work' (*C* 126) (and which constitute the later continuations of the book, *The English Mail Coach* and *Suspiria de Profundis*) was to rehearse and putatively to resolve this problematic. As the episode of the Malay revealed, the *Confessions* are premised on the author's mastery of his own impotence; in accordance with its Brunonian polemic, the opium-eater claims (untruthfully as it turned out) to have 'untwisted the accursed chain' of addiction. And yet this confident claim is qualified by the admission that 'One memorial of my former condition still remains: my dreams are not yet perfectly calm' (*C* 115). The dreams represent, in the haunted rhetoric of *The English Mail Coach*, a 'ratif[ication of] ... the original transgression' as the 'inviolable nature' of European self-presence is overwhelmed by the terror of cultural miscegenation, 'the horrid inoculation upon each other of incompatible natures', whereby the 'horrid alien nature' is revealed as 'the mere numerical double of his own consciousness' (Mass. XIII 304; 291; 292). The weapon De Quincey had used with murderous efficiency against his brother/double Coleridge is turned against himself, as he realized in a passage of 1847:

if I had a *doppel-ganger* who went about personating me, copying me, and pirating me, philosopher as I am I might...be so far carried away by jealousy as to attempt the crime of murder upon his carcase; and no great matter as regards HIM. But it would be a sad thing for *me* to find myself hanged; and for what. I beseech you? for murdering a sham, that was either nobody at all, or oneself repeated once too often. (Mass. XI 460–1)

The anxieties which the dreams rehearse and repeat in fugues of spiralling prose represent warranted murder as suicide, conquest of an 'inorganic' Other as a form of absorption into the Other's materiality, the 'progressive' nature of western civilization as merely repetition, evolution as degeneration, mastery as disintegration. De Quincey's fears exemplify in extreme form the theories of ambivalence and hybridization developed by Bhabha: 'As the chains of civil *substitution* yield to colonial supplementarity, the representative nineteenth-century discourse of liberal individualism loses both its power of speech, and its politics of individual choice.'[94]

The most disturbing element of De Quincey's dream life – which I will consider in the final section of this chapter – is the way that it is quite literally materialized in his later writings about China, Ceylon and the Indian Mutiny. Fear of being mastered by the Other often manifests itself in these writings as a racist psychosis in which De Quincey allowed full reign to the vengefulness of the repressed 'natural Jacobinism' of his own heart. Before we look at his advocacy of the opium wars, consider the following 'dream' passage from De Quincey's 'translation' of the Norwegian writer Ludvig Holberg's novel *Niels Klim*, a satirical travelogue based on *Gulliver's Travels*. This suffices to show that at its most extreme only racial genocide (here another race has become another *species* inhabiting a sub-terranean world) could provide a satisfactory recompense for the opium-eater's sense of impotence, of having 'lain down before the lion'. The passage here quoted, all of it a De Quinceyan increment to Holberg's 'original Danish', describes the narrator's fight against a 'troop of wild apes' who attack him in the subterranean world of rational trees (an adaption of Swift's Yahoos and Houyhnhnms):

My readers of the upper world may rest assured that I did not let this [a boathook carried by the narrator] lie idle... but laid it into these infernal monkeys (*infernal* I may truly call them in a double sense) with right good will, as well for my own particular interest at this moment, as to revenge the horrid affront they were putting on the whole species overhead, which I had the honour to represent in the subterranean world. With the perseverance of fleas or gnats however, as often as they were brushed off, back they swarmed again... I had the satisfaction of bestowing innumerable raps and fractures on some thousands of empty skulls, and strewing the road with heaps of chattering baboons whom I had smashed in vindication of my own insulted honour and that of my species.[95]

De Quincey's dreams are the fantasia of an imperial history characterized (at its worst) by the opium wars and the furious reaction to the Indian Mutiny. If the Mutiny is now in Britain generally laid aside according to the logic of 'an eye for an eye', the former is left, as Kohn puts it, as 'the only episode in imperial history that is generally seen as unambiguously wicked' even after 'the great debriefing that has accompanied the dismantling of the British empire'.[96] To summarize briefly: opium was produced by the British East India Company in India for export to China, as an exchange commodity for China tea. This formed a delicately balanced trade triangle: the Chinese had to pay for Indian opium, Britain's Indian subjects had to pay for the privilege of British rule, and the British consumer had to pay for China tea. These outstanding claims were cancelled one against the other, to the benefit of Britain's worldwide trade. When in 1839 the Chinese, worried by the economics of the international situation and growing indigenous addiction to the illegally imported drug, confiscated a quantity of British opium at

Canton, the British Government maintained that Chinese courts had no jurisdiction over British subjects and could not authorize the seizure of their property. As was the case in India seventeen years later, the cry was for vengeance upon the inhabitants of the subterranean world. War was declared: the British navy seized Hong Kong and bombarded Canton, forcibly opening China to western markets at the Treaty of Nanking in 1842.

British reactions to what would become the biggest narcotics traffic in history were at best ambivalent, at worst hypocritical. Although there was opposition to the trafficking of a drug to which, as our investigations of reactions to the *Confessions* have shown us, medical opinion was increasingly dubious, it was generally considered acceptable as a commodity if labelled 'for external use only'.[97] This attitude was already indicated by Warren Hastings when he wrote that opium was 'not a necessary of life but a pernicious article of luxury, which ought not to be permitted but for the purpose of foreign commerce only, and which the wisdom of government should carefully restrain from internal consumption'.[98] What better instance of 'civility's supplement, democracy's despotic double' can there be than British outrage at the Chinese attempt to staunch the flow of this perilous commodity into Canton? De Quincey, who in a *Blackwood's* essay of 1840 demanded 'war conducted with exemplary vigour', felt that an ambassador should be sent to Peking at the head of a 14,000 man task-force to compel the Emperor's submission, because punitive raids on Chinese ports would have no effect on a country 'defended by its essential non-irritability'. China was 'at present... an inorganic mass – something to be kicked, but which cannot kick again... having... no vital parts, no organs, no heart, no lungs' (Mass. XIV 163; 176).

There is presumably underlying these arguments a link between Chinese 'non-irritability' and racial immunity to prodigious consumption of opium, the argument by which De Quincey salved his conscience with regard to his 'gift' to the Malay. The 'for external use only' label is *only* morally defensible if it can be argued that the coarser oriental nervous system is not vulnerable, as the European one would be, to the poisonous effects of overconsuming the drug. If China and the Chinese lack a nervous system, they also lack the power of will, and are therefore 'incurably savage in the moral sense' (Mass. XIV 193). Referring back as far as 1785, De Quincey substantiated his point by describing the hanging of a British seaman by the Chinese authorities for accidentally firing a cannon which had killed a Chinese citizen, proof that they who 'are bestial enough to think the will and the intention no necessary element in the moral quality of an act, are also savage enough to punish vicariously' (Mass. xiv 192). Because the Chinese have enforced one of their own laws banning the importation of opium, they have to be punished, and because De Quincey cannot think of a better argument, they have to be punished vicariously for an act committed fifty-five years before, the criminality of which lies in its status as a vicarious punishment! Moreover, their refusal of opium, dependence upon which destroys the power of will (a major element of De Quincey's polemic against Coleridge, as we saw above), seems to be an unequivocal example of the assertion of a national will; the Chinese are apparently to be punished for simultaneously possessing and not possessing a will.

De Quincey is in deep waters the moment he begins predicating his argument upon a will, particularly as he has chosen to base his account of the imperial expansion of capitalist markets upon a metaphor of the nervous system independent of the voluntary principle. In 1857 he represented the global expansion of British interests as a kind of inevitable process, a manifest destiny quite independent of will or intention which has 'brought us into a painful necessity of connecting ourselves with the conceited and most ignorant inhabitants of China' (Mass. xiv 350). De Quincey anticipates Sir John Seeley's dictum that 'we seem, as it were, to have conquered and peopled half the world in a fit of absence of mind'.[99] By their manifestation of wilfulness the Chinese are infringing a natural right premised upon a *global* nervous system or free market; it is thus their own fault if they are murdered in consequence, particularly as they are also opium-eaters. Like Coleridge, they are hypocrites whose 'sovereign principle' is based on a lie (De Quincey ignores the fact that his own argument is based on a flagrant contradiction): for their own benefit they must be forced to admit the truth.[100] Echoing the arguments for free trade surveyed in the preceding chapter, De Quincey presents it as a form of global therapy, the healthfulness of unfettered circulation:

It seems clear that the practical liberation and distribution throughout the world of all good gifts meant for the whole household of man, has been confined to the secret sense of a *right* existing in man for claiming such a distribution as part of his natural inheritance. Many articles of almost inestimable value to man, in relation to his physical well-being...such as mercury, Jesuit's bark [quinine],...opium, mineral waters etc. were at one time *locally* concentred. In such cases...the medicinal relief to an hospital, to an encampment, to a nation, might depend entirely upon the right to *force* a commercial intercourse.[101]

War was declared in 1840, and the Chinese opium-eaters were punished simultaneously for their hypocritical act of will and their spineless lack of will. Britain gained Hong Kong and the disdain of the rest of the world; opium flowed freely into China once again, composing, in 1911, just under a staggering half of that huge country's total imports, a drug consumption without precedent in history.[102] By an irony of history, the English opium-eater found that in murdering a sham, he was murdering part of himself; his son Horace, an officer in the 26th Cameronian Rifles, part of the British expeditionary force, died of fever near Canton in 1842 just before peace was declared. Little wonder that De Quincey was 'more than ever confirmed in his bitter hatred of China and all things Chinese'.[103]

TROUBLED DREAMS

As the opium began to take effect, the whole living principle of the intellectual motions began to lose its elasticity, and, as it were, to petrify; I began to comprehend the tendency of madness to eddy about one idea; and the loss of power to abstract – to hold abstractions steadily before me – or to exercise many other intellectual acts, was in due proportion to the degree in which the biliary system seemed to suffer. (*Madness*, Mass. x 447)

The opium wars, like the slave trade and the retribution for the Indian Mutiny, seriously qualified the illusion of British imperialism as a moral crusade 'awakening and organizing' the dark places of the world. The strategy of 'blaming the victims' of imperialist expropriation could barely disguise the fact that, in Victor Kiernan's words, 'the West had become dependent economically on the world, and therefore must make the world dependent politically on it'.[104] Dependence of this kind was the repressed term in imperialist ideology, which rationalized its uncurbed craving for colonial markets in the guise of a civilizing mission. As we have seen, structures of dependence were also very germane to the pathologies of De Quincey's character and writings; the 'John Bull element' in his nature noted by his Victorian editor Alexander Japp is symptomatic, not of 'his love of human nature in its uncorrupted simplicity' (a *non-sequitur* if ever there was one!), but rather of a fear that dependency and corruption were inextricably bound up with the mastery of the world.[105]

In his advocacy of the opium wars, De Quincey is at once the proponent of a civilizing mission which included (external) free trade in opium, considered in term of its *exchange value*, and a 'user' for whom opium was *compulsory* for economic and also personal survival, for *use value*. Although most of the opium sold in England came from Turkey rather than India,[106] and it is possible, with John Barrell, to distinguish a 'near' from a 'far' East in De Quincey's writings,[107] in the case of opium it seems that Turkey, India and China represented a homogeneous Orient. Nevertheless, whether we are talking about a personal dependence on Turkish opium, or a national, economic dependence on Patna opium and the Chinese trade triangle, what has become evident is the fragility of the 'official discourse' which constantly fractures and betrays its repressed term. The equation between the sort of alienation resulting from both the commodity fetishism of capitalism and drug addiction is well drawn by William Burroughs in *The Naked Lunch*. Heroin (the twentieth century's 'technologized' form of opium) is 'the ultimate merchandise... No sales talk necessary... The junk merchant does not sell his product to the consumer, he sells the consumer to his product. He does not improve and simplify his merchandise. He degrades and simplifies his client.'[108]

I will finish by saying some more about the dreams which concluded both the *Confessions* and De Quincey's writing career, dreams which offer a relief, albeit of a nightmarish kind, from the narrative of a life struggling against displacement and dependency. The dreams in the *Confessions* at once *conclude* De Quincey's book, and reveal themselves as the starting point, the occasion, of his narrative; 'because the opium dreams could not always have been understood without a knowledge of these events, it became necessary to relate them...' (Mass. XIII 336). The whole of the *Confessions* can accordingly be seen as a frame for the dreams, at once its end and beginning. De Quincey later described the dreaming faculty 'in alliance with the mystery of darkness, [as] the one great tube through which man communicates with the shadowy' and regarded its exercise as an essential counterbalance to the social, technological and political revolutions of his age, particularly to the threat of 'Red Republicanism'. 'Left to itself,' he added, 'the natural tendency of so chaotic a tumult must be to evil; for some minds to lunacy, for others a reagency of fleshly torpor' (Mass. xiii 335; 334–5). This might seem to beg the question, for the *Confessions*' dreams are hardly soothing. But the opium-eater has an explanation to hand; like the Brutus hairstyle sported by English dandies in Southey's *Letters from England*, De Quincey's dreams, assisted by the 'preternatural' stimulant of opium, themselves represent the lunacy which they are meant to remedy, thereby operating in a *homeopathic* manner upon the mind, inoculating it against its waking anxieties; 'the strength of lunacy may belong to human dreams, the fearful caprice of lunacy, and the malice of lunacy, whilst the *victim* of those dreams may be all the more certainly removed from lunacy' (Mass. xiii 339).

It is perhaps difficult to evaluate the relations of the dreams to the main body of De Quinceyan narrative, particularly as he himself registered their central importance in such contradictory terms. In the introduction I argued that the anxieties of empire could empower as well as disable the functioning of the imperial will. De Quincey sought to rationalize his troubled dreams of dependence and empire as homeopathic agencies, safety valves as it were to draw off his psychic and cultural anxieties. To the modern 'unromantic' reader it seems self-evident that the dreams are very far from living up to De Quincey's wishes, at least in so far as they function as narrative. Such a reader is not obliged to take them in the manner described by De Quincey. The dreams are extremely disturbing, and in one sense their representation of 'lunacy' is the most authentic moment in a body of writing marked by complex narrative displacements and substitutions. The dreams do truthfully register, in the form of a *mise-en-abîme*, the lunacies of De Quincey's engagements with opium and empire, like the 'introvolution' of the 'play within a play' in his 1840 *Theory of Greek Tragedy*. 'The original picture is a mimic, an unreal life. But this unreal life is itself a real life with respect to the secondary picture; which again must be supposed realized with relation to the tertiary picture, if such a thing were attempted' (Mass. x 344).

If then a primary function of the dreams for De Quincey was to realize an 'unreal', inauthentic life by this bizarre contrast (one thinks of the pathos of the transition from the 'unutterable monsters and abortions of my dreams' to the sight of his children at his bedside, 'the sight of innocent *human* natures and of infancy; which causes him to weep and kiss their faces, C 110), the addition of a tertiary picture makes the secondary real by comparison. I propose that the tertiary picture which we must add to De Quincey's text is the material history of imperialism, within the terms of which the contemporary reader is inextricably involved. From the viewpoint of the post-colonial reader, the presence of the tertiary introvolution must restructure our understanding of the dreams; the 'unreal life' of the dreams is the 'real life' of history, so that the racist 'lunacy', psychosis and predatory dependency of imperialism as such (not just De Quincey's particular 'narratives of reparation') can be seen here for what they are.

Two dream structures are particularly salient in the opium-eater's representation of his lunacies, based respectively on *repetition* and *petrifaction*. I mentioned earlier that the dreams represent the De Quinceyan inflection or, to use a more De Quinceyan term, involution of Coleridgean imagination. If Coleridge's self-projection in the *Biographia* was controlled by an act of narrative will, De Quincey's dreams represent the author as *victim* and object of a remorseless involuntary memory, the 'dread book of account' which proclaimed that 'there is no such thing as *forgetting* possible to the mind' (*C* 104). Or rather, De Quincey's dreams articulate the hidden self-knowledge of the *Biographia*, manifest in the fragmentation which comes to a crisis in chapter 13 of that book. Coleridge's 'cor-respondent' describes the 'chapter on Imagination' as a 'Gothic Cathedral in a gusty moonlight night of autumn', its argument like 'the fragments of the winding steps of an old ruined tower' (*BL* 1 301–3). De Quincey's dreams in the *Confessions* are also composed of fragments, because he has been unable to form the 'whole burthen of horrors which lies upon my brain' 'into a regular narrative' (*C* 97).

One of the most striking of these is based upon the celebrated etchings of gigantic classical dungeons by Piranesi entitled *Carceri d'invenzione*, (imaginary prisons) which De Quincey falsely believed to be entitled Piranesi's *Dreams*. To be more accurate, his troubled dream is based upon Coleridge's *account* of the etchings, because De Quincey claimed never to have seen them; as well as symptomatically mistaking their title, he imagines them as 'vast Gothic [rather than Roman] halls'. Groping his way up the massive Gothic staircase of the *carceri*, De Quincey imagines he sees Piranesi himself: 'follow the stairs a little further, and you perceive it come to a sudden abrupt termination, without any balustrade, and allowing no step onwards to him who had reached the extremity, except into the depths below' (*C* 106). The architecture of De Quincey's dream is an accurate representation of Coleridge's chapter 13 letter; his dream is the *doppel-ganger* of Coleridge's correspondent's dream (a correspondent whom, it turns out, is none other than Coleridge shamming). The architect is Coleridge's double (Piranesi had executed the etchings 'during the delirium of a fever'; was he also an opium-eater?), is De Quincey's double, is his own duplicate and triplicate, as the same figure is depicted on different levels of 'the winding steps of the old ruined tower'. De Quincey plagiarizes the plagiarist Coleridge, shams a figure who is already a sham of himself. The figure is always suspended at the moment before plunging into the abyss, and yet he is simultaneously figured plodding up the next stage. The dream is terrible not only because it figures a De Quinceyan 'murder' of Coleridgean idealism. It is also terrible because it betokens the realization that Coleridge is De Quincey's double, and that his symbolic murder of Coleridge is also a self-murder. The Piranesi dream clearly represents the Brunonian article of faith in detoxification (the *Confessions*' assertion that its author had nearly 'unwound the accursed chain' of addiction) as an unqualified illusion.

The 'tertiary introvolution' of a critical/historical reading permits an appreciation of the truthfulness of De Quincey's *mise-en-abîme*, for the drug which he still doggedly believed to be a stimulus turned out to be his permanent incarceration. When De Quincey died in 1859, he was still an addict; in a sense, Coleridge, who had himself died an addict twenty-five years earlier, had had the last word on this article. The dream represents reality as De Quincey, like Coleridge, most feared it might in fact be, as the 'lunacy' of pure repetition, dependence and contingency. On the other hand, this brings a certain relief; liberated from the inauthenticity of the 'primary introvolution', the dream no longer needs to *equivocate* its author's anxiety that every subject is endlessly metamorphosed into its (hated) Other 'that was either nobody at all, or oneself repeated once too often'.

The *Carceri* hallucinates the fantasy of a limitless time composed of endlessly repeated traumas and reparations, very similar to the palingenetic cosmology of the earth described by De Quincey in the 1846 article 'System of the Heavens'; 'Not otherwise by secular periods, known to us geologically as facts, though obscure as durations, *Tellus* [the earth] herself, the planet, as a whole, is forever working by golden balances of change and compensation, of ruin and restoration.'[109] In the same article, Piranesi's imaginary prison is rewritten by De Quincey in a translation of Richter's analect 'A Dream of the Universe', in which a material sublime offers a vertiginous freedom from the gravity of narrative identity and displacement, from the unrelenting positionality of up and down, North and South, West and East: 'Without measure were the architraves, past number were the archways, beyond memory the gates. Within were stairs that scaled the eternities above, that descended to the eternities below: above was below, below was above, to the man stripped of gravitating body: depth was swallowed up in height insurmountable, height was swallowed up in depth unfathomable.'[110]

Perhaps the *Confessions'* most memorable dream-vision, a masterpiece of 'impassioned prose', is the 'May 1818' dream inspired by the Malay. The dominant lunacy of this dream, which in the introduction I argued to have been at least partly inspired by Southey, is the fear of petrifaction, the fear that the organism, through dependence, overconsumption and overstimulation, will become inorganic. The racial corollories of this fear should by now be fairly clear: De Quincey dreaded losing that fragile distinction of 'Englishness' which marked him off from oriental opium-eaters. Put simply, De Quincey believed that imperialism, which entailed the (necessary) abandonment of a civic discourse based on national integrity and moral eminence, would cause Europe to be absorbed by 'inferior' races and cultures. De Quincey's most sanguine imperialism, played out in his first gift to the Malay, envisaged a Europe unified after 1815 by England and the 'secret word', 'Waterloo and Recovered Christendom', fulfilling Kant's dream of 'the establishment of a universal Civil Society founded on the empire of political justice', and, doubtless, global free trade (Mass. IX 433). The racial equivalent of this vision was his idea of a proto-eugenicist interbreeding of the 'nobler' non-European races (such as the Maoris of New Zealand) with their white masters, and the gradual extirpation of the more primitive ones. The whole world would gradually become white, for had it not been decreed, he enquired in 1857, that 'the [European] sons of Japheth shall sit down in the tents of the [Asiatic] Shem?'[111]

And yet there is a recurrent anxiety throughout De Quincey's writing of the innocent white sister, wife, daughter or servant being sacrificed, ravished, polluted by a repulsive miscegenation, 'the horrid inoculation upon each other of incompatible natures', a fear

(manifest in the Malay's threat to Barbara Lewthwaite) which
reaches a crescendo in the 'Dream Fugue' of *The English Mail Coach*.
The sexual threat of an 'inverted' miscegenation (white woman/
black man rather than white man/black woman) is closely linked to
De Quincey's fear of identification with the colonial subject, the
'*un*English' opium-eater/pariah, whom, as John Barrell has argued,
he figures by a recurrent displacement of his own guilt as the
'oriental' murderer of his sister Elizabeth.[112] In the introduction I
discussed another instance of De Quincey's identification with the
Other, the narrative of his elder brother William's imaginary
European kingdom 'Tigrosylvania' annexing and colonizing
Thomas' 'Gombroon' on the grounds that its equatorial inhabitants
had monkey's tails (Mass. 1 98).

Perhaps the humiliation of this recollection justified in De
Quincey's mind the disturbing violence of the passage from *Niels Klim*
considered above, in which the narrator was able to avenge the insult
offered to the inhabitants of the 'upper world' by smashing in the
empty skulls of 'heaps of chattering baboons'. De Quincey can now
identify with the Tigrosylvanians, the denizens of the 'upper world',
and wreak his revenge on the Gombroonians. So much for the
Kantian dream of a 'Cosmopolitic Areopagus' (Mass. IX 441). De
Quincey's 'vengeance' is of course another version of the by now
familiar pattern of 'murdering one's double', although his recurrent
and violent attempts to resolve such psychic traumas in his writings
fully participate in the mood of mid-nineteenth-century thinking
about race and culture. For example, the Victorian scientific racist
James Hunt was horrified in 1870 by a very De Quinceyan anxiety
that 'the almost exterminated savages will be amply revenged by a
slow, gradual degeneracy, and perhaps final extinction, of their...
conquerors'.[113]

The anxiety of petrification which is the dream sequel to the Malay
episode perfectly anticipates the 'return of the repressed' in nineteenth-century imperialist discourse. De Quincey's murderous 'gift
of opium', the means by which he 'commands' the Malay, rebounds
upon his dreams as a multiplication of the latter's image, '[he]
brought other Malays with him worse than himself, that ran 'a-
muck' at me, and led me into a world of troubles'; 'The Malay has
been a fearful enemy for months' (*C* 92; 108). We might note in this
context Marek Kohn's speculation that the fear of a 'yellow peril'
which gripped late Victorian England like a fever was born in part of

a sense of collective guilt for the opium wars. The dream 'intro-volution' allows De Quincey to *confess* the guilt, and suffer the punishment, of his second 'gift' to the Malay without allowing it to impinge upon the narrative confessing of his life:

I came suddenly upon Isis and Osiris: I had done a deed, they said, which the ibis and the crocodile trembled at. I was buried, for a thousand years, in stone coffins, with mummies and sphinxes, in narrow chambers at the heart of eternal pyramids. I was kissed, with cancerous kisses, by crocodiles; and laid, confounded with all unutterable slimy things, amongst reeds and Nilotic mud. (*C* 109)

Underlining the exotic imagery of De Quincey's prose is a terror of *imperialism* as well as of the East. The reductive geographical 'condensations' of the De Quinceyan dream-work (India, China, Egypt) evoke the schematics and 'comprehensive vision' of orientalism as described by Edward Said,[114] but here voided of any will to power. The 'manifest destiny' of political domination and its repressed 'other' of economic dependency are figured as incarceration ('narrow chambers at the heart of eternal pyramids'), petrifaction ('stone coffins') and absorption into the purely material ('laid, confounded with all unutterable slimy things'). European history and geography are cancelled by another version of the 'material sublime' without the boundaries of time and space, this time one defined as Asiatic and unrelentingly oppressive ('over every form ... brooded a sense of eternity that drove me into an oppression of madness'). The ideals of the European nation state and the rights of individuals are forfeited by the imperialist projection, and Malthusian fears of an enormously expanding metropolitan population, as well as of a 'yellow peril', are subliminally represented as concomitants of global capitalism. The European empire-builder sees the future image of his own culture swollen in the mirror of 'the vast empires ... into which the enormous population of Asia has always been cast' (*C* 108–9). De Quincey was so threatened by the scale of these empires that in an 1840 article in *Blackwood's Magazine* called 'Foreign Politics' he tried to persuade his readers (and maybe himself) that the size of the Chinese population was an instance of oriental hyperbole, and therefore more rhetorical than real. Magnitude is wishfully transformed into insignificance in order to minimize the threat of the Other; 'All Oriental nations exaggerate upon impulse. That sort of excess is the uniform disease of debility. They exaggerate also upon principle, and ... to flatter their sovereign. Hence the ridiculous legend of 333 millions in China: a number which betrays its own artificial coinage. We do not believe that China has a population of more than a hundred millions.'[115]

The great anxiety of De Quincey's dream is thus precisely one of *orientalization*. Imperialist and oriental subject are one; conquest is the prelude to revenge and degeneracy ('I was the idol; I was the priest; I was worshipped; I was sacrificed', *C* 109), as well as to fearful, even bestial miscegenations ('I was kissed, with cancerous kisses, by crocodiles'). The repressed fear of the Eurocentric myth of a 'westering' civilization, leaving behind the 'officina gentium' of the Orient with its 'tropical heat and vertical sun-lights' for the temperate north west, is the fear of coming round full circle, of discovering the Other in the Same.[116]

De Quincey would return to this anxiety in the 1846 essay on the 'System of the Heavens' cited above. Technological progress ('the huge four-decker telescope') enables the astronomer to penetrate the extremities of space; what he sees at the limits, in the swirling nebula of Orion, is the scene which, since Herschel's nebular hypothesis, had been theorized as the birthplace of heavenly bodies. Yet De Quincey, in accordance with his cosmological notion of palingenesis, discerns in the nebula the oriental form of the 'young Chinese' or the Malay, the 'antediluvian man renewed' (*C* 108). The vision is not any more comforting than the dream of May 1818; he sees an image of evil in the nebula, a 'detestable phantom', its skull covered by 'an Assyrian tiara', adorned with 'the plumes of a sultan'.[117] The greater the power of conquest, the greater the degree of vengeance to be unleashed. 'Brutalities unspeakable sit upon the upper lip, which is confluent with a snout; for separate nostrils there are none...the lower lip – oh what a convolute of cruelty and revenge is *there*!'[118] The truth which De Quincey discerned in the telescope, as in the dream faculty ('the one great tube through which man communicates with the shadowy'), was that murdering one's double resulted, in the end, in murdering oneself.

Notes

INTRODUCTION

1 *Letters from England, by Don Manuel Espriella* (1807), ed. with an intro. by Jack Simmons (Gloucester: Alan Sutton 1951), letter LXXI, pp. 448–9.
2 Edward Said, *Orientalism* (London and Harmondsworth: Penguin Books 1985), p. 3.
3 *The Works of Sir William Jones*, ed. Lady Jones, 6 vols. (London 1799), I 4.
4 *Orientalism*, p. 70.
5 Homi Bhabha, 'Signs Taken for Wonders', *Europe and its Others*, 2 vols., ed. Francis Barker et al. (Colchester: Essex University Press 1985), I 89–106; 'Sly Civility', *October*, 34 (1985), 71–80. See 'The Word in the Wilderness', chapter 2, for a discussion of Bhabha's work.
6 Nora Crook and Derek Guiton, *Shelley's Venomed Melody* (Cambridge University Press), p. 91.
7 De Quincey, *Confessions of an English Opium Eater*, ed. Alethea Hayter (Harmondsworth 1971), p. 110.
8 Lord Byron, *A Letter to John Murray on William Bowles's Strictures on the Life and Writings of Alexander Pope* (London 1821), p. 45.
9 *Collected Writings of De Quincey*, ed. David Masson, 14 vols. (Edinburgh: Adam and Charles Black 1889), I 89.
10 Ibid.
11 Ibid., I 91.
12 Ibid.
13 Ibid., I 98.
14 Daniel Pick, *Faces of Degeneration: A European Disorder c. 1848–c. 1918* (Cambridge University Press 1989).
15 John Barrell, *The Infection of Thomas De Quincey: A Psychopathology of Imperialism* (New Haven and London: Yale University Press 1991).
16 Cited in *Shelley's Venomed Melody*, pp. 85, 87.
17 Ibid., p. 85.
18 Ibid., p. 94.
19 Ibid., p. 91.
20 Stephen Greenblatt, *Marvellous Possessions: The Wonder of the New World* (Oxford: Clarendon Press 1991), p. 4. Greenblatt continues: 'Those

229

foreign bodies do not disappear altogether but they are drawn into what Homi Bhabha terms the in-between, the zone of intersection in which all culturally determinate significations are called into question by an unresolved and unresolvable hybridity.'

21 Barrell, *Infection of Thomas De Quincey*, p. 7.
22 *Bibliothèque Universelle*, 4 (April 1821), 348.
23 *Eclectic Review*, vii (April 1821) 349.
24 Raymond Schwab, *The Oriental Renaissance: Europe's Rediscovery of India and the East, 1680–1880*, trans. Gene Patterson Black and Victor Reinking with foreword by Edward Said (New York: Columbia University Press 1984), p. viii; p. 16; p. 18.
25 See Roy Porter and Mikulas Teich, *Romanticism in a National Context* (Cambridge University Press 1988), and for a broader approach which considers the question of nationalism in relation to the history of imperialism, Homi Bhabha (ed.) *Nation and Narration* (London and New York: Routledge 1990).
26 J. G. A. Pocock, 'Deconstructing Europe', *London Review of Books*, 13, 24 (10 Dec. 1991), 6.
27 Ibid., p. 10.
28 Gauri Viswanathan, *Masks of Conquest: Literary Study and British Rule in India* (London: Faber and Faber 1989).

1 'BYRON TURNS TURK': ORIENTALISM AND THE 'EASTERN TALES'

1 Jerome McGann, *The Beauty of Inflections: Literary Investigations in Historical Method and Theory* (Oxford: Clarendon Press 1988), p. 278.
2 Ibid., p. 262; Daniel Watkins, *Social Relations in Byron's 'Eastern Tales'* (London and Toronto: Associated University Presses 1987), p. 15.
3 Philip Martin, *Byron: A Poet before his Public* (Cambridge University Press 1982), pp. 53, 51, 62.
4 McGann, *Beauty of Inflections*, pp. 271–6.
5 Schwab, *Oriental Renaissance*, pp. 190–221.
6 Frank Manuel, *The 18th Century Confronts the Gods* (Cambridge, Mass.: Harvard University Press 1959); Elinor Schaffer, *'Kubla Khan' and the Fall of Jerusalem: The Mythological School in Biblical Criticism and Secular Literature 1770–1880* (Cambridge University Press 1975).
7 Said, *Orientalism*, p. 3.
8 D. K. Fieldhouse, *The Colonial Empires* (London: Weidenfeld & Nicolson 1965), p. 75.
9 J. D. Yohannan, 'The Persian Poetry Fad in England 1770–1825', *Comparative Literature*, 4 (1952), 137–60; 138.
10 Martha Pike Conant, *The Oriental Tale in England in the 18th Century* (New York: Columbia University Press 1908), p. xxvi.
11 Ibid., pp. xviii–xix.
12 Barrell, *Infection of Thomas De Quincey*, p. 150.

13 Laura Brown, *Alexander Pope* (Oxford: Basil Blackwell 1985), pp. 9, 13.

14 John Barrell and Harriet Guest, 'The Uses of Contradiction in Pope's *Epistle to Bathurst*', in John Barrell, *Poetry, Language and Politics* (Manchester: Manchester University Press 1988), pp. 79–99.

15 Rana Kabbani, *Europe's Myths of Orient: Devise and Rule* (London: Macmillan 1986), p. 29.

16 Mrs Barbauld, 'On the Poetical Works of William Collins', in *The Poetical Works of Beattie and Collins* (London 1823), p. 233.

17 John Barrell, *The Dark Side of the Landscape: The Rural Poor in English Painting 1730–1840* (Cambridge University Press 1980). See particularly Chapter 1 on Gainsborough.

18 Henry Maty in *New Review*, IX (June–July 1786), 410–12; X 33–9.

19 Kabbani, *Myths of Orient*, p. 54.

20 Ibid., pp. 23, 29; 'the collection of stories commonly referred to as the *Arabian Nights* was never a definitive text in Arabic literature as is generally supposed by a Western reader' (p. 23).

21 *European Magazine*, X (1786), 102–4.

22 *The Poetical Works of Robert Southey. Complete in one Volume* (London: Longmans, Green & Co. 1876), p. 215 n.

23 Ibid., p. xv.

24 Ibid., p. ix.

25 Yohannan, 'Persian Poetry', 155.

26 Conant, *The Oriental Tale*, pp. 230–1.

27 *Edinburgh Review*, LVII (Nov. 1817), 1–35, 2.

28 Patrick Brantlinger, *Rule of Darkness: British Literature and Imperialism 1830–1914* (Ithaca and London: Cornell University Press 1988), p. 136.

29 McGann, *Beauty of Inflections*, p. 260.

30 Martin Bernal, *Black Athena: The Afroasiatic Roots of Classical Civilization*, vol. 1: *The Fabrication of Ancient Greece 1785–1985* (London: Free Association Books 1987), p. 291. See also C. M. Woodhouse, *The Philhellenes* (London: Hodder & Stoughton 1969).

31 *Orientalism*, p. 286.

32 See my 'Pantisocracy and the Politics of the Preface to *Lyrical Ballads*', forthcoming in *British Literary and Visual Responses to the French Revolution*, ed. Kelvin Everest and Alison Yarrington (Leicester University Press 1992). For Coleridge on Wadstrom, see *The Watchman*, ed. Lewis Patton (London and Princeton, NJ, 1970), pp. 134–5.

33 Marilyn Butler, 'Welsh Nationalism and English Poets 1790–1805' (unpublished paper), p. 13.

34 'W. S. Landor' in *De Quincey's Collected Writings*, 14 vols., ed. David Masson (Edinburgh 1890), XI 403–4.

35 Marjorie Levinson, *The Romantic Fragment Poem* (Chapel Hill, University of North Carolina Press 1986): 'The Vision of Columbus: A Poem in 9 Books', in *The Works of Joel Barlow*, 2 vols. Facsimile reproduction with

intro. by William Bottorff and Arthur Ford (Gainesville, Fla.: Scholars Reprints 1970).

36 Byron claimed in the notes to *The Island* that he had never actually read *Gebir*, admitting that he had had it read *to* him by a 'more recondite reader' – almost certainly Shelley, a great admirer of Landor's poem. This reading – or audience – would have postdated the *Eastern Tales*, so clearly Rogers', rather than Landor's, fragment poem was the model for *The Giaour*, cf. *BPW*, p. 903.

37 Although it is worth noting that Landor used the 'oriental' images of the Simoom (p. 93) and of Vampirism, probably derived from Southey's *Thalaba* (p. 89).

38 Greenblatt, *Marvellous Possessions*, p. 51.

39 Preface to the second edition of *The Voyage of Columbus* in *The Poetical Works of Samuel Rogers* (London: Routledge 1867), p. 68 (no line numbers).

40 I disagree here with Marjorie Levinson that *The Giaour*, unlike *The Voyage of Columbus*, 'contains little or nothing (in the way of superstitious machinery) ... that need be legitimized by the postulate of a primitive cultural source' (*Romantic Fragment Poem* p. 116). Byron's concern with the oriental 'materiale' is evident, and, after all, orientalism was in part a discourse of cultural 'primitivism' in terms of the differential between 'East' and 'West', despite Byron's 'exposure' of the equivalence of the values of both.

41 *Voyage of Columbus*, p. 77.

42 Ibid., p. 114 n.

43 Cf. McGann's editorial commentary in *CPW* III 40, 6–24 for further details of the poem's textual genesis.

44 Cf. Robert Gleckner, *Byron and the Ruins of Paradise* (Baltimore: Johns Hopkins 1967), 'Byron carefully identifies pristine Greece with an unstained Leila (the flower images in the description of the latter, for example, are precisely parallel to the flower imagery in the Greece passage)' p. 105.

45 Jerome McGann, *Fiery Dust: Byron's Poetic Development* (Chicago: Chicago University Press 1968), p. 160.

46 Levinson, *Romantic Fragment Poem*, argues that, rather than emulating a 'bardic' performance, *The Giaour* is more closely approximate to 'an early Greek history in the manner of Herodotus' (p. 118). But Byron was not concerned with 'imitating the overall method of [Herodotus'] *History*' (p. 122). The undeniable presence of Herodotus is no more stable in *The Giaour* than the Ovidian sub-text of *The Bride of Abydos*, although the cancelled Herodotean 'principle of non-reductive historical relativism, is clearly of thematic importance. The poem explores the conditions of a world deprived of the Hellenistic 'point de caption'.

47 *Voyage of Columbus*, p. 86.

48 Ibid., p. 96.

49 Ibid., p. 103.

50 Ibid., p. 106.
51 Ibid., p. 111.
52 Ibid., p. 112.
53 *Romantic Fragment Poem*, p. 126.
54 Byron delivers a panegyric to American liberty in the person of Washington 'the Cincinnatus of the West' in his *Ode to Napoleon Buonaparte* (*BPW*, p. 75) and *Childe Harold* IV stanza 96 (*BPW*, p. 240). But he is a poet of the *old* rather than the New World: America never assumes *central* thematic significance for Byron.
55 Levinson's account of the ambivalence of the figure of Themistocles 'both a champion of the people and a social climber' (p. 124) parallels the point that Troy was taken by guile and not by heroism in my discussion of *The Bride*. Byron's scepticism, born of the contemporary world, leads him to a *retrospective* scepticism in questioning the integrity of the idealized origin. Nevertheless, in the early *Tales* at least he does not allow this to undermine the heuristic imperative of an (absent) classical/heroic scene of origin.
56 Jerome McGann, *Don Juan in Context* (London: John Murray 1976), p. 6.
57 Ibid., p. 69.
58 See McGann, *Fiery Dust*, p. 75.
59 Mario Praz, *The Romantic Agony* (Oxford University Press 1933), pp. 67–8, '... any attempt to see in Harold's pilgrimage an image of the *Itinéraire* (1811) – an idea which Chateaubriand himself suggests... does not bear examination of the facts. Apart from the fact that the publication of the *Itinéraire* was later than Byron's own journey (which started in 1809) and the composition of the first cantos of *Childe Harold*, this journey... resolved itself in the end into the Grand Tour which it was the usual custom for Englishmen of rank to take.' Byron cited Chateaubriand in the notes to *The Bride*, a point which Praz has missed, but which does not affect the validity of his point (cf. *CPW* III, p. 441 note to line 389).
60 Chateaubriand, *Travels in Greece, Palestine, Egypt, and Barbary during the Years 1806–7*, trans. Frederick Shoberl, 2nd edn (London 1812), II, 199–200.
61 Carolyn Springer, *The Marble Wilderness: Ruins and Representation in Italian Romanticism 1775–1850* (Cambridge University Press 1987), p. 6.
62 Martin Kelsall, *Byron's Politics* (Sussex: Harvester 1988); Abraham Kriegel, 'Liberty and Whiggery in early 19th Century England', *Journal of Modern History*, LII (1980), 253–78.
63 Kelsall, *Byron's Politics*, p. 56.
64 Leslie Marchand, *Byron: A Portrait* (London: Cresset Library 1971), p. 96.
65 John Keats, 'On Seeing the Elgin Marbles', *Poetical Works*, ed. H. W. Garrod (Oxford University Press 1956), p. 376.
66 *Edinburgh Review*, XXX, LIX (June 1818), 99.

67 See Peter Manning, 'The Tales and Politics: The Corsair, Lara and the White Doe of Rylstone', in *Byron: Poetry and Politics*, ed. Erwin A. Sturzl and James Hogg (Salzburger Studien zur Anglistik und Amerikanistic band 13), p. 212.
68 Kelsall, *Byron's Politics*, p. 95.
69 Robert Ogle, 'The Metamorphosis of Selim: Ovidian Myth in The Bride of Abydos', *Studies in Romanticism*, 20 (Spring 1981), 21–30; 24.
70 Yohannan, 'Persian Poetry', p. 150.
71 *Embassy to Constantinople: The Travels of Lady Mary Wortley Montagu*, intro. by Dervla Murphy, ed. Christopher Pick (London: Century 1988), p. 118.
72 Byron did explore the incest/rebellion theme in *Parisina*, although the forbidden love represented in that poem was between a bastard son and his father's wife, rather than daughter.
73 Kelsall, *Byron's Politics*, p. 150.
74 Peter Burke, 'The Virgin of the Carmine and The Revolt of Masaniello', *Past and Present*, 99 (1983), 3–21; 6.
75 *Biographia Literaria*, ed. James Engell and W. Jackson Bate (New Jersey: Princeton University Press 1983), II 190.
76 *Edinburgh Review*, XXIII, XLV (April 1814), 198–228; 204.
77 *Don Juan in Context*, p. 126.
78 Marina Vitale, 'The Domesticated Heroine in Byron's Corsair and William Hone's Prose Adaptation', *Literature and History*, 10: 1 (Spring 1984), 72–94; 77.
79 John Cam Hobhouse, *A Journey through Albania, and other Provinces of Turkey in Europe and Asia, to Constantinople, during the years 1809 and 1810*, 2 vols., 2nd edn (London 1813), I 300.
80 Norman Bryson, *Tradition and Desire from Delacroix to David* (Cambridge University Press 1987), p. 74.
81 Ibid., p. 73.
82 See Hobhouse, *A Journey*, II, 1027–47 for an account.
83 Kriegel, 'Liberty' 271.
84 Malcolm Kelsall, 'The Byronic Hero and Revolution in Ireland: the Politics of "Glenarvon"', in *Byron: Poetry and Politics*, pp. 137–51; 141.
85 Vitale, 'Domesticated Heroine', 79.
86 Gleckner, *Ruins of Paradise*, p. 164.
87 Ralph Millbanke, Earl of Lovelace, *Astarte: A Fragment of Truth...Concerning Lord Byron*, ed. Mary, Countess of Lovelace (London: Christophers 1921), pp. 20–1.
88 Louis Crompton, *Byron and Greek Love: Homophobia in 19th Century England* (London: Faber and Faber 1985), p. 210.
89 Matthew Lewis, *The Monk*, ed. Howard Anderson (Oxford University Press 1977). See p. 75 for Mathilda's 'revelation'.
90 Crompton, *Greek Love*, p. 123.
91 Manning, 'The Corsair, Lara, and the White Doe'.
92 Brantlinger, *Rule of Darkness*, p. 262.

93 Jürgen Habermas, *The Philosophical Discourse of Modernity*, trans. Frederick Lawrence (Cambridge: Polity Press 1987), p. 110.
94 Ibid., p. 110.
95 Frantz Fanon, *The Wretched of the Earth*, trans. Constance Farrington (Harmondsworth: Penguin 1967), p. 80.
96 Richard Burton, *Narrative of a Pilgrimage to Meccah and Medinah*, 3rd edn, rev. (London and Belfast: William Mullan 1879), p. 7.
97 *A Letter to John Murray on William Bowles' Strictures on the Life and Writings of Pope* (London 1821), p. 49, pp. 45–6.
98 *Don Juan in Context*, p. 124.
99 McGann, *Beauty of Inflections*, p. 286.
100 Jean Starobinski, *1789: Les emblèmes de la raison* (Paris: Flammarion 1979), p. 26.
101 See Caroline Franklin, 'Haidee and Neuha: Byron's Heroines of the South', *The Byron Journal*, 18 (1990), 37–49, for a comparison between 'Neuha, who is man's equal in every way in a state of nature, and the specifically "feminine" moral role enjoined on Northern women of modern civilization, idealized in the portrait of Aurora Raby in *Don Juan*' (48). Thanks to Professor Anne Barton for suggesting the relevance of *The Island* to my reading of the *Eastern Tales*.

2 'SHARP PHILANTHROPY': PERCY BYSSHE SHELLEY AND
ROMANTIC INDIA

1 Thomas Medwin, *The Angler in Wales*, 2 vols. (London: Richard Bentley 1834) II 84.
2 Ernest J. Lovell, *Captain Medwin: Friend of Byron and Shelley* (London: Macdonald 1962), p. 55; *Angler*, II 84.
3 *Angler*, I 4.
4 Lovell, *Captain Medwin*, p. 54.
5 *Collected Letters of P. B. Shelley*, ed. Frederick L. Jones, 2 vols. (Oxford 1964); II 242.
6 Patrick Brantlinger, *Rule of Darkness: British Literature and Imperialism 1830–1914* (Ithaca and London: Cornell University Press 1988); Martin Green *Dreams of Adventure, Deeds of Empire* (New York: Basic Books 1979).
7 See Jerome McGann, *The Romantic Ideology: A Critical Investigation* (Chicago and London: Chicago University Press 1983).
8 See *SL* II 361. The letter in question is now lost. T. L. Peacock later played a crucial role in the development of the East India Company's armoured gunboats – his 'iron chickens' – which were used with lethal results against the Chinese in the first Opium War. See Daniel R. Headrick, *The Tools of Empire: Technology and European Imperialism in the 19th Century* (New York and Oxford: Oxford University Press 1981), pp. 17–57.
9 Quoted by Raymond Schwab in *The Oriental Renaissance: Europe's*

Rediscovery of India and the East, 1680–1880, trans. Gene Patterson Black and Victor Reinking (New York: Colombia University Press 1984), p. 63; Joseph Raban, 'Shelley's *Prometheus Unbound*: Why the Indian Caucasus?' *Keats–Shelley Journal*, XII (Winter 1963), 95–106; 96.

10 Garland Cannon, 'The Literary Place of Sir William Jones', *Journal of the Asiatic Society*, 2, 1 (1960), 47–61; 56.

11 Edward Said, *Orientalism* (London and Harmondsworth: Penguin Books 1985), p. 63.

12 John Barrell, *The Infection of Thomas De Quincey: A Psychopathology of Imperialism* (New Haven and London: Yale University Press 1991), p. 160.

13 *Complete Poetical Works of P. B. Shelley*, ed. Thomas Hutchinson (London: Oxford University Press 1934), p. 447. A similar dichotomy is constructed in Mary Shelley's antisemitic MS 'History of the Jews', probably written in 1815. Here the religion and mythology of the Jews (described by Mary as 'a herd of arrabian [sic] robbers') is unfavourably compared to the Greek. See Jane Blumberg 'A Question of Radicalism: Mary Shelley's Manuscript "History of the Jews"' in *Revolution and English Romanticism: Politics and Rhetoric*, ed. Keith Hanley and Raman Selden (New York and Hemel Hempstead: Harvester Wheatsheaf and St Martin's Press 1990), pp. 131–46.

14 Ronald Inden, *Imagining India* (Oxford: Basil Blackwell 1990), p. 17.

15 *Orientalism*, p. 21.

16 Marilyn Butler, 'Plotting the Revolution: the Political Narrative of Romantic Poetry and Criticism', in *Romantic Revolutions: Criticism and Theory*, ed. Kenneth R. Johnston et al. (Bloomington: Indiana University Press, 1990), p. 135.

17 *SL* 1 563–4.

18 Quoted by Ainslie Embree, *Imagining India: Essays on Indian History* (Delhi: Oxford University Press 1989), p. 36.

19 Javed Majeed, 'James Mill's *The History of British India* and Utilitarianism as a Rhetoric of Reform', *Modern Asian Studies* 24, 2 (1990), 209, 224; 222. Shelley's placement of his poem in a geographical locus *between* metropolitan Britain and colonial India invited the sort of deliberate misreading exemplified by John Taylor Coleridge, the poet's nephew, in his scathing review of *The Revolt of Islam*. 'The laws and government on which Mr Shelley's reasoning proceeds, are the Turkish, administered by a lawless despot; his religion is the Mohammedan, maintained by senile hypocrites; and his scene for their joint operation Greece, the land full beyond all others of recollections of former glory and independence... We are Englishmen, Christians, free, and independent; we ask Mr Shelley how his case applies to *us*? or what *we* learn from it to the prejudice of our own institutions?' *Quarterly Review*, April 1819 (publ. Sept. 1819), in *The Young Romantics and Critical Opinion*, ed. Theodore Redpath (London: Harrap 1973), pp. 337–47; 342. Shelley's Orient was evidently not abstract *enough* to make its allegorical intentions unmistakably obvious and pre-empt literal 'misreadings' such as

J. T. Coleridge's. This *despite* its use of allegorical emblems like the eagle and serpent of Canto 1, or the universalism of Laon and Cythna's idealism. Coleridge's interpretation militates against exactly that Utilitarian and radical 'denial of distinction' discussed by Javed Majeed. See also Majeed's important study *Ungoverned Imaginings: James Mill's 'History of British India' and Orientalism*, (Clarendon Press: Oxford 1992). (Published when the present book was in proofs.)

20 *SL* 1 513. To Byron, Nov. 1816.

21 C. A. Bayly, *Indian Society and the Making of the British Empire* (*The New Cambridge History of India*, II, 1) (Cambridge University Press 1988), p. 170. For an earlier instance of British reactions to rioting and insurrection in colonial India, see William Hickey's account of the Cressy affair in Calcutta in May 1778. Hickey, anticipating De Quincey in his account of Malays, attributed the 'Musselman's' riot ('with a view to a general massacre of the Europeans') to their 'swallowing of large quantities of an intoxicating drug called bang' which 'work[s] them up to a state of absolute madness [during which] they commit great excess' *Memoirs of William Hickey*, ed. Peter Quennell (London: RKP 1975) p. 246.

22 *S Prose*, p. 145.

23 Ibid., p. 146.

24 Bernard Blackstone, *The Lost Travellers: A Romantic Theme with Variations* (London: Longmans 1962), p. 228.

25 *S Prose*, p. 150.

26 See Barrell *Infection of Thomas De Quincey*, p. 127; Barrell's account of the failure of De Quincey's narratives of revenge and reparation 'because the characters which the narratives sought to exonerate, to protect, to accuse and to destroy could so seldom be kept from merging into each other' applies also to Shelley in this case.

27 *Wordsworth's Selected Prose*, ed. John O. Hayden (London: Penguin 1988), p. 99. Preface to *The Borderers*. Wordsworth's play, written in 1796–7 was not published until 1842: the Preface was not published until 1940. I am not suggesting any influence here, although it is not difficult to imagine how Shelley *would* have read the play.

28 Raymond Williams, *The Country and the City* (London: Hogarth Press 1985), pp. 279–88; David Erdman, *William Blake: Prophet against Empire* (Princeton 1954). See Benita Parry, 'Problems in Current Theories of Colonial Discourse', *Oxford Literary Review*, 9: 1–2 (1987), 51–2, for a useful critique of 'the eurovision of the metropolitan left'.

29 Brantlinger, *Rule of Darkness*, p. 27.

30 Homi Bhabha, 'Signs Taken for Wonders: Questions of Ambivalence and Authority under a Tree outside Delhi, May 1817', *Europe and its Others*, 2 vols., ed. Francis Barker et al. (Colchester: Essex University Press 1985), I 89.

31 Cf. Robert Young, *White Mythologies: Writing History and the West* (London and New York: Routledge 1990), p. 144.

32 'Signs Taken for Wonders', I 91.

33 Homi Bhabha, 'The Other Question...; the Stereotype and Colonial Discourse', *Screen* 24: 6 (Nov.–Dec. 1983), 24.
34 Gayatri Spivak, 'The Rani of Sirmur', *Europe and its Others* 1, 131.
35 Parry, 'Current Theories of Colonial Discourse', 41.
36 Cf. Young's excellent discussion of Said in *White Mythologies*, pp. 127–9.
37 Bhabha, 'The Other Question...', 27.
38 Homi Bhabha, 'Sly Civility', *October* 34 (1985), 71–80.
39 David Kopf, *British Orientalism and the Bengal Renaissance* (California University Press 1969); *The Brahmo Samaj and the Shaping of the Modern Indian Mind* (Princeton University Press 1979).
40 Gauri Viswanathan, 'The Beginnings of English Literary Study in British India', *OLR* 9: 1–2 (1987), 2–26. This article reappears as the foundational chapter of her more extensive survey of the role of literature in the nineteenth-century colonial curriculum, *Masks of Conquest: Literary Study and British Rule in India* (London: Faber and Faber 1990).
41 Ibid., 2. See also Chris Baldick *The Social Mission of English Criticism 1848–1932* (Oxford: Clarendon Press 1987), pp. 70–5, on the importance of English literature in the examinations of the India Civil Service. Baldick points out that 'Arnold's conceptions of the humanizing and socially healing power of literary culture had in fact quickly taken root where Homer was unavailable: among women, artisans, Indians and their respective teachers' (p. 72).
42 Eric Stokes, *The English Utilitarians and India* (Oxford: Clarendon Press 1959). As Bhabha points out, Stokes disavows the 'anomalous gaze of otherness' in arguing that 'certainly India played *no* central part in fashioning the distinctive qualities of English civilization', 'The Ambivalence of Colonial Discourse', *October* 28 (1984), 129.
43 See Paul Rabinow, *French Modern: Norms and Forms of the Social Environment* (Cambridge, Mass.: MIT Press 1989) p. 289; Philip Mason, *The Men who Ruled India* (London: J. Cape Ltd 1985), p. 236.
44 Young, *White Mythologies*, p. 139.
45 Peter Stallybrass and Allon White, *The Politics and Poetics of Transgression* (London: Methuen 1986), p. 194.
46 Ibid., p. 193.
47 See Michael Hechter, *Internal Colonization: The Celtic Fringe in British National Development 1536–1966* (London: Routledge & Kegan Paul 1975), and Headrick, *The Tools of Empire*.
48 Although Stallybrass and White are critical of the 'bourgeois romanticism' of Julia Kristeva and Michel Foucault (p. 200), the latter's account of the 'institutional inventiveness' of power (p. 94) runs parallel to their own theorization of the poetics of transgression. Foucault's blindness to the question of imperialism is discussed by Robert Young (*White Mythologies*, chapter 5) and Gayatri Spivak, for whom Foucault is 'a brilliant thinker of power-in-spacing, but the awareness of the topographical reinscription of imperialism does not inform his presuppositions... The clinic, the asylum, the prison, the university – all

seem to be screen-allegories that foreclose a reading of the broader narratives of imperialism' ('Can the Subaltern Speak?' in *Marxism and the Interpretation of Culture*, ed. Cary Nelson and Lawrence Grossberg (London: Macmillan 1988), pp. 271–313; 290).

49 Barrell, *Infection of Thomas De Quincey*. 'The terms self and other can be thought of as superseded by "this" and "that"' in a narrative which now says that there is *this* here, and it is different from *that* there, but the difference between them, though in its own way important, is as nothing compared with the difference between the two of them considered together, and that third thing, way over there, which is truly *other* to them both... what at first seems "other" can be made over to the side of the self – to a subordinate position on that side – only so long as a new, and a newly absolute "other" is constituted to fill the discursive space that has thus been evacuated' (p. 10).

50 Fiona Stafford, *The Sublime Savage: James Macpherson and the Poems of Ossian* (Edinburgh University Press 1988), p. 182.

51 James Mill, *The History of British India*, 4th edn with notes and continuation by H. H. Wilson, 8 vols. (London: James Madden 1840), IV chapter 6, pp. 616–17.

52 Majeed, 'James Mill's *History*', pp. 213–15.

53 See Stokes, *English Utilitarians*, pp. 52–66.

54 Jean Starobinski *J.-J. Rousseau: Transparency and Obstruction*, trans. Arthur Goldhammer, intro. by Robert J. Morrissey (Chicago University Press 1988), xxii.

55 *S Prose*, p. 278.

56 Inden, *Imagining India*, p. 45.

57 Ibid.

58 *Angler*, II 84.

59 Spivak, 'Rani of Sirmur', 133.

60 Thomas Beddoes, *Alexander's Expedition Down the Hydaspes and the Indus to the Indian Ocean* (London: Murray 1792), p. 29–32, lines 251–6, 275–80. My reading of Beddoes' poem differs from that of Roy Porter in *Doctor of Society: Thomas Beddoes and the Sick Trade in late Enlightenment England* (London: Routledge 1992), pp. 166–7.

61 Beddoes, *Alexander's Expedition*, p. 82.

62 *The Poetical Works of Thomas Campbell* (London: Frederick Warne and Co. n.d.) p. 21. Thanks to Marilyn Butler for pointing this out to me.

63 Ibid., p. 13.

64 Bernard Semmell, *The Rise of Free Trade Imperialism: Classical Political Economy, the Empire of Free Trade, and Imperialism 1750–1850* (Cambridge University Press 1970), p. 4.

65 See David Musselwhite, 'The Trial of Warren Hastings', in *1789: Reading Writing Revolution, Proceedings of the Essex Conference of the Sociology of Literature Conference, July 1981*, ed. Francis Barker et al. (Colchester: Essex University Press 1982), pp. 226–51.

66 Stokes, *English Utilitarians*, p. 15.

67 Ibid., p. 18. See my *Politics of Imagination in Coleridge's Critical Thought*

(London: Macmillan 1988), pp. 1–46 for discussion of Coleridge, Wordsworth and the Harrington Agrarian Ideal.

68 Embree, *Imagining India*, p. 100.

69 Bayly, *Indian Society*, p. 116.

70 *Southey's Poetical Works, Complete in One Volume* (London: Longman 1876), p. xv.

71 Ibid., p. 553.

72 This despite the strictures of John Foster, in his review of *Kehama*, *Eclectic Review*, vii (March and April 1811), as discussed in the introduction to this book. Sections of this review are republished in *Robert Southey: The Critical Heritage*, ed. Lionel Madden (London and Boston: RKP 1972), pp. 138–45. My thanks to John Barrell for drawing my attention to it.

73 *SL* 1 154–5.

74 *Eclectic Review*, vii (March 1811), 186.

75 Brantlinger, *Rule of Darkness*, p. 88.

76 See Christopher Pinney, 'Colonial Anthropology in the "Laboratory of Mankind"', *The Raj: India and the British 1600–1947*, ed. C. A. Bayly (London: National Portrait Gallery Publications, 1990), pp. 252–63.

77 S. T. Coleridge, *Biographia Literaria*, ed. James Engell and W. Jackson Bate, 2 vols. (London and Princeton: RKP and Princeton University Press 1983), 1 189.

78 See O. P. Kejariwal, *The Asiatic Society of Bengal and the Discovery of India's Past* (Delhi: Oxford University Press 1988). For an intelligent appraisal of Jones in his intellectual context, see S. N. Mukherjee, *Sir William Jones: A Study in 18th Century British Attitudes to India* (Hyderabad: Orient Longman 1987).

79 John Drew, *India and the Romantic Imagination* (Delhi: Oxford University Press 1987), p. 46.

80 *The Works of Sir William Jones*, ed. Lady Jones, 6 vols. (London 1799), VI 356. Elinor Shaffer describes Jones' work as 'a strange mixture of a new and self-professed accuracy, geographical, linguistic, historical, with unfounded traditional views'. See '*Kubla Khan*' and the Fall of Jerusalem* (Cambridge University Press 1975), p. 117.

81 Revd Sydney Smith, 'On Indian Missions', *Edinburgh Review*, 12 (1808), xxiii 177.

82 Eliza Hamilton, *Letters of a Hindoo Rajah, to which is prefixed a Preliminary Dissertation on the History, Religion and Manners of the Hindoos*, 2 vols. (Dublin 1797), 1 xx.

83 The *Persian Letters* (1721) was the model for another 'Indian' novel very different in its ideological bent from *Letters of a Hindoo Rajah*, the feminism and anti-matrimonialism of which had a profound effect on Shelley. This was James Lawrence's *The Empire of the Nairs, or The Rights of Women, an Utopian Romance, in 12 books* (London: Thomas Hookham 1811). Lawrence was more interested in the polemical possibilities of the matrilinear Nair society of Malabar than in representing India, and his Malabar is really an idealized England devoid of 'oriental materiale'.

See also *SL* 1 323 (17 Aug. 1812 to James Lawrence) and for the influence of the *Nairs* on Shelley's poetry, particularly *The Revolt of Islam*, see Walter Graham, 'Shelley and the *Empire of the Nairs*', *PMLA*, XL (1925), 881–91. In the introduction I mentioned Southey's *Letters from England* in relation to the genre of the *Persian Letters*.

84 The influence of *Shakuntala* on European (particularly German) Romanticism is discussed by Schwab, *Oriental Renaissance*, pp. 57ff.

85 *The Missionary*, II 210–14.

86 *SL* 1 107.

87 Lata Mani, 'The Production of an Official Discourse on *Sati* in Early 19th Century Bengal', in *Europe and its Others*, 1 107–27; 122. See also Spivak, 'Can the Subaltern Speak?', pp. 296–306. For Rammohun Roy's part in the campaign against *sati*, see Iqbal Singh, *Rammohun Roy: A Biographical Inquiry into the Making of Modern India*, 3 vols. (Bombay: Asia Publishing House 1958) I, chapter 9, 'Not for Burning'. Iqbal Singh writes, '...far from acting as deterrents these [British] "regulations" helped to create the ambient impression of official sanction for the rite of concremation...Between 1815 and 1818, recorded cases of *Suttee* in the six divisions of Calcutta, Dacca, Murshidabad, Patna, Benares and Bareilly rose dramatically from 387 to 840; and these statistics must be assumed to have been on the conservative side. Doubtless, there were other reasons for the increase, but it is generally agreed that the ingenious idea of "regulating" ritual murder was an important contributory factor' (1 197).

88 Mill *History*, IV, ch. 5, 511. H. H. Wilson's 1840 edition cuts out Mill's impious reference to the Bible (which I have restored in the text), writing simply that the 'Shasters and Khoran...were just as well calculated for defining the rights of the people of England'. Incidentally, this seems to contradict William Thomas' assertion that Wilson, although he added a substantial body of notes in his 1840 edition, 'left Mill's text unaltered'. See *History of British India*, abridged and with intro. by William Thomas (Chicago University Press 1975), p. xliii. Thomas' abridgement is based on Mill's second edition.

89 Bayly, *Indian Society*, p. 158.

90 See note 47 above.

91 Said, *Orientalism*, p. 19.

92 Spivak, 'Rani of Sirmur', 130; 141.

93 Martin Bernal, *Black Athena: The Afroasiatic Roots of Classical Civilization* (London: Free Association Books, 1987), pp. 169–72.

94 *Orientalism*, p. 82.

95 Constantin Volney, *The Ruins: or A Survey of the Revolutions of Empires*, 2nd edn (London: Joseph Johnson 1795), p. 292.

96 Ibid., p. 229.

97 Thomas Maurice, *The History of Hindostan, its Arts and Sciences, as connected with the History of the other great Empires of Asia, during the most Ancient Periods of the World*, 2 vols. (London 1795–98) 1 359.

98 G. S. Faber, *The Origin of Pagan Idolatry, ascertained from Historical*

Testimony and Circumstantial Evidence, 3 vols. (London 1816), '[The Gentiles] deduced from a *single* destruction and renovation of the world, a *series* of similar destructions and renovations...the vain curiosity of man proceeded to inquire whether matter itself was not eternal, and whether each world through an infinite series could be deemed more than a mere organization of preexisting substance', 111. Byron puts the doctrine of palingenesis in the mouth of Lucifer in his *Cain: A Mystery*, (*BPW*, p. 530, 11, i, lines 153–65).

99 Faber, *Pagan Idolatry*, 1 18.

100 Cf. ibid., 111 77.

101 *SL* 1 45.

102 Bernal, *Black Athena*, p. 230.

103 Reuben Burrow, 'A Proof that the Hindoos had the binomial Theorem', *Supplemental Volumes to the Works of Sir William Jones*, 2 vols. (London 1801), 1 376.

104 Partha Mitter, *Much Maligned Monsters: A History of European Reactions to Indian Art* (Oxford: Clarendon Press 1977), p. 218, and the whole section (pp. 202–20) on German Romantic attitudes to Indian art. Demonstrative of the cross-fertilization of diverse European discourses on India is Mitter's point that 'One cannot afford to underestimate [James] Mill's opinions [on India] for even Hegel was to depend on the English Utilitarian for his remarks on Indian culture' (p. 177). For the views of German 'Higher Critics' like Eichhorn, Heyne, Gabler, Herder and Schelling on India, see Shaffer, *Kubla Khan* pp. 121–44. See also A. Leslie Willson *A Mythical Image: The Ideal of India in German Romanticism* (Durham, NC: Duke 1964). Thanks to John Morrow for this last reference.

105 Schwab, *Oriental Renaissance*, p. 194.

106 Ibid., p. 189.

107 Ibid., p. 236.

108 Bernal, *Black Athena*, p. 227.

109 S. T. Coleridge, *Philosophical Lectures*. ed. with intro. by K. Coburn (London: Pilot Press 1949), lecture XIII, p. 385.

110 Schaffer, 'Kubla Khan', p. 133.

111 *The Friend*, 2 vols., ed. Barbara Rooke (London and Princeton University Press 1976), 1 56; *Phil. Lects.* lecture 11, pp. 91–110.

112 *The Friend*, 1 370.

113 *SPW*, p. 128, lines 3685–6. Henceforth I will quote only line numbers.

114 Stephen Greenblatt, *Shakespearean Negotiations: The Circulation of Social Energy in Renaissance England* (Oxford: Clarendon Press 1988), pp. 4–7.

115 *Edinburgh Review*, VI, xii (1805), 469.

116 *SL* 11 361.

117 *SL* 11 374.

118 *The Poetical Works of Thomas Moore* (London and Edinburgh: William Nimmo 1875), p. 58. No line numbering.

119 Richard Holmes, *Shelley: The Pursuit* (London: Penguin Books 1987), p. 401.

120 For Shelley's *Zeinab and Kathema*, see the *Esdaile Poems: Early Minor Poems from the Esdaile Notebook*, ed. with notes by Neville Rogers (Oxford: Clarendon Press 1966), pp. 96–102; *WJW* IV 534.

121 *Esdaile Poems*, pp. 101, 11, 139–150.

122 *MPW*, p. 76.

123 Ibid., p. 90.

124 For Shelley's Irish expedition, see Timothy Webb, '"A Noble Field"; Shelley's Irish Expedition and the Lessons of the French Revolution', in *Robespierre and Co: atti della ricerca sulla Letteratura Francese della Revoluzione*, ed. Nadia Minerva, 3 vols. (Bologna: Edizione Analisi 1990) II 553–76.

125 *SL* I 239.

126 *S Prose*, p. 46. It is interesting to compare this with Rammohun Roy's editorial on Ireland dated 11 October 1822 in his Persian language weekly *Mirat-ul-Akhbar*. Rammohun attacks the tithe system ('on account of the stipends of the royal clergymen who are appointed to officiate in Ireland, the Government of Ireland exact taxes every year from those who positively refuse to be led by these clergymen in religious matters' and absentee landlordism, both matters with some potential relevance in colonial Bengal. Articles such as this one, and also an 1822 editorial which dealt flippantly with the doctrine of the Trinity in an epitaph on Bishop Middleton of Calcutta, Coleridge's schoolfriend, led to the introduction of draconian measures of press censureship by Lord Hastings' government in March 1823. Saumyendranath Tagore, 'Rammohun: Journalist and Champion of Free Press', in *Rammohun Roy: A Bicentenary Tribute*, ed. Niharranjan Ray (New Delhi: National Book Trust 1974), pp. 113–32; 121.

127 *SPW*, pp. 787–8, VII lines 26–36.

128 Volney, *Ruins*, p. 23.

129 Leigh Hunt, Review of *Revolt of Islam* in the Examiner I, 22 Feb. and 1 March 1818. Republished in Redpath, *The Young Romantics*, pp. 329–33, p. 332

130 Sydney Owenson, Lady Morgan, *The Missionary, an Indian Tale*, 3 vols. (2nd edn London 1811) III 176.

131 See note 83 above. At the conclusion of Byron's *Sardanapalus* (1821), the Greek slave girl Myra immolates herself on the pyre of her master Sardanapalus. Myra *draws* attention to the fact that she is committing a form of *sati*: 'And dost thou think / A Greek girl dare not do for love, that which / An Indian widow braves for custom?' (*BPW*, p. 492, 11. 465–7). Shelley's disavowal of the fact that *his* Greek heroine is committing a form of *sati* (an instance of his working *away* from his source) indicates his unease in relation to both the source and to Indian customs.

132 *The Missionary*, III 183.

133 Karl Marx, 'The British Rule in India', in *Marx and Engels: On Colonialism* (Moscow: Foreign Language Publishing House 1960), pp. 36; 46; 36. For a critique of Marx's orientalism, and particularly of

the notion of the 'Asiatic Mode of Production', see Inden, *Imagining India*, p. 53.

134 *S Prose*, p. 238.

135 Kopf, *Brahmo Samaj*, p. 43. And yet, despite the 'enlightenment' of the Bengali elite, 'it was able to participate only intellectually in the modern movement...because however much British Imperialism disrupted the old traditional order, it did not propel society along the line of material and social development' (p. 46). Shelley's 'anxiety' about the Brahmins exemplifies Kopf's point, and it seems to me (as I will argue below) that Rammohun Roy's cultural negotiation with British power was more complex, and ultimately more radical, than Derozio's, more along the lines of Shelley's *desideratum*. For the *poetic* influence of Shelley on Derozio, see *Poems of Henry Louis Vivian Derozio, a Forgotten Anglo-Indian Poet*, intro. by F. B. Bradley-Burt (Oxford University Press 1923), in particular 'The Poet's Habitation' (echoing *Epipsychidion* and 'Lines written among the Euganean Hills') and 'Leaves'.

136 Rana Kabbani, *Europe's Myths of Orient* (London: Macmillan 1986), p. 67.

137 See Edward Said, 'Orientalism Reconsidered', in *Europe and its Others*, I 23.

138 See, for example, James Notopoulis, *The Platonism of Shelley* (Durham, NC, 1949) for an exemplary case.

139 Cannon, 'Literary Place of Sir William Jones', 57.

140 Drew, *Romantic Imagination*.

141 *S Prose*, p. 292.

142 See Robert Schofield, 'Joseph Priestley, eighteenth-century British Neoplatonism, and S. T. Coleridge', in Everett Mendelsohn, ed., *Transformation and Tradition in the Sciences* (Cambridge University Press 1984), pp. 237–54.

143 C. E. Pulos, *The Deep Truth: A Study of Shelley's Scepticism* (Nebraska 1954), p. 39.

144 *WJW* I 11.

145 Drew, *Romantic Imagination*, pp. 201–6; Joseph Raban, 'Shelley's *Prometheus Unbound*: Why the Indian Caucasus?' *Keats–Shelley Journal*, XII (Winter 1963), 102. See also Michael Rossington, 'Shelley and the Orient', *Keats–Shelley Review*, 6 (Autumn 1991) 18–36; 28–34. (Published when the present study was in proofs.)

146 Bernal, *Black Athena*, p. 229.

147 Pinney, 'Colonial Anthropology', 253.

148 Mary Shelley, *Frankenstein, or the New Prometheus* (New York: Bantam Books 1981), p. 1.

149 *SPW*, p. 15.

150 Joseph Raban, 'Shelley the Dionysian', in *Shelley Revalued: Essays from the Gregynog Conference*, ed. Kelvin Everest (Leicester University Press 1983), p. 27.

151 *SL* I 545.

152 *WJW* I 264. See note 204 below, on the equation between Dionysus, Prometheus and Rama in *Prometheus Unbound*.

153 *Keats' Poetical Works*, ed. H. W. Garrod (Oxford University Press 1956), p. 138, lines 265–7.

154 Ibid., p. 156, lines 984–7.

155 Drew, *Romantic Imagination*, pp. 255–8.

156 *The Missionary*, I 149–50.

157 Ibid., I 78.

158 Ibid., I 48.

159 *SL* I 107.

160 *The Missionary*, I 147, 146–7.

161 *Endymion*, IV, lines 984–6 (*Keats' Poetical Works* p. 156).

162 *SL* I 112.

163 Mary Wollstonecraft, *A Vindication of the Rights of Woman*, intro. by Mary Warnock (London: Dent 1985), p. 100.

164 Ibid.

165 'De Generis Humani Varietate Natura', in *The Anthropological Treatises of Johann Friedrich Blumenbach*, trans. Thomas Bendyshe (London: Longmans 1865), p. 269.

166 *SPW*, p. 511, lines 182–3.

167 In connection with this, see Gayatri Spivak, 'French Feminism in an International Frame', which discusses the 'inbuilt colonialism of First World Feminism towards the Third', in *In Other Worlds: Essays in Cultural Politics* (New York and London: Routledge 1987), pp. 134–53.

168 *Romanticism and Feminism*, ed. Anne Mellor (Bloomington: Indiana University Press 1988), p. 7.

169 Stokes, *English Utilitarians*, p. 39.

170 *S Prose*, p. 238.

171 Mill, *History*, III, ch. 5, p. 517.

172 *Monthly Magazine*, 43 (June 1817), 392.

173 Kopf, *Brahmo Samaj*, p. xiii.

174 Singh, *Rammohun Roy*, I 131.

175 Ibid., I 83–109.

176 Ibid., I 146.

177 Kopf, *Brahmo Samaj*, p. 157.

178 Rammohun's *Precepts of Jesus* are reminiscent of Shelley's lost *Biblical Extracts*. As the poet wrote in Feb. 1812: 'I have often thought that the moral sayings of Jesus Christ might be very useful, if selected from the mystery and immorality which surrounds them; it is a little work I have in contemplation.' David Clark's identification of the *Extracts* with Shelley's *Essay on Christianity* seems to me unwarranted. *S Prose*, p. 196.

179 *The Brahmunical Magazine* (sic) IV (Calcutta 1823), p. 1.

180 Sisir Kumar Das, 'Rammohun: His Religious Thought', in *Rammohun Roy: A Bicentenary Tribute*, p. 83.

181 Kopf, *Brahmo Samaj*, p. 42; Spivak, 'Can the Subaltern Speak?', 284.

182 B. N. Ganguli, 'Rammohun Roy: His Political and Economic Thought', in *Rammohun Roy: A Bicentenary Tribute*, p. 45.

183 Embree, *Imagining India*, p. 136.

184 This point is brought out in Lant Carpenter's *Review of the Labours, Opinions, and Character of Rajah Rammohun Roy, in a Discourse on the Occasion of his Death, delivered in Lewin's Mead (Unitarian) Chapel, Bristol* (Bristol 1833). The common misapprehension in England that Rammohun had converted to Christianity was countered by the discovery of the Brahmin sacred thread around his chest after his death. The wishful thinking of the polite was matched by the orientalist luridity of the impolite, who mistook Rammohun (the first distinguished Indian to visit England) for the only prominent Indian they had heard of: as the landlord of a pub on the road from Liverpool to London in which Rammohun stopped to break his journey put it 'Tippoo Sabe has come to England for to visit King William!' (Iqbal Singh, III 375).

185 Kopf, *Brahmo Samaj*, pp. 43–6.

186 Singh, *Rammohun Roy*, I 316–17.

187 Ibid., I 318.

188 Bhabha, 'Signs Taken for Wonders', 97.

189 *CL* IV, p. 917. It is a sad reflection on Rammohun's subsequent obscurity in the West that the editor of Coleridge's *Collected Letters* should have been unable to identify the 'Luther of the Brahmins'. Thanks to Daniel Roberts for pointing out Coleridge's letter to me.

190 Holmes, *Shelley*, p. 403.

191 *Angler*, II 84.

192 It should be pointed out here that Rammohun formed a temporary alliance with the (Trinitarian) Baptist missionaries at Serampore during his campaign against *sati*, making use of their printing press to publish his pamphlets. He even managed to convert one of their number, the Revd William Adams, to Unitarianism in 1821. But the publication of *The Precepts of Jesus* caused them great offence and ended the brief detente. There is a possibility that this might explain Shelley's uncharacteristic (albeit qualified) sympathy for Christian missionaries in the *Philosophical View*.

193 *S Prose*, p. 238.

194 Drew, *Romantic Imagination*, p. 259.

195 See my *Politics of Imagination*, chaps. 17, 18, 19.

196 *WJW* IV 527–48; 549–62.

197 F. von Schlegel, 'On the Language and Wisdom of the Indians', in *The Aesthetic and Miscellaneous Works of F. von Schlegel*, trans. E. J. Millington (London: H. G. Bohn 1849), p. 525.

198 John Barrell, *The Flight of Syntax: Percy Bysshe Shelley and Tom Raworth* (London: Birkbeck College 1990), pp. 6–19.

199 *S Prose*, p. 277.

200 *SL* II 71.

201 Schlegel, 'Language and Wisdom', p. 466. The influence of German Higher Criticism on the English Romantics, including Shelley, is treated authoritatively by Elinor Shaffer in '*Kubla Khan*'. Shelley's

poem approximates also to Eichhorn's 'advanced' rationalist method, 'in that mythical expressions are understood as historically necessary, rather than as the result of error, superstition or deception' (p. 127).

202 Timothy Webb, 'The Unascended Heaven: Negatives in *Prometheus Unbound*', in *Shelley Revalued*, p. 57.

203 Inden, *Imagining India*, p. 68; Said, 'Orientalism Reconsidered', 23.

204 As well as reorienting the setting of the Prometheus myth, *Prometheus Unbound* assimilates elements of Valmiki's Sanskrit epic *Ramayana* in addition to the Bible, Aeschylus, Dante, Milton, Southey and Wordsworth. It seems to me that there is a (subliminal) paralleling of Valmiki's hero Rama and Prometheus through the Greek Dionysus. Other parallels can be discerned between Ravana and Jupiter, and Sita and Asia, but they are less developed. Joseph Raban ('Shelley the Dionysian', pp. 30–1) points out that 'one of the common etymologies for Dionysus is "the God (Deus, Zeus) of Nyasa"' (ibid. p. 30). This is the same 'Bacchic Nyasa, Maenad-haunted mountain' beyond which is located the cave to which Prometheus and Asia retire to consummate their love, and to which the 'Spirit of the Hour' leads the assembled company after the fall of Jupiter in Act II, lines 152–5. John Drew locates the cave in Kashmir and identifies it with Hilarion's 'cave of congelations' in *The Missionary*, where the hero retires at the end of the novel to dedicate himself to a hybrid cult of Christian and Vedantin doctrine (Drew, p. 273). Both Raban and Drew miss William Jones' equation of Dionysus with the Hindu god Rama. Whereas Dionysus, law-giver and founder of 'navigation and commerce' conquers India with 'an army of *Satyrs* commanded by no less a person than *Pan*', the Aryan conqueror Rama, 'founder of the first regular government in this part of Asia', conquers India with an army of monkeys commanded by Hanuman, the monkey god. Although Jones fails to discover any Indian analogue for Prometheus, it is unlikely that Shelley would have missed Jones' point that the birthplace of Rama, '[Mount] Meros is said by the Greeks to have been a mountain of *India*, on which their DIONYSOS was born ... [and] is also a mountain near the city of Naishada or Nyasa, called by the Grecian geographers Dionysopolis' (*On the Gods of Greece, Italy and India*, *WJW* 1 264). The *differences* between Shelley's Prometheus, Nonnus' Dionysus and Valmiki's Rama are of course just as salient as the similarities; if the latter two are empire-builders in the heroic mould, the former is resigned, pacific, valetudinarian, an empire-abdicator rather than an empire-builder.

205 Bernal, *Black Athena*, p. 220.

206 Cf. Raban 'Shelley the Dionysian', 24.

207 Volney, *Ruins*, p. 197.

208 Schlegel, 'Language and Wisdom', p. 483.

209 See Marilyn Butler, 'Myth and Mythmaking in the Shelley Circle', *Shelley Revalued*, pp. 8–10.

210 *SL* 1 499.

211 Rammohun Roy, *Second Defence of the Monotheistic System of the Veds in reply to 'An Apology for the Present State of Hindoo Worship'* (Calcutta 1817), p. 29.

212 Shelley's handling of the episode alludes to the moment in Aeschylus' tragedy *The Persians* when the ghost of Darius, founder of the dynasty destroyed with Xerxes at Salamis, broods over the collapse of the Persian Empire. The difference here, as I noted, is that Jupiter and the phantasm of Jupiter represent Roman imperialism rather than 'oriental despotism'. Shelley used the device again in *Hellas* (more conventionally and closer to the Aeschylean source) when Ahasuerus summons the Phantom of Mahomet the Second to proclaim the demise of the Ottoman Empire (*SPW*, pp. 471–3).

213 *S Prose*, p. 278. Compare the following passage (from Rammohun's Preface to his translation of the *Kena Upanishad*), 'in the most ancient times the inhabitants of this part of the globe (at least the more intelligent class) were not unacquainted with metaphysical subjects; that allegorical language, or description, was very frequently employed, to represent the attributes of the Creator, which were sometimes designated as independent existences; and that however suitable this method might be to the refined understandings of men of learning, it had the most mischievous effect, when literature and philosophy decayed, producing all those absurdities and idolatrous notions, which have checked, or rather destroyed, every mark of reason, and darkened every beam of understanding' (*Translation of an Abridgement of the Vedant* (London 1817), p. iv).

214 *S Prose*, p. 202.
215 *Second Defence of the Monotheistical System*, p. 47.
216 Webb, 'Negatives in *Prometheus Unbound*', 56–7.
217 *S Prose*, p. 238.
218 *Second Conference between an Advocate for, and an Opponent of, the Practice of Burning Widows Alive* (Calcutta 1820). Quoted by Singh, I 207.
219 *SPW*, p. 272.
220 Drew, *Romantic Imagination*, p. 264.
221 *WJW* I 165; *The Missionary*, I 71. The sceptical immaterialism of the 'Vedantin' philosophy clearly had some influence on Shelley's 'intellectual philosophy' at an earlier stage, although he suppressed the 'oriental' derivation. See, for example, Shelley's *Essay on Life*, *Essay on a Future State*, *A Treatise on Morals*, *S Prose*, pp. 171–94.
222 Drew, *Romantic Imagination*, p. 268.
223 Ibid., p. 269.
224 *S Prose*, p. 201.
225 *Monthly Magazine*, 43 (June 1817), 394, 396; *S Prose*, pp. 282–3.
226 *Monthly Magazine*, 45 (March 1818), 123.
227 Ibid., 123.
228 *Monthly Magazine*, 43 (June 1817), 391.
229 *S Prose*, p. 208.

230 *Southey's Poetical Works*, pp. 626–7.
231 See note 35 above for Drew's identification of Prometheus' cave with Hilarion's.
232 *S Prose*, pp. 259; 240.
233 *S Prose*, p. 277.
234 Ibid., p. 297.
235 *SL* II 357.
236 Rammohun was on cordial terms with the aged Bentham, who greatly admired him, being one of the first to call upon him (contrary to habit) after his arrival in London. William Godwin, who met Rammohun at Basil Montague's, 'sought his help in clarifying the meaning and derivation of certain eastern terms for an off-beat book, *The Lives of the Necromancers*, on which he was working at the time'. Rammohun obliged him with a very full, and very sceptical account, of the function of 'natural magic' in the East (Singh III 492–3). On the other hand, the Rajah argued with Robert Owen, for whilst welcoming Owen's socialist programme in principle, he opposed his vehement rejection of religion as a 'social cement' (*Rammohun Roy*, pp. 23; 53).
237 *S Prose*, p. 292.
238 Stokes, *English Utilitarians*, p. 65–6. Bentham regarded James Mill as a 'disciple' through whom his ideas on legal and administrative reform would bear fruit in India. See Ganguli *Rammohun Roy*, pp. 54–5 and Stokes, pp. 51, 68. As Stokes points out, Bentham's ideas were also very influential at Haileybury, the Company's training college.
239 *S Prose*, p. 292.
240 Ibid., p. 294.
241 Stokes, *English Utilitarians*, p. 18.
242 *The Journal of Edward Ellerker Williams*, intro. by Richard Garnett (London: Elkin Matthews 1902), p. 23.
243 *Angler*, II 67.
244 Ibid., II 73.
245 Ernest J. Lovell, *Captain Medwin: Friend of Byron and Shelley* (London: Macdonald 1962), p. 34.
246 *S Prose*, p. 293.
247 *Angler*, II 70, 79.
248 Spivak, 'Can the Subaltern Speak?', 296.
249 *Prometheus Unbound*, *SPW*, p. 226, I lines 821–3.
250 *Angler*, II 83.
251 Ibid., II 84.
252 For a discussion of European thinking about Indian architecture in the period, and the Ellora and Elephanta cave temples in particular, see Mitter, *Much Maligned Monsters*, pp. 105–88.
253 *Bibliothèque Universelle des Sciences, Belles-Lettres, et Arts*, Faisant suite à la Bibliothèque Britanniques, Redigée à Genève, NS 18, 2 (Sept. 1821), 117.
254 *Angler*, I 72.

255 Bernal, *Black Athena*, chapter v, 'Romantic Linguistics: The Rise of India and the Fall of Egypt, 1770–1880'.

256 *Bibliothèque Universelle*, 2 (Sept. 1821), 120. Medwin's appreciation of the cave sculpture echoes the opinion of the Danish traveller Carsten Niebuhr, who had written (nearly half a century before) of the statues at Elephanta, 'In truth, they are not as beautiful as the bas-reliefs and statues of the Greeks and Roman masters, but far superior to the design and arrangement of Egyptian figures, and besides, very beautiful in relation to their great antiquity' (Mitter, *Much Maligned Monsters*, p. 112). Later commentators like James Forbes (1813) tended to emphasize the sublime rather than the beautiful qualities of the caves. In this respect, Medwin's judgement would seem to be rather behind the times (Mitter, p. 136).

257 *SL* II 183. See Kopf, *British Orientalism*, pp. 222–6 for a discussion of the Calcutta school for burlesque poetry, for which there was a growing demand in England. Kopf writes 'in these poems of "exile" we search in vain for descriptions of the British Civil Servant in contact with the Indian people. We learn instead of relationships between one European and another' (p. 226).

258 *Sketches in Hindostan with other Poems* (London: C. and J. Ollier, 1821), no line numbers, p. 9.

259 Ibid.

260 Ibid., p. 10.

261 Ibid., p. 80.

262 Ibid., p. 81.

263 *SPW*, p. 15.

264 *Sketches in Hindostan*, p. 81.

265 Ibid., p. 11.

266 *Angler*, I 5.

267 Ibid., I 265.

268 Ibid., II 64–5.

269 Ibid., I 4; II 293.

270 Cf. 'The Other Question...' 29.

271 Bayly, *Indian Society*, p. 106.

272 *Angler*, II 303.

273 Bayly, *Indian Society*, p. 172.

274 *Angler*, II 297.

275 Ibid., II 315.

276 Ibid., II 338.

277 Ibid., II 307. Mani, 'Official Discourse of Sati', I 117.

278 Ibid., II 308.

279 Ibid., II 306.

280 Ibid., II 308.

281 Ibid., II 317–8.

282 'A Bengal Yarn' by Capt. Medwin, *Ainsworth's Magazine*, II (1842), 57–63; 60–1.

283 Ibid., 59.
284 Cf. Bayly, *Indian Society*, pp. 188–94.
285 'A Bengal Yarn', 62.
286 Ibid., 63. The conclusion of Medwin's 'Yarn', in relation to his earlier writings, confirms Patrick Brantlinger's observation that Phillip Meadows Taylor's 1872 novel of the Mutiny (significantly) entitled *Seeta* 'is the only Victorian novel about India I know that presents an interracial love affair in a sympathetic light' (Brantlinger, p. 213).
287 *Uncollected Writings of Thomas De Quincey*, ed. James Hogg (London: Swan Sonnenschein 1890), 2 vols., 1 304–5. For De Quincey on the Indian 'Mutiny' see Barrell, *Infection of Thomas De Quincey*, chapter 12, 'Phallalgia: India in 1857', pp. 168–81.
288 Brantlinger, *Rule of Darkness*, p. 200. Chapter 7 of Brantlinger's book offers an excellent general account of British literary reactions to the 'Well at Cawnpore'.

3 'MURDERING ONE'S DOUBLE': THOMAS DE QUINCEY AND S. T. COLERIDGE. AUTOBIOGRAPHY, OPIUM AND EMPIRE IN 'CONFESSIONS OF AN ENGLISH OPIUM EATER' AND 'BIOGRAPHIA LITERARIA'

1 Marek Kohn, *Narcomania* (London: Faber & Faber 1987), p. 36.
2 Virginia Berridge and Griffith Edwards, *Opium and the People: Opiate Use in 19th Century England* (New York and London: Allen Lane and St Martin's Press 1981), p. 53.
3 *Henry Crabb Robinson on Books and their Writers*, ed. Edith Morley (London: Dent & Son 1938), II 767.
4 Grevel Lindop, *The Opium Eater: A Life of Thomas De Quincey* (Oxford University Press 1985), p. 248.
5 *Thomas De Quincey: An English Opium Eater 1785–1859*, intro. and notes by Robert Woof (Cumbria: Trustees of Dove Cottage 1985), p. 113.
6 *Medical Intelligence* XXXII, 3 (July 1822), 290.
7 Lindop, *Opium Eater*, p. 248. Lindop's argument demonstrates the untenability of Terry Parsinnen's claim that 'De Quincey is never presented as an evil influence or moral pariah', a claim which supports his own thesis that opium was a 'non-issue' in the early Victorian period. *Secret Passions, Secret Remedies: Narcotic Drugs in British Society 1820–1930* (Manchester University Press 1983), pp. 7; 8.
8 Lindop, *Opium Eater*, p. 261.
9 Thomas Trotter, *A View of the Nervous Temperament* (London 1807), p. 137.
10 Quoted in Woof, *Thomas De Quincey*, p. 56.
11 Thomas Trotter, *An Essay, Medical, Philosophical, and Chemical on Drunkenness, and its effects on the Human Body* (London: Longman et al. 1810), p. 46.
12 *Essay on Drunkenness*, p. 46.

13 Richard Caseby, *The Opium-Eating Editor: De Quincey and the 'Westmoreland Gazette'* (Cumbria: The Westmoreland Gazette 1985), p. 130.
14 *View of the Nervous Temperament*, p. 171.
15 See W. F. Bynum and Roy Porter (eds.) 'Brunonianism in Britain and Europe', *Medical History*, Supplement No. 8 (London: Wellcome Institute 1988). See particularly the articles by Roy Porter, Christopher Lawrence and Michael Barfoot. Thanks to Simon Shaffer for this reference. See also Berridge, *Opium and the People*, pp. 62–72, 'Opium in Medical Practice'.
16 Christopher Lawrence, 'The Nervous System and Society in the Scottish Enlightenment', in *Natural Order: Historical Studies of Scientific Culture*, ed. Barry Barnes and Steven Shapin (Beverly Hills and London: Sage Publications 1979), pp. 25; 28.
17 John Brown, *Elements of Medicine*, 1795 edn. Quoted by Woof, pp. 55; 54.
18 Matthias Weber and Hinderk Emrich, 'Current and Historical Concepts of Opiate Treatment in Psychiatric Disorders', *International Clinical Psychopharmacology*, 3 (1988), 258. Thanks to Dr Alfonso Martin del Campo for this information. See also Berridge, *Opium and the People*, p. 65.
19 Michel Foucault, *Madness and Civilization: A History of Insanity in the Age of Reason* (London: Tavistock Publication 1967), pp. 156; 173.
20 *Medical Intelligencer*, 117.
21 *Crabb Robinson*, II 740.
22 Lindop, *Opium Eater*, p. 350.
23 *Crabb Robinson*, I 267.
24 'Anonymous Review' (by John Wilson) of Coleridge's *Biographia Literaria* in *Blackwood's Edinburgh Magazine*, II vii (Oct. 1817) 3–17, 5.
25 Ibid.
26 Ibid., 3, 4.
27 Lindop, *Opium Eater*, p. 239. I owe the suggestion that De Quincey might have written at least the first part of Wilson's review of the *Biographia* to Barry Symonds, who was generous in sharing his extensive knowledge of De Quincey with me.
28 *Blackwood's* II vii (Oct. 1817), 4.
29 See note 3 above, on Crabb Robinson.
30 *Blackwood's* II vii (Oct. 1817), 5.
31 *The Posthumous Works of Thomas De Quincey*, ed. Alexander Japp (London: Heineman 1891), I 9; 12.
32 James Gillman, *The Life of S. T. Coleridge* (London: W. Pickering 1838), p. 250.
33 Thomas Colley Grattan, *Beaten Paths: And Those who Trod Them*, 2 vols. (London: Chapman and Hall 1862), II 131. I am indebted to Daniel Roberts for this quotation.
34 Cf. note 1, *BL* I 163 for an account of Coleridge's interest in Brunonian medicine.
35 Foucault, *Madness and Civilization*, p. 157.
36 Michel Foucault, *The History of Sexuality, Volume One: An Introduction* (New York: Vintage Books 1980), p. 59.

37 Ibid. p. 61–2.
38 Christopher Lawrence, 'The Nervous System', 33.
39 *Crabb Robinson*, I 137.
40 For the relations between plagiarism and addiction, as well as a suggestive discussion of the economic underpinnings of De Quincey's imperialism, see Josephine McDonagh 'Opium and the Imperial Imagination', forthcoming in *Reviewing Romanticism*, ed. P. Martin and R. Jarvis (Macmillan). I am grateful to her for letting me read the manuscript of this article.
41 John Beer, 'De Quincey and the Dark Sublime: The Wordsworth–Coleridge Ethos', in *Thomas De Quincey, Bicentenary Studies*, ed. with intro. by Robert Snyder (Norman, Oklahoma, and London: University of Oklahoma Press 1985), p. 172.
42 *A Diary of T. De Quincey 1803*, ed. H. A. Eaton (London: Noel Douglas 1927), p. 194.
43 Nora Crook and Derek Guiton, *Shelley's Venomed Melody* (Cambridge University Press 1986), pp. 10–13.
44 *A View of the Nervous Temperament*, pp. 110–29; *The Cyclopaedia or Universal Dictionary of Arts, Sciences and Literature*, by Abraham Rees (London: Longman 1819), xxv 'Opium'.
45 William Wordsworth, *The 1805 Prelude*, Book xi, lines 326–8.
46 'Dejection: An Ode', lines 45–6, *Coleridge: Poetical Works*, ed. E. H. Coleridge (Oxford Clarendon Press 1912) I 365.
47 Japp, *Posthumous Works*, I 9.
48 Quoted in Lindop, *Opium Eater*, p. 317.
49 Cf. note by editors, *BL* II 190.
50 See my *Politics of Imagination in Coleridge's Critical Thought*, (London: Macmillan 1988) p. 159.
51 Lindop, *Opium Eater*, p. 237.
52 'Emeritus' (De Quincey), 'On the Approaching Revolution in Great Britain', *Blackwood's Magazine*, 30 CLXXXIV (August 1831), pt. 2 313–29: 324.
53 Charles Pollitt, *De Quincey's Editorship of the 'Westmoreland Gazette'. With Selections...from July 1818 to Nov. 1819* (Kendal: Atkinson and Pollitt 1890), p. 38.
54 Ibid.
55 *Specimens of the Table Talk of the late S. T. Coleridge* (London: John Murray 1835), II 129–30.
56 Robert Maniquis, 'Lonely Empires: Personal and Public Visions of T. De Quincey', in *Literary Monographs*, vol. 8, ed. E. Rothstein and J. Wittreich, Jr (Madison: University of Wisconsin Press 1976), p. 50. Maniquis' provocative essay discovers in De Quincey's 'discontinuous selves' 'the presence of guilt, which is always alien, never his'. The paradox of the 'bourgeois pariah' is that he is 'alone in society, but also, by his growing intimation of its totality, one of its purest and most willing representatives'. Thus 'the true revolt for De Quincey is psychic and against the darkness, completing itself, like many revolutions, in the

imperial idea' (pp. 58; 63; 95). The problem with this account is its
possession by a causal model which accepts De Quinceyan guilt as an
existential *a priori* which resolves itself in imperialism. My version of the
relationship is to deconstruct such an essentialist priority by problematizing the relationship, and rather reading the metaphysical rationale
(guilt) as the effect of a material cause (imperialism). John Barrell, in
The Infection of Thomas De Quincey (New Haven and London: Yale
University Press 1991) points the way to a materialist reading such as my
own in criticizing Maniquis' existentialism: 'Why shouldn't we say',
writes Barrell, 'that the meditations on being and existence, the
acknowledgements and declarations (if they can be found) of an
existential guilt, are the symbolic language in which a psycho-sexual
and/or a social guilt are represented, displaced, mystified?' (p. 207).
Barrell refuses to afford priority to either De Quincey's traumatic
'primal scene' or the social guilt of nineteenth-century imperialist
discourse in his fine reading, rather establishing a chiasmic relationship
between private and public representations.

57 A. O. Lovejoy, *Essays in the History of Ideas* (Baltimore: Johns Hopkins
Press 1948), pp. 79–82. David Simpson, *Wordsworth's Historical Imagination. The Poetry of Displacement* (New York and London: Methuen 1987),
pp. 22–55.
58 Frederick Engels, *The Condition of the Working Class in England*, intro. by
Eric Hobsbawm (St Albans: Panther Books 1969), p. 58.
59 William Wordsworth, *Selected Prose*, ed. John O. Hayden (Harmondsworth: Penguin 1988), p. 282.
60 Beer, 'The Dark Sublime', *Bicentenary Studies*, p. 181.
61 Japp, *Posthumous Writings*, II 210.
62 Lindop, *Opium Eater*, p. 345.
63 Pollitt, *De Quincey's Editorship*, p. 45.
64 'On the Approaching Revolution', 324.
65 *Thomas De Quincey, his Life and Writings, with Unpublished Correspondence*,
ed. Alexander Japp (London: John Hogg, 1890) p. 370.
66 Grevel Lindop, 'Innocence and Revenge: The Problem of De Quincey's
Fiction', in *Bicentenary Studies*, p. 236.
67 Alethea Hayter, *Opium and the Romantic Imagination* (London: Faber &
Faber 1968), p. 33.
68 Berridge, *Opium and The People*, p. 28.
69 Karl Marx, *Capital* vol. I, chapter 33, 'The Modern Theory of
Colonisation', in *The Portable Karl Marx*, ed. Eugene Kamenka
(Harmondsworth: Penguin 1983), p. 494.
70 Berridge, *Opium and the People*, pp. 106; 107.
71 Marx, *Capital*, p. 446.
72 Lindop, *Opium Eater*, p. 258.
73 V. A. De Luca, *Thomas De Quincey: The Prose of Vision* (Toronto, Buffalo,
London: University of Toronto Press 1980), p. 24.
74 *Bicentenary Studies*, pp. 72–3.

75 Marjorie Levinson, 'Insight and Oversight: Reading "Tintern Abbey"', in *Wordsworth's Great Period Poems* (Cambridge University Press 1986).

76 Berridge, *Opium and the People*, p. 8.

77 Marx, *Capital*, pp. 489–90.

78 Barrell, *Infection of Thomas De Quincey*, p. 10.

79 De Quincey's 'eudaemonist' imperialism I think challenges Benedict Anderson's thesis in *Imagined Communities* (London: Verso 1983) that the racist element in imperialist discourse has an essentially *aristocratic* provenance. 'Official nationalism was typically a response on the part of threatened dynastic and aristocratic groups – upper *classes* – to popular vernacular nationalism. Colonial racism was a major element in that conception of "Empire" which attempted to weld dynastic legitimacy and national community. It did so by generalizing a principle of innate, inherited superiority on which its own domestic position was (however shakily) based to the vastness of the overseas possessions, covertly (or not so covertly) conveying the idea that if, say, English lords were naturally superior to other Englishmen, no matter: those other Englishmen were no less superior to the subjugated natives' (p. 137). It is true that Count Gobineau, author of the racist's bible, *Inequality of the Human Races*, and amateur sculptor, entered a sculpture of Lord Byron looking down disdainfully on the 'common herd' in an 1875 competition for a 'colossal monument' to the poet. (He lost.) But nevertheless the aristocratic Byron was a far less committed imperialist (and certainly racist) than the 'bourgeois pariah' De Quincey, as was argued in the first chapter of this book. See James Tetreault, 'Heirs to his Virtues: Byron, Blunt, Gobineau', *Byron Journal*, 16 (1988), 68.

80 Lindop, *Opium Eater*, p. 218. See also Victor Kiernan, *The Lords of Human Kind. European Attitudes towards the Outside World in the Imperial Age* (London: Weidenfeld & Nicholson 1969), p. 83.

81 Kiernan, *Lords of Human Kind*, p. 83 and *Works of the Rev. Sydney Smith* (1839), 4th edn, 2 vols. (London: Longmans 1848) I 832–3. Thanks to John Barrell for this quotation.

82 Homi Bhabha, 'The Other Question...; the Stereotype and Colonial Discourse', *Screen*, 24, 6 (Nov.–Dec. 1983), 27–8.

83 Ibid.

84 *The Uncollected Writings of Thomas De Quincey*, with Preface and annotations by James Hogg (London: Swan Sonnenschein & Co. 1890), II 34; 9.

85 René Wellek, 'De Quincey's Status in the History of Ideas', *Philological Quarterly*, 23 (1944), 269.

86 Gayatri Spivak, *In Other Worlds: Essays in Cultural Politics* (New York and London: Routledge 1988), p. 202.

87 Homi Bhabha, 'Of Mimicry and Men: The Ambivalence of Colonial Discourse', *October* 28 (1984), 128.

88 Foucault, *History of Sexuality*, pp. 68–9.

89 See, for example, Kiernan, *Lords of Human Kind*, p. 316.

90 Weber and Emrich, 'Opiate Treatment', 257.

91 Barrell, *Infection of Thomas De Quincey*, pp. 75–6.

92 *Narcomania*, p. 105.

93 Bhabha, 'Of Mimicry and Men', 75.

94 Ibid.

95 '*Niels Klim*, being an incomplete translation by T. De Quincey, from the Danish of Ludvig Holberg', ed. S. Musgrove, *Auckland University College Bulletin* 42, English series No. 5 (1953), 31.

96 *Narcomania*, p. 28.

97 See Elizabeth Lomax 'The Uses and Abuses of Opiates in 19th century England', in *Bulletin of the History of Medicine*, XLVII (1973), 167–76.

98 Quoted in *Narcomania*, p. 26.

99 Brantlinger, *Rule of Darkness: British Literature and Imperialism 1830–1914* (Ithaca and London: Cornell University Press 1988), p. 7.

100 Compare the arguments of *Blaming the Victims: Spurious Scholarship and the Palestinian Question*, ed. Edward Said and Christopher Hitchens (London and New York: Verso 1988).

101 Hogg, *Uncollected Writings*, II 30.

102 *Narcomania*, pp. 27–8.

103 Lindop, *Opium Eater*, p. 347.

104 Victor Kiernan, *Lords of Human Kind*, p. 152.

105 Japp, *Life and Writings*, p. 471.

106 Berridge, *Opium and the People*, pp. 3–4.

107 Barrell, *Infection of Thomas De Quincey*, pp. 10–15.

108 Quoted in *Narcomania*, p. 144.

109 'System of the Heavens, as revealed by Lord Rosse's Telescopes', *Tait's Edinburgh Magazine*, VIII (1846), 566–79; 568.

110 Ibid., 578. See also J. Hillis Miller, *The Disappearance of God: Five Nineteenth Century Writers* (Cambridge, Mass.: Harvard University Press 1975).

111 Hogg, *Uncollected Writings*, I 322–3.

112 Barrell, *Infection of Thomas De Quincey*, p. 59.

113 Christine Bolt, *Victorian Attitudes to Race* (London: Routledge & Kegan Paul 1971), pp. 21–2. See also Daniel Pick, *Faces of Degeneration* (Cambridge University Press 1989). My argument about the 'English Opium Eater' is supported by Pick's critique of an oversimplified dichotomy of self/other in the work of Johannes Fabian and Edward Said; 'the "aggression" of evolutionary discourse may have had as much to do with perceived "terrors", "primitiveness" and fragmentation "at home", as in the colonies...the "other" was outside and inside' (pp. 38; 39).

114 Edward Said, *Orientalism* (London and Harmondsworth: Penguin Books 1985), pp. 72; 239.

115 *Blackwoods Magazine*, xlviii, CCC (Oct. 1840), 546–62, 560–1.

116 As Barrell points out, 'the phrase "officina gentium", "factory where

people are made" is also used by De Quincey...to describe a factory full of "Jacobins" that frightened him in childhood. In the *Autobiographical Sketches* he describes how his brother William and he did battle with the factory boys, using the warcry "Delenda est Carthago", originally used by the Romans against their Carthaginian enemies. "Delenda est Carthago" [De Quincey] intones yet again, when calling upon the British to destroy the "guilty town" of Canton [in the opium wars], the town...of "factories" and swarming myriads: the wars between De Quincey and the factory boys may also have been anticipations (or repetitions) of the Opium Wars' (*Infection of Thomas De Quincey*, p. 60).

117 See Barrell, *Infection of Thomas De Quincey*, pp. 112–14 for a different interpretation of the nebula of Orion. Barrell also notes the ways in which the nebula, 'multiply fissured, infinitely permeable and penetrable (especially by Lord Rosse's 'instrument'), its mouth cracked open, its orifices disfigured from pathways of pleasure into holes of terror' resembles Bakhtin's 'grotesque body' (p. 123). The opposition of the 'grotesque' to the 'classical' body ('a bourgeois ideal, the representation of the body as perfect, smooth, unyielding and – especially – as sealed, inpermeable, *homus clausus* in Norbert Elias' exact phrase', ibid.), is another variety of the Hellenistic/Asiatic binary opposition which has recurred frequently in the course of this book. The manner in which the two bodies are alarmingly 'interchangeable' should also by now be evident.

118 'System of the Heavens', 571. For the background to De Quincey's involvement with astronomy, and the Nicholson/Lord Rosse debate, see Simon Schaffer's article, 'The Nebular Hypothesis and the Science of Progress' in James Moore, ed. *History, Humanity and Evolution: Essays for John C. Greene* (Cambridge University Press 1990).

Index

Abernethy, John, 174, 182
Achilles, 41, 43
Addington, Henry, 182
Addison, Joseph, 18
Adelung, J. C.: *Mithridates*, 210
Adorno, Theodor, 60
Aeschylus, 140, 141, 247: *The Persians*, 73;
 compared to *Prometheus Unbound*, 247–8
Alexander the Great, 124, 141, 143
Altamont, Lord, 191, 195
America, 30
Anderson, Benedict: *Imagined Communities*,
 254–5
'Anglicist' colonial policy in India 78, 82,
 91; *see also* 'Orientalism'
anxiety/anxieties: semantic range of, 3; of
 empire, 2, 7, 227; of racial taxonomy,
 6; of romanticism, 7–12
Aquinas, Thomas: *Summa Theologica*, 147
Arabian Nights, 18, 19, 20–1
Ariosto, 46, 49
Arnold, Matthew, 238
Arrian, 124, 158
Asiatic Society of Bengal, 95, 98, 138
Augustine, Saint, 172
Aurungzebe, 155
Aztecs, 26

Bakhtin, Mikhail, 82, 86, 257
Baldick, Chris, 238
Barbauld, Anna Letitia, 20, 231
Barfoot, Michael, 252
Barlow, Joel, 27, 231
Barrell, John, 8, 19, 20, 87, 141, 208, 214,
 221, 225, 230, 231, 236, 237, 246, 251,
 253–4, 256–7; 'this, that and the
 other', 239; *The Infection of Thomas
 De Quincey*, 6, 191, 229, 230
Baudelaire, Charles, 170, 193
Bayly, C. A., 76, 103, 163, 164, 237, 239,
 241, 250

Beckford, William, 20, 77; *Vathek*, 18, 20,
 21, 58, 74, 97
Beddoes, Thomas, 25, 92–4, 109, 125, 183;
 Alexander's Expedition, 92, 124, 239
Beer, John, 188, 202, 253, 254
Bengali renaissance, 119
Benjamin, Walter, 12
Bentham, Jeremy, 75, 97, 140, 141, 152,
 154, 249
Bentinck, Lord William, 154, 167
Bernal, Martin, 108, 143, 158, 231, 244,
 247; *Black Athena*, 24, 241, 242
Bernier, Francois, 122
Berridge, Virginia, 172, 204, 251, 252, 254,
 256
Bhabha, Homi, 80, 84, 88, 91, 119, 128,
 139, 163, 210, 215, 216, 229, 230, 237,
 246, 255
Bibliothèque Universelle, 69, 158, 249
Blackstone, Bernard, 77, 237
Blackwoods Magazine, 173, 180, 195–7, 205,
 218, 227, 253, 256
Blackwood, William, 203
Blair, Hugh, 27
Blumenbach, J. F., 123, 130, 143, 245
Bolt, Christine, 256
Bonnet, Charles, 106
Booth, Charles, 201
Bounty, mutiny on, 63
Bowles, William, 188
Bowyer, James, 188
Brahmins/Brahminism, 91–2, 95, 103,
 104, 134–40, 158, 164; and Druids,
 107
Brahmo Sabha, 136
Brahmo Samaj, 119, 136, 137
Brantlinger, Patrick, 23, 59, 60, 79, 169,
 250, 251; *Rule of Darkness*, 95, 97, 231,
 235, 237, 256
Broussais, F. J. V., 176
Brown, John, 186; *Elementa Medicinae*, 175,

258

252; 'Brunonian System', 175–9, 200, 204, 215, 224, 251–2
Brown, Laura, 19, 230
Brunell the Attorney, 200, 207
Bryson, Norman, 49, 234
Burton, Richard, 4, 20, 124, 235; *Arabian Nights*, 20; *Pilgrimage to Meccah*, 61
Buckingham, James Silk, 139
Burke, Edmund, 38, 94, 100, 195; *Reflections*, 34
Burke, Peter, 44, 234
Burroughs, William, 170; *Naked Lunch*, 221
Burrow, Reuben, 107, 242
Butler, Marilyn, 26, 74, 231, 236, 247
Byron, George Gordon, Lord, 5, 9, 10, 11, 13–67 passim, 112, 172, 211; anxieties of empire, 58–9; bisexuality, 57; and Loukas Chalandritsanos, 45; his death, 67; on Catholic Emancipation, 39; and Nicolas Giraud, 57; on Greece and Greeks, 22–4, 35, 36, 67; heroines (poetical), 45–54, 56, 66, 165, 166, 235; on imperialism, 16, 37, 59; on incest, 42, 234; on W. S. Landor's *Gebir*; on Luddites, 37, 39; on 'mobility', 16, 63; his orientalism, 59, 61; on Parliamentary Reform, 39; on poetic style, 33; his politics, 53, 56; on Alexander Pope, 62, 86; his satire, 16, 33–37; scepticism about revolutionary democracy, 43, 53
Works: *Age of Bronze*, 39; *Beppo*, 14, 22, 55; *Bride of Abydos*, 14, 24, 38–44, 47, 48; *Cain*, 64, 242; *Childe Harold's Pilgrimage*, 10, 14, 15, 24, 34–7, 40–1, 43, 49, 54, 54, 55, 63; *Corsair*, 14, 45–54, 62, 67, 158, 162, 166; *Curse of Minerva*, 36–7, 46; *Don Juan*, 14, 16, 20, 31, 39, 42, 43, 45, 49, 62, 63, 158; *Eastern (or Turkish) Tales*, 4, 13–67 passim, 74, 84, 158; *English Bards*, 34; *The Giaour*, 14, 25–33, 53, 158; *Hints from Horace*, 34; *Hours of Idleness*, 45; *The Island*, 10, 24, 26, 31, 47, 51, 62, 63–7; *Lara*, 44, 45, 47, 52, 54–62, 67, 78; *Letter to John Murray on Bowles' Strictures*, 62, 229; *Marino Faliero*, 38, 43, 47, 56; *Parisina*, 61–2; *Prisoner of Chillon*, 46; *Sardanapalus*, 47, 243; *Siege of Corinth*, 14, 46, 49, 56, 62, 161; *The Two Foscari*, 385; *Werner*, 55

Caesar, Julius, 66
'Calcutta school' of burlesque poetry, 250
Campbell, Thomas, 20, 25, 94, 109, 239; *Pleasures of Hope*, 93

Cannon, Garland, 236, 244
Carpenter, Lant, 245
Caseby, Richard, 251
caste system, 92, 168
Chateaubriand, François René; *Travels in Greece, Palestine, Egypt*, 34–5, 233
China and opium, 214
Christen, Dr, 172–3
Clapham Sect, 101
Clarke, David, 245
Clement of Alexandria, 158
Cleopatra, 66
Clive, Robert, 97
Colebrook, H. T., 98
Coleridge, John Taylor, 236
Coleridge, S. T., 19, 25; on associationism, 192; on Brunonian system, 184–7; on 'bulls', 191; on 'Clerisy', 198–9; and De Quincey, 170–228; 'dynamic philosophy', 192; his 'egotism', 179; on Genius, 185; on German orientalism, 108, 120, 121, 136; on Imagination, 184, 192; on 'intellectual Jacobinism', 44; on Charles Maturin, 194; on opium addiction, 183; on Peninsular War, 97; plagiarism, 187, 224; political apostasy of, 194; on political economy, 197; his procrastination, 181; projected 'magnum opus', 181, 182, 190; on Rammohun Roy, 139; on Will, 184, 205; on Wordsworth, 190
Works: *Ancient Mariner*, 28, 188, 171; *Biographia Literaria*, 179, 187–194, 198–201, 240; *Conciones ad Populum*, 194; *Essay on Scrofula*, 174; *The Friend*, 108, 194, 242; *Kubla Khan*, 13–14; *Lay Sermons*, 199; *Philosophical Lectures*, 242; *Religious Musings*, 30; *Theory of Life*, 174, 184
Collins, William; *Oriental Eclogues*, 20, 231
Columbus, Christopher, 27, 30
Conant, Martha Pike, 18, 230, 231
Conrad, Joseph; *Heart of Darkness*, 59, 80
Coppola, Francis Ford, 171
Cornwallis, Lord, 94
Cortes, Hernan, 31–2
Crabbe, George, 47
Creuzer, G. F., 107
'Critical Philosophy', 98
Crompton, Louis, 57, 234
Crook, Norah; *see* Guiton, Derek
Cullen, William, 175, 186
Cuvier, Georges, 106

Darwin, Erasmus, 121; *Zoonomia*, 183
Das, Sisir Kumar, 245
David, J-L., *Oath of the Horatii*, 40
degeneration, 6, 7, 227–8
Dell the Moneylender, 191, 195, 200
De Luca, V., 207, 254
De Quincey, Elizabeth, 226
De Quincey, Horace, 220
De Quincey, Margaret (wife), 189, 203
De Quincey, Margaret (daughter), 214
De Quincey, Thomas, 9, 10, 19, 61, 84, 89,
  162, 170–228; Ann of Oxford St,
  189–91, 195, 200, 207; his politics of
  authorship, 187; on China, 216,
  218–20; dream visions of, 216, 221–8;
  his 'eudaemonism' 182; 'Gombroon
  and Tigrosylvania', 5, 226; on
  imagination, 211; on imperialism, 5,
  199, 219, 227; imperialism and
  alienation, 253–4; on India and Indian
  'Mutiny', 168, 212, 216; on W. S.
  Landor's *Gebir*, 26; 'Literature of
  power', 211–12; the Malay, 4, 209–15,
  218, 225, 226, 228; on nervous system
  vs. will, 193, 196, 214–5, 218–20; on
  opium-eating, 176; on Opium War,
  211, 214; on organicism, 190, 195; his
  politics, 195, 196; on political
  economy, 197–8; on professional men,
  200; his racism, 216–19; and venereal
  disease, 189; on women, 213; and
  Wordsworth, 190, 195, 198, 202,
  211–12, on working class, 87, 196,
  201–05
Works: *Autobiographical Sketches*, 5, 191,
  203; 'On the Approaching Revolution
  in Great Britain', 253, 254; *The
  Avenger*, 78, 203; *The Cacador*, 78, 203;
  Ceylon, 212, 216; *Coleridge and Opium-
  eating*, 183; *Confessions of an English
  Opium-Eater*, 4, 97; reviews of, 172–4;
  1856 Confessions, 172, 186, 203, 208,
  214; *Confessions of a Murderer*, 207;
  as critique of *Biographia Literaria*, 182,
  187–94, 229; *English Mail Coach*, 191,
  193, 196, 215, 216, 226; *Foreign Politics*,
  227; *Klosterheim*, 203, *W. S. Landor*,
  231; *Last Days of Immanuel Kant*, 177–8;
  Letters to a Young Man, 187, 198, 199,
  211; *On Murder considered as one of the
  Fine Arts*, 97, 207; *Niels Klim*, 216–7,
  255–6; *The Pagan Oracles*, 196–7;
  Samuel Parr, 201; *The Peasant of
  Portugal*, 203; *The Poetry of Pope*, 211;
  Suspiria de Profundis, 191, 193, 215;

*System of the Heavens, as revealed by Lord
  Rosse's Telescope*, 224, 228, 256; *Theory
  of Greek Tragedy*, 222; *Travelling in
  England in the Old Days*, 196
De Quincey, William, 226
Derozio, Henry, 119, 138; poetry of, 244
Desart, Lord, 191, 195
De Staël, Mme, 13
Dharma Sabha, 119
Dickens, Charles, 201; *Bleak House*, 175
Digby, John, 136, 139
Dionysus' conquest of India, 124–5, 143, 247
Disraeli, Benjamin, 4
Dove Cottage, 209–10
D'Oyly, Sir Charles, 160
Drew, John: *India and the Romantic
  Imagination*, 120, 126, 141, 147, 148,
  240, 244, 246, 247–8
Drummond, Sir William, 121
Dupuis, C. F., 104, 106, 122

East India Company, 68, 71, 77, 84, 87, 88,
  92–3, 136, 137, 161; attitudes to
  Indian culture, 80, 98, 103, 105–7;
  against colonial settlement in India,
  76; demands for reform of, 25;
  'Guardian State', 86, 164; land
  revenues, 95, 163; opium triangle 217
Eclectic Review, 240
Edinburgh Review, 37, 100
Egypt/Egyptiana, 1, 3, 4, 7, 122, 158,
  226–7; French colonial designs on,
  104–5
Eichhorn, J. G., 242, 246
Elephanta, 69, 157; European travellers on,
  249–50
Elephantiasis, 1, 6, 153
Elgin, Lord, and the Marbles, 36–7
Elias, Norbert, 257
Eliot, George: *Middlemarch*, 106
Ellora, 69, 159
Elphinstone, Mountstuart, 94, 95
Embree, Ainslie, 95, 236, 239, 245
Emrich, Hinderk, 252, 255
Encyclopaedia, French, 98
Engels, Frederick: *Condition of the Working
  Class in England*, 201, 254
Erdman, David, 79, 237
Erskine, Lord, 182
Evangelism/Evangelical Movement, 91,
  101, 154, 202
Examiner, 140

Faber, G. S., 105; *Origin of Pagan Idolatry*,
  106, 241–2

Fabian, Johannes, 254
Family Oracle of Health, 174
Fanon, Frantz, 60, 235
Fieldhouse, D. K., 230
Firdausi, 18
Flaubert, Gustave, 58
Flood, Samuel, 204
Forster, E. M., 71
Foster, John, 8, 9, 96, 240
Foucault, Michel, 17, 97, 184, 176–7, 186,
    213, 252, 255; blindness to question of
    imperialism, 238
Freud, Sigmund, 84

Ganguli, B. N., 245
George III, 26
Gibbon, Edward, 98, 155
Gide, André, 58
Gillman, James: *Life of Coleridge*, 183, 252
Gillray, James, 7
Gleckner, Robert, 42, 54, 232, 234
Gobineau, Count Arthur de, 143, 255
Godwin, William, 47, 110, 111, 121, 132,
    151, 249; *Caleb Williams*, 47;
    Mandeville, 140
Goethe, J. W. von, 179
Goldsmith, Oliver, 18, 22
Graham, Walter, 240
Grant, Charles, 96
Grattan, Thomas Colley, 240
Green, Martin, 69, 124, 235
Greenblatt, Stephen, 7, 26, 108, 229, 232,
    242
Guest, Harriet, 19, 231
Guiton, Derek, and Crook, Norah: *Shelley's
    Venomed Melody*, 6, 189, 229, 253

Habermas, Jurgen, 234
Hafiz, 18
Hamilton, Eliza: *Letters of a Hindoo Rajah*,
    72, 100–1, 240
Hartley, David, 192
Hastings, Marquess of, 69, 156, 243
Hastings, Warren, 18, 25, 85, 94, 109, 218
Hayter, Alethea, 170, 254
Hazlitt, William, 151
Headrick, Daniel, 235
Hegel, G. W. F., 104, 107, 242
Hellenism, 32, 211; *see* philhellenism
Herder, J. G., 178, 199–200, 242
hermaphrodites, 52
Herodotus, 232
Heyne, C. G., 242
Hickey, William, 237
Hill, Rowland, 106

Hindu antiquity, 77; compared to Egyptian
    and Greek, 158
Hinduism, modern, 134–40, 158, 169
Hitchener, Elizabeth, 113
Hobhouse, John Cam, 36, 46, 53, 234
Hogg, James, 255, 256
Hogg, T. J., 6, 106, 109, 124
Holberg, Ludwig: *Niels Klim*, 217, 226, 256
Holland, Lord, 38
Holmes, Richard, 110, 242, 246
Homer, 40, 210–11
homosexuality, 57
Horace, 37
Horkheimer, Max, 60
Hume, David, 119, 121, 134, 146;
    Autobiography, 180, 187
Hunt, James, 226
Hunt, Leigh, 115, 140, 151, 243
Huxley, Alduous, 170

imperial heraldry, 8, 22, 70, 125, 172
imperialism: and alienation, 162; 'civilizing
    mission' of, 85, 88, 89, 109, 145; and
    class, 255, 256–7; and economic
    dependence, 220; free trade, 9, 93–4,
    143, 219, 225; as iatrogenic illness,
    215; liberal, 24, 76, 79, 82, 109, 119,
    154; 'manifest' anti-imperialism in
    18th and 19th-century writers, 92–4;
    and nationalism, 86–9, 227; and
    orientalism, 17; as displaced
    revolution, 118–20; as stimulus or
    narcotic, 9, 10, 109, 162, 208; violence
    of, 166
Inden, Ronald, 73, 142, 236, 243, 246
Indian art, romantic attitudes to, 242
Indian Mutiny, 167–9, 217
inoculation, 9
Ireland, 53, 113–14
Istanbul (Constantinople), 72, 74

Jacobinism, 3, 7, 25, 44, 98, 112, 113, 196,
    203–5, 208, 213, 256
Japp, Alexander, 220, 253, 254, 256
Jeffrey, Francis, 22, 44, 54
Johnson, Samuel, 77; *Rasselas*, 18, 20;
    Journey to Western Isles, 87; *Life of
    Savage*, 93
Jones, Sir William, 2, 4, 9, 17, 18, 71, 87,
    96, 100, 101, 105, 106, 113, 125, 135,
    138, 148, 153, 165, 229, 240, 247; on
    Hindu pantheon, 100; on venereal
    disease, 7
    Works: *Essay on the Arts, commonly called
    Imitative*, 95, 98; *On the Poetry of the*

Eastern Nations, 111, 141; *On the Mystical Poetry of the Persians and Hindoos*, 126; *Second Anniversary Discourse*, 121; *On the Philosophy of the Asiaticks*, 126, 128; *Hindoo Hymns*, 95, 98; *Institutes of Hindu Law, or the Ordinances of Manu*, 100; *Shakuntala; or the Fatal Ring*, 102, 165, 241
Juvenal, 34, 37

Kabbani, Rana, 19, 20, 67, 120, 231
Kalidasa: *Shakuntala*, 102, 165, 241
Kant, Immanuel, 178, 198; *Critique of Judgement*, 207, 225, 226
Kashmir, 72, 130, 127, 129–30, 141, 143
'Kayf', 61
Keats, John, 11, 37, 233, 244, 245; his orientalism, 125–233; *Endymion*, 125, 128
Kejariwal, O. P., 240
Kelsall, Malcolm, 37, 38, 40, 43, 233–4
Khoran, 103
Kiernan, Victor, 213, 220, 255, 256
Kipling, Rudyard, 71, 118, 161
Kohn, Marek, 171, 215, 217, 226, 251
Kopf, David, 85, 119, 136, 138, 238, 243, 245, 250
Kreiger, Abraham, 37, 53, 233–4
Kristeva, Julia, 238

Lacan, Jacques, 82
Lamarck, J-B., 106
Lamb, Lady Caroline: *Glenarvon*, 53
Lamb, Charles, 19
Landor, Walter Savage, 18, 25, 26, 94; *Gebir*, 21, 26, 31, 93
Lawrence, Chevalier, J. H.,: *Empire of the Nairs*, 111; and Shelley, 240
Lawrence, Christopher, 175, 251, 252
Lawrence, T. E., 58, 124
Lawrence, William, 7, 174
Lawson, Charles, 200
Leask, Nigel, 239, 253
Lebanon, 72
Leigh, Augusta, 43
Levinson, Marjorie, 27, 32, 207, 231, 232, 233, 254
Lewis, Matthew, 55, 58, 101, 116, 234
Lewthwaite, Barbara, 209, 210, 213, 214, 225
Lind, Dr James, 11, 132
Lindop Grevel, 203, 251, 252, 254, 256
Liverpool, Lord, 195
Liverpool, 206–9
Locke, John, 119, 134, 146

Lomax, Elizabeth, 256
London Magazine, 172–3, 187, 195
Lovell, Ernest, 68, 235, 249
Lovejoy, Arthur, 201, 254
Lowther, Lord, 195
Luxury, economic discourse of, 4, 19, 21, 92, 200, 205, 215

Macaulay, Thomas Babbington, 98, 154, 168; *Minute on Indian Education*, 213
Mackintosh, Sir James, 182
Macpherson, James: *Ossian*, 87–8, 239
Mahabharata, 158
Majeed, Javed, 75, 88, 236
Malays, 209–15
Malcolm, John, 94
Malthus, Thomas, 205
Mani, Lata, 102, 165, 241, 250
Maniquis, Robert, 199, 253–4
Manning, Peter, 233
Manuel, Frank, 17, 230
Marathas, 69, 154
Marchand, Leslie, 233
Marsden, Samuel: *History of Sumatra*, 209
Martin, Philip, 14, 16, 230
Marx, Karl, 204, 206, 208; on India, 109, 118, 128, 243; *Communist Manifesto*, 199
Masaniello, 44
Mason, Philip, 238
Maturin, Charles: *Bertram*, 194
Maty, Henry, 231
Maurice, Thomas, 105–6, 122, 241
Mayhew, Henry, 201
McDonagh, Josephine, 252
McGann, Jerone, 14–15, 24, 30, 34, 45, 63, 230, 231, 232, 235
Meadows Taylor, Philip: *Confessions of a Thug*, 97, 163, 250
Medwin, Thomas, 8, 68–71, 75, 76, 80, 82, 115, 123, 139, 140, 152, 154–69, 235, 249; 'conversion' to Brahminism, 90–1; influence of Byron on, 70; on classical Indian plastic art, 158; orientalism, 165
  Works: *Angler in Wales*, 69, 155, 160; *A Bengal Yarn*, 69, 160, 167–8, 250; *Julian and Gizele*, 69, 162–6; *The Lion Hunt*, 160–1; *Oswald and Edwin*, 69, 160; *The Pindarees*, 161–3; *Sketches from Hindostan*, 69, 160
Medical Intelligencer, 173
Mellor, Ann, 131, 245
Metcalfe, Charles, 94, 100, 154, 166
Metempsychosis, 106
Michaux, Henri, 170

Mill, James, 75, 98, 103, 104, 113, 135, 141, 151, 241, 242; *History of British India*, 75, 87–9, 90, 94, 135, 137, 152, 169, 239 245
Miller, J. Hillis, 191, 256
Milner, Isaac, 182
Mimamsa philosophy, 138
Missionaries in India, 94, 96, 101, 106, 137
Mitter, Partha, 242, 249
Monboddo, Lord, 5
Montagu, Lady Mary Wortley, 42, 234
Montesquieu, Charles de Secondat, Baron de: *Persian Letters*, 7, 18, 101
Montgomery, James, 173
Monthly Magazine, 134, 136, 139, 148, 150, 248
Moore, Thomas, 13, 19, 22, 25, 53, 110, 112, 152, 172, 242; *Lalla Rookh*, 13–14, 58, 74, 97; compared to Shelley's *Revolt of Islam*, 110–14, 140
Morgan, Lady (Sydney Owenson), 119, 148, 153, 243; *The Missionary*, 101–2, 110, 115–18, 126; construction of Hindu religion in, 128, 130, 132, 142, 144, 151, 161, 165; and Shelley's *Alastor*, 126–9; influence on Shelley's 'intellectual philosophy', 248
More, Hannah, 202, 205
Mozart, W. A., 63
Mughal Empire, 72, 155
Mukherjee, S. N., 240
Muller, Johannes, 122
Muller, Max, 123
Munro, Thomas, 94, 95, 100
Murray, John, 14, 62
Musselwhite, David, 239
mythography, Romantic, 104–8, 144

Nanking, Treaty of, 218
Napoleon Bonaparte, 26, 34, 47, 93, 97–8, 105, 113, 122, 232
Naturphilosophie, 108
Neapolitan revolution, 139
Nelson, Horatio, 34
neo-Harringtonian agrarian ideal, 94, 100, 195
New Criticism, 11
Newton, Sir Isaac, 129
Niebuhr, Carsten, 249
Nonnos: *Dionysiaca*, 124, 247
Notopoulis, James, 244
nympholepsy, 10, 125

Ogle, Robert, 41, 234
Ollier, Charles, 69

opium: agent of social harmony, 204–5; effects on nervous system, 176–9; as a commodity of empire, 199, 220; debate about therapeutic effects of, 175–9; and imagination, 206; T. De Quincey on, 170–228
Opium Wars, 217, 219–20, 226
oriental vs. Hellenistic ideals, 4, 53, 59–61, 62, 73, 92, 118
orientalism: and the arts, 8; as eroticism, 20–1, 120, 123, 131; and European nationalism, 103–8; and gender, 142; in Germany, 104; as 'imaginary geography', 72, 91; and imperialism, 137
'Orientalism' vs. 'Anglicism' in colonial India, 9, 23, 77, 85, 94, 96, 102–3, 118, 119, 138, 153, 154, 165
orientalization of Greek culture, 141–3
Otaheite (Tahiti), 64
Ottoman Empire, 23, 24, 36, 248
Otway, Thomas, 32
Ovid, 40–2, 232
Owen, Robert, 152, 249
Owen, Sydney: *see* Lady Morgan

Paine, Tom, 38, 119, 122
Paley, William, 201, 205
Palgrave, William Gifford, 124
palingenesis, 64, 106, 241–2
Pantisocracy, 25, 76
Parry, Benita, 82, 237
Parsinnen, Terry, 251
Pasha, Ali, 24
Pasha, Ibraham, 42
patriarchy, 42–50
Peacock, Thomas, Love, 19, 71, 109, 162; *Melincourt*, 140; *Four Ages of Poetry*, 142, 144, 151, 152, 153; his 'iron chickens', 235
peasants, idealization of Indian, 95, 98
Percy, Thomas, 27
Persian language and literature, 18
Peterloo, 75, 203
philhellenism, 24, 36, 50, 67
Pick, Daniel, 6, 229, 256
Pindaris, 68, 115, 154, 161, 166
Pinney, Christopher, 240, 244
Piranesi, G. B., 223–4
Pizarro, 31–2
Plato: *Symposium*, 147
Plutarch, 38, 158
Pocock, J. G. A., 11, 230
Poe, Edgar, Allen, 170
Political reform, 80, 196

Pollier, Col., 161
Pollitt, Charles, 253, 254
Polybius, 38
Pope, Alexander, 22, 36, 50, 67; *Rape of the Lock*, 19
Praz, Mario, 233
Priestley, Joseph, 121
Prince of Wales's defection from the Whigs, 39
property, Hindu and Mughal ideas of, 95
Pulos, C. E., 121

Quinet, Edgar, 71, 141
Quintius Curtius, 124

Raban, Joseph, 124, 235, 244, 247
Rabinow, Paul, 85, 238
race/racism, 5–6, 10, 79, 169; Aryanism, 107–8; stereotypes of, 210, 225, 226; and class, 255
Radcliffe, Ann, 55, 102
Ramanuja, 138
Ramayana, 85, 158; and Shelley's *Prometheus Unbound*, 247
Rammohun Roy, 68, 84, 134–40; and Baptist missionaries, 246; meets Bentham, Godwin and Robert Owen, 152; supposed 'conversion', 246; on emancipation of women, 147, 180; on European colonialism, 139; influence on Shelley's *Prometheus Unbound*, 146–50; on Ireland, 243; negotiations with colonial power, 244; sufi influence upon, 138; mistaken for Tipu Sahib in England, 245–6; and Unitarians, 137; and Utilitarians, 152, 156, 158, 164, 165, 167, 168, 169, 241
    Works: *The Brahmunical Magazine* [sic], 137; *Precepts of Jesus*, 137, 245; *Translation of an Abridgement of the Vedant*, 136, 137, 139, 140, 148, 248; *Second Defence of the Monotheistical System of the Veds*, 145, 146, 247, 248; *On the Practice of Burning Widows Alive*, 248
Redpath, Theodore, 236
Rees, Abraham, 253
Ricardo, David, 197–9
Richardson, Samuel, 173
Richter, J-P., 225
Ricks, Christopher, 6
Ricouer, Paul, 103
Rig-Veda, 122
Rinaldo, or the Incipient Judge, 160
Robinson, Henry Crabb, 172, 179, 182, 185, 187, 251, 252

Robinson Crusoe, 64
Rogers, Samuel: *Voyage of Columbus*, 25–32, 46
Romanticism/Romantic: autobiography, 190–1; and imperialism, 70–1, 162; problematic modernity of, 28; and nationalism, 11; and orientalism, 10, 11, 104; sublime, 11
Roscoe, William, 152
Rossington, Michael, 244
Rousseau, J-J., 47, 89, 119, 122, 123, 129, 130, 131, 134, 172; *Nouvelle Heloise*, 173, *Confessions*, 180
Ryotwar land settlements, 94, 164

Sadi, 18
Said, Edward, 11, 24, 71–2, 73, 82, 103, 104, 105, 227, 230, 236, 241, 244, 246, 256; *Orientalism*, 2, 10, 17, 74, 91, 107, 229
Sanskrit, language and literature, 10, 18, 98, 105; in Germany, 107
Sastri, Sankara, 136
sati, 69, 95, 103, 116, 156, 165, 167, 241, 243
Saumarez, Richard, 184
Savage, Richard, 93
Schaffer, Simon, 257
Schelling, F. W. J., 104, 107, 108, 187, 242
Schiller, F., 22, 163
Schlegel, F., 107–8, 122, 125, 141, 144, 246
Schofield, Robert, 244
Schwab, Raymond, 10, 11, 107; *Oriental Renaissance*, 17, 230, 235, 241
Scotland, 87–8
Scott, Sir Walter, 19; *Marmion*, 34, 35; *Waverley*, 88
Seeley, Sir John, 219
Semmel, Bernard, 93–4, 143, 239
sensibility, 175–9
Shaffer, Elinor, 17, 108, 230, 240, 242, 246
Shakespeare, William: *Anthony and Cleopatra*, 4
Shankara, 138
Sheffield Iris, 173
Shelley, Mary: *History of the Jews*, 236; *Frankenstein*, 123, 244
Shelley, Percy Bysshe, 6, 7, 8, 9, 10, 11, 211; interest in Alexander's expedition, 124; anxieties of empire, 90, 153; attempt to secure an appointment in India, 71, 109; binary model of imperialism, 89; on Brahmins and Brahminism, 72, 85, 114, 118, 119, 134, 146–52; development of his thought, 120; disavowal of oriental

settings and 'materials', 75; on G. S. Faber, 106–7; fear of elephantiasis, 7; feminism of, 111–12, 122, 129, 130–34; on French materialism, 121; Hellenism of, 73; on Imagination and metaphor, 145–6, 151, 153; on incest, 43, 131; on India, 23, 70–6, 120, 147; scepticism and 'intellectual philosophy' of, 121, 150, 153, 248; and Ireland, 113–14, 243; and Islam, 72; and Medwin's Indian poems, 160; on missionaries in India, 118; on Lady Morgan's *Missionary*, 102, 126, and orientalism, 79; his politics, 110; and revolution, 75; and Utilitarianism, 152; utopian vision, 169; visit to Southey at Keswick, 96

Works: *Address to the Irish People*, 113, 129; *Alastor, or the Spririt of Solitude*, 55, 72, 89, 91, 109, 110, 120, 122–30, 131, 132, 143, 144, 147, 161–3, 164, 166, 168; as poem of empire, 124; and Morgan's *Missionary*, 126–9; *The Assassins*, 72, 76–80, 90, 135, 164; *Defence of Poetry*, 120, 121, 146, 151, 153, 156; *Essay on Christianity*, 146, 148, 151; *Essay on Love*, 131; *Epipsychidion*, 122, 141, 166; *Fragments of an Unfinished Drama*, 71; *Hellas*, 73, 108, 248; *Indian Serenade*, 71; *Julian and Maddalo*, 69, 162; *Mask of Anarchy*, 75, 115; *Mont Blanc*, 144; *Necessity of Atheism*, 106; *Ode to the West Wind*, 108; *Philosophical View of Reform*, 75, 118–19, 134, 136, 140 151; *Prometheus Unbound*, 2, 10, 66, 84, 85, 91, 108, 110, 120, 122, 133, 139, 140–54; and Aeschylus, 248; Prometheus's curse, 145–7; Hindu analogues of Demagorgon, 148, 151, 152, 153, 156, 160; as decolonized account of cultural difference, 166, 169; and *Ramayana*, 247; *Queen Mab*, 73, 89, 110, 114, 115, 129, 140; *Revolt of Islam* (and *Laon and Cythna*), 43, 58, 63, 68, 72, 73, 74, 75, 77, 79, 80, 82, 85, 88, 89, 90, 91, 98, 108–118, 120, 128, 130–34, 137, 138, 139, 140, 142, 143, 144, 146, 153, 154, 156, 160, 164, 166; as 'beau ideal of French Revolution', 74; *sati* in, 116; reviews of, 236; *Songs to the Men of England*, 155; *Triumph of Life*, 129, 130, 155; *Witch of Atlas*, 106; *Zeinab and Kathema*, 71, 111, 118, 128, 242

Simpson, David, 201, 254
Singh, Iqbal, 137, 138, 241
slaves/slavery, 3, 7, 153, 208
Sligo, Marquis of, 191
Smith, Adam, 187
Smith, Sidney, 34
Smith, Rev. Sydney, 100, 209, 240, 255
social anthropology, birth of, 97
Societé Asiatique, 138
Southey, H. H., 7
Southey, Robert, 4, 7, 8, 13, 15, 18, 25, 26, 76, 92, 109, 112, 135, 139, 172, 225, 239; *Curse of Kehama*, 8, 14, 21, 22, 26, 74, 95–8, 148, 151; *Letters from England*, 1, 7, 101, 222 (influence on De Quincey, 4); *Madoc*, 25–6, 30, 78; *Thalaba the Destroyer*, 14, 21, 26, 110, 232
Spanish war against Napoleon, 97–8
Spenser, Edmund, 110, 200
Spenserian burlesque stye, 34
Spinoza, Baruch, 108
Spivak, Gayatri, 82, 91, 104, 137, 156, 212, 239, 241, 245, 249, 255
Springer, Carolyn, 36, 233
Spurzheim, Dr, 152
Stafford, Fiona, 239
Starck: *Hephestion*, 107
Starobinski, Jean, 63, 89, 235, 239
Steele, Richard, 18
Stewart, John 'Walking', 178
Stokes, Eric, 88, 94; *The English Utilitarians and India*, 85, 133, 153, 154, 238, 239, 245, 249
Strabo, 158
Swift, Jonathan, 217
syphilis, 7

Tagore, Saumyendranath, 243
Tait's Edinburgh Magazine, 178, 183, 187
Teich, Mikulas, 230
Tetreault, James, 255
Themistocles, 32, 233
Thermopylae, 66
Thompson, Hunter, 171
Thomson, James: *The Seasons*, 93
Thugee/Thugs, 78, 97
Trelawney, Edward, 209
Trevelyan, Charles, 154
Trotter, Thomas, 173–5, 182, 251
Turkish Spy, 18

Unitarianism, 25, 137, 249
Upanishads, 77, 138; *Kena Upanishad*, 138, 149; Ishopanishad, 136

Utilitarianism, 75, 86, 88, 91, 103, 147, 148, 149, 151, 154, 205
Utopianism, 66, 77, 169

Vedanta school, 136, 156, 248
Vedas, 161
Venice, 32
Vidylankar, Mritunjaya, 136
Vienna, Congress of, 213
Viswanathan, Gauri, 85, 238; *Masks of Conquest*, 12, 230
Vitale, Marina, 45, 54, 234
Volney, Constantin, 98, 104, 106, 110, 113; *The Ruins*, 114–15, 119, 120, 121, 122, 129, 130, 131, 140, 142, 144, 153, 241, 243, 246
Voltaire: *Candide*, 18, 20

Wadstrom, Carl: *Essay on Colonization*, 25, 231
Warburton, William, 105
Washington, George, 31, 253
Watkins, Daniel, 15, 230
Webb, Timothy, 146, 231, 243, 246, 248
Weber, Mathias, 252, 255
Wellek, Rene, 212, 255
Wellesley, Richard, Marquis, 163
West, Benjamin, 30
Westmorland Gazette, 175, 195, 196, 253
Whig ideology, 38–40, 53; 'orientalization of', 58–9; opposition to the evangelizing of India, 100
Wilberforce, William, 96
Wilford, Francis, 107, 122
Williams, Edward Ellerker, 154, 155, 249
Williams, Jane, 154
Williams, Raymond, 79, 237
Wilson, A. Leslie, 242
Wilson, H. H., 98, 241
Wilson, John, 173, 252; on Coleridge's *Biographia*, 180–2, 197
Wollstonecraft, Mary, 130, 245; *Vindication of the Rights of Woman*, 123
Woodhouse, C. M., 231
Woof, Robert, 176, 251
Wordsworth, Kate, 191
Wordsworth, William, 11, 253; and India, 95; his sobriety, 178, 195; 'spots of time', 207 253; *The Borderers*, 78, 237; *Convention of Cintra*, 97; *The Excursion*, 123; *Lyrical Ballads*, 44, 188, 202; *Resolution and Independence*, 176, 201; *Prelude*, 170, 190, 192; *Tintern Abbey*, 207; *White Doe of Rylstone*, 58

Yarrington, Alison, 231
Yohannan, J. D., 18, 230, 231, 234
'Young Bengal' movement, 138
Young, Robert, 237, 238